Problems of a World Monetary Order

Problems of a World Monetary Order

Gerald M. Meier
Professor of International Economics
Stanford University

New York
OXFORD UNIVERSITY PRESS
London Oxford 1974

For Andrew

Preface

"Mystery," "maze," and "muddle" are the words that most frequently follow "international monetary." But international monetary problems are continually being resolved one way or another. And their resolution is crucial in determining the fate of trade liberalization and the prospects for international economic development. This book, the second of three volumes on problems in international political economy, is therefore designed as both a self-contained study of international monetary policy and a bridge connecting the first volume on trade policy with the third volume on development policy.[1]

The policy problems unfolded here relate to the attainment of an international monetary order: the evolution of the postwar international monetary system with its series of currency crises (Problem I), the special role of the dollar as centerpiece of the system (Problem II), and emergence of a reformed Bretton Woods system (Problem III).

These policy problems are not intended to be a record of events but a means of highlighting fundamental issues that call for understanding through the application of basic principles of international monetary economics. The particular events are only significant as indicators of the wider and longer-term issues that dominate the shape of a world monetary order: the amount and distribution of international liquidity, the adjustment mechanism, confidence in different reserve assets, and

1. Volume one is *Problems of Trade Policy* (1973); volume three is *Problems of Cooperation for Development* (forthcoming).

the international harmonization of national policies. As at the Bretton Woods conference in 1944 (described in Problem I), so too were these the major problems of the International Monetary Fund's meeting in Nairobi in 1973 (described in Problem III).

* * *

I have written this book with the same purposes in mind that I expressed in the first volume's introductory words to the student:

From a study of the policy problems in this book I want you to appreciate that economics is still concerned with social betterment; that economic problems cannot be solved in a political vacuum; that qualitative appraisals may be as important as quantitative calculations; and that in public policy formulation, the formal economic principle must usually give way at some point to a value judgment.

These problems do not allow a technocratic approach to policy-making. On the contrary, they emphasize that most policy problems have no natural boundaries and that decision-making is an art as well as a science. Long ago, Keynes observed that economics does not constitute a body of knowledge immediately applicable to policy. Notwithstanding all the advances in the "science" of decision-making, few—if any—economists would yet deny Keynes's dictum. And all who have experienced the complexities of actual decision-making in international economic affairs will appreciate that technical analysis must sooner or later yield to judgment—or to the qualities of imagination and intuition which Keynes believed to be as much a part of economics as logic and fact.

A word on organization. This book begins with a general expository introduction on international monetary affairs that recapitulates some basic principles and provides some perspective of the problems that follow. The materials for each policy problem are then set forth in a way that I thought would best reveal the development of events and the execution of policy decisions. I have tried to unfold the "biography" of each policy situation by presenting an analytical narrative and a set of source materials so that you might gain a sense of the crucial issues in each situation, the types of international conflict involved, and the modes of resolution and cooperation effected. This normally involves placing the problem in its larger context (Section A), followed by the development of the factual situation and the presentation of the actual decisions (Section B). To allow you to discover the major policy issues in the problem, I have tried to use to advantage, documents, reports, and other source materials—while providing continuity with a narrative. Some "seasoning" has been added by giving the observations of the actors, observers, or commentators of the time. Finally, I have provided some questions designed to aid you in analyzing and evaluating the specific policy decisions (Section C) and suggestions for additional readings (Section D).

This method of presenting policy problems is intended to encourage your own thinking about these problems. While materials are offered to illuminate the particular policy problem, it is up to you to identify and analyze the major issues; and you must be prepared to adopt and defend your own policy position with respect to the problem's resolution. You need not worry about a "correct" answer to the problem, but you should be very much concerned about the quality of the reasoning behind your own answer—about the "why" of your conclusion. Your specific recommendations are not as important as your understanding of the complexity of the policy problem and your clarity on criteria for judging the merits of alternatives. Each problem has two objectives: to extend your capacity to evaluate the quality of public policy-making and to suggest ways of improving the process in international economic affairs.

In considering each problem, you will therefore have to exercise your own judgment on a set of questions: What were the crucial policy issues in the problem? How were they resolved? Would another course of action have been preferable? What do you now conclude about the desirable future course of action?

* * *

I am again indebted to my students at Stanford University for enduring early drafts of these problems; their receptivity was most encouraging. Kay Agnew and Edward Ericson provided invaluable assistance. Extracts from the *New York Times* are reprinted by permission, and gratefully acknowledged.

G. M. M.

October 1973
Stanford, California

Contents

Problems of a World Monetary Order

Background: International Financial Diplomacy

International monetary problems are as fascinating as they are perplexing—combining as they do a rich mixture of technical economics, political repercussions, and even the psychology of symbols and beliefs. The process of policy-making in international monetary affairs depends as much on the art of international financial diplomacy as on the rigor of economic analysis or the quantification of econometric relationships. International currency experience has been shaped by the human establishment of international institutional arrangements and multinational negotiations as well as by impersonal economic forces.

Of the establishment of the International Monetary Fund (IMF) at the Bretton Woods conference in 1944, it has been said that "it is difficult even for those familiar with the International Monetary Fund as a working organization to realize what a remarkable achievement its creation was. It came into being as a result of a supreme act of faith—the decision to surrender to an untried and imperfectly visualized international body the supervision of one of the most cherished attributes of national sovereignty, the right to change the rate of exchange. That this surrender was hedged round with safeguards is not surprising;

that it was made at all and was accompanied by vesting in the same body an appreciable fraction of the member's international reserves, can be explained only by the coincidence of the hour and the men." [1]

Now, as the postwar Bretton Woods system becomes outdated, a new order of international monetary conduct is being established. And this establishment of a new world monetary order again calls for high skills of international financial diplomacy. In considering the three Policy Problems in this book, it will be of equal interest to contemplate the political economics of the problem and the "coincidence of the hour and the men."

At the outset, we should draw a distinction between a monetary *system* and a monetary *order*. As expressed by Professor Robert Mundell,

> A system is an aggregation of diverse entities united by regular interaction according to some form of control. When we speak of the international monetary system we are concerned with the mechanisms governing the interaction between trading nations, and in particular between the money and credit instruments of national communities in foreign exchange, capital, and commodity markets. The control is exerted through policies at the national level interacting with one another in that loose form of supervision that we call cooperation.
>
> An *order*, as distinct from a system, represents the framework and setting in which the system operates. It is a framework of laws, conventions, regulations, and mores that establish the setting of the system and the understanding of the environment by the participants in it. A monetary order is to a monetary system somewhat like a constitution is to a political or electoral system. We can think of the monetary system as the *modus operandi* of the monetary order.[2]

1. A TRIAD OF POLICY OBJECTIVES

The reduction of trade barriers is a frequently avowed policy target for most countries; even more vigorously, national gov-

1. J. Keith Horsefield, *The International Monetary Fund 1945–1965*, Vol. I (1965), p. 3.
2. Robert Mundell, "The Future of the International Financial System," in A. L. K. Acheson et al., *Bretton Woods Revisited* (1972), p. 92.

ernments affirm their belief in economic expansion—a satisfactory rate of growth in rich countries and the acceleration of development in poor countries. Attainment of these objectives is, however, strongly conditioned by the type of international monetary system that exists. The design of the international monetary system is more than a matter of instituting a technical mechanism: it necessarily involves policy choices that take international monetary affairs into the political arena, affecting the distribution of benefits and costs among nations, and often requiring the resolution of conflicting interests.

Since the end of World War II, the overriding international economic policy question for most nations has been whether they can attain simultaneously the multiple objectives of high levels of employment, trade liberalization, and balance-of-payments equilibrium with fixed exchange rates. To the extent that these objectives may be incompatible, some policy trade-offs are necessary. In their efforts to achieve full employment, countries have often moved away from trade liberalization by resorting to import restrictions or controls on capital movements. Even though international trade theory would label the advocacy of trade restrictions in order to promote full employment as a "nonargument" or as a "third, fourth, or nth best" policy measure,[3] governmental policies have in reality often had this neomercantilistic character. The pursuit of full employment also can entail balance-of-payments disequilibrium or departure from the condition of fixed exchange rates. As a country undertakes domestic expansion to achieve full employment, its imports may increase or its exports may fall so much that a deficit arises in the country's international payments balance. Some trade-off must then occur between full employment and balance-of-payments equilibrium with fixed exchange rates, or between full employment and trade liberalization. Finally, if a balance-of-payments deficit arises, the country will likely attempt to remedy the situation either by undertaking measures

3. Economists now refer to the theory of the "second best" as a guide to policy norms. See R. G. Lipsey and K. Lancaster, "The General Theory of Second Best," *Review of Economic Studies*, Vol. 24 (1956), pp. 11ff. The objective of the "second best" is to minimize costs of market intervention and to avoid an excess burden when the "first best" is unattainable (because it is impossible to have optimum conditions in every sector of the economy).

that restrict employment and contract income, in order to reduce imports and stimulate exports, or by imposing trade restrictions or controls over capital movements.

When confronted by these policy conflicts, most governments have allowed the objective of full employment to dominate national economic policy even at the cost of a retreat from trade liberalization or pressure on the balance of payments. The central challenge to the operation of the Bretton Woods system during the postwar period, therefore, has been how to allow nations to pursue their domestic economic objectives without having to forgo the gains from trade or to suffer balance-of-payments disequilibrium.

The Bretton Woods conference in 1944 anticipated these problems. It was believed that establishment of the IMF would allow nations to give primacy to their domestic employment policies over balance-of-payments adjustment. The belief that national policies for full employment could be given priority rested on three assumptions of the Bretton Woods system: first, that the IMF would be a source of international liquidity in sufficient amount to allow a deficit country adequate time for the adjustment of its balance-of-payments, without having to resort to deflationary measures or trade restrictions; second, that although exchange rates were to remain fixed in the short run, they would have some flexibility in the long run as the Fund would approve an alteration of exchange rates when a country experiences "fundamental disequilibrium"; third, that deficit countries would not have to bear the sole responsibility for reequilibrating their balance of payments, since surplus countries would share the responsibility. If a surplus country adopted no remedial action and its currency remained in short supply on foreign exchange markets, then the IMF's "scarce currency" clause allowing discriminatory controls against the "scarce currency" could become operative.

In the late 1960's and early 1970's the major assumptions of the Bretton Woods system were being severely tested. For perspective on this challenge we should recognize that any international monetary system can be analyzed in terms of three essential functions: the determination of exchange rates, the adjustment process to a disturbance in the balance of payments, and the provision of international liquidity. Interpretative analysis of these functions is involved in all the Policy Problems in this book: the diagnosis of the postwar international currency crises (Problem I), the evaluation of United States balance-of-payments policy (Problem II), and proposals of international monetary reform that would entail greater exchange rate flexibility (Problem III). Taken together, these problems relate to the political economics of shaping a new international monetary order.

We shall see that international monetary arrangements are the outcome of history, multinational negotiation, and market forces. The history of money shows a long evolution from commodity money toward the increasing use of credit money. A central issue in international monetary reform is how far this trend can now be extended internationally. Even though it may have economic logic, many would contend that a further extension of international credit money is still politically premature. In the past, negotiations among nations have also resulted in the establishment of international monetary institutions such as the IMF, or more recently, swap arrangements among central banks and the inclusion of Special Drawing Rights in the IMF in accordance with the Rio agreement of 1967.

The impact of market forces on the international monetary system has recently been reflected in the extension of multinational corporations, the increased flow of capital internationally, and the emergence in the later 1960's of the Euro-currency market. Although the structure or framework of an international monetary system may be determined through the deliberations of finance ministers, central bankers, and economists, the details of international monetary events will depend on the behavior of private actors—as well as public actors—on international commodity and capital markets.

2. THE NEED FOR REMEDIAL POLICY

Under any international monetary system the most important issues involve decisions about the need for remedial action and the character of this corrective action. For although the accounting of the balance of payments is such that the balance of payments always balances,[4] this does not mean that there is no deficit or surplus in the balance of payments that requires remedial policy.

The crucial consideration is how the balance of payments is brought into balance: what are the "balancing" or "settlement" items? And do they portend the need for remedial policy? If we exclude some transactions—namely, those that act as "settlement" transactions—then the balance of the remaining "ordinary" transactions can be in deficit or surplus. If we refer to "ordinary" or "autonomous" transactions as being "above the line," and consider the "settlement" or "induced" items as being "below the line," then we want to focus on those items below the line that accomplish the financing of any deficit in the ordinary items above the line.[5] Where the line is drawn depends on evaluation of the need for remedial policy—and this is a matter of judgment. Because judgment on a country's need for corrective policies may differ, so too may the interpretation of what is the deficit in the country's balance of payments. In this sense, it has been said that "the balance of payments deficit cannot be measured, it can only be analyzed." [6]

Under the gold exchange standard of the Bretton Woods system (to be explained in Problem I), the changes in gold reserves

4. In balance-of-payments accounting there is always an identical equality between credits and debits, in so far as credit items that result from receipts from sales of goods, claims, or gold and foreign exchange must be matched by debit items that result from payments for purchases of goods, claims, or gold and foreign exchange. For details of balance-of-payments accounting, see B. J. Cohen, *Balance of Payments Policy* (1969), Chap. 1; C. P. Kindleberger, "Measuring Equilibrium in the Balance of Payments," *Journal of Political Economy* (November–December 1969), pp. 873–91; David T. Devlin, "The U.S. Balance of Payments: Revised Presentation," *Survey of Current Business* (June 1971), pp. 24–57.

5. Sometimes items below the line are referred to as "accommodating" or "compensatory" items in contrast to the autonomous "items above the line." This simplifies the problem by implying that the items below the line are "induced" by the sum of the autonomous transactions and occur as the result of the need for residual "financing" to cover a surplus or deficit in the autonomous transactions. It is, however, extremely difficult operationally to determine which transactions are truly compensatory and which are not: it is essentially a question of ultimate motives of the monetary authorities, and this judgment must be inevitably subjective. See Richard N. Cooper, "The Balance of Payments in Review," *Journal of Political Economy* (August 1966), p. 384.

6. Excellent statements of this analytical problem are presented by Cooper, "Balance of Payments in Review"; Kindleberger, "Measuring Equilibrium in the Balance of Payments," p. 873.

act as a balancing item. Monetary gold flow would therefore be placed below the line, and a gold outflow would indicate the size of the deficit or the negative balance above the line. When we consider capital items, however, there can be different interpretations of which capital transactions should be placed above the line and which should be regarded as settlement items below the line. A short-term capital inflow is equivalent to an increase in liabilities to foreigners or a decrease in claims on foreigners. A short-term capital inflow into the United States, for example, is composed of an increase in deposits held by foreigners in American banks, an increase in foreign holdings of United States short-term securities (such as Treasury bills), and a decrease in American-owned deposits in foreign banks. If the increase in liabilities is to foreign official monetary authorities, it is placed below the line. But should an inflow of foreign short-term private capital also be treated as a settlement item in the United States balance of payments in the same way as a gold outflow or inflow of official short-term capital? Or should it be treated as an "autonomous" transaction, primarily in response to market forces, and placed above the line? Analysis of these capital flows will be highly significant in the Problems below.

Depending on how the question of the foreigner's motivation for holding short-term dollar assets is answered, the private short-term capital inflow can be considered as speculative balances so that the private holdings can switch into the official holdings or, instead, as working balances for ordinary transaction purposes. Accordingly, depending upon whether analysis places foreign private short-term capital above or below the line, there will be different measurements of the balance-of-payments position.

One measure is the "balance of official reserve transactions." According to this measure, the United States would have a deficit if there is an inflow of official short-term capital (an increase in liabilities to foreign monetary authorities), a loss of monetary gold (a decline in an American reserve asset), or an increase in the United States net indebtedness position in the IMF.

Another measure is the "net liquidity balance." This incorporates the change in reserves plus the net flow of liquid short-term capital. The net liquidity balance exceeds the official reserve transactions balance when there is a net inflow of liquid short-term capital. (These balances are examined in more detail in Problem II.)

Utilizing the official reserve transactions concept, we may say that a country has a balance-of-payments deficit if its reserve assets are declining and/or if the claims of foreign monetary authorities on the country are rising. To the extent that this deficit cannot be continued indefinitely, but must be corrected, we may conclude that the country is suffering from balance-of-payments disequilibrium. There is pressure on the balance of payments, and unless the deficit country can have unlimited access to sources of international liquidity, the country will sooner or later have to undertake some remedial policy measures to re-equilibrate its balance of payments.

It is, of course, equally correct to say that equilibrium in a country's balance of payments is the absence of a surplus as well as absence of a deficit. A country has a balance-of-payments surplus, according to the official reserve transactions concept, if its reserve assets are increasing and/or if the claims of foreign monetary authorities on the country are decreasing. Although the balance of payments of the surplus country is technically in disequilibrium, the surplus country is not compelled to take corrective action—as the deficit country must do eventually. As is often stressed in the Problems below, it is desirable that the surplus country also take corrective action along with the deficit country. While competitive devaluations by deficit countries handicapped the adjustment mechanism during the 1930's, the competitive nonrevaluations of surplus countries handicapped the adjustment mechanism during the 1960's and early 1970's (see Problems II and III). From the standpoint of facilitating the adjustment mechanism, it is desirable that the surplus country take appropriate action that complements—rather than competes with—action by the deficit country.

Given a situation of disequilibrium in its balance of payments, a government must institute some remedial policy if it cannot look forward to having an actual deficit in its balance of payments supported through "accommodating" capital imports and depletion of gold and exchange reserves, or if it is unwilling to sacrifice other policy objectives and endure unemployment or impose direct controls on trade or capital movements in order to avoid a deficit. By what means can balance-of-payments equilibrium then be restored? How rapidly? And with what repercussions to the domestic economy? These questions dominate the Policy Problems below.

The type of remedial policy that a country will *want* to adopt will depend upon its interpretation of the sources of its balance-of-payments problem and on its other domestic objectives. The country will want to seek the least costly mechanism of adjusting its balance of payments, without sacrificing domestic economic autonomy. It will also be evident that what policy a country *can* adopt will depend upon the type of international monetary system that exists and the code of international economic conduct that the world monetary order imposes.

3. TYPES OF INTERNATIONAL MONETARY SYSTEMS

At various times the world economy has been on a gold-bullion standard, an inconvertible paper standard, and a gold-exchange and reserve-currency system. Under the gold-bullion standard, as it existed in the pre-1914 period and from 1925 to the early 1930's, the exchange rates were fixed and the international reserve asset was gold. Under a paper standard, as it existed in the interwar period, the exchange rates were freely floating and the need for reserves was removed, unless the monetary authorities wanted to intervene to hold the exchange rate fluctuations within limits. Under the gold-exchange and reserve-currency standard as established in the postwar period with the institution of the IMF, and until President Nixon's New Economic Policy of August 15, 1971, exchange rates were fixed but subject to adjustment under conditions of "fundamental disequilibrium," and reserves consisted of a substitute for gold in the form of drawing rights at the IMF. (Details of this will be examined in Problem I.)

Under the various international monetary systems, the sources and amount of international liquidity differ and so does the degree to which the balance of payments exercises discipline on a country. The more it is desired that an international imbalance should exercise discipline on a country's domestic policies, the less access should the country have to international liquidity. The less the country's access to liquidity, the more it must resort either to internal measures to remove its balance-of-payments problem or to external measures. Through a tight monetary policy and budgetary surplus, the internal measures entail deflation if the country is in deficit; to this extent the country loses domestic autonomy over its full employment policies. The external measures constitute the imposition of restrictions on trade and capital movements or a devaluation of the currency; to this extent, the country diminishes its gains from trade or incurs the costs of devaluation.

We shall not here go into the details of the pure gold-bullion standard or paper standard, but instead shall focus in Problems I and II on the postwar Bretton Woods system of the gold-exchange and reserve-currency standard and the changes after August 15, 1971.

4. REFORMING THE WORLD'S MONEY

Along with the problem of the United States balance of payments, there has been a number of international currency crises that have raised questions about whether the international monetary system suffers from fundamental weaknesses and now requires reform. The IMF was established to improve on the process of adjustment to payments imbalance—namely, to avoid the competitive devaluations that had occurred prior to the war and to free domestic policy to achieve full employment by providing a limited amount of additional liquidity through drawing rights with the IMF so that the prewar deflationary bias of the international monetary system might be avoided.

In light of these objectives—and also events during the later 1960's and early 1970's—it is appropriate to recall an observation by Keynes:

> The competitive struggle for liquidity has now extended beyond individuals and institutions to nations and to governments, each of which endeavours to make its international balance sheet more liquid by restricting imports and stimu-

lating exports by every possible means, the success of each one in this direction meaning the defeat of someone else. Moreover, every country discourages capital development within its own borders for fear of the effect on its international balance. Yet it will only be successful in its object in so far as its progress towards negation is greater than that of its neighbours.

We have here an extreme example of the *disharmony* of general and particular interest. Each nation, in an effort to improve its relative position, takes measures injurious to the absolute prosperity of its neighbours; and since its example is not confined to itself, it suffers more from similar action by its neighbours than it gains by such action itself. Practically all the remedies popularly advocated to-day are of this internecine character. Competitive wage-reductions, competitive tariffs, competitive liquidation of foreign assets, competitive currency deflations, competitive economy campaigns, competitive contractions of new development—all are of this beggar-my-neighbour description. The modern capitalist is a fair-weather sailor. As soon as a storm arises he abandons the duties of navigation and even sinks the boats which might carry him to safety by his haste to push his neighbours off and himself in.[7]

This observation related to the world economic crisis of the early 1930's—but in spite of the intervening formation of the IMF, it could also apply to the world economic crisis of the early 1970's. Many economists would contend that the international economy again confronts the same central problems that it did at the Bretton Woods conference in 1944. Many would argue that there has been increasing evidence that the international monetary system of the gold-exchange standard has restrained economic expansion in the major industrial nations and has impeded development in the poor nations. That these unintended effects have occurred can be traced fundamentally to the fixity of exchange rates under the Bretton Woods system at the same time as there has been inadequate growth in international liquidity. The provisions that were originally considered the very virtues of the Bretton Woods system have now come to

7. J. M. Keynes in *The World's Economic Crisis and the Way of Escape,* Halley Stewart Lecture (1931), pp. 73–74.

be considered by many as vices. The IMF increased international liquidity—but only to a limited extent. The alternative creation of liquidity via the United States balance-of-payments deficit is a haphazard method, and raises the confidence problem in acute form. A fundamental question with respect to the international monetary system is therefore whether there is now sufficient internationl liquidity to allow autonomy in national economic policy.

The "pegged rate system" of the IMF also escaped from the extremes of the fixed-exchange-rate system of the pure gold standard and the freely fluctuating rates of a paper standard. But might not the provision for an "adjustable peg" in exchange rates have been a compromise that embodied the worst, rather than the best, features of both the fixed and floating exchange rate systems, entailing neither the certainty of a truly permanently fixed rate nor the flexibility of a floating rate? Were fixed rates no longer a means to the attainment of freer multilateral trade but instead an end in itself, so that governments sought to keep rates fixed even at the expense of trade liberalization?

Finally, the Fund dethroned gold but did not demonetize it. The establishment of the two-tier gold market in March 1968 partially demonetized gold by freezing the monetary gold stock and cutting the link between official dealings in gold and current gold production. But, as asked in Problems II and III, might it not be better to complete the demonetization of gold by having the United States not buy or sell gold at all and instead attempt to establish a dollar reserve standard? Must not the outcome of a gold-based international monetary system be ultimately either an increase in the price of gold or demonetization of gold and the provision of a superior substitute for it?

Answers to these questions are by no means clear-cut, and the issues they raise are very much a matter of controversy, as will be seen in the three Policy Problems that follow. Because national interests do not coincide, the ultimate shaping of a new international monetary order will have to be resolved through multilateral negotiations and the operation of political processes, even though economists may reveal the various alternatives for reform of the world monetary system.

5. POLITICAL ECONOMICS OF MONEY

The establishment of a new international monetary order will require the settlement of political issues for each of its essential components. If by "politics" is meant the process by which conflicting visions of a common purpose are agitated or settled,[8] then politics will enter into the determination of exchange rates, the provision of international liquidity, and the adjustment process. These issues have become a matter of "high politics," no longer simply relegated to the silent level of technically soluble "low politics." Determination of exchange rates involves controversial matters of national prestige and political appearance. Devaluation of one's own currency has never held any political attraction; to the contrary, it has frequently meant the fall of the government or the removal of at least the finance minister.[9] The possibility of several currencies pegging to one currency, for example, the dollar bloc, or a common exchange-rate policy for a regime, such as the European Economic Community, or the formation of an optimum currency area—all these regimes of exchange rate determination are intertwined with political implications in allowing—or denying—different countries various policy options and in bestowing different degrees of economic power to various countries.

Questions involving the sources and amount of liquidity may be even more political, especially because they raise some new issues with no negotiating precedents. If gold is to be replaced by credit international reserve money, who is to authorize the amount of increase in the credit money? And who is to determine its distribution? The advantage of being able to create international reserve money as "negotiated" reserves may at the same time be offset by the disadvantages involved in the politicization of the process of creating reserves through multilateral negotiation instead of having nations rely simply on their

8. E. C. Banfield, in *A Dictionary of the Social Sciences,* edited by J. Gould and W. L. Kolb (1964).

9. Richard N. Cooper, *Currency Devaluation in Developing Countries,* Princeton Essays in International Finance No. 86 (1971), pp. 28–29.

"owned" reserves (such as the nation's own gold stock). If liquidity were now increased, would not countries be able to escape unduly from balance-of-payments discipline? And would not the increase in liquidity impart too great an inflationary bias to the world economy? These reservations were once raised by the United States at the Bretton Woods conference, and other countries raise them again today. The explication of "unduly" and "too great," as expressed in these reservations, is as much a matter of political judgment and social values as economic analysis.

Again, recognizing that the access to an infinite supply of liquidity or the operation of a perfect adjustment mechanism would be perfect policy substitutes for meeting a payments imbalance, we can say that the major task of the international monetary system is to determine the degree of control over this policy trade-off. In doing this, there are bound to be different national positions. In general, surplus countries will seek to minimize liquidity and force deficit countries to adjust. Deficit countries, in contrast, will seek to maximize liquidity and force surplus countries to initiate the adjustment mechanism.

The initiation of the adjustment process may depend not only on the amount and distribution of liquidity, but also on the rules of conduct that can be imposed on countries in deficit or surplus. International coordination is required to ease the adjustment process. The fact of ever-greater international economic interdependence, with the resultant spillover effects of one country's policies on another, also requires evermore coordination of policies. And yet, nations continue to want domestic economic autonomy in the choice of their policies. At what point can national interest be made to be seen as coinciding with the collective interest, and thereby have nations become dependent on multilateral decision-making? It is now a political economics issue of the first order to coordinate policy formation and avoid the competition in policy-making that has plagued international monetary policy in recent years as countries sought to avoid the burdens of the process of adjustment to payments imbalances.

The question of the "appropriate" division of the burden of adjustment among different countries remains as much political as economic. By what criteria are the costs of international adjustment to be distributed? Should the adjustment be through flexibility in exchange rates? restrictive domestic measures in the deficit country? or by some means that compel the surplus country, or give it the incentive, to restore equilibrium in its balance of payments? Depending on how these questions are answered, the costs of balance-of-payments adjustment will appear in different countries in varying degrees through the effects of currency depreciation or appreciation, deflation or inflation, trade restrictions or liberalization.

These political economic issues enter into the major themes that proceed through all the Policy Problems in this book. One theme is the need for policy-makers to operate in the realm of international financial crisis management at the same time as they try to achieve longer-run, more fundamental reformation of the international monetary system. A second theme is the way the benefits and costs of different international monetary arrangements are perceived by the policy-makers of different countries, and how through international financial diplomacy, or market operation, or simply ad hoc or de facto action there does result a certain distribution of these benefits and costs. A third theme is how to reconcile nationalist politics and the desire for autonomy in domestic economic policy-making with international economic forces that are making the world economy evermore integrated in real economic terms. Finally, a fourth theme considers what features of a world monetary order must be politicized and what can be relegated to technical solutions.

Problem I
International Monetary
Experience: Currency Crises

A. THE CONTEXT

1. THE BRETTON WOODS SYSTEM

In the last year of the Second World War, financial experts and delegates from forty-four members of the United Nations convened at Bretton Woods, New Hampshire, to devise international arrangements that would hopefully avoid the monetary problems encountered before the war. The leading industrial nations especially wanted to avoid reoccurrence of the competitive exchange rate depreciations, "beggar-my-neighbor" trade restrictions, and deflationary measures that had been adopted in the 1930's to meet balance-of-payments problems. Pledged to undertake full-employment policies after the war, the countries now wanted to be free to pursue domestic expansion, unconstrained by the balance of payments.

Two plans dominated the negotiations at Bretton Woods—the British plan for an International Clearing Union, presented by John Maynard Keynes, and the American plan for an International Stabilization Fund, presented by Harry Dexter White of the United States Treasury. Another proposal—the key-currency plan—expounded by Professor John H. Williams of Harvard University and the Federal Reserve Bank of New York, created some discussion in unofficial circles, but was not on the Bretton Woods agenda. A brief consideration of the objectives of the three plans may provide a useful background to the provisions that were actually included in the Bretton Woods agreement.

The Keynes Plan was a bold departure from previous monetary systems calling for a new international organization that would operate much like an international central bank for central banks. An International Clearing Union would create a new international reserve asset to be called "bancor" (a term that might appease both the French and adherents of gold). As Keynes envisaged the scheme, the total creation of bancor deposits (overdrafts) available to the members would have been about $26 billion. This was believed to be the amount of international liquidity that would be needed to finance expansion in world trade and postwar recovery, without having to undertake adjustment policies that would limit domestic expansion or inhibit trade liberalization. Although bancor was to be defined in terms of gold, it was not to be convertible into gold: no member would be entitled to demand gold from the Clearing Union, and bancor would be available only for transfer to another clearing account. The value of bancor in terms of gold was to be fixed but not unalterably. Exchange rates would be expressed in terms of bancor, but would not be fixed as under the pure gold standard.

A surplus member's balance of payments would appear as a credit balance on the books of the Clearing Union; a balance-of-payments deficit would appear as a debit balance (comparable to an overdraft in the British banking system). A quota was to be allotted to each country, and it was proposed that a country not be allowed to accumulate a debit balance in any one year larger than one-fourth of its quota. Unlike an ordinary banking system, the Clearing Union was to charge interest on both credit and debit balances, according to the fraction of a member's quota that had accumulated as a debit or credit balance. The novel attempt to charge interest to the surplus country with a credit balance was explicit recognition that a surplus country should also bear some of the burden of the adjustment process.

Keynes's plan went on to specify that when a surplus country had a credit balance exceeding one-half of its quota for a year, it would be required to discuss with the Governing Board of the Clearing Union appropriate remedial measures such as (1) expansion of domestic credit, (2) revaluation of its currency, (3) increase in wage rates, (4) reduction of tariffs and trade restrictions, or (5) making international development loans.

On the other side, for a debtor country, the Governing Board would be empowered to require the member to take measures such as (1) devaluation by a specific amount, (2) imposition of control on outward short-term speculative capital transactions, or (3) payment to the Clearing Union of a suitable proportion of the member's international reserves in reduction of its debit balance.

1.1 *The Keynes, White, and Williams Plans*

PROPOSALS FOR AN INTERNATIONAL CLEARING UNION *

Preface

In preparing these proposals care has been taken to regard certain conditions, which the groundwork of an international economic system to be set up after the war should satisfy, if it is to prove durable:

There should be the least possible interference with internal national policies, and the plan should not wander from the international *terrain*. Since such policies may have important repercussions on international relations, they cannot be left out of account. Nevertheless in the realm of internal policy the authority of the Governing Board of the proposed Institution should be limited to recommendations, or at the most to imposing conditions for the more extended enjoyment of the facilities which the Institution offers.

The technique of the plan must be capable of application, irrespective of the type and principle of government and economic policy existing in the prospective member States.

The management of the Institution must be genuinely international without preponderant power of veto or enforcement to any country or group; and the rights and privileges of the smaller countries must be safeguarded.

Some qualification of the right to act at pleasure is required by any agreement or treaty between nations. But in order that such arrangements may be fully voluntary so long as they last and terminable when they have become irksome, provision must be made for voiding the obligation at due notice. If many member States were to take advantage of this, the plan would have

* Reprinted in J. Keith Horsefield (ed.), *The International Monetary Fund 1945–1965*, Vol. III: *Documents* (1969), pp. 19–22. This is the April 1943 draft of the Keynes Plan (Cmd. 6437).

broken down. But if they are free to escape from its provisions if necessary they may be the more willing to go on accepting them.

The plan must operate not only to the general advantage but also to the individual advantage of each of the participants, and must not require a special economic or financial sacrifice from certain countries. No participant must be asked to do or offer anything which is not to his own true long-term interest.

It must be emphasised that it is not for the Clearing Union to assume the burden of long term lending which is the proper task of some other institution. It is also necessary for it to have means of restraining improvident borrowers. But the Clearing Union must also seek to discourage creditor countries from leaving unused large liquid balances which ought to be devoted to some positive purpose. For excessive credit balances necessarily create excessive debit balances for some other party. In recognising that the creditor as well as the debtor may be responsible for a want of balance, the proposed institution would be breaking new ground.

I. The Objects of the Plan

About the primary objects of an improved system of International Currency there is, to-day, a wide measure of agreement:—

We need an instrument of international currency having general acceptability between nations, so that blocked balances and bilateral clearings are unnecessary; that is to say, an instrument of currency used by each nation in its transactions with other nations, operating through whatever national organ, such as a Treasury or a Central Bank, is most appropriate, private individuals, businesses and banks other than Central Banks, each continuing to use their own national currency as heretofore.

We need an orderly and agreed method of determining the relative exchange values of national currency units, so that unilateral action and competitive exchange depreciations are prevented.

We need a *quantum* of international currency, which is neither determined in an unpredictable and irrelevant manner as, for example, by the technical progress of the gold industry, nor subject to large variations depending on the gold reserve policies of individual countries; but is governed by the actual current requirements of world commerce, and is also capable of deliberate expansion and contraction to offset deflationary and inflationary tendencies in effective world demand.

We need a system possessed of an internal stabilising mechanism, by which pressure is exercised on any country whose balance of payments with the rest of the world is departing from equilibrium *in either direction,* so as to prevent movements which must create for its neighbours an equal but opposite want of balance.

We need an agreed plan for starting off every country after the war with a stock of reserves appropriate to its importance in world commerce, so that without due anxiety it can set its house in order during the transitional period to full peace-time conditions.

We need a central institution, of a purely technical and non-political character, to aid and support other international institutions concerned with the planning and regulation of the world's economic life.

More generally, we need a means of reassurance to a troubled world, by which any country whose own affairs are conducted with due prudence is relieved of anxiety for causes which are not of its own making, concerning its ability to meet its international liabilities; and which will, therefore, make unnecessary those methods of restriction and discrimination which countries have adopted hitherto, not on their merits, but as measures of self-protection from disruptive outside forces.

There is also a growing measure of agreement about the general character of any solution of the problem likely to be successful. The particular proposals set forth below lay no claim to originality. They are an attempt to reduce to practical shape certain general ideas belonging to the contemporary climate of economic opinion, which have been given publicity in recent months by writers of several different nationalities. It is difficult to see how any plan can be successful which does not use these general ideas, which are born of the spirit of the age. The actual details put forward below are offered, with no dogmatic intention, as the basis of discussion for criticism and improvement. For we cannot make progress without embodying the general underlying idea in a frame of actual working, which will bring out the practical and political difficulties to be faced and met if the breath of life is to inform it.

In one respect this particular plan will be found to be more ambitious and yet, at the same time, perhaps more workable than some of the variant versions of the same basic idea, in that it is fully international, being based on one general agreement and not on a multiplicity of bilateral arrangements. Doubtless proposals might be made by which bilateral arrangements could be fitted together so as to obtain some of the advantages of a multilateral scheme. But there will be many difficulties attendant on such adjustments. It may be doubted whether a comprehensive scheme will ever in fact be worked out, unless it can come into existence through a single act of creation made possible by the unity of purpose and energy of hope for better things to come, springing from the victory of the United Nations, when they have attained it, over immediate evil. That these proposals are ambitious is claimed therefore to be not a drawback but an advantage.

The proposal is to establish a Currency Union, here designated an *International Clearing Union,* based on international bank-money, called (let us say) *bancor,* fixed (but not unalterably) in terms of gold and accepted as the equivalent of gold by the British Commonwealth and the United States and all the other members of the Union for the purpose of settling international balances. The Central Banks of all member States (and also of non-members) would keep accounts with the International Clearing Union through which they would be entitled to settle their exchange balances with one another at their par value as defined in terms of bancor. Countries having a favourable balance of payments with the rest of the world as a whole would find themselves in possession of a credit account with the Clearing Union, and those having an unfavourable balance would have a debit account. Measures would be necessary (see below) to prevent the piling up of credit and debit balances without limit, and the system would have failed in the long run if it did not possess sufficient capacity for self-equilibrium to secure this.

The idea underlying such a Union is simple, namely, to generalise the essential principle of banking as it is exhibited within any closed system. This principle is the necessary equality of credits and debits. If no credits can be removed outside the clearing system, but only transferred within it, the Union can never be in any difficulty as regards the honouring of cheques drawn upon it. It can make what advances it wishes to any of its members with the assurance that the proceeds can only be transferred to the clearing account of another member. Its sole task is to see to it that its members keep the rules and that the advances made to each of them are prudent and advisable for the Union as a whole.

The provisions of the White Plan differed from the Keynes Plan on three major points. First, the United States opposed the larger amount of liquidity that would have been provided by the Clearing Union on the ground that it was unnecessary and had potentially unmanageable inflationary effects. A typical reaction was that of the National City Bank's *Monthly Economic Letter* of July 1944 which objected that the Keynes Plan "is likely to serve more as a means of credit expansion than of stabilization—in other words, an application of the principle of deficit-financing translated from the domestic to the international scene." [1] (It is interesting to compare how much liquidity would have been created by the Clearing Union with the amount that was subsequently actually provided by the United States in the form of Marshall Aid to Western Europe, foreign aid to developing nations, and the deficit in the United States balance of payments, as indicated in Problem II below.) Instead of Keynes's bancor, the White plan proposed that the Stabilization Fund should operate with the smaller amount of $5 billion in gold and national currencies contributed by member countries, not in bancor that could be created.

Second, the United States did not welcome the possibility of as much flexibility in exchange rates as the Clearing Union envisaged; instead, the Stabilization Fund proposed that rates be fixed by the Fund and changed only with the consent of 80 per

1. For other objections of this character, see John Blum, *The Morgenthau Diaries*, Vol. III (1967), Chap. V.

cent of the voting power. The third difference was with respect to exerting pressure on a creditor country. The United States wished to limit the liability of the United States as potentially the largest creditor in the postwar world, and the Stabilization Fund had no provision comparable to the payment of interest by a surplus country as in the Clearing Union.

The objectives of the White Plan are outlined in the following excerpt.

PROPOSAL FOR AN INTERNATIONAL STABILIZATION FUND *

There is a growing recognition that progress toward establishment of a functioning democratic world in the post-war period will depend on the ability of free peoples to work together in solving their economic problems. Not the least of these is the problem of how to prevent a widespread breakdown of currencies with resultant international economic disorder. We must assure a troubled world that the free countries will solve these perplexing problems, and that they will not resort to competitive exchange depreciation, multiple currency practices, discriminatory bilateral clearing, or other destructive foreign exchange devices.

These are not transitory problems of the immediate postwar period affecting only a few countries. The history of the past two decades shows that they are continuing problems of vital interest to all countries. There must be a general realization that world prosperity, like world peace, is indivisible. Nations must act together to restore multilateral international trade, and to provide orderly procedure for the maintenance of balanced economic growth. Only through international cooperation will it be possible for countries successfully to apply measures directed toward attaining and maintaining a high level of employment and income which must be the primary objective of economic policy.

The International Stabilization Fund of the United and Associated Nations is proposed as a permanent institution for international monetary cooperation. The resources of this Fund would be available under adequate safeguards to maintain currency stability, while giving member countries time to correct maladjustments in their balance of payments without resorting to extreme measures destructive of international prosperity. The resources of the Fund would not be used to prolong a basically unbalanced international position. On the contrary, the Fund would be influential in inducing countries to pursue policies making for an orderly return to equilibrium.

The Fund would deal only with member governments and their fiscal agents, and would not intrude in the customary channels for conducting international commerce and finance. The Fund is intended to provide supplemental facilities for the successful functioning of the established foreign

* Preliminary Draft Outline, July 10, 1943. Reprinted in J. Keith Horsefield (ed.), *The International Monetary Fund*, Vol. III: *Documents* (1969), pp. 85–86.

exchange institutions and to free international commerce from harmful restrictions.

The success of the Fund must ultimately depend upon the willingness of nations to act together on their common problems. International monetary cooperation should not be regarded as a matter of generosity. All countries have a vital interest in the maintenance of international monetary stability, and in the balanced growth of multilateral international trade.

I. Purposes of the Fund

The United Nations and the countries associated with them recognize, as declared in the Atlantic Charter, the need for the fullest cooperation among nations with the object of securing economic advancement and rising standards of living for all. They believe that attainment of these objectives will be facilitated by international monetary cooperation. Therefore, it is proposed that there be established an International Stabilization Fund with the following purposes:

To help stabilize the foreign exchange rates of the currencies of the United Nations and the countries associated with them.

To shorten the periods and lessen the degree of disequilibrium in the international balance of payments of member countries.

To help create conditions under which the smooth flow of foreign trade and of productive capital among the member countries will be fostered.

To facilitate the effective utilization of the blocked foreign balances accumulating in some countries as a consequence of the war situation.

To reduce the use of such foreign exchange restrictions, bilateral clearing arrangements, multiple currency devices, and discriminatory foreign exchange practices as hamper world trade and the international flow of productive capital.

Differing markedly from both the Keynes and White plans was the "key currency" proposal of Professor John H. Williams who argued that what would really matter for the stability of the postwar international economy would be the position of the dollar and the pound. These would be the key currencies in the sense that they would play dominant roles in world trade, finance, and foreign exchange markets. He emphasized that international stability would depend essentially on monetary control within the United States and Britain, and cooperation between them, because the dollar and pound were the "truly international currencies whose behavior dominates and determines what happens to all the others." [2] Williams suggested that

2. John H. Williams, "Currency Stabilization: The Keynes and White Plans," *Foreign Affairs* (July 1943), pp. 645–58; reprinted in Williams, *Postwar Monetary Plans and Other Essays* (1947), pp. 3–21.

external monetary stabilization should begin with plans for stabilizing the dollar-sterling rate and for measures on internal policy: "the problem of international monetary stability is primarily that of maintaining a state of proper economic health in the leading countries; and . . . this is the only workable answer to the whole conflict between internal and external monetary stability. . . . This means collaboration to maintain both a high level of real income within the leading countries and a high degree of exchange stability between them. If this could be done, the problem of maintaining exchange stability for the other countries, and a reasonable state of economic well-being within them, would probably not present major difficulties."

It is ironical that in the 1970's some of the views that were dismissed at Bretton Woods were receiving another more sympathetic hearing (as we shall see more fully in Problems II and III). The Keynes Plan was revived in the closely related proposals of Professor Robert Triffin for an expanded IMF that would have some attributes of an international central bank.[3] And Williams' key currency plan was echoed by those who advocated a dollar reserve standard (one key currency) or a dollar-European currency standard (two key currencies). As Professor Harry Johnson observes:

> [The key-currency plan] gained no significant hearing in the climate of opinion of the immediate postwar II period; and it has been more or less swamped ever since as an intellectual position by the tendency of both academic economists and practitioners to accept as a framework for argument the fictitious assumption of a large number of equal countries and currencies on which the formal structure of the IMF system is built, and the corresponding assumption that it is useful to discuss the problems of the system in terms of anonymous deficit and surplus countries and their responsibilities towards the system.
>
> Nevertheless, if one looks at the realities of what has been happening in the evolution of the system, the key currency approach helps one to understand a great deal.[4]

3. See Robert Triffin, *Gold and the Dollar Crisis* (1960); *Our International Monetary System: Yesterday, Today and Tomorrow* (1968).
4. Harry G. Johnson, "The Bretton Woods System, Key Currencies, and the 'Dollar Crisis' of 1971," *The Three Banks Review* (March 1972), p. 6.

1.2 Establishment of the IMF

Over the period 1941–44, the United States and Britain engaged in a series of mutual consultations and redrafts of the Keynes and White plans. Finally, in July 1944, the Bretton Woods conference was convened, and after considerable negotiation there was approval of the Articles of Agreement of the International Monetary Fund.

The Articles of Agreement stated the Purposes of the IMF.

ARTICLES OF AGREEMENT *
ARTICLE I. PURPOSES

The purposes of the International Monetary Fund are:
To promote international monetary cooperation through a permanent institution which provides the machinery for consultation and collaboration on international monetary problems.
To facilitate the expansion and balanced growth of international trade, and to contribute thereby to the promotion and maintenance of high levels of employment and real income and to the development of the productive resources of all members as primary objectives of economic policy.
To promote exchange stability, to maintain orderly exchange arrangements among members, and to avoid competitive exchange depreciation.
To assist in the establishment of a multilateral system of payments in respect of current transactions between members and in the elimination of foreign exchange restrictions which hamper the growth of world trade.
To give confidence to members by making the Fund's resources available to them under adequate safeguards, thus providing them with opportunity to correct maladjustments in their balance of payments without resorting to measures destructive of national or international prosperity.
In accordance with the above, to shorten the duration and lessen the degree of disequilibrium in the international balances of payments of members.
The Fund shall be guided in all its decisions by the purposes set forth in this Article.

The accomplishments at the Bretton Woods conference can be interpreted in terms of the uneasy triangle of how to allow nations to pursue their domestic economic goals without being required to forgo the gains from trade liberalization or to suffer the costs of correcting balance-of-payments disequilibrium. In

* For the Articles of Agreement, as established at Bretton Woods, see Horsefield (ed.), *The International Monetary Fund*, Vol. III: *Documents* (1969), pp. 185ff.

the interests of their pledge to full employment, nations would
no longer tolerate—as under the pure gold standard—deflation
as a means of removing a balance-of-payments deficit. Nor did
they want to endure again successive rounds of competitive
currency depreciations. To provide domestic autonomy for the
pursuit of full employment, there must be the possibility of
drawing upon sources of international liquidity other than the
limited amount of gold reserves. To avoid the extremes of a
freely fluctuating exchange rate, or a fixed exchange rate, there
must be initially some fixity of exchange rates, as determined by
the IMF, but subsequently some provision for adjustments in
the value of a country's currency.

To achieve these objectives, the Fund established a detailed
code of international monetary conduct based on four fundamental principles.[5]

First, a country's foreign exchange rate is a matter of international concern; a par value system should be the subject of international scrutiny and endorsement. All member countries of
the Fund must establish par values for their currencies, expressed in terms of gold or of the United States dollar of specified gold content, and may not change them without consultation with the Fund. [See Article IV, pp. 35–37 below.] Exchange
rates should therefore be fixed (ignoring permitted fluctuations
within 1 per cent of either side of the fixed parities). To maintain the stability of its exchange rate, the official monetary authority of a member country should act as the residual buyer or
seller on foreign exchange markets, intervening in the market
as necessary to keep the currency from rising or falling. The
exchange rate may be subject to periodic change—the "adjustable peg" feature of the Fund—but this variation in the exchange rate is allowed by the Fund only to correct a "fundamental disequilibrium" in the member's balance of
payments.

The second basic principle of the IMF is that exchange controls on current international payments should be prohibited,

---

5. These principles are elaborated more fully in W. Scammell, *International Monetary Policy* (1961), pp. 154–70; B. Tew, *International Monetary Co-operation,
1945–1970* (1970); Horsefield (ed.), *The International Monetary Fund 1945–65*, Vol. II:
Analysis (1969), pp. 454–67.

except temporarily under certain extraordinary conditions. [Article VIII (2) (a).] Members were also prohibited from engaging in "any discriminatory currency arrangements or multiple currency practices." [Article VIII (3).] There was also the obligation to convert at par balances of a member's currency held by another member. [Article VIII (4).] A country's currency would be "convertible" when it complied with these Article VIII obligations that were designed to establish a system of stable and unitary exchange rates.

Third, national gold and currency reserves must be augmented so that countries need not be forced to meet short-run balance-of-payments deficits by suffering domestic deflation and unemployment. This should be in the form of prescribed "drawing rights" by a member country on its "quota" at the Fund. [See Article III, pp. 38–39 below.] A member's subscription to the Fund is equal to its quota. The financial resources subscribed to the Fund constitute an international reserve pool of currencies against which members can draw for short-term financial assistance. A member's right to purchase other currencies from the Fund with its own currency is subject to complex rules [Article V]. A member has "drawing rights" up to 125 per cent of its quota, divided into five equal *tranches*. Only the first *tranche*—the "gold *tranche*"—can be drawn upon automatically and unconditionally to achieve international liquidity. Beyond the gold *tranche*, discretionary factors enter into the Fund's decision on whether the member country can exercise its drawing rights and under what conditions. A drawing country must repurchase its own currency from the Fund within three to five years by payment to the Fund in the foreign currency previously acquired or in any other currency acceptable to the Fund. Outstanding drawings are subject to interest charges that increase with the number of credit *tranches* used and with the time for which the drawing has been outstanding. This temporary access to the Fund's financial resources offers only short-term financing to help ease the adjustment process for short-term balance-of-payments problems. For "fundamental disequilibrium," a term left undefined in the Articles, the adjustable peg comes into force.

Finally, the IMF adopted the principle that a balance-of-payments disequilibrium is necessarily two-sided between deficit and surplus countries; the adjustment obligations are therefore the joint responsibility of both surplus and deficit countries. In recognition of this principle, the Agreement permits the Fund to declare that a particular currency suffers from a "general scarcity." [Article VII]. If this "scarce currency" clause is invoked against a country that runs a large and persistent surplus in its balance of payments, members may impose a temporary limitation on exchange of the scarce currency and can practice discriminatory exchange restrictions against it.

A deficit country is still expected to undertake remedial measures to correct a "fundamental disequilibrium" in its balance of payments. These measures should go beyond the temporary use of the secondary reserves provided by the Fund and fall short of alteration of its exchange rate. Pending the adoption of measures to restore equilibrium in its balance of payments, a deficit country has recourse to the international pool of currencies held by the Fund. But the system does not grant a member country immunity from the "discipline of the balance of payments." A member's access to the Fund's resources is contingent upon the member's undertaking some process of adjustment. Balance-of-payments discipline will ultimately be exercised, though a country may gain some "breathing time" by using its drawing rights at the Fund.

It is illuminating to recall Keynes' report after Bretton Woods to the British Parliament, explaining the nature and scope of the Fund. Although the Fund was a compromise, the British had wanted to depart radically from the strictures of the old gold standard, while the United States had advocated a system retaining more features of the gold standard. At the same time as the United States Congress was being told that the dollar was "defined" in terms of gold and that the Fund would operate much like the gold standard,[6] Keynes was insisting that the domestic supply of money would no longer be regulated by gold flows and that the Fund proposals were the "exact opposite of the gold standard."

6. For an account of the Congressional debate before the United States accepted membership in the Fund, see Richard N. Gardner, *Sterling-Dollar Diplomacy* (1956), pp. 129–43.

THE INTERNATIONAL MONETARY FUND *

My Lords, it is almost exactly a year since the proposals for a Clearing Union were discussed in your Lordships' House. I hope to persuade your Lordships that the year has not been ill-spent. There were, it is true, certain features of elegance, clarity, and logic in the Clearing Union plan which have disappeared. And this, by me at least, is to be much regretted. As a result, however, there is no longer any need for a new-fangled international monetary unit. Your Lordships will remember how little any of us liked the names proposed—bancor, unitas, dolphin, bezant, daric, and heaven knows what. Some of your Lordships were good enough to join in the search for something better. I recall a story of a country parish in the last century where they were accustomed to give their children Biblical names—Amos, Ezekiel, Obadiah, and so forth. Needing a name for a dog, after a long and vain search of the Scriptures they called the dog "Moreover." We hit on no such happy solution, with the result that it has been the dog that died. The loss of the dog we need not too much regret, though I still think that it was a more thoroughbred animal than what has now come out from a mixed marriage of ideas. Yet, perhaps, as sometimes occurs, this dog of mixed origin is a sturdier and more serviceable animal and will prove not less loyal and faithful to the purposes for which it has been bred.

I commend the new plan to your Lordships as being, in some important respects (to which I will return later), a considerable improvement on either of its parents. I like this new plan and I believe that it will work to our advantage. . . .

What, then, are these major advantages that I hope from the plan to the advantage of this country? First, it is clearly recognized and agreed that, during the post-war transitional period of uncertain duration, we are entitled to retain any of those wartime restrictions, and special arrangements with the sterling area and others which are helpful to us, without being open to the charge of acting contrary to any general engagements into which we have entered. . . .

Second, when this period is over and we are again strong enough to live year by year on our own resources, we can look forward to trading in a world of national currencies which are inter-convertible. For a great commercial nation like ourselves, this is indispensable for full prosperity. Sterling itself, in due course, must obviously become, once again, generally convertible. . . .

So far from an international plan endangering the long tradition by which most Empire countries, and many other countries, too, have centred their financial systems in London, the plan is, in my judgment, an indispensable means of maintaining this tradition. With our own resources so greatly impaired and encumbered, it is only if sterling is firmly placed in an international setting that the necessary confidence in it can be sustained. Indeed,

* Speech delivered by Lord Keynes before the House of Lords, May 23, 1944.

even during the transitional period, it will be our policy, I hope, steadily to develop the field within which sterling is freely available as rapidly as we can manage. Now if our own goal is, as it surely must be, the general inter-convertibility of sterling with other currencies, it must obviously be to our trading advantage that the same obtains elsewhere, so that we can sell our exports in one country and freely spend the proceeds in any other. It is a great gain to us in particular, that other countries in the world should agree to refrain from those discriminatory exchange practices which we ourselves have never adopted in times of peace but from which in the recent past our traders have suffered greatly at the hands of others. . . .

Third, the wheels of trade are to be oiled by what is, in effect, a great addition to the world's stock of monetary reserves, distributed, moreover, in a reasonable way. The quotas are not so large as under the Clearing Union. . . .

. . . But they are substantial and can be increased subsequently if the need is shown. The aggregate for the world is put provisionally at £2,500,000,000. Our own share of this—for ourselves and the Crown Colonies which, I may mention, are treated for all purposes as a part of the British monetary system (in itself a useful acknowledgment)—is £325,000,000, a sum which may easily double, or more than double, the reserves which we shall otherwise hold at the end of the transitional period. The separate quotas of the rest of the sterling area will make a further large addition to this. Who is so confident of the future that he will wish to throw away so comfortable a supplementary aid in time of trouble? Do the critics think it preferable, if the winds of the trade cycle blow, to diminish our demand for imports by increasing unemployment at home, rather than meet the emergency out of this Fund which will be expressly provided for such temporary purposes?

I emphasize that such is the purpose of the quotas. They are not intended as daily food for us or any other country to live upon during the reconstruction or afterwards. Provision for that belongs to another chapter of international co-operation, upon which we shall embark shortly unless you discourage us unduly about this one. The quotas for drawing on the Fund's resources are an iron ration to tide over temporary emergencies of one kind or another. . . .

There is another advantage to which I would draw your Lordships' special attention. A proper share of responsibility for maintaining equilibrium in the balance of international payments is squarely placed on the creditor countries. This is one of the major improvements in the new plan. The Americans, who are the most likely to be affected by this, have, of their own free will and honest purpose, offered us a far-reaching formula of protection against a recurrence of the main cause of deflation during the inter-war years—namely, the draining of reserves out of the rest of the world to pay a country which was obstinately lending and exporting on a scale immensely greater than it was lending and importing. Under Clause VI of the plan, a country engages itself, in effect, to prevent such a situation from arising again, by promising, should it fail, to release other countries from any obligation to take its exports, or, if taken, to pay for them. I cannot imagine that this sanction would ever be allowed to come into effect. If by no other means than by lending, the creditor country will always have to find a way to square the account on imperative grounds of its own self-interest. For it will no longer be entitled to square the account by squeezing gold out of the rest of us. Here we have a voluntary undertaking, genuinely offered in the spirit both of a good neighbor and, I should add, of enlightened self-interest, not to allow a repetition of a chain of events which between the wars did more than any other single factor to destroy the world's economic balance and to prepare a seed-bed for foul growths. This is a tremendous extension of international co-operation to good ends. I pray your Lordships to pay heed to its importance.

Fifth, the plan sets up an international institution with substantial rights and duties to preserve orderly arrangements in matters such as exchange rates which are two-ended and affect both parties alike, which can also serve as a place of regular discussion between responsible authorities to find ways to escape those many unforeseeable dangers which the future holds.

Here are five advantages of major importance. The proposals go far beyond what, even a short time ago, anyone could have conceived of as a possible basis of general international agreement. What alternative is open to us which gives comparable aid, or better, more hopeful opportunities for the future? I have considerable confidence that something very like this plan will be in fact adopted, if only on account of the plain demerits of the alternative of rejection. You can talk against this plan, so long as it is a matter of talking—saying in the same breath that it goes too far and that it does not go far enough, that it is too rigid to be safe and that it is too loose to be worth anything. But it would require great fool-hardiness to reject it, much more fool-hardiness than is to be found in this wise, intuitive country.

Therefore, for these manifold and substantial benefits I commend the monetary proposals to your Lordships. Nevertheless, before you will give them your confidence, you will wish to consider whether, in return, we are surrendering anything which is vital for the ordering of our domestic affairs in the manner we intend for the future. My Lords, the experience of the years before the war has led most of us, though some of us late in the day, to certain firm conclusions. Three, in particular, are highly relevant to this discussion. We are determined that, in future, the external value of sterling shall conform to its internal value as set by our own domestic policies, and not the other way round. Secondly, we intend to retain control of our domestic rate of interest, so that we can keep it as low as suits our own purposes, without interference from the ebb and flow of international capital movements or flights of hot money. Thirdly, whilst we intend to prevent inflation at home, we will not accept deflation at the dictate of influences from outside. In other words, we abjure the instruments of bank rate and credit contraction operating through the increase of unemployment as a means of forcing our domestic economy into line with external factors.

Have those responsible for the monetary proposals been sufficiently careful to preserve these principles from the possibility of interference? I hope your Lordships will trust me not to have turned my back on all I have fought for. To establish those three principles which I have just stated has been my main task for the last twenty years. Sometimes almost alone, in popular articles in the press, in pamphlets, in dozens of letters to *The Times,* in text books, in enormous and obscure treatises I have spent my strength to persuade my countrymen and the world at large to change their traditional doctrines and, by taking better thought, to remove the curse of unemployment. Was it not I, when many of to-day's iconoclasts were still worshippers of the Calf, who wrote that "Gold is a barbarous relic"? Am I so faithless, so forgetful, so senile that, at the very moment of the triumph of these ideas when, with gathering momentum, governments, parliaments, banks, the press, the public, and even economists, have at last accepted the new doctrines, I go off to help forge new chains to hold us fast in the old dungeon? I trust, my Lords, that you will not believe it. . . .

The question, however, which has recently been given chief prominence is whether we are in any sense returning to the disabilities of the former gold standard, relief from which we have rightly learnt to prize so highly. If I have any authority to pronounce on what is and what is not the essence and meaning of a gold standard, I should say that this plan is the exact opposite of it. The plan in its relation to gold is, indeed, very close to proposals which I advocated in vain as the right alternative when I was bitterly opposing this country's return to gold. The gold standard, as I understand it, means a system under which the external value of a national currency is rigidly tied to a fixed quantity of gold which can only honorably be broken under *force majeure;* and it involves a financial policy which compels the internal value of the domestic currency to conform to this external value as fixed in terms of gold. On the other hand, the use of gold merely as a convenient common denominator by means of which the relative values of national currencies—these being free to change—are expressed from time to time, is obviously quite another matter.

My noble friend Lord Addison asks who fixes the value of gold. If he means, as I assume he does, the sterling value of gold, it is we ourselves who fix it initially in consultation with the Fund; and this value is subject to change at any time on our initiative, changes in excess of 10 per cent requiring the approval of the Fund, which must not withhold approval if our domestic equilibrium requires it. There must be *some* price for gold; and so long as gold is used as a monetary reserve it is most advisable that the current rates of exchange and the relative values of gold in different currencies should correspond. The only alternative to this would be the complete demonetization of gold. I am not aware that anyone has proposed that. For it is only common sense as things are to-day to continue to make use of gold and its prestige as a means of settling international accounts. To demonetize gold would obviously be highly objectionable to the British Commonwealth and to Russia as the main producers, and to the United States and the Western Allies as the main holders of it. Surely no one disputes that? On the other hand, in this country we have already dethroned gold as the fixed standard of value. The plan not merely confirms the dethronement but approves it by expressly providing that it is the duty of the Fund to alter the gold value of any currency if it is shown that this will be serviceable to equilibrium.

In fact, the plan introduces in this respect an epoch-making innovation in an international instrument, the object of which is to lay down sound and orthodox principles. For instead of maintaining the principle that the internal value of a national currency should conform to a prescribed *de jure* external value, it provides that its external value should be altered if necessary so as to conform to whatever *de facto* internal value results from domestic policies, which themselves shall be immune from criticism by the Fund. Indeed, it is made the duty of the Fund to approve changes which will have this effect. That is why I say that these proposals are the exact opposite of the gold standard. They lay down by international agreement the essence of the new doctrine, far removed from the old orthodoxy. If they do so in terms as inoffensive as possible to the former faith, need we complain?

No, my Lords, in recommending these proposals I do not blot a page already written. I am trying to help write a new page. Public opinion is now converted to a new model, and I believe a much improved model, of domestic policy. That battle is all but won. Yet a not less difficult task still remains— namely, to organize an international setting within which the new domestic policies can occupy a comfortable place. Therefore, it is above all as providing an international framework for the new ideas and the new techniques associated with the policy of full employment that these proposals are not least to be welcomed. . . .

1.3 *The Gold-Exchange Standard*

The operation of the IMF and the role played by reserve currencies—dollars and to a much lesser degree, sterling—gave the postwar international monetary system its essential shape. This system is termed the gold-exchange standard, or more accurately, the gold-exchange and reserve currencies standard. The most important features of this international monetary mechanism have turned out to be its system of pegged—but adjustable—rates and provisions for liquidity.

Article IV of the Fund's Articles of Agreement set forth provisions for the exchange rate system.

ARTICLE IV. PAR VALUES OF CURRENCIES

Section 1. Expression of par values. (a) The par value of the currency of each member shall be expressed in terms of gold as a common denominator or in terms of the United States dollar of the weight and fineness in effect on July 1, 1944.

(b) All computations relating to currencies of members for the purpose of applying the provisions of this Agreement shall be on the basis of their par values.

Sec. 2. Gold purchases based on par values. The Fund shall prescribe a margin above and below par value for transactions in gold by members, and no member shall buy gold at a price above par value plus the prescribed margin, or sell gold at a price below par value minus the prescribed margin.

Sec. 3. Foreign exchange dealings based on parity. The maximum and the minimum rates for exchange transactions between the currencies of members taking place within their territories shall not differ from parity

(i) in the case of spot exchange transactions, by more than one percent; and

(ii) in the case of other exchange transactions, by a margin which exceeds the margin for spot exchange transactions by more than the Fund considers reasonable.

Sec. 4. Obligations regarding exchange stability. (a) Each member undertakes to collaborate with the Fund to promote exchange stability, to maintain orderly exchange arrangements with other members, and to avoid competitive exchange alterations.

(b) Each member undertakes through appropriate measures consistent with this Agreement, to permit within its territories exchange transactions between its currency and the currencies of other members only within the limits prescribed under Section 3 of this Article. A member whose monetary authorities, for the settlement of international transactions, in fact freely buy and sell gold within the limits prescribed by the Fund under Section 2 of this Article shall be deemed to be fulfilling this undertaking.

Sec. 5. Changes in par values. (a) A member shall not propose a change in the par value of its currency except to correct a fundamental disequilibrium.

(b) A change in the par value of a member's currency may be made only on the proposal of the member and only after consultation with the Fund.

(c) When a change is proposed, the Fund shall first take into account the changes, if any, which have already taken place in the initial par value of the member's currency as determined under Article XX, Section 4. If the proposed change, together with all previous changes, whether increases or decreases,

(i) does not exceed ten percent of the initial par value, the Fund shall raise no objection;

(ii) does not exceed a further ten percent of the initial par value, the Fund may either concur or object, but shall declare its attitude within seventy-two hours if the member so requests;

(iii) is not with (i) or (ii) above, the Fund may either concur or object, but shall be entitled to a longer period in which to declare its attitude.

(d) Uniform changes in par values made under Section 7 of this Article shall not be taken into account in determining whether a proposed change falls within (i), (ii), or (iii) of (c) above.

(e) A member may change the par value of its currency without the concurrence of the Fund if the change does not affect the international transactions of members of the Fund.

(f) The Fund shall concur in a proposed change which is within the terms of (c) (ii) or (c) (iii) above if it is satisfied that the change is necessary to correct a fundamental disequilibrium. In particular, provided it is so satisfied, it shall not object to a proposed change because of the domestic social or political policies of the member proposing the change.

Sec. 6. Effect of unauthorized changes. If a member changes the par value of its currency despite the objection of the Fund, in cases where the Fund is entitled to object, the member shall be ineligible to use the resources of the Fund unless the Fund otherwise determines; and if, after the expiration of a reasonable period, the difference between the member and the Fund continues, the matter shall be subject to the provisions of Article XV, Section 2 (b).

The United States alone chose to maintain the international value of the dollar by making it interconvertible with gold through transactions with official foreign monetary authorities: it agreed to "freely buy and sell gold" within the prescribed limits [Article IV (4) (b)]. Other countries maintained the value of their currencies by using the dollar as the intervention currency, entering the foreign exchange markets to buy or sell dollars as needed to maintain their currencies within 1 per cent on either side of the par values.

Gold entered into the monetary system in two important ways. First, it constituted an official reserve asset and was a means of ultimate settlement in the balance of payments. Second, the value of local currencies was expressed in terms of gold or the dollar, and the dollar was expressed in terms of gold so that par values connected with gold or the United States gold price. "Convertible currencies" were thus convertible into United States dollars, and United States dollars held by monetary authorities of other Fund members were convertible into gold. This is another sense in which gold was referred to as the "final" or "ultimate" asset. It has been observed that if this "delphic reference to gold as the 'final' or 'ultimate' asset . . . was indeed the theory of the drafters [of the Fund's Articles], they probably assumed the continued invulnerability of the United States dollar and the readiness of other members to hold dollars in the quantities that were likely to become available to them. This view of the world and the assumptions on which it rested were not made explicit in the Articles. For example, there is no obligation under the Articles for the United States or any other member to buy and sell gold for its own currency. The Articles recognize the possibility that the monetary authorities of a member may freely buy and sell gold in fact, within the margins of par established by the Fund for gold transactions, for the settlement of international transactions. If a member engages in this practice, it will be maintaining the value of its own currency in direct relation to gold. . . . The United States is the only member which has informed the Fund that it freely buys and sells gold within the meaning of the provision that recognizes that practice." [7] This practice meant that official monetary authorities could sell gold to the United States Treasury for dollars, and until August 15, 1971, they also had the privilege of converting their holdings of dollars to gold at the United States Treasury.

By being left with these functions, gold was not demonetized under the IMF—even if it was "dethroned" from the central position it had previously occupied under the pure gold standard. The contribution of gold to international liquidity has, however, been limited. By "international liquidity" is meant the aggregate stock of assets held by the national monetary authority that is available unconditionally to settle the country's imbalance in international transactions. At present, official reserve assets consist of official gold holdings, a member country's unconditional drawing rights at the IMF (its gold *tranche*), the special drawing rights allocated to a member country of the IMF (see Problem II), and official holdings of convertible foreign currencies—mainly the United States dollar and pound sterling as reserve currencies.

Drawing rights at the IMF depend on the size of the member's quota. Quotas were specified as follows.

ARTICLE III. QUOTAS AND SUBSCRIPTIONS

Section 1. Quotas. Each member shall be assigned a quota. The quotas of the members represented at the United Nations Monetary and Financial Con-

7. Horsefield (ed.), *International Monetary Fund 1945–65*, Vol. II, pp. 559–60.

ference which accept membership before the date specified in Article XX, Section 2 (e), shall be those set forth in Schedule A. The quotas of other members shall be determined by the Fund.

Sec. 2. Adjustment of quotas. The Fund shall at intervals of five years review, and if it deems it appropriate propose an adjustment of, the quotas of the members. It may also, if it thinks fit, consider at any other time the adjustment of any particular quota at the request of the member concerned. A four-fifths majority of the total voting power shall be required for any change in quotas and no quota shall be changed without the consent of the member concerned.

Sec. 3. Subscriptions: time, place, and form of payment. (a) The subscription of each member shall be equal to its quota and shall be paid in full to the Fund at the appropriate depository on or before the date when the member becomes eligible under Article XX, Section 4 (c) or (d), to buy currencies from the Fund.

(b) Each member shall pay in gold, as a minimum, the smaller of
(i) twenty-five percent of its quota; or
(ii) ten percent of its net official holdings of gold and United States dollars as at the date when the Fund notifies members under Article XX, Section 4 (a) that it will shortly be in a position to begin exchange transactions.

It is noteworthy that at the outset the size of the Fund was limited by the United States and that the initial total of quotas in the Fund, about $8.8 billion, was only about one-third the size of resources which Keynes wished to make available. The American quota was initially $2.75 billion and the United King-

TABLE I. Composition of World Monetary Reserves: 1949–71
(in billions of U.S. dollars)

	1949	1969	1970	1971
I. Gold	33.5	39.1	37.2	39.2
II. Special drawing rights	—	—	3.1	6.4
III. Reserves in IMF	1.7	6.7	7.7	6.9
IV. Foreign currencies	10.4	32.4	44.5	77.6
Dollars	3.2	16.0	23.9	50.7
Sterling	6.9	9.0	6.6	7.9
Euro-dollars, etc.	0.3	7.4	14.0	19.1
V. Total	45.5	78.2	92.5	130.1
United States	26.0	17.0	14.5	13.2
Other countries	19.5	61.2	78.1	116.9

SOURCE: IMF, *International Financial Statistics.*

TABLE II. Gross and Net Reserves of the United States: 1949–71
(in billions of U.S. dollars)

	1949	1969	1970	1971
I. Gross reserves	26.0	17.0	14.5	13.2
of which: gold	24.6	11.9	11.1	11.1
II. External liabilities (−)	− 3.2	−17.0	−25.3	−53.5
to:				
1. IMF and SDR allocat.	—	− 1.0	− 1.4	− 2.8
2. Foreign central banks	− 3.2	−16.0	−23.9	−50.7
III. Net reserves (I + II)	+ 22.8	− 0.1	−10.8	−40.3

SOURCE: IMF, *International Financial Statistics.*

dom's $1.3 billion. The subsequent growth of the Fund has also been restrained: there have been only three general increases in quotas.

There has, however, been increasing use of dollars as reserves, and this has permitted the amount of international liquidity to increase far beyond that which would have been provided by only increases in the total gold stock and Fund quotas. Tables I and II indicate the growth in international reserves and the changing sources of international liquidity over the period 1945–71. As will be seen in Problem II, the growth in the supply of dollars as reserves has been associated with a "deficit" in the United States balance of payments.

2. PRESSURES OF THE 1960's

By the mid-1960's both academic and government economists were expressing ever-greater concern about weaknesses that were becoming increasingly evident in the monetary system. Stresses and strains became more pronounced as nations followed independent monetary policies and divergent rates of inflation; exchange rates were pegged—but the peg was adjustable; and both the dollar and gold served as international monies. As one analyst expressed the problem, "there is no mechanism to ensure that the three major components of the system—the exchange rate system, national monetary and fiscal policies, and the supply of international monies—are consistent with each other." [8]

8. Robert Z. Aliber, *The International Money Game* (1973), pp. 25–26.

2.1 *The System's Vulnerability*

For some, the most vulnerable aspect of the system was that it had become dollar-centered, but the dollar still had to coexist with other reserve assets (sterling, gold). Professor Robert Triffin repeatedly warned that the persistent deficit and piling up of short-term indebtedness of the United States, as a reserve center, were bound to undermine, in the end, the confidence of other countries in the ability of the United States to honor its commitment to redeem dollar holdings in gold. In the early 1960's Triffin was pointing out that

> other countries derived from net U.S. reserve losses nearly 60 per cent of their total reserve increases in 1950-57, and 80 per cent in 1958-62, i.e., in these last five years nearly eight times as much as the amount of reserves derived from gold production in the West.
>
> Nobody can any longer seriously defend such a system—or rather lack of system—as a safe and rational way to regulate the increase of international reserves which must serve as the ultimate basis, particularly under convertibility conditions, for the increases in national money supplies necessary to support growing levels of production and trade in an expanding world economy.[9]

Professor Richard Cooper also provided a clear perspective on weaknesses of the international monetary system in the following Congressional testimony.

GUIDELINES FOR INTERNATIONAL MONETARY REFORM *

Statement of Richard N. Cooper, Associate Professor
of Economics, Yale University

Mr. Cooper. Yes, thank you, Mr. Chairman.
I have submitted a rather lengthy paper. With your permission, I will just read portions of it this morning.

---

9. Robert Triffin, *The Evolution of the International Monetary System: Historical Reappraisal and Future Perspectives*, Princeton Studies in International Finance, No. 12 (1964). Triffin's forecast of forthcoming crises appeared earlier in his *Europe and the Money Muddle* (1957), pp. 296–301; testimony to the Joint Economic Committee on October 28, 1959 [reproduced in his *Gold and the Dollar Crisis* (1960)].

* Hearings before the Subcommittee on International Exchange and Payments of the Joint Economic Committee, 89th Congress, 1st Session, Part 1: Hearings, July 29, 1965, pp. 109–113, 117, 119.

It is customary these days to consider the weaknesses of the international monetary system under three broad headings: defects in the mechanism of international payments adjustment, inadequate means for generating international liquidity, and vulnerability of the composition of international liquidity to crises in confidence. Although every discussion of the need for international monetary reform refers to one or more of these weaknesses, the weights which different observers attach to each vary greatly, and so as a result do the proposed reforms. I will say something general about these weaknesses and then as requested by the subcommittee offer specific guidelines to reform.

International liquidity is needed primarily to finance temporary imbalances in payments and to obviate precipitate action to correct a balance-of-payments deficit. Ample liquidity provides time for more acceptable corrective measures to be taken. Liquidity requirements therefore depend both on the size of disturbances to international payments and on the speed with which imbalances are corrected.

To clarify the relationship between liquidity and adjustment I find it useful to classify the methods for coping with a prospective (ex ante) balance-of-payments deficit under fixed exchange rates—flexible rates have been ruled out by the terms of reference of the subcommittee. Two of these categories involve measures of adjustment, one internal, the other external; one involves financing the deficit, that is, international liquidity.

First, a country confronted with a prospective deficit can use internal economic policies to reduce the deficit. Typically this will involve deflationary policies in the domestic economy; a tighter budget or higher interest rates. Such internal policies influence international payments by lowering the level of domestic activity or raising the yield on assets in the domestic economy.

Second, a country might use external measures to switch expenditures away from imports of foreign goods, securities, and other transactions which involve payments to foreigners. Thus, these selective measures operate directly on international transactions. To help reduce a deficit such actions might include imposing import quotas, raising tariffs, or prohibiting capital outflow.

To the extent that measures within these two broad categories were not taken, the country would experience an actual (observed) deficit which would then have to be financed in some way. Such financing often takes the form of drawing down gold and foreign exchange reserves, but it can also involve compensatory official capital movements from abroad, special borrowing through private markets or commercial banks, or even compensatory sales of goods and services—all motivated by the imbalance in international payments.

The choice among these three methods for coping with prospective imbalances touches on matters of high national importance. We are thus far from indifferent about which types of measure are used.

Most observers want to avoid extreme forms of all of these three categories of action. Many bankers, for example, speak of the need for the "discipline" of the balance of payments; they wish to restrict the means to finance deficits. Liberal economists and people favoring international integration are offended by trade quotas and exchange controls and generally dislike autarkic measures which interfere with trade and payments. Other observers emphasize the need to preserve domestic autonomy in economic policymaking and in particular the ability to maintain full employment or stability in the level of domestic prices.

Economists love diagrams, so true to my profession I have included one. . . .

[Figure 1 indicates] we cannot generally forswear extensive use of external measures, internal measures, and liberal financing simultaneously. Prospective balance-of-payments deficits must be handled in some combination of these three ways, and if we set our standards too high, one or more of them will have to give.

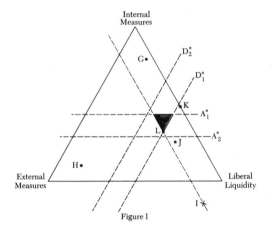

Figure 1

The three broad categories for coping with imbalances—internal measures, external measures, and financing—can be illustrated diagrammatically on a triangle such as figure 1. Each point in the triangle represents some combination of the three types of measure for handling a given ex ante imbalance in the international payments of any country or region under fixed exchange rates during a specified period of time. The three vertices of the triangle represent exclusive use of measures in each of the three categories, and the closer a point is to a vertex, the greater the reliance on measures of that type. Thus point G in figure 1 represents the textbook gold standard, in which domestic deflation is primarily relied on to reduce a payments deficit and domestic expansion to reduce a payments surplus. Temporary financing for deficit countries was often arranged by borrowing, and modest exchange rate flexibility within the gold points could be regarded as a minor external measure. But principal reliance was on adjustments in the domestic economy. By contrast, point H represents heavy reliance on external measures such as exchange control and changes in import quotas. Point J represents a country which has ample ability to finance deficits. Many Europeans claim that the United States is in this position by virtue of its role as a reserve currency country, since foreign countries simply accumulate the excess dollars arising from U.S. deficits. Point K might represent a State within the United States. External measures are totally ruled out—no State can impede interstate commerce or impair contracts made by its residents in U.S. dollars. On the other hand, it acquires liberal financing through many cushioning features of a federal system. A drop in income and employment as a result of a fall in exports reduces tax payments to "foreigners" and increases receipts from "foreigners" in the form of unemployment compensation—both through the Federal fiscal system. Moreover, a State can, up to a point, sell financial claims in the national capital market and it can draw down its stock of cash.

This characterization is extremely rough; there are many variants of each type of measure, and in some instances the differences between various types of external measures may be far greater than between certain external measures and certain internal measures or financing measures. Moreover, the time dimension is important. Virtually all regions have ample sources of finance to cover a short-lived deficit. But if the deficit persists it must arrange extraordinary financing or resort to other measures. Thus it will be most useful to consider the position of regions with reference to some considerable length of time, say 2 to 4 years. Finally, as already noted, the pressures on a surplus country are considerably less than those on a deficit country. A surplus country can if necessary finance its surpluses indefinitely—or, if it is taking gold or other international reserves, at least until the deficit countries exhaust their reserves and must adopt other measures. Thus it is most instructive to consider the position of a country with respect to payments deficits.

The choice among these three methods for coping with prospective imbalances touches on matters of high national importance. We are thus far from indifferent about which types of measure are used.

The postwar evolution of the international payments system can [also] be characterized (as shown in fig. 2) as a steady movement away from reliance on selective or external measures such as import quotas and exchange controls to greater reliance on international financing of deficits (as with the Marshall Plan grants after 1948) and on internal adjustment. The question we now face is where to go from here. A given scope for freedom of trade and capital movements will result over time in greatly increased transactions—and imbalances—among countries. Therefore more frequent and more extensive use must be made of internal policies, or liquidity must increase sufficiently to accommodate the larger imbalances. Alternatively, freedom of trade and capital movements will have to be restricted.

This brings me finally to the question of how urgent is the need for international monetary reform. I will make a conditional forecast which is in two

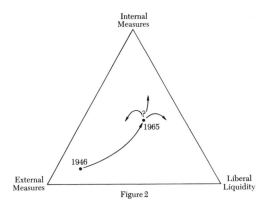

Figure 2

parts. First, unless we improve the means for generating international liquidity and distributing it adequately, we will experience national balance-of-payments "crises" in industrial countries with greater frequency; countries will increasingly find themselves facing balance-of-payments deficits and a weakening of confidence in their currencies, and they will be compelled to adjust domestic policies and/or their barriers to trade and capital movements.

To be sure, in each case it always looks as though the country in question is at fault; its domestic policies may have gotten "out of line" or the public may not be saving enough or something else. But this observation is not sufficient to pass the entire burden of responsibility, or even the major portion of it, to the country in question. At any point in time the positions of some countries will be weaker than others, and any deficiency in the international payments system will show up at their doorsteps first. They are vulnerable, the "marginal" cases. As with general unemployment, it always hits someone, and also like unemployment, there is the danger of confusing the particular case with the general phenomenon.

The second part of the conditional forecast is that we will observe a reversal of the trend toward liberalization of trade and payments and will see greater reliance on selective external measures for eliminating payments deficits. This is not a very daring prediction; we have already seen several moves in that direction: the import surcharges of Canada in 1962 and of Britain in 1964, and the interest equalization tax followed by the program of "voluntary controls" in this country. Countries balk at having to rely too heavily on internal measures to correct imbalances unless such measures also happen to be consistent with domestic objectives of policy, as they were to some extent for Italy last year. This reluctance to use internal measures is as true for surplus countries as it is for deficit countries. Germany has resisted strongly the domestic inflation which is the logical implication of its balance-of-payments surplus under fixed exchange rates; it has relied instead on special devices to induce private short-term investment abroad and on special arrangements with Britain and the United States for purchasing military equipment. But the dilemma is always more acute for the deficit countries. . . .

These then are the crucial questions: How badly do we want liberal trade and capital movements? And how much autonomy in setting and pursuing domestic objectives of economic policy are we willing to sacrifice in order to get them?

2.2 *Financial Crisis Management*

If international liquidity was proving inadequate, there was at the same time a reluctance to rely on the adjustment mechanism of the adjustable peg in exchange rates. In the 1950's, there were few changes in rates, especially for the major currencies in world trade: the United States dollar, pound sterling, French franc, German mark, and Japanese yen. The anticipated political and economic costs and the realization that their currencies were interdependent, made the major countries consider adjustment of rates to be only a last resort device. It should also be remembered that the Fund was not empowered to propose a change of par value to a member; its voice was only a negative one. And a member's own proposal to change the exchange value of its currency was to be "considered only when essential to the correction of fundamental disequilibrium."

Even with the fundamental disequilibrium provision, however, formal devaluations have turned out to be fewer than anticipated at Bretton Woods, and the Fund has found its members reluctant to change their exchange rates even at times when such changes might be the best solution of their difficulties.[10] The pound sterling was devalued in 1949 and 1967, and the French franc was devalued in 1949, 1959, and 1969. Exchange rates of major countries remained fixed between 1956 and 1966 with only three exceptions. In reviewing the international monetary system, Lord Kahn (one of Keynes's closest colleagues) has said that "If one single reason had to be given for the deficiencies in the operations of the international monetary mechanism in the twenty years after World War II it would be the reluctance to contemplate changes in exchange rates." [11]

10. Horsefield (ed.), *International Monetary Fund 1945–1965*, Vol. 1, p. 597.
11. Richard Kahn, "The International Monetary System," *American Economic Review*, Papers and Proceedings (May 1973), p. 181.

Not until after the mid-1960's did exchange rate variations become more frequent. They were then increasingly associated with the build-up of currency crises. Indeed, by establishing the fundamental disequilibrium criterion for adjusting the peg, the Fund clearly presumed that rates would not be changed for a transitory imbalance and that the imbalance would have to persist. In persisting though, the imbalance tended to grow, and speculation against the currency intensified when the adjustment was delayed and could only result in eventually large changes in the rates.

And yet if there was criticism of the system in the 1960's, there was also defense—especially by the Fund:

> the official views of the Fund and also of practically all central banks continued to favor—strongly—fixed exchange rates. Accordingly, when the Group of Ten agreed in August 1964 to study proposals for the reform of the international monetary system, changes in the exchange rate system were explicitly ruled out.
>
> Reluctance to tamper with the par value system reflected at least in part the experience of the Fund and its members during the previous twenty years. . . . [T]here were other arguments in favor of fixed exchange rates—that they put national monetary authorities under pressure to integrate their policies; that they have to be defended by anti-inflationary measures; that they eliminate the danger of competitive depreciation. In addition to these arguments in favor of fixed exchange rates, the Fund had yet another reason for preferring the par value system: in the Fund's view an alternative exchange rate system would make the process of international collaboration more difficult.
>
> As the year 1965 drew to a close, the debates over exchange rates were continuing and becoming more heated.[12] [And currency crises were to become more frequent.]

In the latter-1960's, there were several currency crises in the sense of a severe disequilibrium that threatened the maintenance of value of the currency under attack and the preservation of the international monetary structure. The speculative flights from a currency under pressure to stronger currencies called for financial crisis management. When a country was los-

12. Horsefield (ed.), *International Monetary Fund 1945–1965*, Vol. II, p. 50.

ing international reserve assets at a serious rate—and it was not willing to take remedial measures in the form of deflation or devaluation—it had to manage the crisis by other national measures in the form of direct exchange or trade controls, or else seek international financial assistance. As will be seen in the currency crises examined below, the international assistance can come through a formal system of providing additional liquidity (as in the IMF), or a less formal ad hoc arrangement to meet short-run speculative attacks (as when several central banks cooperate to support a currency under pressure). The imposition of conditions under which this international monetary relief is granted can be highly significant to the recipient country that is trying to manage its economy so as to achieve internal as well as external balance.

As the recounting of the four currency crises below indicates, there is a need to avoid the build-up of the crisis and the need to lessen the cost of crisis management. Short-run management—and provision of "crisis liquidity"—is required to finance or contain the immediate deficit. Beyond that is the longer-term question of monetary reform and provision of "trend liquidity" or other policy action to make the adjustment mechanism more effective.

B. THE ISSUES

3. BRITISH DEVALUATION CRISIS (1967)

Within twenty-four hours of taking office in October 1964, the new Labor Government made a decision not to devalue the pound sterling. Of that first day, the new Prime Minister Harold Wilson recalls that a decision was needed immediately on the three courses that the Treasury had worked out in detail and presented to the new government: devaluation of sterling; quantitative restrictions on imports; or a surcharge on a wide range of imports.

Wilson acknowledges that it was "politically tempting" to devalue at once, "when we could have put all the responsibility on our Conservative predecessors." But he was convinced that "to devalue could have the most dangerous consequences.

. . . [I]n 1964, the true facts of Britain's deficit were not known and politics, rather than economic necessity, would have been blamed." Even more strongly, Wilson believed that a British devaluation "might well have started off an orgy of competitive beggar-my-neighbour currency devaluations . . . which would have plunged the world into monetary anarchy, and left us no better off." Moreover, devaluation "would require a severe and rapid transfer of resources from home consumption, public and private, to meet the needs of overseas markets. This would mean brutal restraints in both public and private expenditure. . . . So devaluation was ruled out by a deliberate decision." [13]

Instead of devaluing, the Government imposed a 15 per cent import surcharge on most imports. A tight money policy was also followed. But there was still heavy pressure on sterling. Wilson recalls that there was daily a heavy drain on reserves, sometimes amounting to more than £50 million in a day while "our total gold and convertible currency reserves barely totalled £1,000 millions. . . . The pound was at its support level. Rumours were reaching feverish proportions." [14]

Compounding the Government's dilemma was the insistence by the Governor of the Bank of England (Lord Cromer) that the government should submit to all-round cuts in expenditure in order to "restore confidence" in the pound. But this would have meant sacrifices in the Government's social and economic priorities. Wilson states that his government

> had to listen night after night to demands that there should
> be immediate cuts in Government expenditure, and particu-
> larly in those parts of Government expenditure which related
> to social services. I said that we had now reached the situa-
> tion where a newly-elected Government with a mandate from
> the people was being told, not so much by the Governor of
> the Bank of England but by international speculators, that the
> policies on which we had fought the election could not be
> implemented; that the Government was to be forced into the
> adoption of Tory policies to which it was fundamentally op-
> posed. [15]

13. Harold Wilson, *The Labour Government 1964–1970, A Personal Record* (1971), pp. 6–7.
14. Ibid. p. 35.
15. Ibid. pp. 34, 37.

Wilson then threatened "to go back to the electorate for a mandate" giving him full powers to handle the crisis and to let the pound float in the meanwhile. Lord Cromer pointed out that the election would occupy about four weeks, the run on sterling would intensify, and "our reserves, which had already fallen considerably, would have run out long before polling day." Wilson, in turn, indicated that the international financial community would be the last to want Britain to float the pound or be forced by speculation into devaluing. He asked Lord Cromer to ask "his central banking colleagues [who] had a vested interest in exchange stability and the strength of sterling" what they were prepared to do to avert a crisis. The next day Wilson received a message that the Governor had successfully raised $3 billion from the central bankers. "He had done a magnificent job," Wilson acknowledged. "Sterling was safe—for a time." [16]

The Bank of England had arranged with the Federal Reserve Bank of New York, the Bank for International Settlements, and the central banks of eight European countries, Canada, and Japan, for facilities to borrow up to $3 billion in various currencies during the next three to six months. In the following interview, Charles Coombs, Vice-President in charge of the Foreign Department, Federal Reserve Bank of New York, recalls how the support for sterling was arranged.

INTERVIEW WITH CHARLES COOMBS *

The Federal Reserve Bank of New York announced an increase in its so-called dollar 'swaps' with other central banks some weeks ago. Could you explain briefly what a 'swap' is and what it is meant to do?

The Federal Reserve swap network is a series of reciprocal credit arrangements now totalling $4.5 billions with 11 central banks and the BIS. The details of these reciprocal credit facilities vary somewhat from agreement to agreement reflecting differing institutional arrangements and operational procedures among the various central banks. However, certain general principles run throughout all of the agreements.

Can you explain what they are?

Yes. Under each standby swap, or reciprocal credit facility, each central bank agrees to exchange on request its own currency for the

16. Ibid. p. 38.
* *The Banker*, November 1966, p. 740, 746–47.

currency of the other central bank up to a maximum amount over a limited period of time, such as three months. If the standby swap facility between the Federal Reserve and the Bank of England of $1,350 millions, for example, were to be drawn upon by the Bank of England in the amount of $100 millions, the Federal Reserve would credit the dollar account of the Bank of England with $100 millions while obtaining in exchange an equivalent credit in sterling on the books of the Bank of England at the prevailing market exchange rate. Both central banks would agree to reverse the transaction on a specified date say, within three months, at the same rate of exchange, thus providing each with forward cover against movement in the market rate, as well as the remote risk of a devaluation of either currency. The central bank initiating the transaction, in this case the Bank of England, might then disburse the dollars so acquired in market operations while the Federal Reserve would retain as a short-term investment the sterling credited to its account on the books of the Bank of England.

You clearly played a major personal part in the sterling crisis of December 1964. Could you describe what contacts you have during the day when there is severe and dangerous pressure on the pound?

Because of the time differential between New York and the European markets, the officers of the Federal Reserve Bank of New York concerned with gold and exchange operations generally find it necessary to be in the Bank at a very early hour whenever sterling or any other European currency becomes subject to speculative pressure. Mr. Roche, our Senior Foreign Exchange Trader, maintains frequent telephone contact with the central bank whose currency has come under attack so that we may be fully informed of developments on an hour-to-hour or even minute-to-minute basis. In such circumstances Mr. Roche would also keep in close touch with official and market opinion in other financial centres abroad. All the information thus collected, and our judgments, would in turn be immediately relayed by telephone to President Hayes and other high-ranking officials of the Federal Reserve and US Treasury.

Could you also describe how exactly the $3,000 millions central bank support for sterling was arranged in November 1964?

The chronology of the $3 billions package of sterling in November 1964 is, to the best of my recollection, roughly as follows: On November 23, the Bank of England raised its discount rate from 5 to 7 per cent. Perversely enough, market reaction to such forceful use of monetary policy by the Labour Government quickly degenerated into fears that the threat to sterling must have reached a truly crisis stage. Whether these reactions might have been averted by earlier bank rate action, more particularly on the usual Thursday date for bank rate announcements, may be debated for some time to come. In any event, the sterling market situation assumed increasingly grave significance on the London afternoon—and the New York morning of Tuesday,

November 24—when a virtual avalanche of selling developed. If sterling were to be rescued, it quickly became clear that a major package of international credit assistance would be required, and I so advised President Hayes shortly before 10 o'clock that morning. President Hayes immediately telephoned Chairman Martin and US Treasury officials and found that their thinking was moving along the same lines.

On the afternoon of the 24th, the Federal Open Market Committee—meeting through a telephone conference—approved the Special Manager's recommendation of an increase in the Federal Reserve/Bank of England swap line from $500 to $750 millions, on condition that credit assistance on a roughly corresponding scale could be secured from other central banks. That evening the Export-Import Bank gave assurance of a $250 millions standby facility while two foreign central banks informally indicated a sympathetic attitude. Beginning early on the morning of November 25, President Hayes and I joined forces with Lord Cromer in explaining by telephone to the governors of other major central banks the magnitude of the danger and the urgency of immediate defensive action in the form of a massive credit package. After roughly ten hours of almost continuous telephone communication, it was announced at 2 p.m., New York time, that a $3 billion credit package provided by 11 countries and the BIS was at the disposal of the Bank of England. Interest in the mechanics of how the money was raised through such teamwork has unfortunately tended to obscure the more fundamental point that each central bank's decision to lend was squarely based on the character and integrity of the Bank of England and its Governor.

During the next three years the government attempted to contain an underlying crisis of confidence in the pound. As Table III indicates, the actual current account balance showed a large deficit only in 1964, 1967, and 1968. But it has been estimated that the deficit would have been much larger every year between 1961 and 1967 if the domestic economy had been allowed to grow at a higher rate of 3 per cent or 4 per cent instead of being held below its full capacity for balance-of-payments reasons.[17] Not only was the government forced to follow "stop-go" policies of restraint on employment, but there were also voluntary and mandatory wage freezes, reduced overseas government expenditure, and tariff surcharges.

17. See David C. Rowan, "Towards a Rational Exchange Policy: Some Reflections on the British Experience," *Review of the Federal Reserve Bank of St. Louis* (April 1969).

TABLE III. Summary Balance of Payments, United Kingdom
(£ million)

	1961	1962	1963	1964	1965	1966	1967	1968	1969	1970	1971
Current account											
Visible trade	−152	−102	− 80	−519	−237	− 73	−557	−648	−143	+ 12	+ 299
Invisibles	+158	+224	+204	+137	+188	+157	+242	+377	+587	+669	+ 741
CURRENT BALANCE	+ 6	+122	+124	−382	− 49	+ 84	−315	−271	+444	+681	+1,040
Currency flow and official financing											
Current balance	+ 6	+122	+124	−382	− 49	+ 84	−315	−271	+444	+681	+1,040
Investment and other capital flows	−316	− 3	− 99	−305	−332	−574	−600	−1,007	−106	+547	+1,839
Balancing item	− 29	+ 73	− 83	+ 8	+ 28	− 57	+244	−132	+405	+ 59	+ 349
TOTAL CURRENCY FLOW	−339	+192	− 58	−695	−353	−547	−671	−1,410	+743	+1,287	+3,228
Allocation of Special Drawing Rights (+)	—	—	—	—	—	—	—	—	—	+171	+ 125
Gold subscription to IMF (−)	—	—	—	—	—	− 44	—	—	—	− 38	—
Total	−339	+192	− 58	−695	−353	−591	−671	−1,410	+743	+1,420	+3,353
Financed as follows											
Net transactions with overseas monetary authorities	+370	−375	+ 5	+573	+599	+625	+556	+1,296	−699	−1,295	−1,817
Official reserves (drawings on + / additions to −)	− 31	+183	+ 53	+122	−246	− 34	+115	+114	− 44	− 125	−1,536

SOURCE: Central Statistical Office, *United Kingdom Balance of Payments 1972*, H.M.S.O. 1972, p. 5.

Nonetheless, the belief persisted that sterling was over-valued, and confidence in the government's ability to maintain sterling parity was diminished as short-term liabilities to foreigners in sterling exceeded greatly the country's gold and convertible currency reserves. There were frequent speculative runs against sterling. Although these speculative attacks were resisted by large short-term government borrowings, a financial crisis of serious dimensions developed in the fall of 1967, aggravated by a Middle East crisis, closure of the Suez Canal, and a series of strikes in Britain. Finally, the government was forced to devalue the pound on November 18, 1967.

Only five days earlier the government had rejected another international support operation which would have involved additional borrowings by the Bank of England from other central banks, but subject to conditions on domestic policy. Prime Minister Wilson recalls that the Secretary-General of the IMF had been consulted about a "massive international operation to back sterling" involving an IMF standby agreement of not less than $3 billion. But since this would amount to 250 per cent of Britain's quota in the Fund, the Secretary-General insisted that the rules of the Fund would require not only the agreement of the members of the General Agreement to Borrow, but also the imposition of conditions on Britain's domestic economic policies. According to Wilson, the Fund "instanced strict credit control, a tightening of prices and incomes policy—presumably statutory—a limitation on growth, and an agreement that, while we might during the currency of the loan decide to devalue, we must pledge ourselves never to float. . . . [S]uch conditions had to be rejected as unacceptable and intolerable."

Of the 1967 crisis, Wilson also reflects on "the suddenness with which we had been overwhelmed by the operations of a speculative market. . . . The financial pages of the press had not been expressed in crisis terms until the very last week. . . . It was a crisis different in kind, shorter in duration and—until the last hours—less intense than those which sterling had weathered in the three preceding years. But this time it was lethal." [18]

18. Wilson, *Labour Government 1964–70*, pp. 453, 460–61.

DEVALUATION: CHRONOLOGY OF A CRISIS *

The first external hint of this year's ultimate crisis came in Rio de Janiero in September from Sir Leslie O'Brien, soft-spoken governor of the Bank of England. The official financial moguls of the non-Communist world were gathered there, in the new waterfront Museum of Modern Art, for the annual meeting of the I.M.F. Sir Leslie told them privately that his country would indeed have to borrow again to make its final payment on the 1964 loan this fall.

Prime Minister Wilson and his Chancellor did not come around to devaluation until last month, but pressure began mounting last spring. The Arab-Israeli war and closure of the Suez Canal were dramatically visible blows to the balance of payments. It is known now that even earlier the payments situation was worsening. The pound began slipping in April.

A critical factor for British policy was that just last year the Government had applied severe restrictions to the economy. Now it could not—or felt it could not—do more. Factors beyond Britain's control arose to make matters worse—West Germany's recession, the high United States interest rates and subsequent economic slowdown, then the war, and then the British dock strikes.

While Sir Leslie was talking about another loan in Rio, an important body of European officials in Brussels—the executive commission of the Common Market—was coming to the conclusion that credits alone would not be enough.

At 2 A.M. on Sept. 29, the commission completed its report on Britain's application for membership in the European Economic Community. The commission concluded, and recommended to the six member Governments, that Britain be admitted. But its 120-page report carried an unmistakable hint that the pound should be devalued.

London had heard this suggestion many times in the last three years, publicly and privately—loudest perhaps from the British press and the French Government. But the report of the Brussels commission, given its official and non-partisan status, had a particular resonance.

October, 1967

In the spartan offices of the massive gray British Treasury building across Great George Street from the Houses of Parliament, the economic staff was beginning to weigh the latest evidence on the balance of payments, and to prepare a crucial report on the outlook.

On Oct. 12, the Government reported that Britain's export-import deficit in September had been the worst in 15 months. The dock

* *New York Times,* December 17, 1967.

strikes were partly to blame, but the pound was shaken nonetheless. A few days later, it hit the lowest level permitted under the rules of the I.M.F.—$2.7825—and the Bank of England had to dig in and buy up everything that came on the market, paying out Britain's precious, inadequate reserves in the process. On Oct. 19, to try to stem the outflow, the bank raised its "bank rate"—Britain's equivalent of the United States discount rate—by one-half point, to 6 per cent.

Nov. 6, 1967

On or about this date, a Monday, the Treasury experts presented their forecast to Mr. Callaghan, the Chancellor, and from this moment the wheels started turning toward devaluation. The experts foresaw still another big payments deficit of close to $1-billion next year. Moreover, they viewed it as a hard-core deficit, not likely to be whittled down as the year progressed.

If Mr. Callaghan had not made up his mind by this time, the experts' report is believed to have done it. He also heard from the Bank of England that official reserves were fast being eaten up by the need to support the pound at $2.80. . . .

For the rest of the week following Mr. Callaghan's decision, he and Mr. Wilson conferred with a handful of other British officials on whether to take the fateful step. A Chancellor can visit the Prime Minister's office 10 times a day without being observed on the outside, because there is a direct passage between the Prime Minister's house at 10 Downing Street and the Chancellor's next door at No. 11.

On Thursday, Nov. 9, the bank rate was notched up another half point, to 6½ per cent—the second increase in three weeks. Both increases were small because the Government feared that the economy was precariously close to being knocked into a serious recession. But both increases were regarded on the outside as inadequate, and the pound failed to strengthen.

On Friday, the 10th, when the ineffectiveness of the second rate increase was apparent, Mr. Wilson decided. Devaluation was on.

A small and select team of Treasury officials was assigned to work it out, measure its implications, and provide the basis for deciding how big it should be. They were not working from scratch. They had been through this exercise before. But this time they worked alone, in utmost secrecy.

Sir Leslie, about to depart for the regular monthly meeting of European central bankers at the Bank for International Settlements in Basel, Switzerland, was informed of the decision and instructed to test the atmosphere without disclosing anything.

Sir Denis Rickett, the competent, classically discreet civil servant who, as Second Secretary of the Treasury, is Britain's regular representative in international money matters, would go to Paris and make hypothetical soundings among the major Western Governments, gathering there the next week for regular economic talks.

Nov. 11-13

Sir Leslie had a bad weekend in Basel, contrary to custom. Basel, in the German part of Switzerland, is a chemical center, the last upstream port city on the Rhine, home of a magnificent modern art museum, the Kunstsammlung, and seat of the Bank for International Settlements since it was founded in 1931.

The B.I.S. is unlike any other bank in the world—a bank for central bankers. Situated in a made-over hotel across the street from the railroad station, it is the quintessence of unhurried tranquility—deep carpets, oak paneling, inconspicuous multilingual guards in gray uniforms, a meeting room and a large sitting room on the ground floor, a small office for each member country upstairs, and quiet throughout.

Sir Leslie had gone there on the second weekend of every month since he took office last year. He and his colleagues from the other major European countries, the United States, Canada and Japan, put considerable stock in the usefulness of their wholly confidential exchanges, pure central-banker talk in language that they alone understand.

This time, Sir Leslie needed support—more support of the sort that the group at Basel had already given Britain several times in recent years. But he didn't get all he wanted.

He got the $250-million loan that he had been talking about in Rio in September. Whether he asked for more is not known for certain, though most evidence indicates that he did. It appears that he also asked for an expression of his colleagues' backing for the pound, perhaps a public statement. He did not get it.

He did not tell the central bankers of Mr. Wilson's decision to devalue. He may even have told them the very opposite, as a matter of routine. But they seemed to sense the reality.

On Monday morning in London—Nov. 13, five days before devaluation—the faded-orange front page of The Financial Times reported rumors of the central bankers' $250-million loan. There was no official confirmation, and the reaction in the City, London's financial district, was that this amount was too small—indeed, a letdown from the powerful central bankers' club, considering the pound's increasingly evident straits.

Sir Leslie flew home. In a plane-side interview at London's Heathrow Airport he made an unconvincing statement that he had "every confidence in the pound."

Back in Basel, on Monday afternoon, the central bank governors of the Common Market countries met among themselves at the B.I.S., as they regularly do after the full membership meeting. They discussed devaluation.

According to one report, their first reaction was to try to prevent it, presumably with another big loan to Britain, perhaps as much as $3-billion. It has been reported that from this meeting an inquiry went to

Pierre-Paul Schweitzer, managing director of the International Monetary Fund in Washington, as to whether the fund might finance such an operation. Mr. Schweitzer was said to have been favorably disposed at first, but rejected the idea after consultation with his staff.

Another version of the Monday afternoon meeting at Basel is that they accepted the inevitability of devaluation, and even the desirability so long as it was properly managed. In any case, they decided that it must be kept within bounds, and that they—the Common Market countries—should maintain a unified position. Jacques Brunet, governor of the Banque de France, made no commitment, but intimated that France would probably not devalue. France's official answer did not come, however, until D-Day.

In London, Prime Minister Wilson spoke at the Lord Mayor's Dinner in the ornate Guildhall Monday night, didn't mention devaluation pro or con, and dismissed the October export-import report—due Tuesday—as "meaningless" because of the dock strike.

In Paris, Jacques Rueff, the 71-year-old economist who is the very embodiment of France's affection for gold and the gold standard, said in a radio interview that the solution to Britain's problems might be found only in Government by decree for awhile—as General de Gaulle had governed by decree in 1958, when he first took office and, on Mr. Rueff's advice, France devalued the franc for the fifth time since World War II and applied strict restraints to the economy.

Nov. 14-16

The October trade figures on Tuesday turned out to be the worst for any month since January, 1964. The Government confirmed the $250-million loan without further explanation. The pound weakened further in the exchange markets.

Preliminary coded cables went out from the British Foreign Office to Her Majesty's Ambassador, The Sunday Times reported, telling them to be ready at an unspecified time to do something quickly on an unspecified matter. Several officials of the Bank of England are reported to have been dispatched to key financial centers to stand by. The Treasury began preparations for another big loan application to the I.M.F.

Sir Denis and Michael Posner, the new economic adviser at the Treasury, took off for Paris to attend scheduled meetings at the Organization for Economic Cooperation and Development. In the O.E.C.D.'s headquarters at the Chateau de la Muette, a spacious old Rothschild mansion close to the Bois de Boulogne on the west side of the city, a group of financial officials known cryptically as "Working Party 3" had been meeting every six weeks or so for the last six years, discussing balance of payments developments in frank detail.

More recently the chateau had also been the meeting place of the "Group of Ten"—the major financial powers, essentially the same as in Working Party 3, who had been negotiating reform of the international money system.

This week, both groups were meeting.

The British delegates took these opportunities to ask selected colleagues, in most guarded terms, what their reaction might be to a devaluation of various amounts—figures of 15 per cent and more were discussed—and to talk about Britain's emerging new crisis and need for more help.

Theirs may have been the first official mention of specific percentages, but actually there had been official and unofficial talk of something in the neighborhood of 15 per cent for months and even years before.

The figure was determined as much by calculations of what size devaluation would force Britain's closest competitors on the Continent to devalue, too, as by calculations of how much devaluation the pound itself needed. It was agreed, always informally, that more than 15 per cent might be too much for others—including the dollar—to withstand, and that less than 15 per cent would not save the pound. The Labor party's left wing wanted 30 per cent, to avoid the need for further restraint on the British economy, but this figure was not seriously contemplated.

Sometime during this week, the United States let it be known that it was opposed to devaluation. Washington has always feared that devaluation of the pound might ultimately bring the dollar down, too. It is reliably reported that Washington tried to arrange another big loan for Britain now, offering $500-million if the Europeans would help commensurately. But only West Germany agreed, it is said, and the idea of the loan as an alternative to devaluation was overcome by events.

France's position remained unknown. For one thing, President de Gaulle had not decided what his position was. For another, the French were, and had long been, ambivalent on the matter. Responsible Paris financial officials believed that the pound really was overvalued. Politically oriented officials would welcome devaluation as a demonstration of Anglo-Saxon weakness. But in terms of economic self-interest, France was uneasy about the possible repercussions for the franc.

An official in London, admittedly biased, said that French officials were "generally surly and hostile throughout" the week of pre-devaluation talks. Rene Larre, the sharp-witted career man who is No. 2 in the French Ministry of Finance, is said to have been intentionally excluded from much of the most confidential discussion.

At 8:50 Wednesday night, London time, a British Broadcasting Corporation news broadcast reported from "sources in Paris" that a $1-billion loan was near agreement—and that there was "absolutely no sign of devaluation." The broadcast strengthened the pound in Thursday's early trading on the exchanges, but it was a brief respite.

Prime Minister Wilson had called the Cabinet to 10 Downing Street Thursday morning to hear and approve his decision to devalue. After the B.B.C. broadcast, Robert Sheldon, a member of Labor's left wing, introduced a private member's question in the House of Commons about the reported loan. At the Cabinet meeting, the government decided to ask the Speaker of the House to disallow the Sheldon question, but not to ask Mr. Sheldon himself to withdraw it. It was a costly decision.

The Speaker refused to act, and the evasive answer that Chancellor Callaghan gave in Commons on Thursday afternoon was all that the City needed to realize that the pound was in real trouble.

British losses suffered heavily Thursday afternoon. So damaging was the day's flight from the pound that the Treasury considered whether to devalue right away, on Thursday night.

Formal notices to other capitals and to the Fund were not made until Friday and Saturday. But officials in Bonn, and presumably elsewhere, received some word sometime Thursday. A second set of coded cables went out to British Ambassadors on Wednesday—before the Cabinet vote—and on Thursday, explaining what the earlier mysterious cables had concealed.

Nov. 17

In Paris, financial officials were still meeting at the Chateau de la Muette. During the morning, Sir Denis and Frederick L. Deming, the United States Under Secretary of the Treasury, took France's Mr. Larre aside and were closeted with him for one and a quarter hours in a room off the chateau's entrance hall. There was still no word on where France stood.

As an indication of the closeness with which the devaluation secret was held, the following scene took place about noon Friday at the cashier's window of the Hotel Continental in downtown Paris, where official United States delegations regularly bed down. George H. Willis, the United States Treasury's top civil servant on international finance, had left the meetings at the chateau and was checking out. He fished a mixture of pounds, francs and dollars out of his wallet to pay his bill.

"I'm sorry, Mr. Willis," said the clerk, "but we cannot accept pounds today." Mr. Willis asked why. The clerk replied: "Mr. Willis, I would have thought that you, of all the people in the world, would know the answer to that."

Le Monde, the prestigious Paris daily, was going on sale in the news kiosks at about this time. It reported, with disturbing accuracy, that Britain was trying to borrow not $1-billion but $3-billion. It was one of several painfully accurate scoops that this newspaper published during the crisis period, leading to the conclusion that the French Government was willfully leaking the news to hurt the pound.

In London, there was turmoil. The Government denied, with disturbing inaccuracy, that it was negotiating new credits. The denial had a worse effect than an assuring confirmation would have had. Gold buying through the London market soared to an estimated 40 tons—about $45-million worth—compared with six or seven tons on a normal day.

All week, forward discounts on the pound had widened, reflecting mounting doubt that the $2.80 value would last, and giving rise to unconfirmed reports of the extraordinary sums that the Bank of England was being forced to commit. One estimate is $7-billion, of which the bank loses about $850-million on the devaluation. This is one figure that may never be revealed.

Amid the turmoil, the Prime Minister and his Chancellor played calm. Mr. Wilson went north to Liverpool to speak at a conference of port industries. Mr. Callaghan went to his home constituency at Cardiff, Wales, to speak at a bankers' dinner.

In Washington, Pierre-Paul Schweitzer, French by birth but an international civil servant now, was first to be officially informed in his capacity as head of the I.M.F., which must approve members' devaluations. He was told at 8 A.M. Soon afterward, President Johnson received a personal cable from Mr. Wilson, and Secretary of the Treasury Henry H. Fowler received one from Mr. Callaghan. . . .

Nov. 18
D—for Devaluation—Day

Sir Leslie O'Brien, governor of the Bank of England, woke this morning in his London flat near St. Paul's Cathedral, a five-minute walk from the bank on Threadneedle Street. Most Friday nights he quits London to spend the weekend at his suburban home in Wimbledon.

In Paris, President de Gaulle met in the forenoon at his office in the Élyseés Palace with his Premier, Georges Pompidou, Foreign Minister Maurice Couve de Murville, and Finance Minister Michel Debré.

There have been reports that the Élyseés meeting was "stormy." If so, the argument was more likely over what aid France might or might not give Britain rather than over whether to devalue. The only certainty is that the decision was against devaluation and in favor of giving some assistance.

One-half hour later, Britain's Ambassadors, having received their final cables from London, personally and simultaneously called on the relevant officials of the governments to which they were assigned, to give them official notice. Some knew already.

At 4 in the afternoon, the Monetary Committee of the six Common Market countries met in Brussels at the Cortenburg, a downtown building of concrete slabs and brick that houses Common Market offices. It was the first time that they had been able to hold a meaningful meeting all week.

In London, at the same moment, Prime Minister Wilson had a teatime rendezvous with a delegation of eight women from the Stretford and Urmston Labor party. They did not discuss devaluation. "He was very relaxed," one of the visitors said afterward, "as though he didn't have a thought on his mind."

The public announcement was set for 9:30 that night, London time—10:30 Continental time, 4:30 in New York. But a Japanese journalist scooped the world by 90 minutes, evidently informed by someone at or close to the International Monetary Fund in Washington.

Unperturbed, the British Treasury made its announcement on schedule. The announcement also revealed that the bank rate would be raised to 8 per cent, corporation taxes would be increased, Government spending cut, Britain's export rebate repealed, and that $3-billion of external aid was being arranged—$1.4-billion from the I.M.F. and $1.6-billion directly from other countries.

B.B.C. television was showing a Doris Day movie. Shaw's "Heartbreak House" was playing at the Lyric, where the manager called out an American who had asked to be notified if the news came during the show. "That does it," said the manager, "I'm emigrating."

As the sun set on the British Empire, the reverberations were already beginning to show.

In Washington the White House announced that President Johnson "unequivocally" reaffirmed the United States commitment "to buy and sell gold at the existing price of $35 an ounce"—that is, not to devalue the dollar. The Federal Reserve Board met in an extraordinary Saturday night session to approve an increase in the discount rate to 4½ per cent, half as a counteraction to London's new 8 per cent bank rate, and half as symbolic notice to the world that the United States was ready to act fast.

The Common Market countries—West Germany, Italy, France, Belgium, the Netherlands and Luxembourg—and Canada, Japan, Norway, Finland, and South Africa announced that they would not devalue, either. Denmark, Ireland and Israel announced that they would.

In Bonn, a special "devaluation team" spent the weekend in the Economics Ministry, assaying developments and nourishing itself on what one member called "English" whisky.

4. FRENCH FRANC CRISIS (1968–69)

A year after the British devaluation, the West German mark and the French franc were subject to large speculative capital flows, based on expectations of a revaluation of the mark and a devaluation of the franc. In the three days November 16–19,

1968, the Deutsche Bundesbank (German central bank) acquired approximately $1.8 billion in efforts to hold the mark at its ceiling—an inflow unprecedented in the history of the Federal Republic. Much of the massive inflow was in the form of French francs. On November 18, 1968, the French Premier Maurice Couve de Murville addressed a nationwide television audience and laid the immediate blame for the current monetary crisis on the "frenzied—I would say phenomenal" speculation in the mark. He did not mention speculation in the franc, but took the extraordinary step of advocating change in another country's currency parity: the mark must be revalued.

Just before his address, the French had refused to accept an emergency loan of $1 billion from the Basel group of central bankers of eleven major industrial nations. This refusal was designed to put another form of pressure on West Germany and to indicate a position of strength on the part of France. It was true that French reserves were still more than $4 billion, but they had declined by $3 billion since the national strikes during May and June 1968, and some action would eventually be necessary to stop the flow of "hot money" from France to West Germany. At a Group of 10 meeting in Bonn on November 20, 1968, a West German spokesman said that any reversal of its decision not to revalue the Duetsch mark was "out of the question." The only action taken by the German government was to impose a 3 per cent tax on exports and rebate on imports—a measure equivalent to a small fiscal revaluation of the mark.

The negotiations at Bonn are summarized in the following account.

THE THREE HECTIC DAYS OF THE
NEGOTIATIONS IN BONN *

PARIS, Nov. 25—France never committed herself to devaluing the franc, reserving the right to take this decision herself as a national, sovereign prerogative, according to participants in the international monetary conference in Bonn last week. But there was the widespread belief that, barring an upward revaluation of the mark, which the West German Government excluded, there could be no credible solution to the problem of the franc without devaluation.

* *New York Times*, November 26, 1968.

The French delegates, led by Finance Minister François-Xavier Ortoli, gave the impressions that they shared this view, even after telephone conversations with Paris.

That was the explanation offered by some of those who participated in the talks for the extraordinary turn of events in which the world expected devaluation last Saturday only to find that the parity of about 20 cents had been maintained.

A Machiavellian Plot?

What actually happened Thursday night, Friday and Saturday that produced such a decision against devaluing? Did it represent some Machiavellian plot by President de Gaulle?

The meetings of the central bankers and Finance Ministers from the 10 leading financial nations were held under strict security precautions in the three-story white stucco Economics Ministry building in the western part of Bonn. More than 200 newsmen, restricted to the lobby of the building and a second-floor press room, gathered information from the few delegates willing to risk pushing their way through the throng.

Though there was a lack of much precise knowledge about what was going on, those in the lobby Thursday night and early Friday were aware that something extremely important was taking place.

The West German delegation, led by Dr. Karl Schiller, the Economics Minister, repeatedly said the mark would not be revalued. At 7 P.M. Thursday Mr. Ortoli requested a suspension of the meeting while he conferred with Paris.

Then, A Major Deadlock

The French delegation never considered the issue of mark revaluation closed and there was a major deadlock as delegations retired to caucus chambers at the rear of the building. The negotiations did not resume until 10 P.M., and the pressures were becoming intense on all delegations to try to resolve the dispute.

France, Britain and the United States took the position that the West German Government had not done enough to halt the flow of speculative funds into West Germany. They demanded an increase in the value of the mark by 7.5 per cent.

The Germans had announced tax changes aimed at curbing their huge trade surplus and had taken action to make it unattractive for West German banks to hold speculative funds of nonresidents.

Dr. Schiller and the West German Finance Minister, Franz Josef Strauss, said that the Germans had shown their international responsibility by acting in this fashion and that it was up to the debtor countries to act.

Without revaluation of the mark, the French were in trouble. They had taken enormous losses of reserves in the turn-around of the franc's fortunes following the national strikes and student protests of May and June. From being one of Europe's strongest currencies, it had become one of Europe's weakest.

Revaluation of the mark would have helped France by ending the flow of volatile funds into West Germany and by making France's exports more competitive with those from Germany.

With the West Germans ruling out revaluation, the conversations after 10 P.M., when the sessions resumed, turned to the franc and what should be done to help it over a difficult period.

At Basel, where central bankers had met the previous weekend, credits were offered France, but these were refused as part of the war of nerves to get a revaluation of the mark.

The question of credits came up again Thursday night, and with this an exchange of ideas about a French devaluation. It was the view of nearly all the delegations that a change was unavoidable.

The Choices Considered

These were the choices under consideration:

¶A devaluation and a Draconian program of austerity enforced on all Frenchmen to defend the rate. This was viewed by most of the delegates as politically unacceptable for General de Gaulle, who had promised broad reforms for the French people after the strikes.

¶A large devaluation, which would have probably touched off a chain reaction of competitive devaluations by other countries and even a wave of speculation against the dollar in the gold markets. Monetary order would have turned to chaos and a world recession could have developed. France would be no better off, and probably a lot worse off, except for the consolation that she had not devalued unilaterally.

¶A small devaluation, which could have been accepted by other countries, followed up by temporary and not overly severe austerity measures to help support the franc at the new rate until the effects of devaluation—lower export prices or increased export profitability—would begin working toward rebuilding French reserves.

According to those present at the sessions, hours and hours were spent discussing parity changes. Meanwhile, the nine other participating Governments pledged $2-billion in short-term credits for France to reinforce her reserve position. There were no conditions attached, but the credits were considered by the Governments offering them to be providing the means for France to devalue in the area of 10 per cent.

The United States Secretary of the Treasury, Henry H. Fowler, pointedly told the French Finance Minister that France would not be justified in devaluing by more than 10 per cent in view of the new credits, plus the drawing rights on the International Monetary Fund worth $985-million more.

As the participants recalled the crucial encounters that night, they pointed out that the delegates seemed to get lost in the technicalities of devaluation, forgetting the politics of it and a man named deGaulle.

On Nov. 13 the French leader had said that "to accept the devaluation of our currency would be the worst possible absurdity." That statement was to be the key to what followed.

At 1 A. M. on Friday, Mr. Ortoli threw a bombshell into the meeting. France, he said, will devalue by 20 per cent—the large devaluation everyone was afraid of. With this move the French were reopening the debate, putting pressure on the West Germans to revalue and threatening the world with a new monetary crisis unless Bonn reconsidered.

Working on Ortoli

From then until 3:15 A. M., when the meeting broke up, the others, led by Mr. Fowler, worked on Mr. Ortoli to try to get him to reduce the figure to around 10 per cent. As the session wore on, it appeared that the arguments were making an impression on Mr. Ortoli, and by the end it appeared that he had been won over to the view that there should be a devaluation of 10 per cent.

The West Germans held firmly to their earlier position, and as the French figure was being whittled down, they seemed to have won the battle.

It was unclear whether Mr. Ortoli spoke directly with General de Gaulle that night; most sources doubted it. Nevertheless, the fact that the French Minister, supported by officials of the Bank of France, appeared to accept the 10 per cent figure after having consulted Paris was viewed as a sign that the action would probably be confirmed at the Cabinet meeting in Paris last Saturday.

When the session resumed at 10:15 A.M. Friday, the delegates began work on a communiqué. The key section dealt with France, and some time was spent trying to determine what to say. There were those who wanted the word "devaluation" in the communiqué but the French refused.

Eventually this wording was settled on: "The French Economic and Finance Minister explained the situation of the French currency, the measures already taken toward a restoration of internal and external equilibrium, and the problems still to be solved."

Anyone reading the communiqué in Bonn that day would construe the words "problems still to be solved" as an allusion to the expected devaluation.

By Saturday morning there were articles in newspapers around the globe forecasting imminent devaluation and indicating a French surrender to the West Germans.

Participants at the meeting only speculate on this point, but it seems apparent to them now that when General de Gaulle read the reports about what France intended to do, he must have been enraged.

In their view he must have been particularly nettled by this statement by Finance Minister Strauss Friday afternoon in a radio interview: "My impression is that there will be a French decision to devalue, and very soon." That statement caused a good deal of German embarrassment, and Bonn issued a formal denial later in the day.

General de Gaulle is well known for his capacity to surprise. He showed this in his veto of Britain's entry into the European Common Market in January, 1963, after having allowed negotiations to continue for a year and a half. He showed it by saying nothing when speculation was rampant that he was about to resign during the May–June disorders. He showed it again Saturday.

Minister Kept in the Dark

Did he deliberately allow his ministers to mislead the others at Bonn to intensify and dramatize the decision he knew all along he would make? There was some speculation to this effect; the answer may never be known. . . .

General de Gaulle's broadcast to the French nation follows:

ADDRESS BY GENERAL CHARLES DE GAULLE *

The monetary crisis undergone by France is the consequence of the moral, economic and social upheaval that she suddenly suffered last May and June, because the cooperation of all participants could not in time replace the sterile battle of interests.

When, in the midst of world competition, a country—and I am speaking of ours—that was in a state of growing prosperity and that had one of the strongest currencies in the world, stopped working for weeks and weeks; when she was for a long time deprived of trains, ships, public transportation, mining products, postal communications, radio, gasoline, electricity; when, to escape from death through asphyxiation, she had all at once to impose enormous wage burdens on her economy, crush her budget with the weight of suddenly increased spending, exhaust her credit in hurriedly prodigal subsidies to firms that were heading toward bankruptcy, nothing can make that country—even if she was able to stop on the brink of the abyss—find her equilibrium immediately.

But, until she has recovered her equilibrium, nothing can prevent there being a number of people, both inside and outside, who suspend the confidence they had in the country and try to put their own interests ahead of the public interest. Naturally, it is the national currency that then risks paying the price for this odious speculation.

However, despite the foul blow that it suffered, our economy recovered.

* Broadcast, November 24, 1968, Ambassade de France, Service de Presse et d'Information.

Work began again everywhere. Expansion developed once more. Foreign trade grew. All that thanks to the natural resilience of our people and to certain appropriate measures.

Furthermore, the richest states have just opened considerable credits to us that can still be increased and that supplement our own reserves.

Finally, one sees the day coming when, following one unhappy experience after another, the whole world will agree to establish an impartial and reasonable monetary system sheltering every country—so long as it merits it—from sudden and absurd speculatory movements.

In short, we have, in all truth, for the present and for the future, all that is necessary to complete the recovery that has begun and to take the lead once more.

That is why, all factors weighed, I, with the Government, decided that we must complete our recovery without having recourse to devaluation.

In the both troubled and hopeful situation in which we find ourselves today, such an operation would run the strong risk of being not a remedy at all, but a ruinously easy and momentary device and the reward paid to those who gambled on our decline.

But, alongside certain competitors who are very active and in very good shape, the maintenance of our currency absolutely demands that we place ourselves, in all respects and in all domains, in complete equilibrium.

From the standpoint of the economy, this means that, without putting into question the increase in salaries as it was fixed in the spring, we refuse in this respect to impose new burdens on our economy so long as they would prevent it from becoming vigorous and competitive again.

This means that, simultaneously, we intend to maintain the prices of finished goods, food and services. This means that, to make our balance of payments positive, we are going to increase outright the capacity of our business firms, notably by relieving them of certain taxes that weigh excessively on their cost prices.

From the standpoint of finances, the deficit in the 1969 budget, which had first been estimated at more than $2.3 billion, will be reduced to under $1.3 billion, thanks in particular to a reduction in the operating expenses of our government services, in the subsidies given to nationalized concerns, and in our present ambitions regarding our civil, military and university equipment.

At the same time, funds granted by the State will be adapted and limited to the real needs of national expansion. It goes without saying that the necessary controls will have to be implemented rigorously, both as regards foreign exchange and the actual collection of all existing taxes.

From the standpoint of public order—because the crisis started from the moment it was disturbed and will not end if there can be doubts that it can be maintained—the necessary measures must be taken so that henceforth be finished, in our universities and schools as in the streets of our cities and on the roads of our countryside, all agitation and demonstrations, all tumult and parading, which prevent work and offend sensible people, and so that each individual who has a duty to perform, a post to hold, a function to fulfill, may do so conscientiously.

Frenchwomen, Frenchmen, what is happening as regards our currency proves to us, once again, that life is a struggle, that effort is the price of success, that salvation demands victory.

If—as we can and as we must—we win this struggle by participating in it all together, then we shall be able successfully to accomplish, as is necessary, the transformations, reforms and progress that will make us, in all certainty, a great exemplary people of modern times. For, through our trials, whatever they are or whatever they might be, such is the national goal.

Long live the Republic!
Long live France!

By the following March, however, the belief was intensifying that France could no longer refuse to devalue. New wage negotiations were being undertaken, and unions had called a national strike to back up wage demands the Government considered inflationary. There had been continual deficits in the French balance of payments, and reserves were only half of what they had been a year previously. Nonetheless, international credit facilities available to France were still sizeable, with approximately $4 billion available from these sources: $3 billion of short-term central bank credits and $1 billion of conditional credits (half of which would be almost automatically available from the IMF).

In April, General de Gaulle resigned. The new post-de Gaulle government reversed de Gaulle's stand and finally bowed in August to the pressure of massive reserve losses, a continuing trade deficit, and inflationary pressures: it was decided to devalue the franc by 12.5 per cent.

DEVALUATION OF FRENCH FRANC *

The Government of France has proposed, and the International Monetary Fund has concurred, in a change in the par value of the French franc to be effective August 10, 1969. The new par value, expressed in terms of gold and in terms of the U.S. dollar of the weight and fineness in effect on July 1, 1944, is as follows: 0.160000 gram of fine gold per French franc; 194.397 French francs per troy ounce of fine gold; 5.55419 French francs per U.S. dollar; 18.0044 U.S. cents per French franc.

Corresponding changes have been made in the par values of the separate currencies in France's non-metropolitan territories, with the exception of the

* Press release, No. 755, International Monetary Fund, August 10, 1969.

par values for the currency that circulates in the territory of the Afars and the Issas and the French currency of the condominium of the New Hebrides.

Summary of statement by the French Minister of Finance and Economic Affairs, Mr. Giscard d'Estaing, on August 8, 1969.

The Minister of Finance and Economic Affairs, Mr. Giscard d'Estaing announced on Friday August 8 that the French Government had taken the initiative in modifying the parity of the franc. This decision, he said, would be followed by discussions over the weekend with members of the European Economic Community, the countries of the franc area and the international monetary authorities. On August 10, the value of the franc would be changed to 0.16 gram of fine gold, instead of the 0.18 gram that it had been established at since 1958.

Explaining the reasons for the devaluation, the Minister said that, in the first place, the Government had had to acknowledge that on foreign markets the franc was being sold at a discount, and that on the forward market the discount amounted to 11–12 per cent. During the second half of 1968, the country had lost reserves at an average monthly rate of $500 million; in the first half of 1969, losses still amounted to an average of $300 million a month. Faced with the prospect of seeing its reserves dwindle to practically nothing by the end of the year and to a negative balance in mid-1970, the Government had chosen to take preventive action. Furthermore, an attempt to defend the former par value of the franc against international speculation would have resulted in an overvalued currency, making France less competitive in world markets.

Secondly, the decision to devalue the franc was not an isolated one. The Government had already taken several important steps toward re-establishing equilibrium. Credit ceilings had been applied and a number of budget appropriations (amounting to F 4 billion) had been frozen in order to dampen demand. As a result of these measures, reserve losses in July had declined to $138.8 million, less than half the monthly average in the first half of 1969. Also in July the rate of growth of exports exceeded that of imports for the first time in 1969. The trend of savings, which had declined in May and the first two weeks in June, had been reversed. Since the Government was not relying solely on adjustment of the parity of the franc to enable the country's economy to return to equilibrium but also on budgetary and credit measures, it had been possible to decide on a moderate rate of devaluation. Such a rate, the Minister added, was in the interest of international cooperation.

Thirdly, devaluation would be followed by other measures designed to contribute to the re-establishment of equilibrium. Credit restrictions would be observed and exchange controls maintained until the uncertainties in the international monetary situation had been cleared up. A balanced budget would be adopted for 1970. Early in September, further measures would be announced as part of the over-all program to be presented in connection with the budget. These would consist of measures that, on the one hand, were necessary to guarantee a fair allocation of resources within the national community, including measures to protect the most disadvantaged, and, on the other hand, would encourage savings and international competitiveness so that the French economy might pursue its course of development and modernization.

5. GERMAN MARK CRISIS (1969)

Two months after the franc devaluation, the German mark was revalued. Revaluation had been a major issue in the political campaign of September 1969, and when the Social Democrats were elected they allowed the mark to float in exchange markets. The free-floating mark was achieved by the government's directive to the Bundesbank to stop selling marks every time a wave of buying sent the price more than 1 per cent over the fixed rate of 3.98 marks to the dollar.

Commending the action as a "float for freedom," *The Economist* stated:

> All the world should welcome last Monday's floating of the D-mark. It is another sign that, in the very last resort, even international economic problems do now tend to be handled with a saving common sense. It is a pity that solemn assurances had had to be given that this will not last for long, so that the International Monetary Fund has been promised that "Germany will resume maintenance of the limits around par at the earliest opportunity." But, even in the very brief interval during which this floating of a major currency has been allowed, one can dare to hope that a process of economic education has been set afoot, which is likely to lead towards wider and wiser use of more flexible exchange rates in the future. . . . Britain, with its pretensions to running the less-favoured of the two big international currencies, has suffered particularly from the pains inflicted by the fixed rate system. That is why there has for some time been a strong argument that Britain should act first to break the nexus by moving sterling to a more flexible exchange rate. But since the British Government would not move, and the Americans could not move (although some of President Nixon's advisers are eager for reform), it had also become clear that the second best country to break the ice would be Germany.[19]

The annual meeting of the IMF coincided with Germany's action. At this meeting, Dr. Otmar Emminger, deputy governor

19. *The Economist* (October 4, 1969), p. 14.

of the Bundesbank said, "A system of fixed exchange rates can only be maintained if the major countries of the world are prepared to co-ordinate their monetary and fiscal policies. But this they have dismally failed to do, with the common market countries among the worst offenders." This led Dr. Emminger to question whether there is not a better alternative to the present jumpy and costly method of occasional, large, ad hoc parity changes.[20]

The question became how long Germany would allow the mark to float and at what value would it repeg. This was of especial concern to the EEC countries.

REVALUED MARK PLEDGED BY BONN *

LUXEMBOURG, Oct. 6—West Germany's Economics Minister, Karl Schiller, pledged to the European Economic Community today that the new German Government would move toward an early formal upward revaluation of the mark.

While declining to commit himself on timing, or the rate, Professor Schiller told an emergency session of the Community's Council of Ministers that the revaluation decision, which now becomes a formal commitment, would be one of the new Government's first acts.

The coalition of Social Democrats, whom Dr. Schiller represents, and Free Democrats is expected to assume power around Oct. 21.

That parity decision would terminate the present "floating" rate for the mark, under which it has been unhooked from fixed pegs and left to move to a 6 per cent premium in the exchange markets.

While it was not so stated, central banking sources attribute softening in the community position to the realization that the new coalition would revalue the mark by a higher rate than the present caretaker government of Christian Democrats, who blocked revaluation efforts earlier, and the Social Democrats, who have supported a higher parity for months.

New Rate Estimated

Frankfurt banking sources expect the revaluation rate to be somewhere between 6 and 8 per cent above the present value of 25 American cents.

The higher the rate, the more Germany's partners inside the Community—France, Italy, Holland, Belgium and Luxembourg—stand to benefit in foreign commercial competition with the Germans, as well as in sales inside the German market.

20. Ibid. p. 67.
* *New York Times*, October 7, 1969.

Revaluation, with its effects of reducing prices of imports and inflating prices of exports, is also expected to help foreign sales of the United States and reduce competitiveness of German products in the American market.

With today's agreement, the Germans also won Community approval to continue charging a tax on imports of agricultural products.

But the tax will be more limited in scope, applying to fewer products than the Germans had initially envisaged when it was imposed by a Bonn Cabinet decision a week ago.

The tax is aimed at providing relief to German farmers whose domestic markets are threatened by the premium for the mark.

The threat arises because farm exporters to Germany now earn more money. The marks they get will buy more French or Belgian francs or Italian lira.

The Community's Executive Commission saw the tax as one more obstacle to the free movement of community products and declared it illegal last week.

The executive body was motivated by the desire to pressure the Germans to end the mark's "floating" rate venture and return the currency to fixed intervention points under the rules of the International Monetary Fund.

Raymond Barre, vice president of the Commission for Monetary Affaires, told the council today that flexible rates and a customs union looking toward full economic union were incompatible.

Decision Is Explained

He won general agreement on this point from the assembled finance ministers of the six countries. They later decided to try to work out a common community position on the issue of rate flexibility for debates within the broader context of studies now underway in the Monetary Fund in Washington.

Professor Schiller explained that the German decision to "float" the mark temporarily had to be seen within the context of the political split over revaluation and that anything else, barring of course revaluation, would have been "no more effective (in controlling speculation) than a drop of water on a hot stone."

That said, the economics minister, who will be a dominant figure in the new coalition, gave his agreement to end the experiment "in the shortest possible time."

Mr. Barre said that a system of flexible rates would provide an element of uncertainty that would disturb community commerce, levels of competition, the mobility of labor and capital, and the common agricultural policy based on uniform prices.

At the Monetary Fund's annual meeting in Washington last week, there was a good deal of discussion about greater rate flexibility as a means of getting round the political obstacles to parity changes that have brought unsettled times to the monetary world.

Should the community adopt a hard line against flexibility, such as that taken by Mr. Barre today, it could mean any new reform ideas would have difficulty getting off the ground.

The United States has taken a neutral position on the issue, its lack of enthusiasm for new reform motivated by fears that greater flexibility might mean a chain reaction of devaluations leaving the dollar exposed.

Under international monetary rules, currencies fluctuate against the dollar, within fixed margins set up to 1 per cent above or 1 per cent below parity. The dollar can be altered only by changing the official price of gold, now fixed at $35 an ounce.

Mr. Barre said that under this system the community discriminates against its own currencies in favor of the dollar. What he meant was that community currencies fluctuate more widely among themselves than they do against the dollar and that the dollar is therefore favored as a medium of international exchange.

This is an argument in favor of locking the parities of the six member states so that they would fluctuate as a bloc, but far greater economic and monetary cooperation is required before this action, long sought by the commission as a step towards economic unity, is realized.

Loss of Face Suffered

On the question of the German tax on agricultural imports, the commission suffered some loss of face. It had recommended that the Germans abolish the "illegal" tax and put into effect instead a ban on all agricultural imports.

This was impossible for the Germans to accept. It would have deprived the heavily populated Ruhr area, for example, of its traditional sources of food supplies.

Although there had been support for the commission's stand last week, this melted away today as the Germans promised to get rid of the tax as soon as they went back on a fixed-parity basis.

The government finally decided to establish a new par value for the mark at 9.29 per cent above the previously established par.

MARK IS REVALUED *

BONN, Oct. 24—The West German mark was revalued upward today to 27.3224 American cents in the first major act of Chancellor Willy Brandt's Social-Democratic-led coalition Government.

* *New York Times,* October 25, 1969.

The decision, which lifts the external rate by 9.2896 per cent above the old parity of 25 cents, was taken after more than a year of speculation in exchange markets, some of it so frenzied that it threatened to topple the international monetary system of agreed-upon parities.

The new parity is higher than had been expected. Economics Minister Karl Schiller, announcing the Cabinet decision tonight, said it was a "courageous rate, but certainly not a foolhardy one."

Surplus Reduction Seen

The more valuable mark should have the effect, although it may be slow in coming, of reducing West Germany's huge trading surplus.

It will also accelerate an outflow of capital—funds that had been pumped into West Germany by speculators all over the world in anticipation of today's revaluation.

All West Germany's trading partners should reap an advantage because a higher mark will mean higher-priced German goods in world markets. France is West Germany's biggest trading partner, followed by the United States and the Netherlands.

Troop Cost to Rise

For the United States, the higher parity brings with it the disadvantage of increasing the $1-billion annual cost of garrisoning American troops here. Washington may seek to negotiate an adjustment.

The mark had been worth 25 cents from December, 1961, until the Federal elections last month that ended 20 years of Christian Democratic leadership. The elections nullified what had been in recent months a virtual veto by the Union parties against a parity change.

On Sept. 29, one day after the Federal elections, the caretaker Cabinet, acting to forestall what almost certainly would have been a new monetary crisis, decided to detach the mark from its internationally set pegs and let the rate float.

This was in anticipation of a formal revaluation by the Social Democrats when, as was then the expectation, they would become the dominant force in a new coalition. As the minority partners in the old coalition, they had been in favor of revaluation since last March.

With careful manipulation by the Bundesbank, the West German Central Bank in Frankfurt, which fed out dollars in a steady stream to keep the mark on a slow-but-steady upward course, the rate had moved over the last four weeks from the official 25 cents to 27.02 at today's formal fixing in Frankfurt. This came six and one-half hours before the revaluation announcement.

Members of the International Monetary Fund—most of the non-Communist world—are committed to maintaining rates for their currencies within limits of 1 per cent above and 1 per cent below parity.

Exception Allowed

An exception was made for the West Germans because of their special political problems and because they announced their intention to return to a fixed parity system in the near future.

Central banks control the rate movements by intervening in the exchange markets to buy their currencies with dollars if the rate slides to the lower limit, or in reverse, selling their currencies for dollars if the rate climbs toward its upper limit.

With the parity set at 27.3224 cents, the new upper limit for the mark is 27.5040 cents and the new lower limit is 27.1. This represents a fluctuation of .82 per cent either side of parity—well within the one per cent limit.

Fewer to the Dollar

Because the mark is now worth more in terms of dollars, the standard yardstick of the monetary system, the dollar necessarily buys fewer marks.

There had been four marks to the dollar under the old parity. Now there are 3.66. This means that the dollar buys eight and a half per cent fewer marks, even though the mark's value has been increased by 9.2896 per cent.

There is nothing inconsistent here. It is simply that a different base is used in computing the two percentage adjustments.

The same principle applies, for example, if a merchant raises the price of a product by 25 per cent, then offers a 20 per cent discount. The price is back where it was.

European Dealings Differ

With the parity at 3.66 marks to the dollar, the new limits have been fixed at 3.69 and 3.63 marks. European banks deal in these terms, while American banks quote the mark's value in terms of American cents.

The big question now is whether there will be upper revaluations by other "strong" currencies.

The Dutch guilder, for one, has been pressed hard against its upper limits, and foreign-exchange dealers said that in today's dealings the Dutch central bank might have bought as much as $100-million to keep the ceiling from being breached.

Guilder Is Sought

The general expectation had been that the Dutch would be able to hold their rate with anything under a 10 per cent revaluation by the West Germans.

But since so much Dutch trade is with West Germany, upward pressure may remain on the guilder for a while. The Dutch followed the Germans in the 1961 revaluation.

Austrian schillings and Swiss francs were also in demand, on the theory that these countries also might be forced into upward parity adjustments.

The theory is based on the fact that the substantial West German exports to these countries will be priced higher and therefore will add to inflationary pressures unless there is a counterbalancing parity adjustment.

Schiller Comments

Asked whether other countries might feel it necessary to adjust their parities, Economics Minister Schiller said their problems were taken into consideration in setting the new rate.

But he added, "We came through alone in this matter," referring to the sovereign right of nations to make parity changes as they saw fit.

The West Germans, however, did engage in some preliminary consultations. While the Cabinet was meeting, lower-level West German economic officials were in Luxembourg at a specially convened session of European Economic Community's monetary committee to inform the five other member states of the decision before it was announced.

France Criticized

The six member states are committed to this under the Common Market's rules. France was criticized in community councils for not having fulfilled this commitment when she devalued the franc from 20.255 United States cents to 18.004 cents in August.

The International Monetary Fund in Washington was also notified in advance, Dr. Schiller said, adding that "I have no doubt it will give its approval to this long-awaited step."

The executive directors of the IMF immediately issued a statement "concurring in the change in the par value of the Deutschmark." France's Finance Minister called the decision "a positive act" and, referring to the floating of the mark in recent weeks, he stated that "the demonstration has been provided that the absence of monetary parity was not compatible with good functioning of international exchanges, particularly within the Common Market." The United States Treasury also welcomed the revaluation, stating that it should resolve uncertainty in foreign exchange markets.

6. CANADIAN DOLLAR CRISIS (1970)

The float of the D-mark was followed shortly by the floating of the Canadian dollar in June 1970. This was the second time Canada floated its currency. Indeed, Canada has had a flexible exchange rate for almost half the period since Bretton Woods, from 1950 until 1962, and since June 1970.

The 1950 decision to adopt a floating rate for the Canadian dollar was taken under conditions similar to the German float in 1969. The Canadian dollar was undervalued in the face of a heavy inflow of foreign investment, and the expectation of a revaluation stimulated speculation on a scale that the Canadian monetary authorities could not control. The inflow of capital was adding to the money supply, and tending to lower interest rates, thus augmenting inflationary forces. The Canadian authorities therefore obtained the approval of the IMF to float, but the floating rate was intended as a temporary device to determine what the market would establish as a new parity rate. Although the Fund requested the re-establishment of an effective par value as soon as circumstances warranted,[21] the Canadian dollar actually continued to float until 1962. The Fund's ultimate objective was to create the conditions for the restoration of a stable and unified exchange rate, and the fluctuating rate was regarded only as a temporary means to an end. In effect, Canada's exchange rate fluctuated by only 3 to 5 per cent, and for practical purposes the benefits commonly associated with exchange rate stability were not lost.

The more general opposition of the Fund to a fluctuating rate was stated, however, in 1964, by the deputy manager director, as follows:

> Some economists argue the case for freely fluctuating rates of exchange as an instrument for balance-of-payments adjustment. But financial officials in most countries today—even in those developing countries which temporarily have fluctuating rates—have been convinced by experience that greater flexibility than that sanctioned by the Fund's Articles of Agreement would be undesirable and impractical. Fluctuat-

21. Horsefield (ed.), *International Monetary Fund 1946–65*, Vol. II, pp. 159–73.

ing rates create great uncertainty for traders and investors and set up stresses in the financial and economic relationships within a country and in its international position. Moreover, far from being simple, the problems of managing a flexible rate are no less complex than those which arise in maintaining an effective par value, and in addition present their own mixture of financial, economic, and political difficulties. Indeed, countries which have endeavored to conduct their affairs on the basis of a fluctuating rate have found it extremely hard to let the exchange rate perform its intended functions. It also is generally true that exchange rate policy under a system of flexible rates tends to become much more a matter of unilateral action, which would make the whole process of international collaboration in financial matters far more difficult.[22]

Again, in June 1970, Canada decided to float under conditions broadly similar to those of 1950—a general belief that the Canadian dollar was undervalued, a massive inflow of short-term funds, and a desire to pursue domestic anti-inflationary policies. The speculative inflows made it extremely difficult for the Bank of Canada to avoid an inappropriately expansive monetary policy. In order to free domestic monetary policy from the balance-of-payments situation, the government abandoned the fixed parity of United States 92.5 cents.

OTTAWA'S DECISION *

PRINCE ALBERT, Saskatchewan, June 1—Ottawa's decision for the second time since World War II to let the Canadian dollar find its own level in foreign-currency dealings may prove to have important implications for the international monetary system.

The Canadian action is significant in that it represents two types of change. Primarily, it is a step away from the rather rigid system of fixed currency parities drawn up at the 1944 International Monetary Conference at Bretton Woods, N.H. Second, Canada is attempting to achieve greater independence in the management of her own economy. In the past, the fixed-parity system sometimes forced governments, in Canada and other countries, to pursue for external reasons policies that ran counter to domestic requirements.

22. Speech by Frank A. Southard, Jr., Dallas, Texas, March 27, 1964, in *International Financial News Survey* (April 3, 1964), pp. 115–16.
* *New York Times*, June 2, 1970.

Canada evidently wants to manage her affairs more in keeping with her own needs. For example, one immediate effect of the floating dollar, which promptly gained more than three cents in early trading today, will be to intensify import competition in Canadian markets, thereby dampening inflationary pressures.

In Canada the dollar closed around 97 cents to the United States dollar.

If Ottawa lets the Canadian dollar float indefinitely, events might prove that Canada nudged the world along a new monetary path.

If after a while Ottawa reintroduces a specified parity, yesterday's move may prove to have been at least an important modification of the old system.

Edgar J. Benson, the Finance Minister, refused to be committed at yesterday's news conference on whether a specified parity might be re-introduced later.

It is not difficult to imagine that in floating their dollar, the Canadians, basically a cautious people, were only seeking temporary relief from the heavy cost imposed on them in recent months by the strength of their currency. To keep it from trading above 93.25 United States cents, the effective upper limit under the old rules, Canada had spent hundreds of millions of her own dollars—selling them in the market for American dollars.

The drain on the Federal Government's cash balance complicated the tasks of managing the Government's debt and the over-all domestic monetary policy.

Mr. Benson said yesterday that disclosure in a day or two of the huge May increase in foreign-exchange reserves, $262-million, would almost certainly have drawn large speculative sums into Canadian funds. That is what happened to West Germany last year under similar circumstances, which also led Bonn to allow the mark to float.

After allowing the mark to find its own level, Bonn froze it at 27.3224 United States cents. However, whether Ottawa will freeze her currency at a new, higher level is doubtful. Mr. Benson commented that Canada's circumstances might not be the same.

Behind that remark lay the concern of Government economists that Canada's trade position, strong in recent years, might weaken in the nineteen-seventies. Two special factors helped Canada's exports in the nineteen-sixties—the devaluation near the beginning of the decade and the mid-decade auto trade pact with the United States.

Weakening Trade Possible

Analysts see no such special lift to exports in the nineteen-seventies, and they are afraid that United States trade policy will become more protectionist, hurting Canada's exports. Some Ottawa experts would not be surprised if Canada's trade position turned appreciably less robust before the end of the year.

That possibility invites speculation that Ottawa will put the peg back in, so to speak, when the upward pressure on the Canadian dollar abates and it drifts back to the range of 92.5 United States cents, the abandoned official parity. In other words, it is possible that yesterday's action was privately regarded by its authors as a temporary expedient.

Such essential conservatism would be characteristically Canadian. Canada, however, has been showing signs of greater independence, particularly when it comes to differing with the United States. Her actions with respect to Communist China, the Atlantic Alliance and Arctic pollution all displease Washington, in varying degrees.

Consequently, it would not be surprising if Canada, having pulled the monetary peg, throws it away. There was considerable clamor for a floating exchange rate in 1968, when Canada was forced to borrow hundreds of millions of dollars abroad to prop up her currency, and the Canadian dollar did float from 1950 to 1962 when other currencies were fixed. After Bretton Woods, the Canadian dollar was pegged at $1 in 1946 and in 1949 devalued to 90.91 cents. In May, 1962, Canada returned to the fixed-parity system, pegging the dollar at 92.5 cents, where it stood until yesterday.

As a country doing considerable business with Japan, Britain, West Germany and the United States, Canada is bound to make an impression, intellectually and financially, by yesterday's action. It is possible that unpegging the dollar will hasten the introduction of flexibility in the international financial system.

The Bank of Canada reported on official reserves.

EXCHANGE RATE AND OFFICIAL RESERVES *

In the first five months of 1970 the combined strength of the current and capital accounts put upward pressure on the Canadian dollar and Canada's official international reserves rose sharply. When the maintenance of the official parity margins was suspended at the end of May, reserves were U.S. $853.4 million higher than they had been at the beginning of the year, excluding the initial allocation of SDRs amounting to U.S. $124.3 million. In addition, U.S. $360 million had been acquired for future delivery so that the combined increase in spot and forward positions, excluding the SDR allocation, was about U.S. $1.2 billion.

The exchange rate of the Canadian dollar rose sharply at the beginning of June after the parity limits were abandoned. By the end of the month the Canadian dollar had appreciated by more than 3½ per cent, and by the end of

* Bank of Canada, *Annual Report, 1970,* pp. 71–72.

December it had risen to 98.89 U.S. cents, an appreciation of 6 per cent. From the end of May to the end of December official reserves rose by U.S. $595 million, including U.S. $360 million delivered under forward contracts undertaken before the end of May. A substantial part of the increase excluding deliveries on maturing forward contracts occurred at the beginning of June. On January 1, 1971 Canada's reserves were augmented by the receipt of its share of the second allocation of SDRs in the amount of U.S. $117.7 million. Reserves rose a further U.S. $53.6 million to the end of February and the exchange value of the Canadian dollar at that time was 99.32 U.S. cents.

The forward exchange rate for the Canadian dollar was at a small discount early in the year, moved to a large premium in June and remained at an appreciable premium until late in the year. It then fell sharply and was at a considerable discount by February.

Official International Reserves
(month-ends—millions of U.S. dollars)

	Dec. 1968	Dec. 1969	May 1970	Dec. 1970
Foreign currencies				
U.S. dollars	1,964.9	1,743.6	2,526.3	3,022.1
Other currencies	11.6	12.3	17.4	14.5
Gold	863.1	872.3	879.5	790.7
Special Drawing Rights	—	—	138.1	182.1
Reserve position in the IMF	206.2	478.1	522.5	669.6
Total	3,045.8	3,106.3	4,084.0	4,679.0

At the time of the float, the IMF merely noted "the current situation in Canada" before going on to emphasize the responsibility that rests on all members to promote exchange stability and maintain orderly exchange arrangements with one another. A *New York Times* editorial was, however, commendatory:

Canada's move should have important educational value for other countries with undervalued currencies. For instance, Japan's trade problems vis-à-vis the United States and Western Europe could be greatly eased if the Japanese also permitted their currency to find its true market value. An appreciated Japanese yen could help to forestall the imposition of rigid quotas or other artificial barriers to trade.

In fact, a more flexible exchange rate system adopted by all nations could prevent the growing wave of protectionism from wrecking the international market for goods and capital which took so long to rebuild after the Depression and World War II.

The world's finance ministers and central bankers, a notoriously conservative group, would be extremely ill-advised to try to persuade the Canadians to abort an experiment with so much educational value to other nations in terms of both domestic and international economic policy. The longer the Canadian experiment lasts, the better.[23]

The *Wall Street Journal* also emphasized the importance of Canada's "experiment."

CANADA'S CRUCIAL EXPERIMENT *

The Canadian government last week found it necessary to affirm, once again, that it has "no plans at the moment" to return its dollar to a fixed exchange rate. The financial community finds it hard to accept that Canada does indeed intend to let its dollar float freely in exchange markets, at least for some time to come.

In the current International Currency Review, Professor Harry G. Johnson of the University of Chicago and the London School of Economics explains why the Canadians are in no rush to return to a fixed rate. The basic reason is that they see a floating rate as the only way to escape the economic troubles that currently beset the U.S.

With the Canadian economy closely geared to the American economy, Canada recently has been having even more inflation than the U.S., along with unusually high unemployment. Canada might tighten money and thus produce higher domestic interest rates to curb inflation, but—with a fixed exchange rate—this would only attract an inflationary inflow of capital.

That was exactly what was occurring last spring, after Canada tightened credit to check inflation. "From the standpoint of checking inflation in Canada," says Professor Johnson, "the flotation of the Canadian dollar was probably the only sensible policy open to the Canadian authorities."

"The floating rate," he continues, "will bring pervasive competitive pressures to bear on Canadian wage and price fixing, as exporters feel the pressure of an appreciated exchange rate on their profit margins and domestic industry feels the pressure of lower-priced competition from imports. These pressures may prove sufficiently strong and effective to allow the government to take expansionary measures to improve the unemployment situation."

23. Editorial, *New York Times* (June 3, 1970).
* *Wall Street Journal*, August 4, 1970.

There is, unfortunately, a great deal of pressure from the U.S. and elsewhere for Canada to return to a fixed exchange rate. "Few, if any, Americans," says Professor Johnson, "understand that a floating Canadian dollar is far more advantageous to the United States than a pegged Canadian dollar.

"Given the high degree of economic and financial integration of the two economies, together with some room for independence of Canadian economic policy, the existence of a fixed exchange rate . . . necessarily implies large-scale and highly volatile movements of capital and of international resources between the two countries." In recent years the U.S. has had to obtain various ad hoc financial agreements from the Canadians to keep the capital flows from further unbalancing the American payments accounts.

With a floating Canadian dollar, transactions with Canada no longer accentuate the U.S. payments deficit, and there's no need for repetition of the frantic and frequent consultations of the recent past. "With luck," says Professor Johnson, "the Canadians may be able to get away with a floating exchange rate . . . and thus enjoy both more independence of economic policy and more self-respect in relations with the United States. But it would take a lot of luck."

If Canada does give in to the pressures for a return to a fixed exchange rate, it would damage if not destroy the movement toward greater exchange rate flexibility around the world. For the Canadians and a great many other people, the current floating rate experiment may well be crucial.

From the outset of the float, the Canadian authorities had stated they did not intend to let the exchange rate adjust completely to market forces, but reserved the right to intervene on exchange markets to keep the Canadian dollar from rising too rapidly and to stabilize the rate. Thus, the governor of the Bank of Canada stated:

> The exchange rate is a very important price in a country that trades with the outside world on the scale that Canada does: changes in it have important effects on the level and nature of economic activity in Canada, particularly on the position of industries that export and that compete with imports. It is not therefore possible to ignore it, even when it floats. Public financial management must continue to be concerned that the exchange rate is broadly suitable to the development of Canada's international trade, and compatible with the desired structure of our balance of payments, in particular the

size of the balance on current account. . . . If the exchange
rate moves or threatens to move outside that range it will be
prudent to review the mix of financial policy in Canada to see
if some other mix would be more appropriate. Whether it will
be monetary policy or fiscal policy or both that will need to be
changed will depend on the circumstances.[24]

In following a policy of first keeping the rate down and then
stabilizing it, Canada's Exchange Fund Account intervened to
purchase United States or Canadian dollars as needed "to maintain orderly conditions in the market." Canadian foreign exchange reserves increased by approximately $850 million in
1971, indicating that the float was not "clean" but subject to intervention by the Canadian authorities to keep their dollar from
rising above the United States dollar.

Finally, in a favorable review of Canada's experience with
exchange flexibility, one student has concluded that Canadian
policy did not violate reasonable standards of international economic conduct:

> Canadian exchange rate policy has been developed with
> the needs of the domestic economy in mind. In early 1970,
> the Canadian dollar was allowed to float upward in order to
> avoid the degree of monetary expansion which would have
> been necessary to maintain the pegged rate of 92.5¢. This did
> not, however, signal an abrupt shift towards restriction, but
> rather was a way of responding to the balance of payments
> pressures created by very strong merchandise trade develop-
> ments. Expansive domestic policies were then able to pro-
> ceed in a measured manner, with the exchange rate adjust-
> ment reducing immediate inflationary problems and
> mitigating the unemployment-inflation dilemma. In order to
> prevent further pressures on industries heavily engaged in
> international trade, the government resisted upward move-
> ment of the currency, thereby reaching a compromise be-
> tween a fully flexible exchange rate and the maintenance of a
> fixed par.
>
> Because it represented a middle-of-the-road poasition, a
> rather strong *a priori* case can be made that Canadian ex-
> change rate policy met reasonable standards of good interna-
> tional behavior.[25]

24. Bank of Canada, *Annual Report, 1970*, pp. 9–10.
25. Paul Wonnacott, *The Floating Canadian Dollar* (1972), p. 79.

7. BRETTON WOODS, TWENTY-FIVE YEARS AFTER

After twenty-five years experience with the IMF, its managing director took the occasion "to look back . . . to appraise the handiwork of its founders and to see what lessons intervening experience holds for the future conduct of international monetary management."

THE BRETTON WOODS SYSTEM: AN APPRAISAL *

If I dwell tonight rather on the weaknesses associated with the system created at Bretton Woods, I do not mean to disparage its achievements, which are recognizably outstanding. The dream of Bretton Woods—or, as many cynics were to say for more than a decade after the conference, the illusion of Bretton Woods—was the unrestricted convertibility for current transactions of at least the major currencies. This became a reality some ten years ago and in many cases was extended also to capital transfers. The real output of the membership of the Fund, their trade in goods and services, and the flow of investment capital among them have expanded beyond all expectations and with barely any interruption. The achievements of the system and of the related revolution in national policies have changed our whole way of describing the economic climate. We talk much less of the business cycle, much more of rates of growth in real income. Insofar as the economies of member countries are still subject to cyclical phenomena, we no longer describe these in the terms used thirty years ago— "prosperity and depression." The problems have been transposed to a different key and we speak now of "overheating" and—occasionally— "recession."

Yet in recent years the system has betrayed signs of strain in a notorious series of currency crises. Less spectacular but more ominous have been the introduction in some cases of restrictions on current transactions, the tinkering with border taxes, the reimposition or tightening of capital controls, and the sluggish growth of aid. These developments have given rise to a keen debate on the adequacy of the system established a generation ago. As I said, I propose tonight to concentrate on those aspects of the system where performance has been less satisfactory. In that context, I shall deal first with exchange rates, second with the adjustment process, and third with the provision of adequate reserves.

* Address by the managing director of the IMF, Mr. Pierre-Paul Schweitzer, June 2, 1969. Reprinted in *International Financial News Survey*, June 6, 1969.

Par Value System

The current controversy has centered chiefly on the exchange rate regime. It has been seriously questioned whether the par value system and its limited freedom for market rates to move on either side of parity is not unduly rigid and outmoded in the present world. This system was intended to provide a stable environment which, by encouraging commercial interchange, would stimulate the growth and sharpen the efficiency of the world economy and its constituent parts. Stability, as the Fund has stressed in the past, does not mean rigidity. Specific provision was written into the Articles of Agreement for changes in par values; and where countries—in deficit or surplus— can no longer maintain broad equilibrium over time in their external payments without having to incur undue unemployment or price inflation, it is wholly proper that this provision should be used.

Yet in some instances, despite the existence of this provision, exchange rates that had ceased to be appropriate have been maintained. And this has contributed to the persistence of payments disequilibria, the encouragement of speculation, and crises in the exchange markets. Moreover, the rigidity of exchange rates in this sense has sometimes led to corrective measures of a kind that deny the very purposes which the par value system seeks to promote.

It is also true that the present framework differs in at least one important aspect from the world envisaged when the Articles of the Fund were agreed. The drafters were well aware that a country might have to alter its exchange rate in response to relative changes in its real economic position. But they did not envisage that a country would have to be so much concerned about the public's changing views on the strength of its currency. Speculative capital movements were to be suppressed rather than financed; indeed, limitations were put on members' access to the Fund to finance capital outflows. While the liberalization of payments for capital transactions has been a major factor in bringing about an integrated world economy, it has also greatly increased the possibility of sudden pressures on exchange rates, notably when underlying economic developments give reason to suppose that an adjustment would be appropriate. In their efforts to minimize speculative capital movements, moreover, countries have frequently felt obliged to make firm pronouncements on the fixity of their exchange rates, and this has inevitably made it more difficult for policy to respond to changed economic conditions.

The strains thus experienced by the system have led to suggestions that it might function better if there were more room for exchange rates to change. Various possibilities have been advocated for various kinds of flexibility intended either to facilitate adjustment in the basic balance of payments or to provide more incentive for equilibrating speculation or to combine these two objectives in some degree.

These suggestions deserve careful study in the full context of the achievements of the present system, of its weaknesses to be sure, but also of the grave disturbances of which the drafters at Bretton Woods still had the most immediate and vivid recollections. It is true that the world's financial system has been badly rocked in the last few years; and it would be foolish to minimize these disturbances. But it is also true that they have been overwhelmingly financial, not economic, in kind.

It seems to me that the essential characteristics of the par value system remain valid now as they were twenty-five years ago. Stability of exchange rates has made a key contribution to the balanced expansion of the world economy. The major advance toward international cooperation in the economic field that was achieved at Bretton Woods was that the rate of exchange for each currency was made a matter of international concern. It is only by bringing exchange rates under international jurisdiction that the risk of competitive depreciation and other forms of currency warfare can be avoided. It is true that since the end of the war this risk has not manifested itself as a serious one; but this experience at least partly reflects the success of the Bretton Woods system and in no wise justifies dismantling the protection provided by the Articles of the Fund.

In this connection I should like to make one very general point. Governments have in the postwar period increasingly accepted responsibility for the performance of their national economies in terms of employment, output, price stability, and other major economic variables. The rate of exchange has a major impact on all these aspects and is bound to be politically sensitive. In my view, it is therefore unrealistic to suppose that governments would be prepared to accept alternative regimes that would put the rate of exchange at the mercy of market forces alone. Almost certainly rates would continue to be managed and common rules would have to be agreed to forestall any possibility of a reversion to anarchic practices. It is at least open to doubt, however, whether generally acceptable criteria could be worked out in this area.

I believe that any case for change must be convincingly made in light of the interrelated aims—growth and stability—which any system should serve. Beyond this I have no wish to prejudge the outcome of the various studies that are being made on this matter. Nor do I wish to predict whether in the end any changes that might be found desirable would involve primarily some loosening of the provisions of the Articles or a somewhat readier use of the possibilities for par value changes that the Articles contain. In this last respect there might be advantages in members proposing changes in parities whenever there were substantial evidence of fundamental disequilibrium and without necessarily waiting until such evidence was overwhelming.

Adjustment Process

Although I have so far dwelt almost exclusively on exchange rates, it would of course be wrong to consider this matter in isolation. Changes in exchange rates are one element in the broader mechanism that has come to be called the adjustment process. In certain circumstances rate changes are an indispensable condition for the correction of economic maladjustment, but even so they are part only of what must be a concerted attack on that problem.

The Fund is very much concerned with the adjustment process, as Article I makes plain. One of the purposes of the Fund, in accordance with its other objectives, is "to shorten the duration and lessen the degree of disequilibrium in the international balances of payments of members." It is inevitable that countries should from time to time develop deficits or surpluses in their external payments; and it is important for the member concerned and, in the case of the main trading countries, for the system as a whole that these should be contained and corrected within a reasonable period of time and in a manner consistent with the other objectives of the Fund. Unfortunately, members' imbalances have not always been notable for the brevity of their duration or the modesty of their size. The long-standing deficits of the United States and the United Kingdom and the surpluses of some continental European nations are serious cases in point.

Against this background some commentators have argued that the international community should formulate and adopt uniform rules for financial policy to introduce an element of automaticity into the adjustment process. That approach tends to underrate the complexities of this world. In seeking to achieve simultaneously a variety of economic objectives of differing degrees of compatibility, countries need leeway to apply that combination of policies which is best calculated to overcome their particular difficulties and takes account also of the range of instruments at their disposal. A mechanistic formula, even if it were operationally feasible or politically acceptable, would inhibit this flexibility of response. At the same time there can be no question that, in the pursuit of their domestic objectives, countries should give adequate weight to the evolution of their external payments. This means that countries should be prepared to coordinate and temper their economic policies in light of the implications that these have for other countries and the world economy.

The responsibilities of surplus and deficit countries in the adjustment process have been extensively discussed in the Fund and in Working Party 3 of the Organization for Economic Cooperation and Development. This interchange has been fruitful in identifying problems of common concern and in increasing understanding as to appropriate responses. Having said this, I am bound to add that there remains a gap between understanding and practice. This stems partly from imperfections in economic diagnosis and forecasting. At the same time the tools for implementing policy are often cumbersome to use and lacking in precision when applied.

Yet, after due allowance is made for such difficulties, there remains a basic problem which is political in nature and which has not infrequently impeded prompt and appropriate action. It consists broadly in a reluctance to dampen down excessive aggregate demand until the inflationary process has caused substantial damage; and also in an unwillingness to make necessary adjustments in exchange rates not simply for reasons of national prestige but also because this is no easy option in terms of its effect on the real income of particular sectors of the community. It is not readily apparent to me how this problem, in light of its nature, can be resolved simply by changing the monetary system. To the extent that political will is engaged, it seems necessary that countries should accept that timely action is in their own self-interest in all but the very shortest term. It may be that this is being, or will become, more widely recognized as a result of experience over the last several years. If the chaos of the 1930's could be followed by the incomparably more responsible approach of the postwar period, I am inclined to believe that the improvement can be carried further.

It is possible to take encouragement from the fact that countries have made and are making the effort to adjust. The two major deficit countries of past years, the United States and the United Kingdom, have shown much determination in this respect. To improve the severe imbalance in the system, however, persistent action on their part will be necessary for some long while ahead. At the same time the policy reactions of a wide range of other countries will be hardly less important. As the United States and the United Kingdom move into surplus, the payments positions of many other countries will become less easy. This expectation has been confirmed by developments in the first quarter of 1969. During this period the United States, although in record deficit on the liquidity basis, had a large surplus on official settlements account; and the United Kingdom also was running a moderate over-all surplus. This situation had an immediate impact on the payments and reserve positions of a number of industrial countries and began to provoke certain defensive reactions.

Adequacy of Reserves

These recent developments underline an essential requirement of the international monetary system which, though understood by some at Bretton Woods, was not provided for in the structure that emerged. This is the need for a continuing accrual over the longer run of global reserves in a quantity sufficient to permit countries that conduct their international transactions in a responsible fashion to increase their reserves adquately as those transactions expand.

This need was satisfied in the earlier years of the system created at Bretton Woods, although it would perhaps be too generous to say that its architects had clearly foreseen how this aspect would work. The increase in reserves during the 1950's through the early 1960's was not statistically very large. The annual rate of growth was about 2½ per cent, against an increase of trade in the order of 6 or 7 per cent a year. The main explanation for the fact that reserve growth was nevertheless adequate is found in the massive redistribution of reserves that took place during the period. The United States especially, and a number of developing countries, that had ended the war with very large accumulated reserves could well afford an absolute decline in their stock. The small amount held by foreign countries in the form of claims on the United States could readily be expanded without hesitation on the part of debtor or creditor. These adjustments, together with accruals of newly mined gold, permitted the combined reserves of countries outside the United States to grow roughly in proportion to the expansion of their trade. In these circumstances countries were able to sustain that rapid expansion, to liberalize current and—in many cases—capital transactions, and to devote resources to assisting developing countries.

The process of reserve growth that I have just outlined ceased to function some five years ago. Such reserve growth as there has been since then—and it has been small—has been in the form of monetized credits to countries in balance of payments deficit. It is clear that this is no basis for the long-run growth of world reserves.

Fortunately the imagination which twenty-five years ago produced the Articles of Agreement of the Fund has not been wanting in recent years. The proposed Amendment to the Articles provides a constructive solution to the need for deliberate reserve creation that is now materializing as the traditional process ceases to function. The discussions and negotiations that preceded agreement on the special drawing rights facility were protracted and by no means easy. Nevertheless, I think that we can take some satisfaction in the fact that a procedure has been worked out and will soon be available to meet an emerging defect of the system, without the world economy having had to provide the proof, through large-scale misery and dislocation, that adequate reserves are the required lubricant of that system.

It would be strange if we were not deeply concerned about the international monetary scene at a time when financial crises seem almost to have become a regular feature. But it is possible to be too discouraged. A rational means of injecting liquidity into the system has been agreed; and this was a striking instance of cooperation which has been evident, though in widely differing degrees, in other areas. Countries have made the effort to adjust, even if action has too often been tardy. There is certainly need for a less defensive attitude toward exchange rate changes. Beyond that, there remains the basic need for countries to put more emphasis on financial stability in recognition of the economic benefits that this confers. Without that policy disposition, experience will be unhappy under no matter what system. Paradoxically, the very difficulties of these latter years, which have mercifully been still financial in character, may have served to make this increasingly understood.

C. QUESTIONS

1. a. What do you think should be the norms or standards of an international monetary order?

b. During its first twenty-five years, did the Bretton Woods system contribute to the attainment of these norms?

c. How strict a code of international monetary conduct did the IMF impose upon its members? Has this code served its purposes?

2. a. Do you think the Articles of the IMF and the International Bank for Reconstruction and Development were drafted according to economic logic alone without political considerations? What would it mean to say that the IMF should be "politically neutral?" Could it be?

b. At the inaugural meeting of the Boards of Governors of the Fund and the Bank in 1946 Keynes delivered a reflective speech in which he evoked the assistance of the good fairies to watch over the new-born Bretton Woods twins. But at the end he hoped that no malicious fairy, no Carabosse, had been forgotten at Bretton Woods, lest coming uninvited she should curse the children. "You two brats," he visualized her saying, "shall grow up politicians; your every thought and act shall have an *arrière-pensée;* everything you determine shall not be for its own sake or on its own merits but because of something else." [The full speech is reproduced in R. F. Harrod, *Life of John Maynard Keynes* (1951), pp. 631–32.]

Do you think the Fund has grown up more politician than economist? Have the practices of the Fund retained the confidence of the international community? Should international monetary reform proceed through the Fund, or should the Fund be liquidated?

3. What were the principles of adjustment implicit in the Bretton Woods system? Did these prove adequate up to the early 1960's? Why were there more difficulties in the adjustment experience after the mid-1960's?

4. Consider the IMF's provisions for a change in exchange rates.

a. A member alone can formally "propose" a change in the par value of its currency, and the IMF may simply "concur or object."

Would it have been better if the Fund had been given the initiative to propose a change and to impose sanctions if the proposal was not followed?

b. The criteria under which it is necessary "to correct a fundamental disequilibrium" [Article IV (5) (6)] were left highly vague rather than being made precise. Do you think this was necessary because the criteria could not be defined, or was it because of the political compromises necessary to secure a consensus at the Bretton Woods conference?

c. If you were an IMF official, how would you decide if there were a "fundamental disequilibrium?" Would you now propose other presumptive rules for adjustment? [Compare pp. 266–73 below.]

5. Why has the IMF's scarce currency clause [Article VII (3)] never been invoked? Could other sanctions have been imposed on surplus countries to share some of the burden of adjustment?

6. How did the IMF relate to the promotion of development? What political power did the less-developed countries have at the Bretton Woods conference? Should the Fund have made more provision for development finance, or should this have been left solely to the International Bank for Reconstruction and Development? [Compare pp. 224–35 below.]

7. To what extent has the process of policy making between members of the IMF and the IMF as an organization been based on consultation, negotiation, or definite rules of economic conduct?

8. a. Recall that some of the original provisions of Keynes's plan for a Clearing Union were the creation of bancor as an international currency, the inconvertibility of bancor into

gold, interest charges on the accumulation of credit balances by surplus members, and the right of a member to change the par value of its currency by 5 per cent a year without consent of the Governing Board of the Clearing Union.

Would the adoption of these provisions at Bretton Woods have avoided the international currency crises of the 1960's? Would you have argued for their adoption at Bretton Woods? Why were they not adopted?

b. Do you think the international currency crises since the mid-1960's indicate that there has been insufficient international liquidity to make the pegged exchange-rate system viable? Insufficient harmonization of national policies?

9. The success of a devaluation usually depends as much on a number of supplementary policies which accompany devaluation as the devaluation itself. Consider how this is demonstrated by conditions of the French economy in 1969.

10. How do changes in exchange rates among countries in the European Economic Community (such as Germany's revaluation or France's devaluation) complicate the EEC's policies? What are the implications for a European monetary union?

11. Was Canada's relative success with a fluctuating rate because of the uniqueness of the country's circumstances (especially the close relations to the United States economy)? Would you argue that Canada's experience is not a precedent for other countries because their circumstances with respect to trade and normal capital movements and domestic fiscal and monetary policies would be quite different from Canada's?

12. In reviewing Canada's experience with a floating rate, Deputy Governor Lawson of the Bank of Canada said that

> the most important question for a government in respect of exchange policy is not should the exchange rate be "fixed" or should it float, but what should the exchange rate be? . . . I am aware that some people seem to believe that if the exchange rate is determined in a free market without direct official intervention it will inevitably be the right rate, but this view seems to me to be a considerable oversimplification. A floating rate may be influenced indirectly

in a variety of ways to make it float freely at quite different levels. A decision to float does not therefore offer an escape from the fundamental question—what should the exchange rate be? . . . Good exchange rate policy is thus a blend of economics and politics; it requires analysis of the costs and benefits of the exchange rates that are possible in the circumstances, and then a choice between them.

Would you agree with this view? If you were Governor of the Bank of Canada, under what conditions would you recommend that the Bank intervene in the foreign exchange market to contain the limits within which the Canadian dollar might float? Why not rely simply on the law of supply and demand in foreign exchange markets? What other norms may there be for exchange-rate adjustment?
13. What lessons do the British, French, German, and Canadian currency crises provide for financial crisis management? What are the implications for longer-run international monetary reform?

D. READINGS

Acheson, A. L. K. et al., *Bretton Woods Revisited* (1972).

Aliber, R. Z., *The International Money Game* (1973).

Caves, R. E. and Associates, *Britain's Economic Prospects* (1968), Chap. IV.

Cohen, B. J., *Balance of Payments Policy* (1969).

Conan, A. R., *The Problem of Sterling* (1966).

Cooper, Richard N., *The Economics of Interdependence* (1968).

Davis, T. E., "Exchange Rate Adjustment Under the Par Value System 1946–68," Federal Reserve Bank of Kansas City, *Monthly Review* (September–October 1969).

Dunn, Robert M., Jr., *Exchange Rate Rigidity, Investment Distortions, and the Failure of Bretton Woods* (Princeton Essays in International Finance No. 97, February 1973).

Gardner, R. N., *Sterling-Dollar Diplomacy* (1969).

Grubel, Herbert G., *The International Monetary System* (1969).

Hirsch, F., *Money International* (1969).

Hirsch, F., *The Pound Sterling: A Polemic* (1965).

Horsefield, J. Keith (ed.), *The International Monetary Fund 1945–65*, Vol. I: *Chronicle*, Vol. II: *Analysis* (1969).

Johnson, H. G., and Nash, John, *Floating the Pound* (1969).

Loftus, M. L., "The International Monetary Fund, 1968–1971: A Selected Bibliography," *IMF Staff Papers* (March 1972).

Stern, R. M., *The Balance of Payments* (1973).

Strange, Susan, *Sterling and British Policy* (1971).

Tew, Brian, *International Monetary Cooperation 1945–70* (1970).

Triffin, Robert, *The Fate of the Pound* (1969).

——, *World Monetary Maze* (1966).

——, *Our International Monetary System* (1968).

Wonnacott, Paul, *The Floating Canadian Dollar* (1972).

——, *Canadian Dollar, 1948–1962* (1965).

Yeager, L. B., *International Monetary Relations* (1966).

Problem II
Balance of Payments Policy: The Dollar Problem

A. THE CONTEXT

1. FROM "DOLLAR SHORTAGE" TO "DOLLAR GLUT"

The dominant factor shaping international financial diplomacy since the end of World War II has been the evolution from "dollar shortage" in the immediate postwar years to "dollar glut" since the mid-1950's. Many economists have believed that while the dollar was undervalued until the mid-1950's, it then became overvalued until the devaluations of August 1971 and February 1973. Of all the postwar currency crises, the dollar crisis of August 1971 has had the most far-reaching implications—making the need for reform of the international monetary system obvious. But there has been a wide range of opinion among government officials, the international financial community, and academic economists as to the causes and the cures for the dollar "deficit."

As one authority has summarized the period since the war:

> On August 15, 1971, the United States placed the world on a virtually pure dollar standard by suspending indefinitely the convertibility of the dollar into U.S. reserve assets. . . .

The postwar monetary system is now in its third phase. The first phase lasted through 1958, when only the dollar among major currencies was convertible into other currencies and into the reserve assets of the issuing country. The second phase lasted from 1959 until August 1971, when the currencies of all major countries were convertible both into one another and into their own reserves. The third phase began in August 1971, when the dollar alone among those major currencies became inconvertible into the reserves of its issuing country—though through the actions of the private markets and other countries, it remained convertible into other currencies. So the dollar has moved from being the only *convertible* major currency to being, at least in part, the only *inconvertible* major currency.[1]

Certain features stand out in the international monetary history of the past quarter-century:

(i) From 1950 to the 1971 crisis there was a persistent "deficit" in the United States balance of payments (except for a single surplus in 1957).

(ii) The foreign holdings of dollar assets rose markedly throughout the period, and the United States gold stock diminished from $23 billion in 1957 to less than $11 billion at the time of the gold crisis in March 1968.

(iii) But while the "deficit" in the United States balance of payments served to provide additional liquidity to the international monetary system, the very creation of the "deficit" also undermined confidence in the future exchange-rate stability of the dollar.

(iv) Nonetheless, the dollar—possessing some functions of international money—retained a unique position in the gold-and-dollar reserve system.

(v) For the United States, however, there was no readily available mechanism of adjustment to balance-of-payments disequilibrium.

Considering the political economics of the United States balance-of-payments deficit, one student of the problem has observed:

---

1. C. Fred Bergsten, *Reforming the Dollar: An International Monetary Policy for the United States* (1972), pp. 5–6.

Two of the most sensitive areas of sovereign power are defense and money: The former determines a nation's security, and the latter influences its allocation of material resources. When seen in this light, it is not coincidental that, given the absence of an over-all political consensus, major problems confronting the Atlantic community have to do with the control of nuclear weapons and international liquidity.

[T]he clear-cut U.S. superiority in military technology persists, a fact which effectively keeps European fingers off the alliance's nuclear button. But the similarity in the Atlantic problems ends as soon as the U.S. nuclear stockpile is compared with its gold stockpile. The former has grown bigger and better in the 1960's, while the latter has been decimated. The European offensive for authority in monetary affairs and the U.S. reaction have understandably reflected the fact that this country's international economic performance has not been as successful as its military performance. Nuclear warheads have been produced in greater quantities than gold bullion. . . .

To say that the U.S. balance-of-payments deficit is extraordinary is a classic understatement. Its causes, severity, duration, method of financing, impact on other countries, and means of elimination are all without comparison in international monetary history.[2]

The emphasis on control of nuclear weapons and international liquidity is not purely rhetorical. In the early 1960's these were precisely the problems that were of major concern to the Kennedy Administration. It has been reported that:

The balance of payments remained a constant worry to Kennedy. Of all the problems he faced as President, one had the impression that he felt least at home with this one. He used to tell his advisers that the two things which scared him most were nuclear war and the payments deficit. Once he half-humorously derided the notion that nuclear weapons were essential to international prestige. "What really matters," he said, "is the strength of the currency. It is this, not the *force de frappe*, which makes France a factor. Britain has nuclear weapons, but the pound is weak, so everyone pushes it around. Why are people so nice to Spain today? Not because Spain has nuclear weapons but because of all those lovely gold reserves." He had acquired somewhere, perhaps

2. Stephen D. Cohen, *International Monetary Reform, 1964–69* (1970), pp. 19–20.

from his father, the belief that a nation was only as strong as the value of its currency; and he feared that, if he pushed things too far, "loss of confidence" would descend and there would be a run on gold. But he was determined not to be stampeded into restrictive domestic measures, and he brought steady pressures for remedies which would not block expansion at home. The problem perhaps constrained him more in foreign affairs. He thought, for example, that the continuing payments deficit gave France, with its claims on American gold, a dangerous international advantage; and at times he even briefly considered doing things which would otherwise run athwart his policy, like selling submarines to South Africa, in the hope of relieving the strain on the balance of payments.[3]

To reach an understanding of the causes of the dollar "deficit" and to appraise the significance of the accumulation of foreign holdings of dollars and the gold outflow, we must first appreciate the special position of the dollar in the world monetary system.

2. THE DOLLAR AS AN INTERNATIONAL CURRENCY

Whatever passes as "money" is supposed to meet three basic needs: a unit of account, a medium of exchange, and a store of value. These needs relate just as much to international money as they do to domestic currency. It is important to recognize the extent to which the dollar, by fulfilling certain functions, has acquired the characteristics of an international currency.

2.1 *International Roles of the Dollar*

Under the Bretton Woods system the dollar came to fulfill several functions more effectively than any other currency, being essentially a world currency. The dollar is widely used as a transactions or "vehicle" currency. A large portion of world trade is invoiced and transacted in dollars, and the dollar has had a dominant medium-of-exchange function in international transactions.

The dollar has also been central to the IMF system because the United States was the sole country to peg its currency to gold, and other countries pegged their currencies in relation to

3. Arthur M. Schlesinger, Jr., *A Thousand Days: John F. Kennedy in the White House* (1965), pp. 654–55.

the gold value of the dollar. The dollar thereby became a *unit-of-account currency*, in the sense that exchange rate parities were initially expressed in terms of the dollar as the unit of account. This function is, however, tenuous because it is on a de facto rather than de jure basis. Article IV of the IMF gave legal status to the gold value of the dollar on July 1, 1944—that is, on 0.888671 grams of fine gold. No choice between the dollar and gold as a legal unit of account need be made as long as the price of the dollar in terms of gold remains fixed. But when the dollar is devalued in terms of gold, governments then have to decide whether to maintain the de facto price relationship of their currency vis-à-vis the dollar, or the de jure price relationship of their currency vis-à-vis gold.

Another major role of the dollar is as an *intervention* currency. It will be recalled that the original IMF agreement obligated governments to maintain their exchange rates "within the limits of plus or minus 1% of the defined parities of the currencies." To keep their currencies pegged within this narrow band, governments bought and sold in the dollar exchange market to offset discrepancies between demand and supply of their own currencies. When intervening as residual buyers or sellers, governments use the dollar as the intervention currency.

Most important, the dollar has also been the primary *"reserve currency"* insofar as the dollar has been useful for a store-of-value purpose in official reserve assets. Convertible currencies, under the Fund Agreement, are convertible into dollars; and dollars held by official monetary authorities were convertible into gold at a known price until the crisis of August 1971.

2.2 *Asymmetries in International Financial Relations*

Given the special roles of the dollar, the international monetary policy of the United States has differed from that of other countries in an important respect. Until August 1971, the United States maintained its exchange rates within the parity band by freely buying and selling gold against dollars offered by foreign monetary authorities at a fixed price of $35 per ounce [under Article IV, sec. 4(b) of the IMF Agreement]. The United States was the only government committed to selling gold at a fixed price. Because other countries used the dollar as a unit of account and an intervention currency, the United States monetary authorities were technically unable to change the relationship between the dollar and other major currencies. It was the *other* currency that had to be devalued or revalued—or maintained within the set margins of parity—vis-à-vis the dollar. Other countries had to change the price at which *they* bought and sold dollars to bring about a change in the exchange rate of the dollar.

In analyzing United States balance-of-payments policy, many economists have emphasized the international asymmetry in the adjustment of balance-of-payments disequilibria as between the United States and the rest of the world. A strong statement of this follows:

> At the moment . . . it is a dollar world, just as 1913 was a sterling world. In the view of some American economists . . . , this produces certain asymmetries in financial relationships which are an inherent part of the present system. Put baldly and with some exaggeration, these are:
>
> (i) The dollar is the world medium of exchange, unit of account, store of value, standard of deferred payment. It is the vehicle currency through which French francs are transferred into Deutschmarks, for example, and lire into Danish kroner. No other currency performs a similar role on a similar scale.
>
> (ii) If the dollar is a world money, the United States is a bank and not a firm as other countries are. The difference between a firm and a bank, of course, is that the liabilities of the former are expected to be paid off at regular intervals, while those of the latter are passed from hand to hand as money, and tend to be permanent in fact, despite being "demand" in form. . . . To the extent that a country is a bank and not a firm, its balance of payments must be viewed from a different perspective, with equilibrium, deficits and surplus measured on a different basis.
>
> (iii) The dollar is a money's money, a numéraire for foreign exchanges, and cannot be regarded as other currencies. It cannot float, except as other currencies float against it, and its value is the reciprocal of the value of all other currencies, not its price in one.
>
> (iv) The United States can change the value of gold, but not the price of the dollar. Other countries can readily change the value of their currencies against the dollar, but not the price of gold.[4]

4. C. P. Kindleberger and Andrew Shonfield (eds.), *North American and Western European Economic Policies* (1971), pp. xiii–xiv.

The extent to which these asymmetries actually existed and were controlling in the formation of balance-of-payments policy is a fundamental question throughout this Problem. In differing degrees, many American economists would have regarded the statement of these asymmetries as objective statements of fact, but many European economists would view them merely as subjective claims by the United States to preferred treatment. In opposing these claims, it is difficult to sort out how much of the negative reaction in Europe is objection to the economic analysis, and how much objection to the political dependence of Europe implicit in the asymmetrical or hierarchical relationship.[5]

2.3 Benefits and Costs of a Dollar-Centered International Monetary System

In acquiring functions of an international currency, the dollar reaps some benefits, but also some costs. The major benefit is that when foreigners are willing to accumulate dollars, the United States is able to sustain a larger balance-of-payments deficit than would otherwise be possible. Instead of losing gold, the United States can finance its deficit through voluntary accumulations of dollar liabilities held by foreigners. As long as confidence is retained in the dollar, this allows the United States to run a larger cumulative deficit over time than it otherwise could. It has been said that by financing its deficit through its own creation of international money, the United States obtains a kind of "free" command over real resources which can be used to enlarge its purchases of foreign goods, services, and assets (including interest-paying reserves).[6] This benefit is sometimes likened to the gain from "seignorage"—the reference being to an earlier period when the state treasury gained

5. Ibid. pp. xiv–xv.
6. Benjamin J. Cohen, *The Future of Sterling as an International Currency* (1971), p. 35. The benefits and costs of an international currency are discussed in greater detail by Robert Z. Aliber, *The Future of the Dollar as an International Currency* (1966), chap. III; Ronald I. McKinnon, *Private and Official International Money: The Case for the Dollar*, Princeton Essays in International Finance (1969), pp. 17–23; Robert A. Mundell and Alexander K. Swoboda (eds.), *Monetary Problems of the International Economy* (1969), part 5.

the difference between the circulating value of a coin and the cost of bullion and its minting. By running a cumulative deficit in its balance of payments, the United States can create internationally held dollars in a costless fashion and gain an increase in real national expenditure relative to national income.

On the other side, however, the major cost of being a reserve currency country is the opportunity cost in policy-making—the policies that the country must forgo in order to prevent the withdrawal of past foreign accumulations of its money. To the extent that there is an "overhang" of dollar liabilities, the United States may have to forgo the use of expansionary monetary and fiscal policies that would otherwise be undertaken for domestic economic objectives, but which if undertaken might lessen the foreigners' confidence in the United States government's ability or willingness to maintain dollar convertibility at a fixed rate of exchange.

An appraisal of the benefits and costs of having some functions of international money is in the background of United States international monetary policy. When the benefits become less than the costs, it might be expected that the United States would recognize that reform of the international monetary system is essential to remove pressure on the dollar and allow greater freedom in domestic policy formation.

3. MEASURING THE "DEFICIT"

The basic quantitative information for this problem must come from statistics of the balance of payments. The measurement of the "deficit" in the balance of payments is in itself a large part of the problem's formulation. The payments deficit of the United States is usually measured by the "liquidity" definition or the alternative "official settlements" definition. Attention is also frequently focused on the "balance-of-current account," and the "basic balance."

In 1971, the Department of Commerce revised its presentation of balance-of-payments data in hopes of letting the "underlying" trend show through more clearly.

REVISED PRESENTATION OF BALANCE
OF PAYMENTS *

The results of a review of the presentation of U.S. balance of payments statistics, which was begun in 1970 by the Interagency Committee on Balance of Payments Statistics, convened by the U.S. Office of Management and Budget, were adopted and used for the first time with the presentation of the balance of payments for the first quarter of 1971.

New Format

There are three new groups of balances in the revised presentation.

Balance on goods, services, and remittances. This balance measures the net export of goods and services and takes into account unilateral transfers other than U.S. Government grants. It is often used as a rough indicator of net receipts available to offset U.S. Government aid and other capital flows.

Balance on current account and long-term capital. This balance is the sum of the current account (net exports of goods and services minus all unilateral transfers to foreigners) plus net flows of private long-term capital and of U.S. and foreign government capital other than changes in U.S. official reserve holdings and foreign official reserve holdings in the United States. This new overall measure is intended as a rough indicator of the long-term trends in the U.S. balance of payments.

Net Liquidity Balance. This balance focuses on changes in the liquidity position of the United States and replaces the so-called gross liquidity balance that had been used for many years. It is the sum of the balance on current account and long-term capital plus net flows of short-term nonliquid private capital, allocations of SDRs, and errors and omissions. Alternatively, one may focus on the below-the-line items that finance the net liquidity balance, and from this perspective it is measured by net flows of U.S. and foreign private liquid funds plus changes in U.S. reserves and in foreign reserves held in the United States. . . .

The *balance on current account* (previously the balance on goods, services, and unilateral transfers) and the *official reserve transactions balance* both continue to be calculated as before.

Both the balance on current account and long-term capital and the net liquidity balance attempt to focus on more fundamental, longer-term trends in the external position of the United States. However, neither is quite successful, inasmuch as the results are affected not

* *International Financial News Survey*, Vol. XXIII, No. 29, July 28, 1971.

only by the limitations of the statistical reporting system and other technical difficulties but also by the complications resulting from the dollar's role as an international currency. That role results in considerable ambiguity as to what measure, if any, and what level of the measure, would indicate fundamental long-term equilibrium in the external accounts of the United States. For instance, a deficit on the net liquidity balance would not necessarily imply disequilibrium in the external position, because a net buildup in liquid dollar holdings by private foreigners may simply reflect the use of the dollar as an international medium of exchange. Because of the difficulties involved, there was some question as to whether either balance should be calculated. Nevertheless, given the need for indicators of underlying trends, it appears that the two balances in combination, particularly when they move together, are the best available, although neither is of a theoretical or statistical quality sufficient to carry the weight of being *the* balance of payments, nor is there a presumption that either should be zero.

The net liquidity balance plus net flows of U.S. and foreign private liquid capital sum to the official reserve transactions balance. As in the past, this balance is financed by changes in U.S. official reserve assets plus changes in liquid and nonliquid liabilities to foreign official agencies. It is intended to indicate the net exchange market pressure (either favorable or adverse) on the dollar, during the reporting period, resulting from international transactions of the United States. (Exchange market pressure, in this sense, reflects the net influence of all transactions above the line in the calculation of the official reserve transactions balance.) Of course, foreign central banks themselves may wish to increase or decrease their dollar holdings, and to that extent a deficit or surplus does not necessarily indicate disequilibrium in the U.S. position.

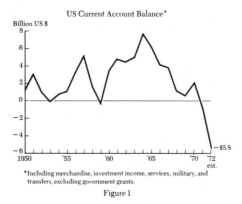

US Current Account Balance*

Billion US $

*Including merchandise, investment income, services, military, and transfers, excluding government grants.

Figure 1

It should be noted that certain types of transaction between foreigners in the Euro-dollar market could have the effect of increasing dollar liabilities. Thus the dollar could come under pressure in the exchange

Summary of U.S. International Transactions
(in millions of dollars)

	1968	1969	1970
Merchandise trade			
balance	624	660	2,110
Services (net)	1,866	1,351	1,480
Balance on goods			
and services	2,489	2,011	3,592
Remittances, pensions,			
and other transfers	−1,168	−1,266	−1,410
Balance on goods, services,			
and remittances	1,321	745	2,182
U.S. Government grants			
(excluding military)	−1,707	−1,644	−1,739
Balance on current account	−386	−899	444
U.S. Government capital			
flows (net), and nonliquid liabilities			
to other than foreign official			
reserve agencies	−2,161	−1,930	−2,029
Long-term private capital			
flows (net)	1,198	−50	−1,453
Balance on current account			
and long-term capital	−1,349	−2,879	−3,038
Nonliquid short-term			
private capital flows (net)	231	−602	−548
Allocations of SDRs	—	—	867
Errors and omissions (net)	−493	−2,603	−1,132
Net liquidity balance	−1,610	−6,084	−3,852
Liquid private capital			
flows (net)	3,251	8,786	−5,969
Official reserve transactions			
balance	1,641	2,702	−9,821

market even though transactions of U.S. residents with foreigners and the official reserve transactions balance were in equilibrium.

Although the official reserve transactions balance may be the most important indicator of changes in the U.S. external position over the longer run, it is too volatile to serve in the short run as an indicator of underlying, more fundamental developments.

Figure 1 indicates the "current account balance" over the period 1950-72. This balance measures the difference between United States purchases of foreign goods and services, and sales of United States goods and services abroad; it includes the "balance of trade" plus the balance on invisible transactions, of which earnings on foreign direct investment are most important. This account was in surplus every year between 1960 and 1970, although there were wide variations as can be noted in Figure 1.[7]

The "basic balance" adds private long-term capital movements and government grants and capital transactions to the current account balance. As Figure 2 indicates, the basic balance was in deficit in the $1.5-$3 billion range between 1950 and 1970. The large net outflow on capital account more than offset the surplus on current account; for example, in 1970 a current account surplus of $2.2 billion was outweighed by a deficit of $5.3 billion on the grants and long-term capital account, producing a basic balance deficit of approximately $3.0 billion.

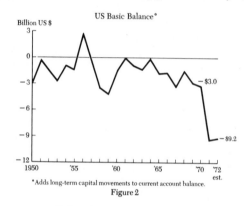

*Adds long-term capital movements to current account balance.
Figure 2

The persistence of the basic balance deficit contributed significantly to the accumulation of foreign reserves and United States dollars abroad. Table 1 summarizes the international liquidity position of the United States in the period 1961-70. It can be noted that external liquid liabilities increased from $23 billion in 1961 to almost $47 billion in 1970 (line 4, Table 1); of this total in 1970, official holdings amounted to approximately $24 billion and private holdings to approximately $22 billion, but the gold stock was only $11 billion (line 1a, Table I).

7. Figures 1–3 are from the Council on International Economic Policy, *International Economic Report of the President,* March 1973. For more details of the United States balance of payments, see *Survey of Current Business* (December issue, annually); *IMF Financial Statistics* (annual).

TABLE I. International Liquidity Position of the United States

International Liquidity		1961	1962	1963	1964	1965	1966	1967	1968	1969	1970	1971	1972
Monetary authorities reserves	1	18.75	17.22	16.84	16.67	15.45	14.88	14.83	15.71	16.96	14.49	13.19	13.15
Gold	1a	16.95	16.06	15.60	15.47	14.06	13.23	12.07	10.89	11.86	11.07	11.08	10.49
SDRs	1b							—	—	—	.85	1.19	1.96
Reserve position in the fund	1c	1.69	1.06	1.04	.77	.60	.33	2.35	3.53	2.78	.63	.28	.24
Foreign exchange	1d	.12	.10	.21	.43	.78	1.32	.42	1.29	2.32	1.94	.63	.46
Fund position													
Credit tranche position: stand-by	2a	4.12	4.12	4.12	4.12	4.12	5.16	5.16	5.16	5.16	6.70	7.27	7.27
Credit tranche position: other	2b	5.81	5.19	5.16	4.89	4.73	5.49						
Net draw./fund sales (−) to date	2dc	−.64	−.03	−.02	.23	.38	.91	.79		−1.05	−.30	1.17	1.38
Quota	2f	4.12	4.12	4.12	4.12	4.12	5.16	5.16	5.16	5.16	6.70	7.27	7.27
External liabilities	4	22.94	24.07	26.32	29.00	29.12	29.78	35.67	38.47	45.91	46.96	67.81	82.90
Central banks & governments	4a	11.83	12.71	14.35	15.42	15.37	13.66	18.19	17.34	16.00	23.78	50.65	61.50
Canada	4aa	2.48	3.11	1.79	1.61	1.53	1.19	1.31	1.87	1.62	2.95	3.98	4.28
Western Europe	4ab	9.56	9.27	8.44	9.22	8.61	7.49	10.32	8.06	7.07	13.62	30.13	34.20
Latin America	4ac	1.20	1.20	1.06	1.24	1.50	1.13	1.58	1.87	1.91	1.68	1.43	1.72
Asia	4ad	2.84	3.29	2.73	3.02	3.30	3.34	4.43	5.00	4.55	4.71	13.82	17.57
Africa	4ae	.34	.43	.15	.16	.19	.28	.25	.25	.55	.41	.42	.78
Other	4af			.18	.18	.24	.23	.30	.30	.29	.41	.87	2.96
Other banks & other foreigners	4b	8.36	8.36	9.20	11.06	11.48	14.21	15.76	19.38	28.23	21.77	15.09	19.77
of which: short-term to banks	4ba	5.38	5.25	5.71	7.22	7.36	9.86	11.08	14.47	23.64	17.17	10.95	14.82
International agencies	4c	2.75	3.00	2.76	2.52	2.26	1.92	1.71	1.75	1.68	1.41	2.07	1.63
By type: short-term	4d	19.48	21.16	22.14	24.72	24.75	26.79	29.91	30.95	39.45	41.39	55.19	60.95
Marketable	4e	2.65	2.11	2.68	2.40	2.33	1.71	1.47	.93	.87	.86	2.40	5.66
Nonmarketable convert.	4f			.70	1.08	1.20	.26	.71	.70	.56	.43	6.09	12.11
Fund gold deps. & invest.	4g	.80	.80	.80	.80	.83	1.01	1.03	1.03	1.02	.57	.54	
Nonliquid liabilities	4h		.26	.25	.35	.48	1.31	2.55	4.86	4.02	3.72	3.59	4.18
External claims	6	6.85	7.32	9.00	12.24	12.25	12.02	12.53	12.28	12.92	13.88	16.94	20.45
Short-term	6a	4.82	5.16	5.98	7.96	7.74	7.84	8.61	8.71	9.67	10.80	13.28	15.54
Long-term	6b	2.03	2.16	3.03	4.28	4.52	4.18	3.92	3.57	3.25	3.08	3.66	4.91

SOURCE: IMF, International Financial Statistics, 1972 Supplement.

Trends in the net liquidity balance and the official settlements balance are shown in Figure 3. The surplus in the official settlements balance in 1968 and 1969 is explained by the large inflow of short-term funds when United States interest rates were higher than foreign rates. In 1970, United States interest rates were below foreign rates, and the outward flow of short-term capital funds was so large that the official settlements deficit was nearly $10 billion.

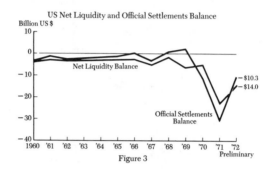

Figure 3

4. ANALYZING THE "DEFICIT"

When announcing the new presentation of balance-of-payments data, the Commerce Department stated that "it isn't possible to define a single balance which can adequately represent the underlying position of the U.S. . . . and equilibrium in the external position of the U.S. cannot be equated with zero in any of the possible balances, in either the short run or long run." [8] The accountant's measurement of the "deficit" is no substitute for the economist's analysis of the "deficit." [9] The accountant's measurement is of transactions ex post; the economist's analysis involves the more difficult attempt to identify the motives of the transactors. The economist tries to analyze the ex ante disequilibrium in "autonomous" transactions (as contrasted with the "induced" or "accommodating" transactions that finance the deficit). Analysis of the deficit requires interpretation of cause and effect relationships within the accounts, and the determination of whether remedial policy

8. *Wall Street Journal* (July 7, 1971), p. 6.
9. See pp. 8–11 above.

measures are required—and if so, what measures are desirable and feasible. This analysis is complex and has an inescapable judgmental quality.

As we turn to the specific issues involved in the problem of the dollar deficit, we should respond to the economist's task of analysis by keeping in mind some fundamental analytical, as well as the political, questions:

Does a deficit necessarily represent a disequilibrium among currencies? If we define an equilibrium situation as a constellation of forces that can be maintained, can we argue that the United States balance of payments can be in equilibrium even though there is a deficit in one of the measures of the balance?

Even if we do contend that there can be an economic equilibrium with a deficit, is this also a political equilibrium—or do political forces require some adjustment process?

If remedial policies are required, should they be in the form of changes in the level of national income and expenditure, or price changes, or exchange rate variations? And should the adjustment be forced through unilateral actions or negotiated through international consultations?

B. THE ISSUES

5. A RANGE OF VIEWS

If in the postwar period economists narrowed their differences on domestic stability policy, the same could not be said for international monetary policy. In the case of the United States balance of payments, the range of views was exceptionally wide. Since 1959, American officials introduced a series of measures to meet the United States balance-of-payments problem. But among economists, there were differences in interpreting whether the United States really had to adjust to a balance-of-payments disequilibrium; whether the essential problem was one of "adjustment" or "liquidity"; whether the dollar could—or should—be made the preferred asset to gold or other reserve assets. There was also wide diversity in interpretation—and prescription—among the international business and financial community, central bankers, and government officials.

5.1 *Contingency Planning*

Five years before the dollar crisis of 1971, the Subcommittee on International Exchange and Payments of the Joint Economic Committee decided to canvass "expert private opinion on what the United States should do to protect its international payments position" in the event that prospects for international cooperation on monetary reform are not fulfilled. In his letter to a number of economists, Chairman Reuss noted that "the only policy package that has been used so far is that of marginal improvisations within the existing order; we need to examine the merits of other arrangements, be they unilateral, bilateral, group or multilateral." [10]

The 1966 letter asked for replies to the following questions:

1. Supposing that there were to be no agreement in the immediate future, would you regard the process of adjustment as being, probably, adequate under the present system, with no intolerable stresses on the U.S. domestic economy, with adequate extensions of intercentral bank borrowing rights and with no adverse effects on the growth of trade and the provision of aid? Can we muddle through?

2. If, on the other hand, you regard a crisis as inevitable, how long do you think it would be before it came, and what would be the principal reasons for it?

3. Assuming that we are anticipating a crisis in which we shall have exhausted the possibilities of joint action, can we now, at this date, undertake any useful advance planning for our unilateral action, either to mitigate the crisis or to turn it to use in creating a better situation? Do you think we must plan to undergo a crisis before we can assure the future?

4. Next, assuming that a crisis is a risk but not a certainty, should we try actively to avoid it if we can? If so, what kinds of policy would be feasible, in regard to international investment flows, trade, and gold transactions?

5. Finally, is the threat of a crisis an opportunity to make U.S. policy effective? Is there any unilateral action or planning by the United States which might be undertaken now or soon and whose effect would be enough to induce international cooperation to avert a crisis and to speed the process of adjustment?

Excerpts from some replies follow:

10. *Contingency Planning for U.S. International Monetary Policy, Statements by Private Economists,* submitted to the Subcommittee on International Exchange and Payments of the Joint Economic Committee, 89th Congress, 2d Session (1966), pp. 1–2.

STATEMENT BY EDWARD M. BERNSTEIN *
President, EMB, Ltd., Research Economists, Washington, D.C.

Reserve and Payments Problems and Policies

Does the United States have a Payments Deficit?

Q.1. In a recent lecture in Australia, Professor Kindleberger reaffirmed the view "that the United States balance of payments was not in deficit, in a meaningful sense, because the definitions of equilibrium used were not the right ones." Is this view justified?

The concept of a deficit in the balance of payments is extremely complex and there is always considerable scope for reasonable differences of opinion on the amount of the deficit and, at times, whether there is a deficit. Unfortunately, it is not possible to say that the balance of payments of the United States is not in deficit at this time.

Professor Kindleberger emphasizes that the interpretation of the balance of payments cannot be the same for a country whose international transactions consist almost entirely of exports and imports of goods and services (a trader) and a country that not only engages in an enormous volume of trade but also is an enormous foreign investor and has large short-term foreign assets and foreign liabilities (a banker). "Banks [as distinguished from traders] are in the business of owing money. They have reserves, to be sure, generally of the order of 1 to 5 between their primary reserves and their demand liabilities. For the rest they are in the business of financial intermediation, or lending long and borrowing short. A definition which asserts that a bank is in disequilibrium every time its deposits rise without a parallel [equal?] rise in primary reserves would come as a shock to most bankers, although they do not protest when the Department of Commerce applies this definition to the United States."

When a trading nation buys more goods and services than it sells, it can meet the excess of its payments by drawing down its reserves (gold and foreign exchange), borrowing from the IMF or other central banks (reserve credit), or by securing long-term or short-term credit from foreign financial centers. A trading country that meets its deficit on goods and services by borrowing long-term (through security issues) or short-term (through bank credit) is regarded as having a capital inflow. Its deficit on goods and services is offset by a surplus on capital account. The overall balance of payments is neither in surplus nor in deficit. On the other hand, when a trading country draws down its reserves or secures reserve credit, its overall balance of payments is in deficit.

The deficit of a banking nation is far more difficult to define acceptably. . . .

The pragmatic test of a deficit is whether the balance of payments could be continued indefinitely with the existing relationship of the accounts. Ob-

* *Contingency Planning*, pp. 3–5.

viously, a deficit on the liquidity definition could be continued indefinitely. Foreigners do want to accumulate dollar assets. As Kindleberger has emphasized, they are attractive assets, denominated in a currency whose foreign exchange value is assured, earning a good return, and easily bought and sold (or deposited and withdrawn) in a broad financial market. Even the Commerce Department experts recognize that a deficit on the liquidity definition of an average of $500 million to $800 million a year could be continued indefinitely—it is an equilibrium position requiring no change.

On the other hand, a reserve transactions deficit either depletes the reserves of a country (and cannot be continued indefinitely) or increases its reserve liabilities and confronts it with the risk of a sudden drawing down of its reserves in the future by conversions of foreign official holdings of its currency. This is an uncertain risk, although the United Kingdom has been confronted by it from time to time, and even the United States has had such conversions in 1965 and 1966. Nevertheless, it could be argued that there is a normal growth in foreign exchange reserves in the form of dollars that other countries would find necessary and acceptable, and such an increase in the holdings of a reserve currency could be regarded as capital inflow. Even so, for a banking nation that is a reserve center, there is no escaping the definition of the deficit as a decline in its reserve assets (including short-term reserve credit), for it cannot continue indefinitely a balance of payments that depletes its reserves.

The Kindleberger thesis is replete with description and analysis of the role of the United States as a financial intermediary—that is, a banker. There is much that is enlightening in this discussion. He fails, however, in his attempt to draw an analogy between the position of a commercial banker and the position of the United States as a reserve center. Of course, commercial banks are very happy to increase their liabilities and their assets—that is how they make profits as bankers. But a commercial bank could not continue to make loans (capital outflow in the balance of payments analogy) if it were to find that as a consequence of increasing its income-earning assets it were confronted with an unfavorable balance with other banks at the clearinghouse or withdrawals of cash over the counter (reduction of reserves in the balance of payments analogy). It might have no objection to borrowing from the Federal or buying Federal funds (incurring reserve liabilities), provided it could do so without assuming undue risk. But if the Federal is reluctant to let it borrow and it cannot buy Federal funds, it will have to curtail its acquisition of income-earning assets, however profitable its lending and investment operations may be.

That is the situation of the United States. We have acquired a large amount of very valuable income-earning assets abroad. Our earnings from net exports of goods and services, after U.S. aid, have not been sufficient to pay for our foreign investments. This is true even after allowing for the increase of foreign banking claims in this country. As a consequence, we have been drawing down our reserves, and this no country (and no banker) can do indefinitely. It is futile to say, as Kindleberger does, "that the dollar has no need for adjustment, if financial intermediation is properly understood." This would seem to imply that foreign countries would always want to acquire as much dollars as the United States would wish to invest abroad in excess of its balance on other transactions—a thesis of doubtful validity. So long as the United States continues to pay out reserves, it has a deficit in its balance of payments, however much we may rationalize our role as a banker. The proof that we have a deficit is that we cannot continue the present balance of payments without ultimately being confronted with an exchange crisis.

STATEMENT BY EMILE DESPRES *

Professor of Economics, Stanford University

The grave danger inherent in existing international monetary arrangements is not that they are likely to break down but that they may endure for a long time, with highly damaging economic and political consequences.

The restoration of current account convertibility by the principal European countries at the end of 1958, following devaluation and stablilization of the French franc, brought to a conclusion the postwar reconstruction of international economic and financial relations. Import quotas had been eliminated or greatly relaxed, currencies had been stabilized and a relatively liberal system of multilateral trade without restriction on international payments for commercial purposes was established. This fulfilled a longstanding objective of American foreign economic policy, which rested on the postulate that a regime of nondiscrimination (apart from customs unions and free trade areas) and convertibility would not only serve the direct economic interests of the United States but would be broadly conducive to healthy economic and political development of the non-Communist world.

It is ironical that the whole period since the restoration of convertibility has been one of contained crisis and intense balance-of-payments preoccupations. Existing international monetary arrangements not only provide protection against an acute crisis leading to breakdown but also assure continuation of low-grade, contained crisis lasting indefinitely into the future. This is their basic defect. The long-run dangers inherent in this situation are substantial retardation of economic growth of both the industrially advanced and the low-income countries, and an increasingly mercantilist tendency in economic policies. Second only to the U.S. military involvement in Vietnam, balance-of-payments preoccupations have exerted a widely pervasive and undesirable constraining influence on both foreign and domestic policy. Even if the gold outflow is halted for a time, anxious preoccupation with the balance of payments will continue to weigh heavily upon major foreign policy and domestic economic policy decisions since, in the climate of attitudes which has now become entrenched, we shall continue to regard our liquidity position as delicate, maintaining that our position as world banker will not

* *Contingency Planning*, pp. 25–29.

permit us to relax our guard. The present international monetary system is defective not because it is likely to collapse but because of the harmfulness of the financially restrictive and mercantilist measures which are applied to defend the system.

The main source of present difficulties is the inflated world demand for gold. The substantial private speculative accumulation of gold, motivated chiefly by the desire to profit from an anticipated devaluation of the dollar and other currencies, has been derivative in nature. The basis for these speculative anticipations and the originating source of the inflated total demand for gold has been the evident preference of most Western European central banks for gold rather than dollars as a reserve medium. Although fears of dollar devaluation may have played a part, the preference for gold is not due primarily to this cause.

In the special case of France, political factors have undoubtedly played a part in demands for gold; since the 19th century French governments have regarded all forms of foreign lending, whether private or official, as an instrument of foreign policy to be used for political purposes. In the case of other European countries, however, it does not appear that political considerations have been a factor.

The main source of European desires to limit accumulation of official reserves in the form of dollars is the heritage of obsolete theories regarding the way in which an international monetary system based on fixed exchange rates should function. According to traditional doctrine, which is still professed by many economists and generally accepted by central bank and financial officials, it would interfere with the proper working of a fixed exchange standard if the United States were relieved of the pressures and the discipline which a strained liquidity position entails. Consequently, although demands for gold have been limited by the general desire not to subject the international monetary mechanism to intolerable strain, within this limit demands for gold have been maintained at a sufficient level to keep pressure on the United States to balance its payments. Our evident anxiety in the face of gold losses has made this not too difficult a task.

The trouble is that the orthodox theory simply does not conform to the economic realities of the present-day world. My reasons for this view were stated in hearings before the Subcommittee on International Exchange and Payments on September 9, 1966 ("New Approach to United States International Economic Policy," pp. 10–14, 28–33), and I also submitted a proposal for shifting prevailing asset preferences from gold to dollars through certain steps which would result in a partial demonetization of gold (pp. 39–42). It seems unnecessary to repeat these views and this proposal here. A few supplementary observations are given below.

Under a regime of fixed exchange rates, generally low tariffs and convertible currencies, and an unrestricted international market for loan capital, quite substantial upward or downward fluctuations in aggregate domestic demand for goods and services can be accommodated without serious inflationary or deflationary consequences. In an open economy of this sort, a growth in domestic demand which outpaces the growth of output is largely compensated by shifts in the external trade balance, thus minimizing the domestic inflationary consequences which excess demand in a closed economy, or an economy in which imports competitive with domestic production are restricted by high tariffs or quotas, would produce. In an open economy the inflow of goods responds sensitively and limits the rise in prices. Provided the country enjoys good credit standing, the shift in the trade balance can be financed by attracting foreign capital through a moderate rise in interest rates.

This capital inflow not only permits domestic investment to outrun domestic saving by financing increased imports; the gross capital inflow serves also to meet a part of the growing demand for liquid assets which accompanies economic expansion. Within a stable external environment this process of rising capital inflow can continue so long as the general growth of productivity, including appropriate expansion of efficient export earning and import substitution activities, is sufficient to give no grounds for questioning the country's ability to service its rising external debt. It should be noted that in this typical case, the balance of payments moves into surplus through buoyant growth of demand since the external financing meets some of the growing demand for liquid financial assets as well as for goods and services.

By the same token, a retardation in domestic demand relative to output will shift the trade balance toward net exports, lower interest rates, reduce capital inflow and move the balance of payments toward reduced surplus as domestic banks and other intermediaries meet a larger share of the diminished growth in demand for liquid assets.

The foregoing simplified analysis has been put forward to illustrate the accommodating role of international capital movements which traditional doctrine largely ignores. With a properly functioning international capital market countries with good credit standing need owned reserves only in amounts sufficient to assure prospective lenders of their credit worthiness. Subject only to credit standing, the international ebb and flow of capital frees them of any balance-of-payments discipline as this is conventionally defined. The accommodating role of capital movements permits flexible adaptation of the current account to changing domestic economic circumstances.

A properly functioning international capital market cannot be sustained, however, if gold is demanded on a large scale in exchange for the liquid claims which its financial intermediation generates. Such demands result in restriction of capital outflow, tight money or both. The balance-of-payments discipline imposed on the financial center thus reacts back upon the clients.

It is important to note the close interrelationship which must exist between the international mobility of goods and of loan capital. If goods movements are restricted by high tariffs and quotas, shifts in the trade balance cannot do much to mitigate domestic inflationary or deflationary tendencies. Under these circumstances, a high degree of international mobility of loan capital would be undesirable since it would complicate the task of the central bank in attempting to curb inflation or deflation by monetary policy.

By the same token, it is hard under present day conditions to conceive of a regime of low tariffs integrating national markets for goods into a world market without a parallel international mobility of loan capital. Although much of theory of international trade assumes a close balancing of imports and exports, it is conspicuously evident that countries with limited credit standing almost invariably rely heavily on import controls to balance their international payments. If the primary cause of impaired credit standing is inflation and currency overvaluation, as in several Latin American countries, a major benefit of financial stabilization would be to facilitate import liberalization and attract private loan capital.

A fundamental and insufficiently discussed issue is whether to encourage or limit severely the international mobility of untied loan capital. Severe limitation goes hand in hand with increasing restriction of trade. The likely outcome would be a division of the world economy into rather insulated economic blocs within each of which goods movements and financial movements would be relatively free. This seems to me highly undesirable, but it should be recognized that the other alternative involves major problems. It needs to be complemented by further reduction of tariff barriers lest the mobility of loan capital between the United States and Europe outrun the mobility of goods.

It is widely recognized that centralized economic planning of the Soviet type has been biased toward self-sufficiency since planning of international trade raises special complications and involves some loss of control. It is now becoming evident that the aggregative type of national economic planning through monetary and fiscal policy which is generally practiced in the mixed private enterprise economies of the non-Communist world introduces some desire for insulation of capital markets in order to avoid impairing the usefulness of monetary policy for domestic stabilization. International mobility of loan capital limits the scope for national differences in open market interest rates. The United States, as the financial center, would determine through its monetary policy the level of interest rates around which interest rates elsewhere would have to cluster.

Decisions on U.S. monetary policy would have to be made in collaboration with other members of the Group of Ten on the basis of general requirements of free world economic stability. The remaining task of achieving strictly domestic economic stabilization would be left chiefly to fiscal policy in each country, although special controls over residential mortgage rates and agricultural credit, as well as tax incentives to industrial investment, would still be instruments of domestic stabilization. The dangers of undue reliance on monetary policy as a domestic stabilization device have recently become apparent, however, both in the United States and several other countries, and it is evident that a shift in policy mix is desirable on other grounds.

STATEMENT BY FRITZ MACHLUP *
Professor of Economics, Princeton University

Although the really decisive actions concerning the future price of gold, or concerning the people's expectations with regard to the future price of gold, must be international in scope and based on international agreement, there are some possibilities for unilateral action by the United States. Any such action, however, should be previously discussed and explained to all interested national and international monetary authorities. It should be fully understood that the purposes sought are mutually beneficial and, if agreement can be reached, preparatory to cooperative or collective action.

Declarations to the effect that the price of gold will not be increased have widely been disbelieved. To repeat such declarations without taking any action that makes them credible is useless. People know too well that anything of which the supply falls short of the demand can only gain, not lose, in value; and it has been too obvious that most monetary authorities, including our own, desire to hold more gold, not less. The only way to reverse people's impressions is to reverse our own attitude: we must be glad to get rid of gold.

I do not mean to propose a big bluffing game. Every serious student of the subject knows that the value of the dollar (in terms of what it can buy) does not depend on its gold backing, whereas the value of gold (in terms of dollars) depends on the willingness of the United States to buy any excess supply that it is offered and to hold on to any of its stocks that are not demanded by private or official buyers. There is no present demand for the $13 billion of gold now held by the United States. We could not get rid of all our gold at $35 an ounce, and still less at a slightly lower price, since at the slightest price decline several billions worth of gold from private holdings would urgently seek buyers. I do not say this to threaten anybody and do not propose that we actually throw all the $13 billion worth of gold on the market.

I do propose, however, that the Congress take action to indicate that we are not eager to hold large amounts of gold as reserves, and that we would be glad to use substantial amounts of our gold to reduce our liabilities to official foreign holders of dollars and to reduce thereby our payments of interest on these liabilities. This would involve the following two steps: (1) abolish the requirement for the Federal Reserve Banks to hold a reserve of gold certificates for 25 percent of Federal Reserve notes in circulation; and (2) invite the monetary authorities of all foreign countries to convert into gold any amounts of dollars they hold in excess of what they prefer to hold for reasons of yield or expediency.

If these actions are taken after full and open discussion about the future of gold as a part of the international monetary system, of the prospective supply of gold from new production, of the potential industrial demand for gold at various prices, of the magnitude of gold hoards in private hands, and of the

* *Contingency Planning*, pp. 81–82.

intention to open an international exchange of ideas on the possibilities of slight downward adjustments of the price of gold (or at least of the buying price of gold), then the appropriate bearishness regarding the future of gold is likely to emerge.

What ought to be better understood by all is that the value of gold, as of everything else, is a matter of supply and demand, and that there is now an entirely artificial demand for gold to the tune of $42 billion held in official vaults—for merely historical reasons, fortified by tradition and superstition. If all monetary authorities decided suddenly to reduce their gold stocks by as little as 5 percent, there would be no private demand that could absorb such an excess supply. The demand for gold as a metal for strictly industrial purposes is at best $200 or $300 million a year. Without one-way expectations of a price increase, private purchases could not absorb but a fraction of the annual new production. No doubt the time will come when the nations of the world will have to come to an agreement not to sell their gold stocks at a rate that would make it impossible to maintain the artificial support price for this precious metal, so overabundant as soon as the governmental buffer stocks are discontinued.

Since the facts are so very different from the myth believed by the people, I submit that the Congress, and your committee in particular, have a responsibility for setting popular ideas straight. . . .

People all over the world might learn that, with proper public policies, the dollar is safer than gold.

STATEMENT BY MILTON FRIEDMAN *

Professor of Economics, The University of Chicago

I expect no significant reform in international monetary arrangements to occur in the near future. The widespread agreement that reform is desirable conceals complete lack of agreement about the specific character that reform should take. In my opinion, this is a good thing, not something to be regretted, since the leading current proposals for international monetary reform seem to me undesirable both nationally and internationally.

As long as we and other countries continue to try to maintain fixed exchange rates and also to retain independence in domestic monetary policy an international monetary crisis is always a possibility. Such a crisis might erupt at any time as a result of a widespread demand for conversion of dollars into gold, or, indirectly, as a result of a crisis in sterling. However, such a crisis is not inevitable and I believe there is no way to predict with any confidence whether or how soon it will occur.

The key reason a crisis remains a possibility is because we have an international system of pegged exchange rates. The single and only effective way to make a crisis of this kind impossible is to introduce a system of free market

* *Contingency Planning*, pp. 30–31, 36.

exchange rates. That would provide an automatic and effective adjustment mechanism for changes in international trade.

We shall be exceedingly unwise if we wait for a crisis and then adopt panic policies. We should proceed on our own to set free the price of the dollar in terms of other currencies to find its own level in world markets. Almost exactly 3 years ago, I testified to this effect before the Joint Economic Committee in connection with its hearings on the balance of payments. I believe now, as I did then, that the system of floating exchange rates is the only feasible way to eliminate balance-of-payments problems and at the same time promote liberalization of international trade. I have nothing new to add to that statement, whose final paragraph indicates the policy that I would follow with respect to gold.

The experience of the past 3 years has only strengthened my belief that my earlier statement outlines the most desirable policy for the United States to follow.

Professor Friedman's 1963 Statement before the
Joint Economic Committee

Discussions of U.S. policy with respect to international payments tend to be dominated by our immediate balance-of-payments difficulties. I should like today to approach the question from a different, and I hope more constructive, direction. Let us begin by asking ourselves not merely how we can get out of our present difficulties but instead how we can fashion our international payments system so that it will best serve our needs for the long pull; how we can solve not merely *this* balance-of-payments problem but *the* balance-of-payments problem.

A shocking and indeed, disgraceful feature of the present situation is the extent to which our frantic search for expedients to stave off balance-of-payments pressures has led us, on the one hand, to sacrifice major national objectives; and, on the other, to give enormous power to officials of foreign governments to affect what should be purely domestic matters. Foreign payments amount to only some 5 percent of our total national income. Yet they have become a major factor in nearly every national policy.

I believe that a system of floating exchange rates would solve the balance-of-payments problem for the United States far more effectively than our present arrangements. Such a system would use the flexibility and efficiency of the free market to harmonize our small foreign trade sector with both the rest of our massive economy and the rest of the world; it would reduce problems of foreign payments to their proper dimensions and remove them as a major consideration in governmental policy about domestic matters and as a major preoccupation in international political negotiations; it would foster our national objectives rather than be an obstacle to their attainment. . . .

It is not the least of the virtues of floating exchange rates that we would again become masters in our own house. We could decide important issues on the proper ground. The military could concentrate on military effectiveness and not on saving foreign exchange; recipients of foreign aid could concentrate on how to get the most out of what we give them and not on how to spend it all in the United States; Congress could decide how much to spend on foreign aid on the basis of what we get for our money and what else we could use it for and not how it will affect the gold stock; the monetary authorities could concentrate on domestic prices and employment, not on how to induce foreigners to hold dollar balances in this country; the Treasury and the tax committees of Congress could devote their attention to the equity of the tax system and its effects on our efficiency, rather than on how to use tax gimmicks to discourage imports, subsidize exports, and discriminate against outflows of capital.

A system of floating exchange rates would render the problem of making outflows equal inflows into the market where it belongs and not leave it to the clumsy and heavy hand of government. It would leave government free to concentrate on its proper functions.

In conclusion, a word about gold. Our commitment to buy and sell gold for monetary use at a fixed price of $35 an ounce is in practice the mechanism whereby we maintain fixed rates of exchange between the dollar and other currencies—or, more precisely, whereby we leave all initiative for changes in such rates to other countries. This commitment should be terminated—as the corresponding commitment for silver already has been. The price of gold, like the price of silver, should be determined in the free market, with the U.S. Government committed neither to buying gold nor to selling gold at any fixed price. This is the appropriate counterpart of a policy of floating exchange rates. With respect to our existing stock of gold, we could simply keep it fixed, neither adding to it nor reducing it; alternatively, we could sell it off gradually at the market price or add to it gradually thereby reducing or increasing our governmental stockpiles of this particular metal. Personally, I favor selling it off (which would involve removing the present gold reserve requirement for Federal Reserve liabilities) and simultaneously removing all present limitations on the ownership of gold and the trading in gold by American citizens. There is no reason why gold, like other commodities, should not be freely traded on a free market.

5.2 *Financial Intermediation and the "Deficit"*

The Despres proposal to demonetize gold, referred to in the preceding statements, is related to the international financial intermediation hypothesis about the United States balance of payments. In 1966, a celebrated article presented "a minority view" on the United States balance of payments and world liquidity.[11] Exception was taken to the consensus in Europe

11. Emile Despres, C. P. Kindleberger, and Walter S. Salant, "The Dollar and World Liquidity: A Minority View," *The Economist* (February 5, 1966), pp. 526–29. A later elaboration is presented by Salant, "Financial Intermediation as an Explanation of En-

and the United States that the United States deficits were no longer available as a generator of liquidity because the accumulation of dollars had gone so far that it had undermined confidence in the dollar, and that to forestall headlong flight from the dollar, it is necessary above all else to correct the United States deficit. In opposition, the minority view focused on the United States' role as a financial intermediary as an explanation of the "deficit." Financial intermediation could give rise to a "deficit" that is compatible with equilibrium. Thus, it was stated:

> While the United States has provided the world with liquid dollar assets in the postwar period by capital outflow and aid exceeding its current account surplus, in most years this excess has not reflected a deficit in a sense representing disequilibrium. The outflow of U.S. capital and aid has filled not one but two needs. First, it has supplied goods and services to the rest of the world. But secondly, to the extent that its loans to foreigners are offset by foreigners putting their own money into liquid dollar assets, the U.S. has not overinvested but has supplied financial intermediary services. The "deficit" has reflected largely the second process, in which the United States has been lending, mostly at long and intermediate term, and borrowing short. This financial intermediation, in turn, performs two functions: it supplies loans and investment funds to foreign enterprises which have to pay more domestically to borrow long-term money and which cannot get the amounts they want at any price; and it supplies liquidity to foreign asset-holders, who receive less for placing their short-term deposits at home. Essentially, this is a trade in liquidity, which is profitable to both sides. . . . Such lack of confidence in the dollar as now exists has been generated by the attitudes of government officials, central bankers, academic economists, and journalists, and reflects their failure to

during 'Deficits' in the Balance of Payments," in *International Mobility and Movement of Capital*, Fritz Machlup et al. (eds.) (1972), pp. 607–59. No econometric model exists for quantitative estimates of how much of the United States liquidity deficit can be accounted for by a comparative advantage in the provision of financial-intermediary services. But Salant's "own guess would be, on the one hand, that financial intermediation by the United States does not account for all of the liquidity deficit of the past two decades, but, on the other hand, that the increase of liquid liabilities of the United States willingly held by nonofficial foreigners—$11.6 billion in the period 1960 to 1968, or 58 per cent of the total liquidity deficit of $20.0 billion—implies that it does account for much of that deficit." (p. 650).

understand the implications of this intermediary function. Despite some contagion from these sources, the private market retains confidence in the dollar, as increases in private holdings of liquid dollar assets show. Private speculation in gold is simply the result of the known attitudes and actions of government officials and central bankers.[12]

This view diminishes the emphasis placed on the liquidity deficit, and it also indicates that the adjustment problem involves not only the current account but also the capital account. Attempts to correct the "deficit" by deflation or direct controls on trade and capital movements are likely to make the cure of the balance-of-payments policy worse than the disease of balance-of-payments deficit. The more appropriate policy, it was argued, would be to deny foreign holders of dollars the option of switching from dollars to gold to dollars. The dollar would then become the preferred asset. And unlike any new internationally created reserve asset which would meet only the need for external liquidity, an increase in the liquid liabilities of the United States in response to a growing total "stock demand" would meet the needs of savers for internal liquidity and of borrowers in the same country for long-term funds. It was therefore concluded that:

> Mutual recognition of the role of dollar holdings would provide the most desirable solution, but if, nevertheless, Europe unwisely chooses to convert dollars into gold, the United States could restore a reserve-currency system, even without European cooperation in reinterpreting deficits and lifting capital restrictions. The decision would call for cool heads in the United States. The real problem is to build a strong international monetary mechanism resting on credit, with gold occupying, at most, a subordinate position. Because the dollar is in a special position as a world currency, the United States can bring about this change through its own action. Several ways in which it can do so have been proposed, including widening the margin around parity at which it buys and sells gold, reducing the price at which it buys gold, and otherwise depriving gold of its present unlimited convertibility into dollars.[13]

12. Ibid. p. 608.
13. Ibid. p. 658.

6. GOLD CRISIS OF 1968

The minority view, however, had few adherents in official circles. Perhaps Secretary of the United States Treasury Fowler came close to it when on March 17, 1967, before a meeting of the American Bankers Association at Pebble Beach, California, Secretary Fowler chose to issue a statement that was interpreted as an ultimatum to the Group of 10 to create a substitute for the dollar in the form of a new international reserve or else face the prospect of a reconsideration of the United States commitment to its current gold policy. Secretary Fowler declared that the United States feels impelled to find more ways to "neutralize" the threat of a gold loss, and he warned that lack of enough reserves to support growing world trade would mean "retreat into stale and timid and destructive restrictionism."

A substitute reserve asset—eventually in the form of Special Drawing Rights (SDR's)—was not to be actually created for another two years. And while the supply of gold remained insufficient to serve as the only external reserve, the dollar confronted a confidence problem as questions were raised how long the dollar could continue to be the major source of liquidity and endure a rising ratio of official liabilities-to-gold-reserves without endangering the foreign exchange value of the dollar. In this situation, the world's monetary authorities would have to choose—sooner or later—among three courses of action: (i) to raise the price of gold and thereby increase the value of gold as a reserve asset in the system; (ii) to demonetize gold in favor of the reserve currency as the fundamental reserve money in the system; (iii) to create through international negotiation a new international reserve money to substitute for both gold and the dollar.

In September 1967 the Group of 10 and the executive directors of the IMF finally agreed to submit to the annual IMF meeting an outline agreement that could lead to the creation of a new reserve asset (see pp. 218–21 below). Less than two months later, however, the pound sterling was devalued (see pp. 54–62 above). Devaluation of sterling led to speculation on a devaluation of the dollar in terms of gold, and there began a speculative rush into gold. Private demand for gold increased, and the United States gold stock fell as the seven-nation Gold Pool attempted to support the price of gold in private markets. Washington also reacted with more restrictions on international payments by tourists and foreign investors.

In contrast to official action, a few economists continued to advocate that the United States should stop buying gold and allow exchange rate flexibility. The following letter again expresses this view.

STRONG DOLLAR SEEN IN FREE MARKETS *

To the Editor:

A few days ago the pound was devalued by the arbitrary margin of 14.3 per cent. This happened after long-drawn-out and wasteful efforts to maintain a sterling rate that was clearly incompatible with the requirements of economic equilibrium. The abrupt devaluation that occurred on Nov. 18 is apt to cause substantial dislocations. These could have been avoided if sterling, instead of having been pegged, had all along been allowed to find its true equilibrium level by gradual adjustments in the market.

Will other countries, including the United States, continue to make costly efforts to maintain an administratively determined exchange-rate structure many elements of which are wholly arbitrary by market criteria?

These efforts would involve senseless sacrifices at the expense of significant economic objectives. Furthermore, it is highly questionable whether the administrative controls that would be needed to preserve this artificial structure would be effective even by their own standards. The obvious objective of these controls is to suppress the forces of the market, and this is neither a laudable nor a promising objective.

Flexible Exchange Rate

As is well known, many economists have favored exchange rate flexibility in free markets for a long time. Recent events have further strengthened our own conviction that policy makers at home and abroad should put flexible exchange rates promptly into effect, with allowance for the probable desire of some countries to form larger currency areas.

As for the United States, we favor letting the market determine the dollar rates without pegging operations of any sort. For a specified final period the American monetary authorities should continue to

* *New York Times,* November 26, 1967.

offer conversion into gold at $35 an ounce for such foreign official dollar holdings as were acquired prior to Nov. 18. Our present standing offer to buy gold should stop at once. Thus we should make the dollar independent of gold and should cease to link our currency to foreign currencies at rates that do not satisfy the conditions of international equilibrium.

The United States has the most widely used currency in the world. The strength of the dollar has been obscured by the administrative restrictions of recent years, but it would express itself very clearly in free, unmanipulated markets, unless we should adopt irresponsible monetary and fiscal policies for an extended period of time. There is no reason whatever why we should have to pursue such policies, but if we should nevertheless do so, then the present artificial and wasteful pegging arrangements would collapse anyway.

WILLIAM FELLNER
MILTON FRIEDMAN
HARRY G. JOHNSON
FRITZ MACHLUP

New Haven, Nov. 22, 1967

The writers are professors of economics at universities here and abroad.

In the last quarter of 1967, gold losses from the United States mounted to more than $1 billion and to more than $1.5 billion in January and February 1968. Countries in the gold pool found it increasingly difficult to support the London gold price. By mid-March, the gold drain reached crisis proportions.

GOLD POOL MEETING *

A Wall Street Journal News Roundup

The frenzied London gold market was ordered closed today as top international financial officials were summoned into an urgent weekend meeting in hopes of keeping the monetary crisis from toppling the Free World into economic disaster.

Almost simultaneously with last night's announcements, the Senate in Washington acceded to intense Administration entreaties and sent to the White House the "gold cover" repeal bill making clear that none of the U.S. gold stock need be tied up as "backing" for domestic currency.

* *Wall Street Journal,* March 15, 1968.

When President Johnson signs the bill, the historic link will be broken and the $11.4 billion of gold that's left, as of last count, in the U.S. stocks will all be unquestionably available for dollar-propping sale to foreign governments and central banks.

In announcing the exceptional assembly of finance officials from the seven countries active in the London "gold pool," the Treasury said the "temporary closing of the London market doesn't affect the U.S. undertaking to buy and sell gold in transactions with monetary authorities at the official price of $35 an ounce."

While the wording assured that the governmental gold dealings that are the underpinning of world currency stability aren't to be disturbed—at least for now—it pointedly stopped short of assuring that the seven nations would continue pouring gold into hands of private speculators and hoarders through the pool. Whether to continue incurring the immense drain this policy has caused in recent days undoubtedly is the key question before the meeting.

Last night's moves came after a furious day of gold buying in London and European markets sent volume to avalanche proportions, surpassing by well over 100% the record turnover of Wednesday.

And, after the closing of the London gold and securities markets was announced, a bank holiday in Britain was declared. From London, however, the Associated Press said that British banks would be supplying domestic customers with their normal cash requirements in sterling; but that only.

In Washington, a U.S. Treasury spokesman made clear the closing of the gold exchange was at "the suggestion of the U.S." because the London gold market "had become disorganized and didn't permit the handling of business in a reasonably orderly fashion."

Canada also asked its banks and other financial institutions not to deal in gold today, pending the weekend meeting of central bankers on the gold situation.

Canada's relatively small gold market has been flourishing recently, along with markets in the rest of the world. The nation isn't a member of the international gold pool that supplies London.

Invitations From Fowler, Martin

Treasury Secretary Fowler and Federal Reserve Board Chairman William McChesney Martin jointly invited the European banking officials "to consult with us on coordinated measures to insure orderly conditions in the exchange markets and to support the present pattern of exchange rates based on the fixed price of $35 an ounce of gold."

On the guest list—with the meeting place late last night tentatively planned to be Federal Reserve headquarters in Washington—are Hubert Ansiaux, governor of the Belgian National Bank; Guido Carli, governor of the Bank of Italy; J. Zijlstra, president of the Netherlands Central Bank; E. Stopper, president of the Swiss National Bank; Sir

Leslie O'Brien, governor of the Bank of England, and Karl Blessing, president of the German Central Bank. . . .

Close Vote in Senate

The Senate vote to remove the 25% gold backing of domestic currency was a dramatically close 39 to 37.

The bill removing the gold cover, passed earlier in identical form by the House, would make the Treasury's entire $11.4 billion gold stock available to support the dollar's international value. The Senate approved the bill without amendment under the lash of Administration arguments that putting up the entire gold supply for potential international sale at $35 an ounce could help calm speculative gold-buying fever in Europe.

The rule requiring a $1 gold reserve for every $4 in Federal Reserve currency in circulation has tied up about $10.4 billion of gold, leaving a rapidly dwindling cushion of "free" metal for sale to foreign central banks and governments, and to meet the U.S. contribution to the London gold pool.

After the emergency meeting of the Gold Pool countries, it was decided to terminate gold sales to the private market, and establish a two-tier gold price arrangement by maintaining the official price of $35 for transfers of gold among official monetary authorities while allowing the private market to find its own level without any government dealings with private holders of gold. The following communique was issued.

CENTRAL BANKERS' COMMUNIQUE AND IMF STATEMENT *

Communique

The Governors of the central banks of Belgium, Germany, Italy, the Netherlands, Switzerland, the United Kingdom, and the United States met in Washington on March 16 and 17, 1968 to examine operations of the gold pool, to which they are active contributors. The Managing Director of the International Monetary Fund and the General Manager of the Bank for International Settlements also attended the meeting.

The Governors noted that it is the determined policy of the United States Government to defend the value of the dollar through appropriate fiscal and monetary measures and the substantial improvement of the United States balance of payments is a high priority objective.

* *New York Times*, March 17, 1968.

They also noted that legislation approved by Congress makes the whole of the gold stock of the nation available for defending the value of the dollar.

They noted that the United States Government will continue to buy and sell gold at the existing price of $35 an ounce in transactions with monetary authorities. The Governors support this policy, and believe it contributes to the maintenance of exchange stability.

The Governors noted the determination of the United Kingdom authorities to do all that is necessary to eliminate the deficit in the United Kingdom balance of payments as soon as possible and to move to a position of large and sustained surplus.

Finally, they noted that the governments of most European countries intend to pursue monetary and fiscal policies that encourage domestic expansion consistent with economic stability, avoid as far as possible increases in interest rates or a tightening of money markets, and thus contribute to conditions that will help all countries move toward payments equilibrium.

The Governors agreed to cooperate fully to maintain the existing parities as well as orderly conditions in their exchange markets in accordance with their obligations under the Articles of Agreement of the International Monetary Fund. The Governors believe that henceforth officially held gold should be used only to effect transfers among monetary authorities, and, therefore, they decided no longer to supply gold to the London gold market or any other gold market. Moreover, as the existing stock of monetary gold is sufficient in view of the prospective establishment of the facility for Special Drawing Rights, they no longer feel it necessary to buy gold from the market. Finally, they agreed that henceforth they will not sell gold to monetary authorities to replace gold sold in private markets.

The Governors agreed to cooperate even more closely than in the past to minimize flows of funds contributing to instability in the exchange markets, and to offset as necessary any such flows that may arise.

In view of the importance of the pound sterling in the international monetary system, the Governors have agreed to provide further facilities which will bring the total of credits immediately available to the United Kingdom authorities (including the IMF standby) to $4-billion.

The Governors invite the cooperation of other central banks in the policies set forth above.

Statement

During their meeting in Washington over the past two days, the active members of the gold pool have decided to stop supplying gold from monetary reserves to the London gold market or any other gold market.

This decision is readily understandable as a means of conserving the stock of monetary gold, which has recently been subject to heavy drains through such operations in the London market.

The decision, of course, involves no departure from the obligation of these countries to maintain the par values of their currencies established with the IMF.

Countries adhering to the Articles of Agreement of the Fund undertake to collaborate with the Fund to promote exchange stability and to maintain orderly exchange agreements with each other. It is most important that the monetary authorities of all member countries should continue to conduct gold transactions consistently with this undertaking, and that they should cooperate fully to conserve the stock of monetary gold. Such action will be an important contribution to the functioning of the international monetary system.

In the longer run, it will not be sufficient simply to conserve global reserves. In this connection, it is to be noted that work on the establishment of the Special Drawing Rights facility in the Fund is proceeding on schedule. It is to be hoped that this facility will enter into force with the least possible delay in order to make it possible to supplement existing reserve assets as and when needed.

With this communique, the world's monetary authorities had taken a major step towards the demonetization of gold. The result of this decision could be interpreted as putting the world de facto on an international dollar standard, since it was obvious that the United States could also at any time refuse to convert dollars into gold for official holders of dollars. The action of the Gold Pool also left ambiguous the future role of gold and made its price uncertain.

7. MAKING OF THE CRISIS

At the same time as the United States was supporting negotiation for creation of the Special Drawing Account in the IMF, the Administration began stressing the need for balance-of-payments discipline and emphasized the connection between "domestic economic management" and the country's external payments position.

TEXT OF NIXON STATEMENT ON
BALANCE OF PAYMENTS *

Washington, April 4—The following is the text of a statement issued today by President Nixon on the United States balance-of-payments problem:

In my fiscal message to the Congress on March 26, I called for a strong budget surplus and monetary restraint to curb an inflation that has been allowed to run into its fourth year. This is fundamental economics, and I pointed out that we intend to deal with fundamentals.

* *New York Times,* April 5, 1969.

Similarly, the problem of regaining equilibrium in the United States balance of payments cannot be solved with expedients that postpone the problem to another year. We shall stop treating symptoms and start treating causes, and we shall find our solutions in the framework of freer trade and payments.

Fundamental economics call for:

Creating the conditions that make it possible to rebuild our trade surplus.

Ultimate dismantling of the network of direct controls which may seem useful in the short run but are self-defeating in the long run.

Capital Inflow Included

The United States balance of payments showed a surplus last year. But this surplus included an unusually high and probably unsustainable capital inflow. Our trade surplus, which reached a peak of $6.5-billion in the mid-sixties, declined sharply and all but disappeared.

That trade surplus must be rebuilt, and it can only be rebuilt by restoring stable and noninflationary economic growth to the United States economy. Inflation has drawn in a flood of imports while it has diminished our competitiveness in world markets and thus dampened our export expansion.

This is why our program of fiscal and monetary restraint is as necessary for our external trade as for restoring order in our domestic economy.

Effort in Key Areas

Building on the solid base of a healthy, noninflationary economy—a base that only the fundamentals of fiscal and monetary restraint now can restore —we are planning a sustained effort in several key areas:

In export expansion, we have tentatively set an export goal of $50-billion to be achieved by 1973. This compares with 1968 exports of about $34-billion. This is primarily the task of American private enterprise, but Government must help to coordinate the effort and offer assistance and encouragement. We must also call on the productivity and ingenuity of American industry to meet the competitive challenge of imported goods.

In trade policies, we will be working with our major trading partners abroad to insure that our products receive a fair competitive reception.

In defense activities, we will also work with our friends abroad to insure that the balance-of-payments burden of providing for the common defense is shared fairly.

In travel, we will encourage more foreign travel to the United States. Here, as in other areas, we will be relying heavily on the support of the private community. We seek no restrictions on the American tourist's freedom to travel.

In international investment, we will review our own regulations and tax policy to assure that foreign investment in the United States is not discouraged; for example, we should move now to eliminate from our laws the prospective taxation of interest on foreign-held bank deposits.

In the international financial area, we will be continuing to work with our friends abroad to strengthen and improve the international monetary system. An expanding world economy will require growing levels of trade with adequate levels of reserves, and effective methods by which countries can adjust their payments imbalances. In particular, we look forward to ratification by the International Monetary Fund members of the special drawing rights plan and its early activation.

Steps Are Listed

I am confident that measures in these areas, coupled with the cooling of the economy through fiscal-monetary restraint, will move us in an orderly manner toward true balance-of-payments equilibrium. Accordingly, I have begun, gradually but purposefully, to dismantle the direct controls which only mask the underlying problem.

Specifically:

First, I have today signed an executive order reducing the effective rate of the interest-equalization tax from 1¼ per cent to ¾ of 1 per cent. This measure was designed to close a large gap—which has now narrowed—between foreign and domestic interest rates. I shall, however, request the Congress to extend the President's discretionary authority under the interest-equalization tax for 18 months beyond its scheduled expiration in July.

Second, I have approved a recommendation to relax somewhat the foreign direct investment program of the Department of Commerce. This means that most firms investing abroad will have substantially more freedom in planning these investments.

Third, I have been informed by chairman [William McChesney] Martin of modifications in the Federal Reserve program which will provide more flexibility for commercial banks, particularly smaller and medium-sized banks, to finance United States exports.

Realities Recognized

These are prudent and limited steps that recognize the realities of our present balance-of-payments situation.

The distortions created by more than three years of inflation cannot be corrected overnight. Nor can the dislocations resulting from a decade of balance-of-payments deficits be corrected in a short time.

But the time for restoring the basis of our prosperity is long overdue. We shall continually direct America's economic policy, both foreign and domestic, at correcting the root causes of our problems, rather than covering them over with a patchwork quilt of controls.

By facing up to fundamental economic needs, the inflationary tide and the trade tide can be turned and the United States dollar continued strong and secure.

7.1 *The Eurodollar Slop*

In considering the interaction of political and economic factors, causes and responses during the events of 1971, one analyst has said:

The underlying source of trouble in the winter of 1970-71 was what some journalist graphically described as "the Eurodollar slop," the large and ever-expanding pool of expatriate credit funds which, though free to move around the globe, tended mostly to slosh back and forth across the Atlantic. This was partly because most Eurocurrencies were dollars and partly because the major dealers in the market were the foreign branches of American banks, and their parent banks in the United States could easily raise or lower their total liabilities to them. Clearly, the Eurodollar slop made it increasingly difficult for the United States both to manage its domestic economy, whether by promoting growth or restraining inflation and, at the same time, to avoid sudden explosive increases in its external deficit.[14]

EURODOLLAR TRANSMISSION BELT *

The Eurodollar market acts as an efficient transmission belt linking the U.S. and European money markets. Interest rates in the Eurodollar market respond almost immediately to changes in U.S. interest rates, while short-term funds move out of European countries and into Eurodollars, and back again, on the basis of small interest-rate differentials.

In the last two years, changes in the volume of Eurodollars used by banks in the United States have played a crucial role in the transmission of U.S. monetary influence to Europe. When the Federal Reserve adopted a highly restrictive policy, banks in the United States increased their takings of Eurodollars by $7 billion. Eurodollar rates rose steeply and funds flowed out of the European banking systems into the Eurodollar market. In Britain, France and Germany, the outflow contributed to a slowdown in monetary expansion, the effect of which has been felt on business activity this year.

The decline of U.S. short-term interest rates this year and the backflow of Eurodollars released by U.S. banks as domestic monetary conditions have eased have pushed Eurodollar rates down, creating a strong incentive for firms in Germany and other European countries to borrow Eurodollars. For domestic interest rates in Europe this year have been generally higher and credit tighter than in the United States. The resulting inflow of funds has hampered European, especially German, monetary authorities in their struggle with inflation.

14. Susan Strange, "The Dollar Crisis," *International Affairs* (April 1972), p. 198. For a fuller understanding of the operation of the Eurodollar market, see A. K. Swoboda, *The Euro-Dollar Market: An Interpretation*, Princeton Essays in International Finance (February 1968); F. H. Klopstock, *The Euro-Dollar Market: Some Unresolved Issues*, Princeton Essays in International Finance (March 1968).

* *Monthly Economic Letter*, First National City Bank, November 1970.

If the Eurodollar market did not exist, changes in U.S. monetary policy probably would not be felt as strongly in Continental Europe. The effects would be transmitted through more traditional channels, such as international lending by banks and the U.S. securities markets. These channels are neither as efficient international movers of short-term funds nor as free of regulation as the Eurodollar market—which, of course, is why the Eurodollar market came into existence.

European central banks could doubtless reduce the consequences of dollar ebbs and flows through more effective open-market operations or by changes in the reserves required to be maintained by commercial banks. Yet, given the size of the movements of funds into and out of European currencies relative to the size of bank reserves in these countries, such measures would often be difficult to apply with sufficient vigor and foresight to prevent large changes in local monetary conditions, when conditions in U.S. money markets were changing rapidly.

In any event, the more fundamental political issue remains. Sovereign nations are likely to find irksome, and some of them may in time find unacceptable, a relationship in which their money supplies are partly determined by the vagaries of U.S. monetary policy. . . .

Europe's malaise about the dollar has been greatly intensified by the experience of the last five years. The excessive expansion of the U.S. money supply in the 1965–68 period and its inflationary impact in Europe made Europeans much more aware than they had been previously of the transatlantic monetary leverage of a U.S. payments deficit. The impact of the Federal Reserve's restrictive monetary policy in 1969 on European interest rates and central bank reserves was another sharp reminder of monetary interdependence.

Particularly troublesome was the impact on European interest rates last year, which was greater than it would have been in the absence of the Federal Reserve's Regulation Q and the U.S. Commerce Department's restrictions on foreign investment. Regulation Q forced U.S. banks to borrow heavily in the Eurodollar market and the investment controls had the same effect on U.S. subsidiaries abroad. As a result, Eurodollar rates shot up considerably faster than U.S. rates, putting strong upward pressure on domestic rates in European countries.

A marked improvement in U.S. domestic economic management such as now seems to be in the making—avoiding phases of excessive monetary growth as well as phases of extreme stringency—will improve the present transatlantic monetary atmosphere. Yet the question will remain whether, even if U.S. stabilization policy is successful, European countries will be indefinitely reconciled to living with the dollar on the present basis if a working alternative can be found.

During the decade of the 1960's the Eurodollar market had increased from some $3 billion to an estimated $50 billion.

While national capital markets were regulated, the growth in the unregulated Eurodollar market was viewed by many as a source of potential trouble.

7.2 *A Policy of Benign Neglect?*

Despite—or precisely because of—the continuing United States deficit and the taking of additional restrictive measures to suppress the deficit, two provocative studies appeared in early 1971 advocating that the United States should pursue a passive balance-of-payments strategy.[15]

One proponent of this strategy stated that passive policy was meant to mean two things: first, that domestic monetary, fiscal, and other general economic policies are guided by domestic policy objectives—price stability, employment, growth—and not by balance-of-payments considerations; second, that intervention in the exchange rates is left to other countries. A passive policy was not, however, meant to mean lack of interest in the organization of the international monetary system, neglect of the interests of other countries, or indifference to the dangers of inflation.[16]

Another proponent emphasized that the case for a passive balance-of-payments policy did "not grow out of arrogance of the United States," but was intended to allow the United States to fulfill its international responsibilities for the viability of the dollar-centered international monetary system. It was explicitly stated that "the United States, because of its relative wealth, has a responsibility to provide real resources to other countries. The policy actions required to do this are straightforward: appropriations for foreign aid and a willingness to permit and possibly even to encourage the outflow of long-term private capital." [17] At the same time, the invocation of the adjustment process should be left to other countries through the exchange rate adjustments that they initiate, instead of having the United

15. Gottfried Haberler and Thomas D. Willett, *A Strategy for U.S. Balance Payments Policy* (1971); Lawrence B. Krause, "A Passive Balance-of-Payments Strategy for the United States," *Brookings Papers on Economic Activity*, No. 3 (1970).

16. Gottfried Haberler, "Prospects for the Dollar Standard," *Lloyds Bank Review* (July 1972), p. 2.

17. Krause, "Passive Balance-of-Payments Strategy for the United States," pp. 342–43.

States continually resort to deficit-suppressing measures that create distortions and inefficiencies in their effort to restrain the outflow of dollars.

But will not other countries want the United States to continue to suppress or "correct" its deficit? Will not other countries ask such questions as these: "Doesn't America want to pay her own way in the world? Is it really fair for American firms to buy out European businesses with dollars that European central banks are subsequently forced to hold against their better judgment? Shouldn't the U.S. also bear some of the burden of adjustment when it is in deficit even though it bears less burden than other countries?"

An advocate of a passive policy replies:

> The proper response by the U.S. to this attack is to recognize the realities of the situation and to evaluate correctly its responsibilities and its ability to meet them. An American deficit, if it did exist, can be perpetuated only if other countries maintain undervalued currencies relative to the dollar. Unlike the U.S., other countries can change their exchange rates. If they want to end a U.S. deficit, they can do so; but if they want to maintain undervalued currencies, there is no effective U.S. policy to force an end to their surpluses. Americans can buy foreign assets at bargain prices only because of a lack of competition by foreigners for their own assets or because of undervalued currencies. Both conditions are correctable only by foreign governments. The U.S. unquestionably will bear a burden when a deficit is adjusted, for Americans will be able to absorb fewer real resources from abroad; only the mechanism for effectuating the adjustment is in dispute. The real burden that the United States must shoulder should not be confused with the problem of invoking the adjustment mechanism, which does fall to others.[18]

The Nixon administration remained unimpressed, however, by the advocacy of a policy of "benign neglect" of the payments deficit. A *Wall Street Journal* report stated: [19]

> But within the Nixon administration—and especially at the independent Federal Reserve Board—many responsible of-

18. Ibid. pp. 356–57.
19. *Wall Street Journal* (February 19, 1971).

ficials argue that the U.S. still can't afford to adopt a completely devil-may-care posture on the payments problem. Even if continental countries never stage an ultimate "run" on the U.S. gold stock, they would be more apt to keep demanding modest amounts of gold to keep the pressure on the U.S., these officials note.

More importantly, an avowed passive policy would gravely strain U.S. diplomatic relations across-the-board, making it much harder for the U.S. to get its way in military and trade matters, the officials assert. And instead of the constructive monetary responses Mr. Haberler envisions, they fear that foreign countries more likely would retaliate against the U.S.—by stiffening their resistance to upward revaluations, becoming less likely to cooperate in mutually helpful swaps of currencies, dealing a death blow to the IMF's paper gold or special drawing rights mechanism that now gives governments a rationally managed form of new money for settling up payments deficits.

7.3 Dollar Outflow

While stating that he did not want to engage in "malignant preoccupation" (the opposite to "benign neglect"), Nobel Laureate Paul A. Samuelson nonetheless chose to call attention to the "shakey dollar" in his *Newsweek* column in April 1971. Samuelson wrote that "by every rational test the dollar has been an overvalued currency for almost fifteen years now," and that the situation is not improving.[20]

Capital outflows during the latter part of 1970 had begun to put additional pressure on the dollar. To promote more investment and expansion in the American economy, the United States undertook an easing of monetary policy in the autumn of 1970. But tight monetary conditions in France, Italy, the United Kingdom, and most particularly, Germany encouraged large capital inflows from the United States to these nations. By late 1970, Germany's foreign exchange reserves had risen to $13½ billion—a larger amount than before the 1969 revaluation of the mark and almost twice what they had been earlier in the year. Contrary to the dictates of domestic stabilization policy which called for an anti-inflationary tight money policy, the Bundesbank was forced to reduce its discount rate in order to stem the

20. *Newsweek* (April 19, 1971).

inflow of dollars. Germany was confronting a dilemma situation in its mix of internal and external policy objectives. Moreover,

> just when the worst of the outflow of Euro-dollars was narrowing, the foreign exchange markets began to get the jitters. After an Easter lull, the French finance minister started the gold market price upward by calling for a rise in the official price, and the Bundesbank announced it was no longer supporting the dollar by buying in the forward market. Then, when Germany's chief economic institutes suggested on May 3 that the only answer to the dollar inflow was another DM float, the dollar-selling bandwagon began to roll in earnest. In two and a half days, before the Bundesbank closed the foreign exchange market forty minutes after it had opened on the morning of Wednesday, May 5, $2,000 million in dollars had flowed into Germany, half of it in those last forty minutes.[21]

In the following selection, a report of the Bundesbank summarizes the events leading to the floating of the mark in May 1971.

NEW MEASURES OF MONETARY POLICY *

After monetary conditions entered a new acute phase in the first few days of May, marked by heavy speculative dollar inflows into Germany and other European countries and leading to the temporary closure of the foreign currency exchanges, the Bundesbank was released on May 10, 1971 until further notice from its obligation to intervene against the U.S. dollar. Since then the exchange rate for the Deutsche Mark has been formed freely on the foreign exchange markets without Bundesbank intervention. The dollar rate has dropped distinctly below the lower limit of DM 3.63 and has fluctuated quite considerably from day to day. In addition, in accordance with Article 23 of the Foreign Trade and Payments Law, the payment of interest on the financial investments of non-residents was made subject to approval by the Bundesbank.

The Necessity for Safeguards against External Influences

The release of the Bundesbank from its obligation to intervene and the introduction of the ban on interest payments are both measures to safeguard the Federal Republic of Germany from money inflows from the rest of the world endangering its stability. In adopting such measures the Federal Gov-

---

21. Strange, "The Dollar Crisis," p. 20.
* *Monthly Report of the Deutsche Bundesbank*, May 1971, pp. 7–9.

ernment is complying with the commitments laid down in the Law on Economic Stability and Growth (Article 4), which states that the instruments of economic policy available to preserve external equilibrium are to be applied whenever overall economic equilibrium is disturbed by external influences and this disturbance cannot be rectified by domestic measures or by means of international coordination. The two last-mentioned remedies proved to be unrealisable.

The necessity for safeguards against external influences derived primarily from the fact that the ample supply of dollars on international financial markets increasingly thwarted the attempts to keep money and credit in Germany as tight as was desirable in the light of domestic economic conditions and the growing threat to the value of money. During 1970 and the first few months of 1971 the Bundesbank had of course endeavoured to neutralise as far as possible the domestic repercussions of the massive dollar influx. Its efforts were, moreover, successful, inasmuch as interest rates in Germany were kept relatively high and the domestic supply of credit remained relatively tight over a fairly long period. Nevertheless, the credit shortage in Germany was increasingly undermined by recourse to borrowing abroad. The longer the inflows of foreign exchange persisted, the smaller became the scope for the Bundesbank's monetary policy to perform its statutory duty in accordance with Article 3 of the Bundesbank Law to regulate the supply of money in such a manner that the currency can be kept stable. In 1970 it had been possible to mitigate the contradiction between domestic goals on the one hand and exchange rates, permitted under the present monetary system to move only within narrow margins, on the other, by lowering domestic interest rates as far as the slight relaxation in economic tensions allowed. But the most recent reduction in the discount rate on March 31, 1971 was motivated solely by external considerations; it was no longer in conformity with domestic conditions. By this time there was no mistaking the fact that the tendency for economic activity to slacken, which had been evident from the late autumn of 1970 up to then, had come to a halt, at least for the time being. The overtaxing of domestic productive resources, especially the labour market, was diminishing only sluggishly; the rise in costs and prices was continuing unabated, and actually quickening in the case of consumer prices. It was hardly possible any longer to erect barriers to keep the inflationary trends in check; this would have required, in particular, a squeeze on the money and credit supply. Moreover, the spate of foreign funds did not reverse direction, despite the latest reduction of the discount rate, but actually intensified further, although on different grounds.

The main reasons for the decreasing effectiveness of monetary and credit policy lay in the following:

1. Since the beginning of 1970 the United States has been pursuing a policy of cheap money with the aim of strengthening economic growth at home and reducing the high level of unemployment. By means of a large creation of central bank money by the Federal Reserve System the level of interest rates

in the United States, particularly in the short-term lending field, has been sharply lowered, so that for roughly the last year it has been substantially below the level in Germany.

2. In view of the freedom of international capital transactions this tendency for interest rates to fall spread increasingly to other industrial countries, mainly through the Euro-dollar market, which acts as a "distribution centre" and "money creation multiplier". The dollar exodus from the United States and the supply of credit on the Euro-markets led to a particularly massive swamping of Germany, which kept its borders completely open in capital transactions with the rest of the world, but had to make efforts, in the light of its own domestic situation, to keep the level of interest rates high and the supply of credit scarce. The German and U.S. balances of payments largely assumed the status of opposite poles. The record deficit of over $10.5 billion in the U.S. balance of official reserve transactions in 1970 was accompanied by a record surplus of $6 billion in the German balance of payments (in each case exclusive of special drawing rights allocated). The huge volume of the Euro-dollar market, estimated at not less than $50 billion, gave rise to fears of a further increase in the raising of money and capital.

3. Since the beginning of 1971 the dollar efflux from the United States has intensified, although there have been certain fluctuations. The capital inflows prompted by interest rate considerations were now joined by flows due to speculative financial investment in Germany—all the more so, in fact, the more frequently measures of exchange rate policy were discussed. In view of the Bundesbank's obligation to intervene on the foreign exchange markets, financial investment in Germany entailed no risk of loss for the foreign investor; indeed, seeing that domestic interest rates were relatively high, it even yielded a good return. At the same time, foreign investors were hoping for a chance of making profits in the event of a de facto or de jure revaluation of the Deutsche Mark. Between January and end-April 1971 Germany's central monetary reserves (excluding special drawing rights allocated) went up by another $3 billion, and between May 3 and May 5 alone a further sum of over $2 billion flooded in. Thus the Bundesbank's monetary reserves rose by roughly $5 billion within little more than four months, compared with a growth of $6 billion, as noted, during the whole of 1970. . . .

Measures to Safeguard the Economy against
External Influences

In order to insulate the Bundesbank's monetary policy against further inflows of foreign funds, and in general to secure for it a greater freedom of movement, the Federal Government adopted two safeguarding measures against external influences:

1. The Bundesbank was requested temporarily to suspend its interventions on the foreign exchange markets. This means that the exchange rate of the Deutsche Mark was set free to float.

2. By means of an Order the payment of interest on deposits on the accounts of non-residents at banks in Germany, the acquisition of money mar-

ket paper by non-residents, and the conclusion of security transactions under repurchase agreements with non-residents were all made subject to approval.

In taking these measures the Federal Government was acting in conformity with the agreement reached in the Council of Ministers of the European Communities on May 9, 1971. Admittedly, the Council stated that the present situation and the prospective future course of the balances of payments of member countries did not warrant any changes in parities and expressed the member countries' determination to retain these parities. At the same time, however, the Council intimated that it appreciated that countries with excessive capital inflows might for a limited period extend the margins of fluctuation of the exchange rates of their currencies, as compared with the present par values, even though "under normal circumstances" a system of flexible exchange rates within the Community was not compatible with the efficient operation of the Community. The member countries also agreed to hold consultations before July 1, 1971 on appropriate measures to discourage the excessive capital inflows and to neutralise their impact on domestic monetary conditions.

As already mentioned, and also clearly expressed by the Federal Government, the Deutsche Mark has been floated primarily for reasons of credit policy and not with the intention of effecting a revaluation. If, as in 1961 and 1969, the situation had been one calling unequivocally for a revaluation, this could have been achieved much more readily by changing the parity, especially as in such a case no international commitments, not even ones towards the EEC, stand in the way of a parity change. That the Federal Government chose to release the Bundesbank from its obligation to intervene against the U.S. dollar as a means of safeguarding the economy from external influences accords with the fact that Germany's balance of payments is not at present in fundamental disequilibrium and that the disturbance from abroad is due to the inflow of short-term capital. The Bundesbank is now no longer obliged to purchase any amount of dollars offered to it at a floor rate, to create central bank money by this means, and thus of necessity to run counter to the aims of its own credit policy.

7.4 *Balance-of-Payments Mess*

A calm view of the May 1971 international monetary "flurry" was taken by both the chairman of the President's Council of Economic Advisers, Paul W. McCracken, and the Under Secretary of the Treasury for Monetary Affairs, Paul A. Volcker. Addressing the International Economics Forum in Chicago on May 3, Mr. McCracken said there were "heartening signs that the worst may be over" in the outflow of short-term capital, and that "both logic and the facts of experience" suggest that the over-all United States balance of international payments will get better, not worse, with an expanding domestic economy. At the same meeting, Mr. Volcker said that "national views converge" on the proposition that the short-term capital problem should be handled "by cooperative arrangements within the basic framework of the convertible currency system at stable exchange rates." Both Mr. McCracken and Mr. Volcker put the "basic" deficit at about $2.5 billion in 1970. Citing the $2.5 billion figure, Mr. Volcker said this was equal to "about 3 per cent of our total trade and less than 2 per cent of our total international transactions. A deficit of that magnitude should certainly be manageable for a time, whether viewed from the standpoint of its effect on our international liquidity position or its impact on flows of funds to other countries. The size is not so great as to appear prohibitive in terms of achieving adjustment over a reasonable period." [22]

Only a few weeks later, however, the Joint Economic Committee was conducting hearings on what it chose to call "The Balance-of-Payments Mess."

OPENING STATEMENT OF CHAIRMAN REUSS [*]

Chairman REUSS. Good morning.

The Subcommittee on International Exchange and Payments will be in order for the first of several hearings on the balance-of-payments mess. Spokesmen for the Treasury, the Council of Economic Advisers, and the Federal Reserve System have been denying for a decade that the U.S. external payments situation is a mess; instead they have been maintaining that one more regulation or a minor adjustment in interest rates would buy the time required until a fundamental recovery took hold. Now, however, the time has come to candidly acknowledge the extent of our problem.

One of President Kennedy's first responsibilities after his election was to quiet a flurry of foreign central bank requests for conversion of dollar balances into gold. In 1961 the duty-free allowance for American travelers returning from abroad was reduced from $500 to $100. In the same year, the Executive instituted the "gold budget" procedure for reducing foreign expenditures by Government agencies. The following year, the Defense Department instituted a procedure under which procurement would be made

22. *New York Times* (May 4, 1971).

* *The Balance of Payments Mess*, Hearings before the Subcommittee on International Exchange and Payments of the Joint Economic Committee, 92nd Congress, 1st Session, June 16, 1971, pp. 1–2, 316–24, 382–85, 409–16.

abroad only if the domestic price of comparable goods and services exceeded the foreign price by more than 50 percent.

In 1963 legislative authorization was requested for the interest equalization tax to discourage foreign borrowing in the United States; the tax was subsequently enacted retroactive to the date of the President's request. In fiscal 1964, 80 percent of U.S. AID commitments were tied to the procurement of goods in the United States, and this percentage rose to 85 percent by 1965.

From 1962 on the Executive has engaged in a number of special transactions designed to veil the true dimensions of our payments deficits. Chief among these special transactions have been the issuance of special notes and bonds to foreign monetary authorities, the prepayment of debt by foreign countries, and advance payment by other governments for military purchases here.

In 1965 voluntary controls were introduced on direct investment abroad by U.S. corporations and on lending to foreigners by American commercial banks. In 1968, the direct investment control program, administered by the Commerce Department, was made mandatory. At the same time, the ceilings on bank lending to foreigners, supervised by the Federal Reserve System, were tightened.

Also since 1960, we have seen the gold pool come and go, and the institution of a two-tier price system for dealings in gold. These changes in the treatment of gold are also largely the result of persistent U.S. payments deficits. The most recent initiative by the Executive to mitigate the effects of excessive dollar outflows have been borrowings by the Export-Import Bank and the Treasury together of $3 billion in Europe to prevent these claims on the United States from falling into the hands of foreign central banks.

Despite all these ad hoc measures, U.S. balance-of-payments deficits are larger than ever and massive international flows of short-term dollar assets have grown into a new problem provoking widespread concern. The Treasury now admits that the United States has a chronic basic payments deficit of $2 to $3 billion annually. The true figure is undoubtedly somewhat larger, since the controls and measures introduced over the last decade tend to mask its proper dimensions. It would certainly seem that the time has come to lay aside palliatives and to consider fundamental adjustment mechanisms to correct the U.S. balance of payments. The role of the dollar as the chief reserve currency in the international monetary system makes decisive corrective action especially urgent.

Earlier this week Mr. Jelle Ziljlstra, chairman of the board of directors and president of the Bank for International Settlements, said in a speech, "The dollar cannot remain the basic currency of the system if the United States does not participate fully in the adjustment process." The purpose of these hearings is to determine whether the United States has participated in the adjustment process as fully as it should. In addition, we will apply the same question to the actions of other nations—in particular to the amount of payments by Germany for the maintenance of U.S. troops in Europe and to the external value of the yen as maintained by Japanese monetary authorities.

Senator Javits has suggested, and I concur, that these issues should be discussed and I would hope resolved in an international monetary conference. Unfortunately, the administration seems to be opposed to the idea of such a conference. In addition, I have suggested that if no conference is held, the United States should formally sever the link between the dollar and gold and permit the dollar to temporarily float in exchange markets until an appropriate realignment of rates has occurred, upon which time we would continue to support the parity value of the dollar through exchange operations. These proposals by Senator Javits and myself will also undoubtedly come up for discussion during the course of these hearings.

Senator JAVITS. Thank you very much, Mr. Chairman.

Chairman REUSS. I will now ask Mr. Bergsten, Mr. Halm, and Mr. Willett to come forward.

Gentlemen, we thank you for coming. We now would like to ask each of you to proceed either to summarize or to read your prepared statements.

We will start out first with Mr. Bergsten.

STATEMENT OF C. FRED BERGSTEN

*Visiting Fellow, Council on Foreign Relations, and
Guest Scholar, The Brookings Institution*

Mr. BERGSTEN. These hearings are obviously triggered by the events of May 1971. It is therefore appropriate to begin with a short discussion of the causes of those events, and their implications for the future, before turning to more fundamental issues.

The huge hot money flows of late April-early May, which led to exchange rate actions by five countries, had one immediate, one intermediate and two underlying causes. The immediate cause was the resumption in late April of public discussion in Germany, by both Government officials and respected research institutes, of the need to revalue the deutsche mark to help combat internal inflation. The massive flows into Germany were almost wholly due to this development. The large flows into several other European countries were based on market judgments that, because of their close economic ties to Germany and their own inflationary problems, their currencies would follow any upward move of the mark.

The intermediate cause was the huge movement of short-term capital eastward across the Atlantic from early 1970 through early 1971, motivated almost entirely by the emergence of sizable differences between U.S. and European (including Eurodollar) interest rate. These differences were in turn due to the fact that the United States and Europe were at opposite points of the business cycle during that period, and that both relied heavily on monetary rather than fiscal policy to deal with unemployment and inflation, respectively. . . . German balance-of-payments surplus and the U.S. balance-of-payments deficit ballooned as a result. . . .

The deeper causes were the persistent deficit in the underlying U.S.

balance-of-payments position, and the related concern in some quarters that it would be perpetuated because the U.S. authorities had adopted a policy of "benign neglect." Both produced an underlying uneasiness about the viability of the entire structure of world exchange rates, since all major currencies are quoted in terms of U.S. dollars.

The recent events had virtually no economic effect on the United States. In Germany and a few other European countries, however, the money flows did complicate efforts to combat internal inflation, and the resultant exchange rate moves raised important issues for the evolution of the Common Market. In addition, the disturbances caused important international political disagreements—within Europe, and between Europe and the United States—over who was to blame and what should be done.

Since there are some costs to such disturbances; since hot money flows are certain to occur periodically under the rules of the present international monetary system; and since such flows are likely to become ever larger in the future, it would be desirable to improve the ability of the system to deal with them if sufficiently low-cost methods could be found. In addition, it would be desirable to meet directly the short-term problems caused by these short-term flows, to avoid their confusing the more fundamental international monetary situation. Controls over the Eurodollar market are not among my recommendations for such action. Controls limited to the Eurodollar market could only reduce the size and rapidity of international capital flows to a marginal extent, and are therefore not worth the complex negotiating effort that would be needed to institute them; controls extending beyond the Eurodollar market could be effective if they were quite comprehensive, but they would then represent a significant setback to the maintenance of a liberal world trading and payments system.

There are, however, steps that could be taken. National authorities should consult more closely on the timing of changes in their monetary policies, although it is illusory at this point in history to contemplate real coordination of monetary policies or of mixes between fiscal and monetary policies. Monetary authorities in both the United States and Europe could seek to alter the relationships between short-term and long-term interest rates in their own money markets and in the Eurodollar market—a la Operation Twist in this country—to minimize international flows. An extension of the maturities of the present swap lines to at least 12–18 months, and perhaps a further increase in the size of the network, could counter any serious effects of the temporary flows on national reserves.

Most important, however, the permissible margins around existing exchange rate parities should be widened from the present 1 percent on either side of parity to at least 3 percent on either side, as discussed approvingly in the September 1970 Report on Exchange Rates by the Executive Directors of the International Monetary Fund. . . .

The fundamental international monetary issue to any particular country is the degree of control which it can exercise over the liquidity-adjustment tradeoff in the system as a whole. Liquidity and adjustment are perfect substitutes. An infinite supply of liquidity obviates any need for adjustment, and a perfect adjustment process obviates any need for liquidity. Deficit countries usually seek to maximize liquidity and force surplus countries to initiate the process of adjustment. Surplus countries usually seek to minimize liquidity and force deficit countries to initiate adjustment. Both seek to impose their own economic and foreign policy preferences on the other in the process. This essentially political question underlies all of the issues raised for the present hearings.

The adjustment mechanism in the present international monetary system is weak. Countries increasingly orient their domestic economic policies to their domestic needs, which frequently conflict with the needs of external equilibrium. Exchange rate changes are traumatic, psychologically and politically and even in real economic terms, as the recent events remind us once more—although these events also remind us that exchange rates in fact will change. Controls over international transactions are thus the path of least resistance, and hence the most likely response to payments imbalances. Yet these controls vitiate the basic objective of the fixed exchange rate system— to maximize the freedom of international trade and capital movements; are usually inefficient in achieving their objective and therefore tend to proliferate rapidly; and, at this point in history, could easily tip the scales toward protectionist trade policies in the United States and elsewhere, with disastrous economic and international political consequences.

Countries thus wish to avoid adjustment of their imbalances, and none is sufficiently powerful to force adjustment on others. In addition, most want to run continual surpluses to build their reserves as protection against future deficits. The result is that the international monetary system needs lots of liquidity.

Gold now provides very little new liquidity, and will soon provide none since production is stagnant and industrial demand is rising rapidly. Special drawing rights were, of course, created to meet this very need, and are adding about $2 billion yearly to "owned" reserves—the 70 percent of gross allocations which need never be "reconstituted." Under the present international monetary system, the only other major source of additional reserves is the dollar.

The U.S. balance-of-payments position must be seen in this context. I agree with the official calculation that there is a basic deficit of about $2.5–$3 billion annually in the U.S. balance of payments, and has been for many years. The underlying deficit may be a bit larger, in fact, since some U.S. capital outflows have been suppressed by the existing control programs. This deficit long preceded the Vietnam war. It not only preceded our present inflationary excesses, but coexisted with our remarkable price stability of the early 1960's. It has been a permanent feature of the postwar world, through all combinations of cyclical situations and despite dramatic structural changes in the world economy. The basic issue is whether it represents a disequilibrium in any meaningful economic or political sense.

It is impossible to provide a quantitative answer with precision. However, I believe that any U.S. disequilibrium, in the framework of the present international monetary system, is small if indeed it exists at all. Private foreigners clearly want to add to their dollar holdings by at least $1 billion annually, in view of the dollar's unchallenged use as the world's chief transactions currency and the steady growth of the need for such a currency. The revealed desires of foreign monetary authorities to accumulate reserves clearly "justify" additions of at least $1.5 to $2.5 billion annually to world reserves in dollar form, beyond the present level of SDR allocations, as recognized in the IMF analysis of world reserve needs on which the first SDR allocation was based. An underlying U.S. payments imbalance of $2.5 to $3 billion thus appears reasonably close to equilibrium, defined in global economic terms.

The same conclusion holds if we ask the more proper question in assessing the situation of the dollar: Are any major foreign countries in disequilibrium on the surplus side? Switzerland and Austria have just revalued. Canada, Germany, and the Netherlands are floating and will probably eventually repeg at revalued levels, although the very small appreciation of the floating mark—especially prior to Bundesbank intervention—the guilder, and the Belgian "financial franc" raise doubts over the degree of disequilibrium which exist even there. Japan is the only major country with a clearly undervalued exchange rate at this time. Any U.S. disequilibrium on the deficit side is thus matched by disequilibrium on the surplus side only by Japan, and perhaps a few less important countries where exchange rate changes would not have much effect anyway.

Finally, the U.S. balance-of-payments "problem" has never been a direct function of our own balance-of-payments deficits. A real "problem" has occurred for the United States only when surpluses accrued to countries unwilling to hold their reserve increments in dollar form. We could be in surplus on any accounting definition yet have a "problem" if unwilling dollar holders were also in surplus. Fortunately, only a few major countries are consistently unwilling to add to their dollar balances and their persistent surpluses are relatively small even in relation to our sharply reduced stock of reserve assets. Over time, there easily appear to be enough willing dollar holders to maintain the equilibrium situation outlined above: underlying U.S. deficits averaging $2.5 billion annually.

The United States should therefore adopt no new unilateral measures in an effort to reduce its balance-of-payments deficit. In fact, recent econometric studies indicate that our balance of payments could gain well over $1 billion from the recent exchange rate moves, assuming that the Canadian dollar eventually settles near its present level and that the mark and guilder settle 5 percent above their present parities. The additional improvement we would get from an adequate revaluation of the Japanese yen would seem to nail down beyond much doubt the absence of any U.S. balance-of-payments disequilibrium.

I strongly oppose the proposal for a unilateral U.S. effort to change our exchange rate by unpegging the dollar from gold. Such a move is certainly unnecessary at this time. It would be extremely disruptive politically, at home, and especially abroad. It might not even result in any exchange rate changes, since other countries could simply maintain their present dollar intervention points. It would provide no lasting improvements in the adjustment process, even if we were never to repeg to gold but at some point assumed instead the obligations of "current account convertibility" under the Articles of Agreement of the IMF, and it would drastically hurt our efforts to achieve such improvement. U.S. action of this type would clearly be seen as an effort to build our trade balance and hence alter the structure of our balance of payments, which would be all too reminiscent of the competitive devaluations of the 1930's and thus hurt badly, rather than help, the crucial effort to combat protectionism around the world. . . .

The topic of today's session is "More Muddling, Bretton Woods Revisited, or U.S. Unilateral Action." I have indicated my view that there is no need for unilateral U.S. action and that such action would be extremely costly; it can be viewed only as a last resort, though its availability should avoid the need for such a resort. I have also concluded that the international monetary system today stands very close to an equilibrium situation, from a purely economic standpoint, so the United States and others can continue to "muddle through" for quite a while longer; this is my second choice. But the present system clearly contains serious problems, essentially of a political nature but which could cause serious economic difficulties, and my preference is to begin now the trip toward revisiting Bretton Woods.

It will be a long and complicated trip—both politically and technically. However, it is a necessary component of the adjustment of the United States and the rest of the industrialized world to the post-postwar period. Now is a good time to start. Three major exchange rates are floating, and the need to amend the international rules to bring national exchange rate changes under effective international surveillance should be obvious. The need to permit wider margins around parities, so clear from the events of May, makes it necessary to undertake the time-consuming task of amending the Articles of Agreement of the International Monetary Fund anyway and thus presents an opportunity for broader reform which typically occurs only about once per decade. The next allocation of SDR must be negotiated soon, and should encompass the considerations cited here concerning their magnitude and possible new uses. From the standpoint of the United States, the continued preeminence of the dollar as the world's top currency makes it a good time to begin to move, before the achievement of monetary unity in Europe and the continued development of Japan reduce further our international monetary power. I commend this subcommittee for its contribution toward beginning the journey.

Thank you, Mr. Chairman.

Chairman REUSS. Thank you very much, Mr. Bergsten. . . .

We will now finally hear from Mr. Willett. Would you proceed in any way you choose. You may wish to summarize part of your prepared statement.

STATEMENT OF THOMAS D. WILLETT
Associate Professor of Economics and Public
Affairs, Cornell University

Mr. WILLETT. The prepared statement is rather long so I will try to briefly summarize some of the major points.

I am particularly happy to be here today because I think these hearings are quite important. I think the international monetary system is at an important crossroads because we no longer have an international monetary system, I think, in the sense of coherent set of principles such as those layed out at Bretton Woods, which are adhered to by the major participants of the system. The Bretton Woods system in the last few years has finally proved unworkable and is currently on its last legs, if it is not its ghost that we are currently observing.

Clearly the gold exchange portion of the Bretton Woods system is by sheer numbers no longer working. The dollar liabilities outstanding greatly exceed our gold supply and the idea of a gold exchange standard is no longer workable. Likewise, the exchange rate mechanism of adjustable pegs envisioned in the Bretton Woods system is under serious doubt both from the action of member countries and from academic arguments.

It is most appropriate that we do consider what directions the future international monetary system will go. I think it is entirely possible that the present system will continue to muddle on for quite awhile. This would be an undesirable result in which we would keep getting current financial crises that we have seen too frequently in recent years.

In looking at the alternatives for possible directions in which the international monetary system might go, it would be helpful to begin with the question of basic objectives of the system, at least what would be a major objective with which we would want the system to be consistent. For the most important objective we suggest the freedom of macroeconomic policy to be geared to the dictates of domestic economy.

The major cause of tensions and problems in the present international monetary system is where you get deficits resulting from supply side phenomena emanating from the United States. It would be hard to argue that all of the U.S. measured deficit in recent years was a result of the increase in foreign countries' demand for dollars. Certainly it in part was a reflection of the Vietnam war and the concomitant inflation and serious deterioration in the trade balance. This was clearly a case in which we forced a dilemma on other countries, either they had to accept unwanted dollars or take measures to correct deficits themselves or the United States would have to take measures.

I think that this will be less of a problem in the future as countries begin to use greater exchange rate flexibility. If we go that route with other countries we are back to a monetary system in which we treat the dollar like all other currencies. And I might add this point, this doesn't make a lot of economic sense because there are very real economic reasons why the dollar reached the position it did. It was really a result of private entrepreneurs actions in response to this, not some political scheme on the part of the United States, that put the dollar in its present position. But if we say largely for political reasons we don't want a system in which the United States is an inconvertible center of the system, we want to rely on special drawing rights or an international Federal Reserve System to manage international liquidity, then we are going to have to find some way to restore effective exchange rate adjustment for the United States.

I won't go here into different ways this might be done. There might be some possibility for increased adjustment by using crawlings pegs for the United States, but the main constraint on the United States using exchange rates is not international law, but the fact that the United States is so large and an important part of trade in the international community that it is very hard to believe that the United States could devalue without most other countries following suit because they would not want to suffer a large deterioration in their trade balances. This in part you could get around by making use of a crawling peg for the United States, making small more direct adjustments, if we did have a disequilibrium. I agree with Mr. Bergsten that I don't think we are in much of an economic disequilibrium at present but I am sure at some point again we probably will be.

The essence of the problem would be in some form or another to get international agreement that if the United States did want to change its exchange rate, that it could effectively do so, that other countries or most other countries would refrain from following suit. For this it would be necessary to get an informal or formal agreement from the international community.

Now, what I am arguing is that there are only two reasonable types of international monetary systems. One would be a system in which we have some sort of a full passive U.S. balance-of-payments policy and we tell everybody else to adjust or finance deficits. The other one is one in which we are treated like every other country, we have the same adjustment responsibilities as other countries but we have to also be given the same adjustment techniques. If you are looking at the criteria for flexible exchange rates, the criteria for ranking countries as better or worse candidates for using exchange rate adjustments to correct their balance of payment, the United States is the leading candidate. It would not really in any sense be reasonable to try to run an international monetary system in which the United States does have adjustment responsibility but doesn't have necessary techniques to carry it out.

Now, the problem is that these are sort of two polar systems and, as you well know, in politics you tend to muddle around in the middle. In the last few years we have moved first in one direction, a little bit toward a dollar standard, and then moved a little bit toward a SDR standard, and you have the tremendous problem of having a case which tends to combine the worse features of the two prototype systems rather than the best features. Now, between the two systems, these two polar systems which I think are the most reasonable, I don't think it makes a great deal of difference to the United States which system was chosen.

I think the major U.S. interest could be secured in either way. We would not have to worry about the balance of payments as a severe constraint on domestic economic policies or need to resort to controls to correct our balance of payments. We get out of this problem under either system and in fact the sort of differences in the two systems are probably much more important for our European neighbors than they are for us because a major part of the choice concerns how useful is the dollar to others as an international transaction currency and how repugnant to the Europeans are the political implications of the use of the dollar. Really the decision between the two polar positions is a question that we could well leave to the international community to decide. But what the United States does need to do is to force a decision because otherwise we will just continue to muddle through. Hopefully, some increase in exchange rate flexibility and the SDR creation will be a distinct improvement over the way the system has been running in the last few years, but still I think a very much second-best solution.

How can the United States force in effect the international community to face up to the choice? Well, I think that is very simple because the United States could just say we are going to follow option No. 1, that is the passive U.S. balance-of-payments policy, until such time as the international community might decide that they wanted to switch to option No. 2, back to a new Bretton Woods system in which the United States was guaranteed effective use of its exchange rate. I think that would very nicely force the choice. I don't think we necessarily need to go formally inconvertible to force the choice because clearly an ideal solution is to reach agreement in a cooperative fashion. Just announcing that we are going to follow a passive policy may be sufficient. However, we have come close to a passive policy in recent years, certainly much more passive than in earlier years. And this hasn't forced the issue yet.

Perhaps rather than going inconvertible the best response would be to take off the capital controls. This would be a clear political act on the United States to make it completely clear that we are going to be following a passive policy until such a time as the international community decided they want to follow such other reasonable alternative.

Thank you, Mr. Chairman.

Chairman REUSS. Thank you very much. I guess I will start my questioning with you, Mr. Willett, since you ended up in a provocative manner.

My difficulty is with your proposition that we try to move others toward a new Bretton Woods which would permit adjustment of the dollar by saying we are going to vigorously continue the passive approach. The passive approach is one in which we say to the other countries, "Look, we can't adjust under the present system, therefore, you adjust, or if you don't want to adjust, finance our deficit."

I think there are real difficulties with that posture which I would like to present to you and see whether I can diminish your enthusiasm for what we will call the passive policy.

In the first place, we can say, you adjust, but they don't adjust. Japan, for example, won't adjust, it isn't adjusting, it says it won't adjust. A lot of intelligent people think that it is not going to adjust for a good long time.

Japanese exports to this country in the high technology field—steels, automobile, radio, television, and electronics—as well as things like textiles, are taking over increasing shares of our domestic and world markets. Nobody has worked out a system, unless Milton Friedman has, whereby Americans will do nothing, will be idle and happy, and our sole industry will be printing greenbacks so that the Japanese central bank may accumulate them. We don't really have a system of living without working in this country. Nobody has thought of one.

In the absence of such a philosopher's stone, we find labor and vast segments of business getting so protectionist that they inspired Mr. Bergsten to write the very perceptive if somewhat pessimistic article in Foreign Affairs which I have just read, so I don't think a passive policy is so glorious.

I haven't even mentioned that under a passive policy various gold bug countries, which shall be nameless, can give us the jitters by slicing off pieces of salami from time-to-time and cause us to do all kinds of foolish things domestically, which cause unhappiness, men thrown out of jobs, and produce inadequate growth.

So really can we afford to just keep on with the passive policy in the hope that the ridiculousness of it will induce others to move toward a new Bretton Woods?

Mr. WILLETT. Let me try some answers to that. I would defend the passive system as a reasonable alternative. It is the system which economically probably makes the most sense for world economy. The conception of passive policy that I have in mind is really very close to the functional equivalent of an inconvertible dollar or flexible exchange rate for the dollar, except that most countries would presumably stay pegged to the dollar, but that would be their decision.

Chairman RUESS. But a country that for neomercantilism reasons is just whacky about exports and thinks that a central bank, bulging with dollars, is a good thing to have, can frustrate the whole benign arrangement.

Mr. WILLETT. It certainly can in one sense.

Chairman REUSS. And is frustrating it right now.

Mr. WILLETT. I would tend to put that in the category of trade policy rather than balance of payments.

Chairman REUSS. Why, you could get the Japanese to abolish their import quotas and capital restraints and everything else, but if the yen is still fundamentally undervalued, we can't compete with them or with any other country in such a position.

Mr. WILLETT. That is quite true. But that type of problem is really probably the stickiest in a sense to get agreement on because it is really a trade problem. It is not an overall employment problem in the United States because what the passive policy will do, flexible exchange rate, if you want to call it that, in which we don't force other countries to appreciate against us because we really don't have any way to do that, means that our domestic policies are free to run the domestic economy the way we want to. And if we want to look over the past decade at causes of unemployment in the U.S. economy, I am sure that there has been much greater unemployment caused by not enough expansionary policies in the late 1950's and early 1960's than we have gotten from import competition from Japan and similar situations.

In other words, I don't think within the sort of conceivable range of mercantilism policies that other countries would follow we need be worried about American labor being unemployed except in the transitional basis, in response to a changing structure of—

Chairman Reuss. If the Japanese, due to an undervalued yen, take over the manufacture of steel, automobiles, electronics, textiles, to name a few, I wish you would tell me what you are going to do with those unemployed steelworkers, autoworkers, electronic workers, and textile workers? They are not mobile, they aren't going to leap into the services industries over night.

Mr. Willett. That is certainly true.

Chairman Reuss. And we don't have any mechanism for letting them remain idle and for compensating them out of revenues perhaps obtained from a huge sales tax on Japanese steel and automobiles and electronics and textiles which come in so cheaply they could stand a sales tax. If someone would work out such a proposition and table it then we can all discuss it, but it is really quite far out. So what we are left with is the prospect of considerable distress and unemployment and, what is worse, the prospect of a real protectionist lobby in this country which can set us on the downward paths of the 1930's.

Mr. Willett. I certainly do not want to underestimate the protectionist sentiment in this country but I think it really is important to distinguish between the trade aspect and a monetary aspect. In practice we may want to blend the two. But my remarks were directed primarily to the monetary aspect in which I think we have serious problems and I suggested an alternative by which we could deal with them.

I think you are correct in the area of trade problems. I think I tend to be somewhat more optimistic than you on the amount of transitional adjustment problems that will take place from the type of competition we are likely to get from Japan in the future but I certainly agree it is a very real problem. But if we hang reforming the international monetary system on solving that problem, I am very afraid we won't go anywhere. So I guess, being somewhat pragmatic, I would like to see us get progress where we may be able to.

If I could make just one other brief comment on the problem of the gold bugs, under a passive policy the way I mean it, we wouldn't worry if people came and bought our gold. The passive policy would be to not respond to people that did that. Let them take all the gold or maybe want to save a billion dollars or two. Say if you want the gold up to that amount come and take it.

Chairman Reuss. As you know, I am the antithesis of a gold bug. However, I am not at all sure that we would want to let all of our gold go or let it go down to a billion dollars worth. I would feel more comfortable in a world in which we don't have the new Bretton Woods as yet. I feel much more comfortable with a large chunk of the silly stuff still around unless somebody else, I won't mention any names, gets such a large part of the world monetary gold. Then gold price raising monkeyshine might be a feasible policy for them.

I think we should regard gold for that purpose as a strategic metal and be very thoughtful about what we do with it. So I don't think we are as immune from salami tactics as you do.

Mr. WILLETT. I would certainly agree with your basic point, but I mentioned a billion dollars. We can set it at $5 billion, $8 billion, whatever we decide for strategic purposes. We can even let it be known that if people want to convert dollars into gold up to *x* amount we will be glad to do that, after that we will go formally inconvertible. That to me would be the passive policy.

Chairman REUSS. Mr. Bergsten, in your statement you specifically reject the benign balance-of-payments policy and then you say, "The United States should adopt no new unilateral measures in an effort to reduce its balance-of-payments deficit."

I am not suggesting that those statements are necessarily inconsistent, but on the thought that they might be I want to ask you a few questions.

You suggest in your statement that we should phase out our present capital restraints. Well, I find much that is attractive in phasing these out. But if we did phase out our restraints on bank lending abroad and the Department of Commerce's foreign investments program, wouldn't that action add quite a bit to our basic deficit?

Our basic deficit, as you have said, is $2½ to $3 billion, and you go on to say that you think we can live with that while we are going for a new Bretton Woods.

Well, if you take off capital controls, certainly there has been testimony in our hearings here that our basic deficit would go up a good deal? Therefore, could we get by with no new unilateral measures?

Mr. BERGSTEN. Let me answer the first question first. As I understand the advocates of benign neglect, they would not only take no new measures but would do away with all existing measures immediately, including the present capital controls of the type you mentioned, the buy American policy, and presumably all other balance-of-payments controls which have sprung up over the years, in addition to not changing domestic economy policy on balance-of-payments grounds. I wouldn't interpret as benign neglect my saying that I would have no new policies aimed at reducing the balance-of-payments deficit (in a conventional sense), because I am not saying undo the present controls all of a sudden.

Chairman REUSS. Who in your judgment is a neglector so benign that he falls into this category?

Mr. BERGSTEN. Professor Willett here is a spokesman for the school and I could ask him whether he and some of his colleagues take the view. Some of the writings of Haberler and Willett, and Larry Krause, who are the main advocates in writing on benign neglect as of this date, would take that approach.

Mr. WILLETT. I would certainly say I would favor an orderly but swift withdrawal of the control measures.

Mr. BERGSTEN. It may be a timing difference. When I talk about a deliberate elimination I mean over a period of years, hopefully phasing them out as we phase in the basic changes in the monetary system which I advocated. Incidentally that is my other answer to your point.

I certainly am not advocating benign neglect when I advocate, from the U.S. national standpoint, a policy of negotiating the roles for the dollar for the first time, in an effort to achieve an effectively functioning monetary system. It seems the antithesis of benign neglect if one is willing to push, down the road, for basic changes in the system, including basic changes in the role of the dollar in an effort to get a better functioning system.

Chairman REUSS. Don't all of the benign neglectors want a new Bretton Woods the same as you? Mr. Halm does; Mr. Willett does.

Mr. BERGSTEN. Well, again it is a matter of—

Chairman REUSS. Far from trying to foment discord, I am trying to induce accord here.

Mr. BERGSTEN. Well—

Chairman REUSS. If you, for instance, say that you don't believe in benign neglect because you come out very strong for a new Bretton Woods, I suggest that as thus defined there really aren't any benign neglectors.

Mr. BERGSTEN. That would please me a great deal, Mr. Chairman.

Chairman REUSS. Anyway—

Mr. BERGSTEN. I think it may be a matter of the tactical approach to the second Bretton Woods.

Mr. Willett was just suggesting the possibility of shocking the rest of the world in that direction by abolishing the capital controls immediately.

Some people have suggested forcing the world toward a Bretton Woods by bringing down the gold window very rapidly. I think those are polar extremes. One would attempt to force adjustments by getting the U.S. exchange rate into a different position. Another would try to force adjustment by throwing out more dollars onto the rest of the world, and forcing them to change their exchange rates. Those are polarized tactical choices. . . .

Chairman REUSS. Your new broadened IMF or whatever would, if we had it now, have the power to recommend to Japan whatever adjustment of the yen rate is necessary to remove the fundamental disequilibrium. That is what you meant by presumptive rules.

Mr. BERGSTEN. A set of agreed rules that would point to the need. I would presume, whatever those rules were, they would now single out Japan as a candidate for revaluation.

Chairman REUSS. In the adjustment regime which would be part of the new Bretton Woods arrangement, would the dollar have the same capability of adjustment as other major currencies?

Mr. BERGSTEN. I think it probably should have. It certainly could technically, there would be no technical bar to it, with one exception though which should be mentioned.

And here I differ slightly with Professor Willett, who commented in his notion of a new Bretton Woods that the dollar would be just like all other currencies. I think it is impossible under any conceivable change in the monetary system for the dollar to wind up just like all other currencies. Even if you abolish totally the reserve currency role, the dollar would clearly continue to be used as the intervention currency and held at least in working balances by most other monetary authorities, and would continue to be used as the primary private transactions currency. So there would still be some asymmetry in the system because of those uses of the dollar. In any event, given the continued use of the dollar as an intervention currency, the means through which other countries intervene in the exchange markets to change their own exchange rates, there would have to be some special rules which govern exchange rate changes in the dollar.

Chairman REUSS. Like what?

Mr. BERGSTEN. When the dollar was contemplating an exchange rate change under presumptive criteria, other countries would have to be brought into the act; in fact, they would then have to intervene at different points in the exchange markets than they had the day before. The United States, technically, simply could not change the rate change. It all gets back to the fundamental point that it is more efficient, economically, for other countries to do the exchange rate changing, as long as the dollar remains the intervention currency. That raises some of the political problems I mentioned earlier but it remains a fact. This is one of the reasons I would oppose our unilaterally ending convertibility of the dollar into gold as an effort to get exchange rate changes now, since other countries could frustrate any efforts on the part of United States to change our exchange rate under whatever regime as long as the dollar remains the intervention currency, simply by maintaining the intervention points that they now do. . . .

Chairman REUSS. In your statement, Mr. Bergsten, you say that:

> United States action of this type would clearly be seen as an effort to build our trade balance and hence alter the structure of our balance of payments, which would be all too reminiscent of the competitive devaluations of the 1930's and thus hurt badly, rather than help, the crucial effort to combat protectionism around the world.

What in the world is wrong with the United States altering by an adjustment process the structure of its balance of payments? The suggestion isn't that the United States get into a great surplus position, but what is wrong with—

Mr. BERGSTEN. Well, I think there is—

Chairman REUSS (continuing). Trying to end the deficit?

Mr. BERGSTEN. There is nothing necessarily wrong with trying to change the structure of our balance of payments. This statement is in the context of the particular measure proposed to do so, and the comment refers to a tactical point. My view is that if we did unilaterally at some point in coldblood eliminate gold convertibility de jure, as has been suggested, that this would be read by the rest of the world as a policy similar to the beggar-thy-neighbor approaches of the earlier period. If one agrees with my earlier analysis, that our overall payments position is close to equilibrium, then I think such a move could be seen only as that. If you could psyche out the rest of the world to think that we do have a big overall balance-of-payments problem, and that this particular measure was necessary to solve it, even if we, therefore, got a sizable increase in our trade surplus that would be all right. However, I am afraid that would not be the reaction and that such a coldblooded move for ostensibly monetary reasons would be seen as part of the overall offensive we have launched, and I think properly so, to take a much tougher position on our trade policy.

7.5 *Other Disturbing Events*

The outlook for the dollar remained precarious even after the revaluations of the European currencies. The United States Treasury's gold stock was diminished by conversions of dollars into gold by France and Belgium in mid-May, and the *Wall Street Journal* disclosed that these purchases of gold reduced the Treasury's gold stock "to what is probably its lowest level since the end of World War II. Unless offset by undisclosed U.S. purchases of gold from other countries, the sales . . . would leave the U.S. gold stock at about $10.6 billion." [23] Speculation in gold intensified, and by mid-May the price of gold in private bullion markets reached the highest level since October 1969.

Few economists (outside of South Africa and France) advocated a rise in the price of gold. A notable exception was Sir Roy Harrod, biographer of John Maynard Keynes. Although Keynes had earlier denigrated gold as a "barbaric relic" and had sought its demonetization at Bretton Woods,[24] Harrod's view was now quite different.

TRIPLE THE DOLLAR PRICE OF GOLD*

To the Editor:

The gyrations of the world currency crisis of the last few days have been formidable. We may expect further crises in the future, unless something is done about it.

There is a very simple solution, which would, I feel quite confident, free us from crises of this kind for a few decades ahead. The Americans, by agreement with the International Monetary Fund, should raise the dollar price of gold.

We are supposed to be, but for some years have not in fact been, liv-

23. *Wall Street Journal* (May 13, 1971).
24. See pp. 33–35 above.
*Letters to the Editor, *New York Times*, May 18, 1971.

ing under the Bretton Woods system. This has two parts. One is that countries have to maintain exchange rates within fixed limits within their own territories. For this purpose they have been using the dollar as "the currency of intervention"; this is a convenient system, which has, however, no official sanction. The other part is that each country is obliged to pay gold in exchange for accumulations of its currency in the hands of other members. This obligation applies to all member currencies and not, as is sometimes asserted, to the dollar only. (Article VIII, 4a of Articles of Agreement of I.M.F.)

In recent years some countries have refrained from asking the Americans for gold in exchange for unwanted dollars, sometimes perhaps out of consideration for the Americans, sometimes perhaps under political pressure and recently because it was evident that there was not enough gold in Fort Knox to enable the Americans to honor their obligations.

Thus the Bretton Woods system has ceased to function. It will take many years for the Special Drawing Rights to become a sufficient substitute.

For some twenty years I have advocated a doubling of the dollar price of gold. But as the average of the dollar prices of goods has gone up about three times since President Roosevelt fixed the existing dollar price of gold, a trebling would seem to be appropriate ($105 = one ounce of gold). This would make the gold stock in Fort Knox worth about $36 billion.

And then a remarkable thing would happen. Much of the desire by other central banks to convert dollars into gold would fall right away. Recently there has been restiveness about holding dollars because of what is called "a credibility gap"; but with $36 billion of gold in Fort Knox this would end.

And then the dollar could indeed become the world's currency for practical purposes, which it certainly is not at present. Nothing could be more wrong-headed than to see gold as a sort of rival to the dollar. On the contrary it is via gold that the dollar could achieve its maximum usefulness in the world.

Some Americans have told me that owing to statements by Presidents Kennedy, Johnson and Nixon they feel bound in honor to maintain the dollar at $35 = one ounce of gold. There is no sense in this when the rest of the world does not want them to do so. It is as though a father promised an infant son a horse when he attained the age of twelve. When the boy does so, it turns out that he is entirely unathletic, would not go near a horse, still less ride on it. But the father says, "I have promised my son a horse and a horse he shall have." Further to this, the Americans have not been making the dollar de facto gold convertible at will. They have only provided a painted, wooden horse.

There might be some question of compensation. The sums involved would not be large in relation to the new situation.

Nothing said above is inconsistent with the idea of having more flexible exchange rates, which I have not discussed.

ROY HARROD

An economics correspondent of the *New York Times* wrote that

> after the second floating of the German mark last month, Mr. Connally (U.S. Secretary of the Treasury) assailed the Germans for unpegging their exchange rate "for domestic reasons" and threatening to tear apart "the essential fabric of the system and institutions that serve us all."
>
> By contrast, the President's economists have privately hailed the floating of the mark as a victory for United States policy, which they dislike calling "benign neglect," because it upsets foreigners.[25]

The report went on to note that

> pressure has been building on Japan to revalue the yen upward. But as long as the yen stays pegged at 0.27777 United States cents, the Administration's economists cannot regard the recent crisis as having been truly "constructive. . . ." Mr. Connally has pledged that the dollar will not be devalued. Similarly, Premier Sato of Japan has pledged that the yen will not be revalued upward.
>
> But, if the dollar is overvalued in relation to the yen and other currencies, as Administration economists think it is, American goods suffer in international markets—and even in their domestic market against foreign competition.[26]

Reports of the United States balance of trade were certainly underscoring the difficulties of the United States trading position, particularly vis-à-vis Japan. In April, May, June, and July, imports exceeded exports, and the balance of trade threatened to show an annual deficit for the first time since 1893. For the four months the trade deficit averaged almost $280 million per month or an annual rate of more than $3.3 billion. For the first seven months of 1971 there was a trade deficit of $676 million,

25. Leonard S. Silk, "Monetary Challenge," *New York Times* (June 9, 1971).
26. Ibid.

whereas there had been a surplus of almost $2 billion in the same period in 1970.

In contrast, during the first six months of 1971, Japan had a large current account surplus, and at the end of June, official reserves amounted to $7.8 billion, compared with $2.0 billion at the end of 1967, and $3.7 billion at the end of 1969.[27] Almost two-fifths of the United States over-all deficit and 70 per cent of its trade deficit in the first half of 1971 was with Japan.

Finally, Rep. Henry S. Reuss gave the authority of his Joint Economic subcommittee to demands for altering the exchange value of the dollar. On June 3, 1971, Reuss introduced a "sense of Congress" resolution in the House of Representatives that would formally end the United States commitment to sell gold to foreign central banks at $35 an ounce and would eventually have the Federal Reserve System support the exchange value of the dollar, as other countries do, by operations in the foreign exchange market. Reuss proposed an interim period during which the dollar would float, with the aim of removing present "disequilibrium" in exchange rates, particularly against the Japanese yen. He stated; "The United States under the present monetary system unnecessarily cripples itself by its inability to alter its exchange rate with other countries. . . . Only by closing the gold window and letting the dollar find a newer and sounder relationship with the yen can we avoid the deterioration of our trading position and a return to trade autarky." [28]

A spokesman for the Treasury, however, was quick to state that the Reuss plan was "certainly not the position of the United States Government." He pointed to a statement by Treasury Secretary Connally the previous week in Munich that "we are not going to devalue the dollar."

Again, on August 6, Representative Reuss' subcommittee reported that based on hearings held by the subcommittee in June, the subcommittee came to the "inescapable conclusion" that the dollar is "overvalued" in relation to most other currencies, and that a "new external value for the dollar" had to be found. The United States should urge the IMF to pressure other countries to revalue their currencies upward, the subcommittee

27. International Monetary Fund, *1971 Annual Report*, pp. 12, 93.
28. *New York Times* (June 4, 1971).

said, but warned that if the IMF continues to fail to take such strong actions, "the U.S. may have no choice but to take unilateral action to go off gold and establish new dollar parities." The report said that the United States could announce that it will no longer be the only country stabilizing its currency by dealing in gold and will intervene by dealing in foreign currencies as other countries do. The subcommittee also suggested that the United States might resort to a "transitional float or a controlled rate of depreciation until the reestablishment of an appropriate U.S. balance-of-payments position." [29]

In response to this report, the Treasury once again insisted that the "limited hearings" did not reflect or develop any wide body of congressional opinion in support of the views expressed earlier by Representative Reuss. The Treasury reaffirmed its position: "No discussions are planned or anticipated with respect to exchange-rate realignments at the IMF or elsewhere." [30]

On the same day—August 6—that Representative Reuss' subcommittee recommended exchange-rate realignment to eliminate the United States deficit, the United States Treasury reported a loss of gold and other reserve assets totaling more than $1 billion. Over the following week, the flight from the dollar sharply accelerated as $3.7 billion moved across the exchanges and into central bank hands.[31]

At the close of the week, on August 14, an editorial in *The Financial Times* (London) was headlined "The $ Under Pressure."

> The troubles of the dollar have become a permanent part of the international scene, but its difficulties during the past week have been worse than ever. It has been weak in relation to all the main European currencies, and the steady pressure has been so strong at times, that central banks, including the Bank of England, have offered support in the market. The D-

29. *Action Now to Strengthen the Dollar*, Report of the subcommittee on International Exchange and Payments of the Joint Economic Committee, 92nd Congress, 1st Session (August 1971).

30. *Wall Street Journal* (August 9, 1971).

31. Charles A. Coombs, "Treasury and Federal Reserve Foreign Exchange Operations," *Monthly Review of Federal Reserve Bank of New York* (October 1971), p. 215.

Mark has floated upwards to a premium of more than 8 per cent above its original dollar parity. . . . When the Swiss authorities, the sternest custodians of the fixed exchange system, limit dollar convertibility, as they did briefly at one point in the week, it may be assumed that uncertainty is unusually great. . . .

The American symptoms are familiar by this time—a continuing deterioration of the trade balance, a steady outflow of the capital account and a dwindling gold reserve. This last problem has become particularly ominous during the last few months as the gold reserve shrunk towards the magic $10,000 million figure which the authorities have traditionally regarded as the minimum safety level. The reluctance of other countries to accept further accumulations of dollar holdings is once again becoming acute. . . . In the light of all this there is a general disposition to agree with the Reuss Committee's diagnosis that the dollar is overvalued.

No one doubts that the objective must be to produce a more realistic exchange relationship between the dollar and the currencies of America's chief economic partners. The difficulty is to find a way of achieving this which does not meet apparently insuperable political objections.[32]

The next day the *New York Times'* economics analyst wrote:

There is one overriding feature of the present situation of monetary turmoil that must be reported: Nobody really knows what to do. . . . In this kind of situation, what happens is that each government must react on a very short-term basis to the events that threaten its own situation—its economy's internal liquidity, the competitiveness of its export industries, its rate of inflation, the problem of imports. . . . [It is] a time when very good minds are groping and when nations sometimes find themselves forced into actions by the pressure of events rather than collective judgment.

It is not, as far as can be seen now, the kind of time when a meeting of the "Group of Ten" big financial powers can settle everything, or even anything. It is a time, perhaps, when events are in control and when no predictions are worth very much.[33]

32. *Financial Times* (August 14, 1971).
33. Edwin L. Dale, Jr., "Monetary Strife: No One Wants It, But . . ." *New York Times* (August 15, 1971).

That night—Sunday, August 15, 1971—President Nixon announced on television his New Economic Program of domestic and international economic measures. The private and public pressure to convert the dollar into other assets—foreign currencies and ultimately reserve assets or their equivalent—had become overwhelming.[34] Action was being forced by "the pressure of events rather than collective judgment": market pressures across the international exchanges—not the collective judgment of another Bretton Woods conference—were dictating policy reactions.

7.6 August 15, 1971

On August 15, 1971, President Nixon suspended convertibility of the dollar into gold. The United States Treasury ceased selling gold to other governments at $35 an ounce in order to bring about devaluation of the dollar by allowing the dollar to float. Other measures were also announced to protect the nation's trade and payments position: a temporary surcharge of generally 10 per cent on goods imported into the United States; a 10 per cent cut in foreign aid; and a request to other nations "to bear their fair share of the burden of defending freedom around the world." Coupled with the international measures were a freeze on wages and prices and some changes in domestic taxes.

The President called his range of actions "the most comprehensive new economic policy to be undertaken in this nation in four decades." On international monetary arrangements he stated,

> We must protect the position of the American dollar as a pillar of monetary stability around the world.
> In the past seven years, there has been an average of one international monetary crisis every year. Who gains from these crises? Not the workingman, not the investor, not the real producers of wealth. The gainers are the international money speculators. Because they thrive on crises, they help to create them.
> In recent weeks, the speculators have been waging an all-out war on the American dollar. The strength of a nation's

34. *Economic Report of the President* (January 1972), p. 148.

currency is based on the strength of that nation's economy—
and the American economy is by far the strongest in the
world. Accordingly, I have directed the Secretary of the Treasury to take the action necessary to defend the dollar against
the speculators.

I have directed Secretary Connally to suspend temporarily
the convertibility of the dollar into gold or other reserve assets, except in amounts and conditions determined to be in
the interest of monetary stability and in the best interests of
the United States.

Let me lay to rest the bugaboo of devaluation. What does
this action mean for you? If you want to buy a foreign car, or
take a trip abroad, market conditions may cause your dollar to
buy slightly less. But if you are among the overwhelming majority who buy American-made products in America your dollar will be worth just as much tomorrow as it is today. The effect of this action will be to stabilize the dollar.

This action will not win us any friends among the international money traders. But our primary concern is with the
American workers, and with fair competition around the
world.

To our friends abroad, including the many responsible
members of the international banking community who are
dedicated to stability and the flow of trade, I give this assurance: The United States has always been, and will continue
to be, a forward-looking and trustworthy trading partner. In
full cooperation with the International Monetary Fund and
those who trade with us, we will press for the necessary reforms to set up an urgently needed new international monetary system. Stability and equal treatment is in everybody's
best interest. I am determined that the American dollar must
never again be a hostage in the hands of the international
speculators.[35]

FUND NOTIFIED OF U.S. DECISION ON GOLD *

The U.S. authorities, in a letter from the Secretary of the Treasury to the
Managing Director, have notified the International Monetary Fund that, effective August 15, 1971, the United States no longer, for the settlement of international transactions, in fact, freely buys and sells gold. The United States
will continue to collaborate with the Fund to promote exchange stability, to
maintain orderly exchange arrangements with other members, and to avoid
competitive exchange alterations. The Fund notes that exchange transac-

35. IMF, *International Financial News Survey* (August 25, 1971).
* *IMF Press Release No. 853*, August 20, 1971.

tions in the territories of the United States have been occurring outside the limits around par, and the actions taken by the U.S. authorities do not at the present time ensure that transactions between their currency and the currencies of other members take place within their territory only within the limits around par.

The Fund notes the circumstances which have led the U.S. authorities to take the actions described above. The Fund emphasizes the undertaking of members to collaborate with it to promote exchange stability, to maintain orderly exchange arrangements with other members, and to avoid competitive exchange alterations, and therefore welcomes the intention of the U.S. authorities to act in accordance with this undertaking.

The Fund will remain in close consultation with the authorities of the United States and the other members with a view to the prompt achievement of a viable structure of exchange rates on the basis of parities established and maintained in accordance with the Articles of Agreement.

An analyst summarized the political aspects of the New Economic Policy in these terms:

> In the circumstances, the combined requirements of domestic economic management and of domestic political strategy for a President who clearly wanted re-election for a second term in 1972 were compelling. To these, clearly, international political objectives took third place; Dr. Henry Kissinger was not present and the State Department was not represented at Camp David where the package of August 15 was prepared. Mr. Schweitzer of the Fund was told only half an hour before the President went on television. The United States had decided that a forcing bid would anticipate trouble in the market and subdue the recalcitrance of the surplus trading partners. The main parameters of this policy were therefore ideological or political rather than narrowly financial or economic. The United States did not want to lose any more gold. It did not want (or feel able) to correct its balance of payments deficit by cutting either its capital outflow or its military spending abroad. Mr. Nixon badly needed to reinforce public belief in his own leadership. The co-operation of the rest of the Group of Ten was needed if the stability of the system was to be preserved against the depredations of the market. If this co-operation could not be obtained by persuasion, then it must be obtained by using such leverage as the wealth and military power of the United States gave it. The question was how susceptible the allies would prove to this leverage." [36]

36. Strange, "The Dollar Crises," p. 204.

The tariff surcharge, severance of the gold-dollar link, and investment tax credit for purchases of domestic capital machinery affected the United States' international economic obligations under the GATT and IMF. About these obligations, an international law expert wrote:

> The violation of international obligations by major countries is always a worrisome thing. The impact of such actions on the general international legal system causes justifiable concern whenever the departure from such obligations occurs. Yet in the specific actions [of the United States] . . . there are some remarkable parallels. As to the tariff surcharges and the floating exchange rates, the parallels are most strong. In these cases both the GATT and the IMF norms have been departed from on a number of previous occasions without meaningful sanction. In fact a sort of *de facto* tolerance of the practices has appeared to develop. In each of the circumstances where the actions occurred, including the most recent departures, there is a respectable body of opinion that the "illegal" practice was desirable and even necessary from an economic policy viewpoint. Yet despite this, the treaty norms have not been amended or changed to keep pace with changed circumstances and current thinking, partly because of the relative rigidity and difficulty of amendment of the international institutions.[37]

8. DEVELOPMENTS AFTER AUGUST 15

According to the Council of Economic Advisers, the actions and the positions taken by the United States in subsequent negotiations linked the questions of improved access to foreign markets for United States exports and a better sharing of the financial burdens of mutual security to "the basic issue of exchange-rate realignment."

THE ISSUE OF EXCHANGE RATE REALIGNMENT *

The issue of exchange-rate realignment immediately raised some fundamental questions.
1. How should realignment be achieved? Should it be done through market forces (freely floating rates) or through negotiations?

37. John H. Jackson, "The New Economic Policy and United States International Obligations," *American Journal of International Law*, (January 1972), p. 117.
* *Economic Report of the President*, January 1972, pp. 149–50, 154–56.

TABLE I. U.S. Balance of Payments, 1960–71
(Billions of dollars)

Type of Transaction	1960–64 Average	1965–69 Average	1968	1969	1970	1971 Fi 3 Quarte
Merchandise trade balance	5.4	2.8	0.6	0.7	2.1	−1.7
Exports	21.7	31.3	33.6	36.5	42.0	44.3
Imports	−16.2	−28.5	−33.0	−35.8	−39.9	−46.1
Military transactions, net	−2.4	−2.9	−3.1	−3.3	−3.4	−2.7
Balance on investment income [2]	3.9	5.8	6.2	6.0	6.2	7.5
U.S. investment abroad	5.1	8.6	9.2	10.5	11.4	12.0
Foreign investments in the United States	−1.2	−2.8	−3.0	−4.6	−5.2	−4.6
Balance on other services	−1.0	−1.2	−1.2	−1.3	−1.4	−1.4
BALANCE ON GOODS AND SERVICES [3]	5.9	4.4	2.5	2.0	3.6	1.6
Private remittances and government pensions	−.7	−1.1	−1.2	−1.3	−1.4	−1.4
BALANCE ON GOODS, SERVICES, AND REMITTANCES	5.2	3.3	1.3	.7	2.2	.1
Government grants [4]	−1.8	−1.8	−1.7	−1.6	−1.7	−1.9
BALANCE ON CURRENT ACCOUNT	3.3	1.5	−.4	−.9	.4	−1.8
Balance on direct private investments	−1.8	−3.0	−2.9	−2.4	−3.5	−5.9
U.S. direct investments abroad	−1.8	−3.3	−3.2	−3.3	−4.4	−5.5
Foreign direct investments in the United States	.1	.3	.3	.8	1.0	−.3
Balance on other long-term capital flows [5]	−2.2	−.6	1.9	.4	([6])	−2.5
BALANCE ON CURRENT ACCOUNT AND LONG-TERM CAPITAL	−.7	−2.2	−1.3	−2.9	−3.0	−10.2
Balance on nonliquid short-term private capital flows	−1.1	−.2	.2	−.6	−.5	−2.6

2. If the realignment were to be arranged through negotiations, how large an improvement in the U.S. balance would be required? How should the counterpart of this improvement be shared among other nations? And, finally, what set of changes in exchange rates would this require?

Starting in September, the United States pursued both approaches to realignment. The second required an explicit analysis of the U.S. balance of payments.

Balance-of-Payments Analysis

Any analysis of the nature and size of U.S. external disequilibrium must begin with an examination of balance-of-payments accounts. These data, for

Type of Transaction	1960–64 Average	1965–69 Average	1968	1969	1970	1971 First 3 Quarters [1]
rrors and unrecorded transactions	− 1.0	− 1.0	− .5	− 2.6	− 1.1	− 11.4
locations of special drawing rights					.9	.7
:T LIQUIDITY BALANCE	− 2.8	− 3.4	− 1.6	− 6.1	− 3.8	− 23.4
ansactions in U.S. liquid short-term assets, net	− .1	.1	− .6	.1	.2	− 1.0
ansactions in U.S. liquid liabilities to other than foreign official agencies, net	.8	3.3	3.8	8.7	− 6.2	− 6.7
'FICIAL RESERVE TRANSACTIONS BALANCE	− 2.2	([6])	1.6	2.7	− 9.8	− 31.2
nanced by change in: Nonliquid U.S. Government and U.S. bank liabilities to foreign official agencies [7]	.1	.7	2.3	− 1.0	− .3	− .7
Liquid liabilities to foreign official agencies	1.1	− .6	− 3.1	− .5	7.6	28.5
U.S. official reserve assets, net	1.0	([6])	− .9	− 1.2	2.5	3.4

[1] Average of the first 3 quarters at seasonally adjusted annual rates.
[2] Includes direct investment fees and royalties.
[3] Excludes transfers under military grants.
[4] Excludes military grants of goods and services.
[5] Excludes official reserve transactions and includes transactions in some short-term U.S. Govern-
ent assets.
[6] Less than $0.05 billion.
[7] Excludes U.S. Government nonliquid liabilities to foreign official agencies other than official re-
rve agencies.
NOTE: Detail will not necessarily add to totals because of rounding.
SOURCE: Department of Commerce.

the first 3 quarters of 1971 (at seasonally adjusted annual rates) and for earlier periods, are shown in Table 1.

Balance on Current Account and Long-Term Capital

The current account balance combined with the balance on long-term capital account plus Government grants provides an important yardstick (sometimes called the "basic balance") for measuring and assessing the fundamental position of a nation relative to other countries. Starting in mid-1971
the official U.S. presentations of balance-of-payments data have begun to
recognize the importance of this yardstick, and it is now published as a separate "balance."

In 1970 the United States was in deficit on basic balance by $3.0 billion. Between 1970 and the first 3 quarters of 1971 the balance worsened by $7.1 billion to reach an annual rate of $10.2 billion. Of this, $2.2 billion was due to a worsening of the balance on current account and $4.9 billion to a net increase in the long-term capital outflow. Although the basic balance generally reflects underlying forces, it is sometimes subject to short-run movements. This appeared to be the case in 1971.

The Size of the Required Correction

Negotiations on exchange-rate realignments which began soon after August 15 required an answer to the question: By how much should the United States improve its basic balance in order to achieve a stable equilibrium? The U.S. representatives presented an analysis which showed that the required turnaround was about $13 billion.

Alternative Routes to Realignment

Developments after August 15 made one fact clear: The immediate operational issue facing governments was a realignment of the pattern of exchange rates, especially a realignment of the U.S. dollar relative to the other major currencies.

Among the questions associated with this operation were these:

1. How should the industrial nations arrive at a new set of equilibrium exchange rates? One route was to let all currencies float freely for a transitional period until a new set of equilibrium rates emerged. The other was to negotiate a multilateral shift to a new set of fixed rates.

2. If the second route was to be used, should the United States "contribute" to the realignment by a formal devaluation of the dollar against gold? Or should negotiations concentrate on exchange rates among currencies, expressed in dollars, with the question of the gold price being left to subsequent negotiations on longer-range issues?

3. How large was the readjustment required to restore the U.S. balance of payments to an equilibrium position? How large an average change in the dollar's exchange rate did this require? How should the effect of the proposed readjustment in the U.S. position be shared among other nations?

Mutually acceptable answers to all of these questions depended in part on related issues. The inclusion of trade practices and the question of mutual security costs as part of the overall negotiations involved other members of foreign governments besides financial officials. This affected the tempo and procedure as well as the substance of the negotiations.

When foreign exchange markets opened a week after August 15, the situation was described as follows.

WIDELY DIFFERING MONETARY POLICIES *

LONDON—The world appeared little, if any, closer to a new monetary system after a week's closedown of major foreign exchange markets and a hasty round of conferences and discussions among major nations.

Instead, world money markets will reopen today under an "every man for himself" basis of widely differing national monetary policies. There will be controlled floats, fixed parities with wider bands on each side of the rigid figure, two-tier systems and, in one case, the worst action from the standpoint of the U.S. balance of payments: an outright devaluation against the dollar. Israel cut the dollar value of its pound 20%.

Not one major industrial nation has yet accepted the course of action which President Nixon recommended a week ago when, cutting the dollar's tie to gold, he urged foreign nations with strong currencies to raise the stated value of their currencies against the dollar.

The U.S. would like such increases in the parities of strong currencies since politically this would be the easiest way to, in effect, devalue the sick dollar. Such currency revision would improve the U.S. trade balance by raising the cost of imports into the U.S. while cutting the price of America's goods on the world marketplace.

This outcome may be difficult to arrange. Common Market nations still are split after their abortive attempt to devise a joint monetary policy. Japan welcomes Europe's disunity, using it to stall its own monetary decisions. Cautious Switzerland is so worried that it may keep its money markets closed all today until money trends become evident.

While it's impossible to predict just what will happen to the dollar when foreign exchange markets reopen, an unofficial and spotty survey of foreign exchange dealers here and on the Continent shows expectations of some improvement in dollar rates at the start of trading.

This may be due to technical features of the market. People in international finance were dumping dollars so assiduously just before markets closed that they may have oversold their positions, dealers say. There are bills to be paid in dollars and this may require some dollar buying at the start of trading.

Moreover, there are indications that some central banks are ready to intervene in markets should the dollar seem likely to decline sharply. This, it's hoped, may preserve some semblance of order in the markets.

The currency uncertainties have, of course, led to massive flows of short-term capital out of the U.S. In a report on world financial mar-

* *Wall Street Journal*, August 23, 1971.

kets, economists for Morgan Guaranty Trust Co. estimate such flows at
$13 billion so far this year, making up more than half of the $22 billion
deficit estimated for the U.S. balance of payments on an official settlements basis so far in 1971.

While European moneymen generally favor a return to fixed parities as soon as it can be arranged, nobody is very hopeful about quick
return after seeing the way Common Market nations split in Brussels.
Some American government sources have expressed the belief that it
may take until the end of this year or into 1972 before money markets
sort themselves out and a new monetary system can be introduced.

Some sources in Europe, however, think the world may stumble
along a lot longer before finding a solution, and even then it may be
only a jerry-built affair. "We have missed an important opportunity,"
says Sicco Mansholt, vice president of the Common Market governing
body, speaking about the Brussels meeting that saw the six nations attempt to work out a joint policy flounder on division between France
and Germany.

France insisted on sticking to a two-tier system that, if it works, effectively would cancel out any trade advantage America had hoped to
gain by floating its dollar. Germany sought a joint float of all Common
Market currencies against the dollar and tight parities within the bloc.

New developments aren't expected on the Common Market front
until the next meeting of the group's finance ministers Sept. 13 in
Brussels. "It isn't unreasonable to give oneself a certain delay for
reflections," comments Valery Giscard d'Estaing, France's finance
minister.

That nonchalant attitude causes many to believe that France, along
with Japan, will be the biggest footdraggers when it comes to reform
of the monetary system. France wants gold to play an important role in
any such reform and would like to downgrade the dollar. . . .

In capsule form, here is how major nations will be handling foreign
exchange when markets reopen today:

Britain—Pound sterling will float from a base of $2.38 to the pound,
a base which will be protected by the Bank of England.

West Germany—Deutschmark will continue the float that was in effect when markets closed Aug. 13.

France—A two-tier market is being introduced, with the official
franc parity of 5.55415 to the dollar being maintained for commercial
transactions. The rate for financial, tourist and other transactions will
float.

Italy—The market will open with the lire at its old official parity of
625 to the dollar. As the Bank of Italy says it won't intervene in the
market, however, the dollar will float. But Italy will hold the tourist
dollar at 618.5 lire at least through Monday evening.

Switzerland—Money markets won't open this morning although
they might in the afternoon if the monetary situation is clarified.

Netherlands—The guilder will continue to float against other currencies as it had been doing up to closing of markets Aug. 13. However, Belgium, Holland, and Luxembourg will seek to maintain pre-crisis rates among themselves, thus creating a two-tier system, but one far different from France's.

Belgium—Francs will float with the central bank expected to intervene to control that float and to maintain intra-Benelux parities.

Norway—The krone will be revalued when the exchange market opens today. The new exchange rates are expected to be announced before noon.

Japan—Money markets, open all last week, again will open with yen parity unchanged. The Bank of Japan, however, probably will have to continue massive dollar purchases to keep the yen's dollar value from rising. (Such purchases have already boosted Japan's holdings of gold and foreign exchange, mostly dollars, $3.7 billion since Aug. 1 to a total of some $11.6 billion, United Press International reports.)

It's evident in Europe that Japan welcomes the Common Market's inability to formulate a joint monetary policy. "We can't act until Europe does something," says a Japanese official observer of the Brussels meeting. He explains that if West European nations raise their parities, Japan could go along, confident that it could retain its European markets. But if Japan alone raised the value of its yen, it would lose European as well as American markets.

There seems to be another reason why Japan will stall as long as it can before making any change in its parity. Customarily, Japanese businessmen use dollars in writing their international trading contracts. In recent days, Japanese have been writing in clauses to protect themselves against a yen revaluation.

But there still are tens of thousands of contracts that don't have such protection clauses. Thus, Japanese businessmen with such contracts would have to take the losses of the currency changes, without any chance of passing them along to customers under the old contracts.

DEMAND PRESSURES ON THE YEN *

The worldwide speculation against the dollar building up in late July and early August [1971] led to even greater demand pressures on the yen than before. Even though the Bank of Japan was holding the yen rate at its upper limit by absorbing dollars daily, the exchange control apparatus left much of the demand for yen unsatisfied, and the apparatus itself was subjected to great strain. Because of the time difference, when President Nixon announced the United States mea-

* Charles A. Coombs, "Treasury and Federal Reserve Foreign Exchange Operations," *Monthly Review of Federal Reserve Bank of New York*, October 1971, pp. 233–34.

sures on Sunday night, August 15, it was already Monday morning in Tokyo and the market was open for trading. The Japanese authorities nevertheless kept the market open the remainder of that day and through the rest of the week as well.

With dealers all around the world now convinced more than ever that a revaluation of the yen was imminent, the Bank of Japan had to absorb dollars on a massive scale over the following days, despite reinforcement of exchange control policies. Japanese banks, in particular, liquidated their long positions in dollars by converting into yen the dollars they were borrowing from every possible source in the United States as well from the Euro-dollar market. Finally, after further very large exchange gains on August 26 and 27, the Japanese authorities decided to "suspend temporarily the existing fluctuation margin for buying and selling quotations of foreign exchange, while maintaining the present parity of the yen". The vast inflow during August was reflected in a $4.4 billion gain in official reserves for the month as a whole.

In Tokyo, on August 28, the spot yen immediately rose to a premium of 4.7 per cent over the ceiling. The rate pushed gradually higher through September, despite substantial further purchases of dollars by the Japanese authorities and some additional tightening of exchange control measures. . . . The Japanese authorities subsequently eased their restrictions slightly, but some payments problems persisted through September. By early October the yen rate had risen to a premium of almost 8 per cent over the previous ceiling."

8.1 *"Group of 9" Plus United States*

During the six weeks between the announcement of August 15 and the annual meeting of the IMF at the end of September, there was considerable sparring between the United States and the other members of the Group of 10—the other leading industrial nations of the world, notably the EEC countries and Japan.

The EEC countries could not agree on a united position after the announcement of August 15. The French preferred a two-tier exchange market, and agreement on a joint float among Common Market currencies was impossible. A correspondent for *The Times* (London) philosophized: "What went wrong? After the best part of 15 hours discussion together of how to respond to the dollar crisis, the Common Market countries, ended up where they started, with no common position. When the exchange markets open on Monday, every country—including Britain—is going to go its own way.

Yet here was an opportunity—literally a golden opportunity, since the American decision to break the dollar's link with gold was what the crisis was all about—for the Six to hammer out a European approach. . . .

After all, the idea of European nations coming together to deal on equal terms with the United States is part of the rationale of the European Community. The crisis meeting was a chance to do so, not for theoretical reasons, but because there was a clear and urgent need for combined action. . . .

The truth is the meeting went wrong for the simple reason that the French and the Germans did not agree, and national positions, whether right or wrong in logic, prevailed as they usually do over Community theory.[38]

At meetings of the Group of 10, Treasury Secretary Connally insisted that the United States should acquire a $13 billion annual improvement in its balance-of-payments position, with a favorable trade balance of $7 to $8 billion annually. "It isn't being produced as a negotiating figure, it states our position accurately," Connally said in contending that the $13 billion surplus goal was a conservative figure.[39] And to achieve this, Connally was intent on using the import surcharge as a bargaining weapon. He told the finance ministers of the other nations present that they were making too big an issue about the surcharge. He denied that the surcharge was a political action, aimed at garnering votes in the next presidential election. But he refused to specify any timetable for removing the surcharge. "The issues involved, correcting our balance of payments, are more important than the time factor for the surcharge," Connally said. He did emphasize, though, that the surcharge was introduced "as a temporary measure." It will be removed, he stated, when it becomes clear that progress is being made toward a realignment of currencies and toward a sharing of United States political and military burdens around the globe.[40]

The other countries requested not only removal of the surcharge but also devaluation of the dollar directly through an increase in the price of gold above the official $35 an ounce. Japanese Finance Minister Mizuta was especially emphatic

38. *The Times* (August 20, 1971).
39. *Wall Street Journal* (September 16, 1971).
40. Ibid.

that a precondition to any Japanese contribution to a currency-parity realignment would be that all countries take part in it, including the United States.

8.2 *Position of the IMF*

Recognizing the serious implications for the future of the IMF, Mr. Pierre-Paul Schweitzer, managing director of the IMF, responded quickly to the announcement of President Nixon's new economic policy. In a cable sent to the 118 governors of the IMF, he said,

> The recent developments which have overtaken the international monetary system give great cause for concern but at the same time create the opportunity for strengthening the system.
> Unless prompt action is taken, the prospect before us is one of disorder and discrimination in currency and trade relationships which will seriously disrupt trade and undermine the system which has served the world well and has been the basis for effective collaboration for a quarter of a century. We must not sacrifice the efforts and achievements of the postwar period, which I fear are in jeopardy.
> Piecemeal approaches to change are not likely to yield beneficial results even for a single or a few countries, and much less for the whole community of countries represented in the fund. In my view, it is vitally important to take prompt collective and collaborative action in the interest of the prosperity of all members.[41]

At the opening of the IMF's annual meeting, Schweitzer again argued that it would "be desirable" if "all the major countries involved were to make a contribution to the realignment of currencies." He also declared that "real dangers are inherent in a prolongation of the present impasse," citing especially the possibilities of "serious disarray" in currency and trade affairs and "an abandonment of rules of law providing for orderly and just international economic relations."

At the close of their meeting, the board of governors of the IMF unanimously adopted the following resolution:

41. *The Times* (August 20, 1971).

TEXT OF RESOLUTION BY IMF GOVERNORS *

Washington, Oct. 1—
Whereas the present international monetary situation contains the dangers of instability and disorder in currency and trade relationships but also offers the opportunity for constructive changes in the international monetary system; and

Whereas it is of the utmost importance to avoid the aforesaid dangers and assure continuance of the progress made in national and international well-being in the past quarter of a century; and

Whereas prompt action is necessary to resume the movement toward a free and multilateral system in which trade and capital flows can contribute to the integration of the world economy and the rational allocation of resources throughout the world; and

Whereas consideration should be given to the improvement of the international monetary system and the adjustment process; and

Whereas the orderly conduct of the operations of the International Monetary Fund should be resumed as promptly as possible in the interest of all members; and

Whereas all members of the fund should participate in seeking solutions of the aforesaid problems;

Now, therefore, the board of governors hereby resolves that:

[I]

Members of the fund are called upon to collaborate with the fund and with each other in order, as promptly as possible, to

(a) Establish a satisfactory structure of exchange rates, maintained within appropriate margins, for the currencies of members, together with the reduction of restrictive trade and exchange practices, and

(b) Facilitate resumption of the orderly conduct of the operations of the fund.

[II]

Members are called upon to collaborate with the fund and with each other in efforts to bring about

(a) A reversal of the tendency in present circumstances to maintain and extend restrictive trade and exchange practices, and

(b) Satisfactory arrangements for the settlement of international transactions which will contribute to the solution of the problems involved in the present international monetary situation.

[III]

The executive directors are requested:

(a) To make reports to the board of governors without delay on the measures that are necessary or desirable for the improvement or reform of the international monetary system; and

* *New York Times*, October 1, 1971.

(b) For the purpose of (a), to study all aspects of the international monetary system, including the role of reserve currencies, gold, and special drawing rights, convertibility, the provisions of the articles with respect to exchange rates, and the problems caused by destabilizing capital movement; and

(c) When reporting, to include, if possible, the texts of any amendments of the articles of agreement which they consider necessary to give effect to their recommendations.

8.3 *A Way Out?*

Although no definitive action was taken at the IMF's annual meeting, the United States began to adopt a more conciliatory posture. In his speech at the meeting, Secretary Connally offered to remove the 10 per cent import surcharge "if other governments will make tangible progress toward dismantling specific barriers to trade over coming weeks and will be prepared to allow market realities freely to determine exchange rates for their currencies for a transitional period." It was clear that the United States was now concerned about the "widely varying degrees of intervention and controls" that resulted in "dirty floats" instead of allowing free floating according to "the objective, impersonal forces of the market place." [42] The United States still wanted a greater appreciation of other currencies, particularly the yen and mark.

On foreign demands that the United States formally devalue the dollar by raising the official $35-an-ounce gold price, Mr. Connally was also more conciliatory than before the IMF meeting. He still attacked the idea as "patently a retrogressive step in terms of our objective to reduce, if not eliminate the role of gold in any new monetary system"; but he was also willing to describe a change in the gold price as "of no economic significance."

Why the change in the United States's negotiating stance? Perhaps it was realized, as one commentator suggested, that,

> One mistake the Nixon Administration may be making is overestimating its bargaining strength. There are signs of that in connection with the 10 per cent import surcharge imposed in violation of agreed international rules. There seems to be

42. *Wall Street Journal* (October 1, 1971).

an assumption that other countries, especially Japan, will find the surcharge so painful that they will have to come to terms.

But Japan is not so dependent on trade as we may think: exports are just 10 per cent of her fast-rising gross national product. And Japan is skillful and flexible enough so that she may well be able to reorient her trade and wait out the surcharge.[43]

Again, a report from the IMF meeting stated:

The language of diplomats runs to understatement and euphemism. Yet the worry is genuine here—and people are expressing it in the corridors and lounges—that if prompt action is not taken to end this crisis, the world economy and the political and military alliances among Western nations will be seriously damaged.

One seasoned observer here contends that warnings of these dangers have been getting through to President Nixon—and that this is the basic reason for the moderation of the United States tone at this meeting.

Spokesmen of other nations are also striving to reduce the tensions and to work out constructive solutions to the immediate and longer-term problems of the international monetary system. . . . But building a new system will be a challenge of the first magnitude to the intellectual ability, diplomacy and political skill of the United States and its major partners.[44]

Two months later the Group of 10 finance ministers again met in Rome. But now the G-10 meeting was overshadowed by the forthcoming summit meetings between President Nixon and President Pompidou of France, Prime Minister Heath of Britain, and Premier Sato of Japan. In a press conference after the meeting, Secretary Connally said that the meeting had discussed a great many hypothetical situations and had dealt with specific percentages and figures relating to the over-all magnitude of the currency realignment. He said that "there were no offers and no acceptances." But the frank discussion that had taken place could be viewed as useful enough to warrant another meeting of the G-10 in Washington on December 17 and 18.

43. Anthony Lewis, "Beyond the Bankers," *New York Times* (September 24, 1971).
44. *New York Times* (October 1, 1971).

President Nixon held lengthy discussions with President Pompidou and agreed on moves toward devaluation of the dollar and realignment of other currencies, widening of the band within which exchange rates could move, and removal of the import surcharge. Only two days before the Group of 10 were again to meet in Washington, President Nixon and President Pompidou issued this joint statement:

TEXT OF JOINT STATEMENT *

ANGRA DO HEROISMO, THE AZORES, Dec. 14

President Nixon and President Pompidou reached a broad area of agreement on measures necessary to achieve a settlement at the earliest possible date of the immediate problems of the international monetary system. In cooperation with other nations concerned, they agreed to work toward a prompt realignment of exchange rates through a devaluation of the dollar and revaluation of some other currencies. This realignment could, in their view, under present circumstances, be accompanied by broader permissible margins of fluctuation around the newly established exchange rates.

Aware of the interest in measures involving trade for a lasting equilibrium of the balance of payments, President Pompidou confirmed that France, together with the Governments of the other countries which are members of the European Economic Community, was preparing the mandate which would permit the imminent opening of negotiations with the United States in order to settle the short-term problems currently pending and to establish the agenda for the examination of fundamental questions in the area of trade.

President Nixon underscored the contribution that vigorous implementation by the United States of measures to restore domestic wage-price stability and productivity would make toward international equilibrium and the defense of the new dollar exchange rate.

The Presidents agreed that discussion should be undertaken promptly in appropriate forums to resolve fundamental and interrelated issues of monetary reform.

9. THE SMITHSONIAN AGREEMENT (DECEMBER 1971)

From the meetings of the Group of 10 at the Smithsonian Institution in Washington from December 16–18, 1971, there emerged agreement on realignment of the world's major currencies, widening of the margins of exchange rate fluctuation to 2.25 per cent above and below the new "central rates," and an

* *New York Times,* December 15, 1971.

increase in the monetary price of gold to $38 per ounce—
thereby devaluing the dollar by 8.57 per cent. And the 10 per
cent surcharge on imports was removed by President Nixon on
December 20.

The communique issued at the conclusion of the meetings of
the Group of 10 follows:

AGREEMENT ON INTERNATIONAL MONETARY ARRANGEMENTS *

1. The Ministers and Central Bank Governors of the ten countries participating in the General Arrangements to Borrow met at the Smithsonian Institution in Washington on December 17 and 18, 1971, in executive session,
under the Chairmanship of Mr. J. B. Connally, the Secretary of the Treasury of
the United States. Mr. P. P. Schweitzer, the Managing Director of the International Monetary Fund, took part in the meeting, which was also attended by
the President of the Swiss National Bank, Mr. E. Stopper, and in part by the
Secretary-General of the Organization for Economic Cooperation and Development, Mr. E. van Lennep, the General Manager of the Bank for International Settlements, Mr. R. Larre, and the Vice-President of the Commission of
the European Economic Community, Mr. R. Barre. The Ministers and Governors welcomed a report from the Managing Director of the Fund on a meeting held between their Deputies and the Executive Directors of the Fund.

2. The Ministers and Governors agreed on an interrelated set of measures
designed to restore stability to international monetary arrangements and to
provide for expanding international trade. These measures will be com-
municated promptly to other governments. It is the hope of the Ministers and
Governors that all governments will cooperate through the International
Monetary Fund to permit implementation of these measures in an orderly
fashion.

3. The Ministers and Governors reached agreement on a pattern of exchange rate relationships among their currencies. These decisions will be announced by individual governments, in the form of par values or central rates
as they desire. Most of the countries plan to close their exchange markets on
Monday. The Canadian Minister informed the Group that Canada intends
temporarily to maintain a floating exchange rate and intends to permit fundamental market forces to establish the exchange rate without intervention
except as required to maintain orderly conditions.

4. It was also agreed that, pending agreement on longer-term monetary
reforms, provision will be made for 2¼ per cent margins of exchange rate
fluctuation above and below the new exchange rates. The Ministers and Governors recognized that all members of the International Monetary Fund not
attending the present discussions will need urgently to reach decisions, in

* Press Communique issued December 18, 1971.

consultation with the International Monetary Fund, with respect to their own exchange rates. It was the view of the Ministers and Governors that it is particularly important at this time that no country seek improper competitive advantage through its exchange rate policies. Changes in parities can only be justified by an objective appraisal which establishes a position of disequilibrium.

5. Questions of trade arrangements were recognized by the Ministers and Governors as a relevant factor in assuring a new and lasting equilibrium in the international economy. Urgent negotiations are now under way between the United States and the Commission of the European Community, Japan, and Canada to resolve pending short-term issues at the earliest possible date, and with the European Community to establish an appropriate agenda for considering more basic issues in a framework of mutual cooperation in the course of 1972 and beyond. The United States agreed to propose to Congress a suitable means for devaluing the dollar in terms of gold to $38.00 per ounce as soon as the related set of short-term measures is available for Congressional scrutiny. Upon passage of required legislative authority in this framework, the United States will propose the corresponding new par value of the dollar to the International Monetary Fund.

6. In consideration of the agreed immediate realignment of exchange rates, the United States agreed that it will immediately suppress the recently imposed 10 per cent import surcharge and related provisions of the Job Development Credit.

7. The Ministers and Governors agreed that discussions should be promptly undertaken, particularly in the framework of the International Monetary Fund, to consider reform of the international monetary system over the longer term. It was agreed that attention should be directed to the appropriate monetary means and division of responsibilities for defending stable exchange rates and for insuring a proper degree of convertibility of the system; to the proper role of gold, of reserve currencies, and of special drawing rights in the operation of the system; to the appropriate volume of liquidity; to re-examination of the permissible margins of fluctuation around established exchange rates and other means of establishing a suitable degree of flexibility; and to other measures dealing with movements of liquid capital. It is recognized that decisions in each of these areas are closely linked.

As compared with the rates that prevailed on May 1, 1971, the currency realignment of the Smithsonian agreement initially resulted in an appreciation of the Japanese yen against the dollar by 16.9 per cent, the German mark by 13.6 per cent, the French franc and British pound by 8.6 per cent, and the Italian lira by 7.5 per cent.

President Nixon hailed the agreement as "the most significant monetary achievement in the history of the world." Walter

Scheel, the German Foreign Minister, said in a radio statement that "we have, especially with our European neighbors, a new currency relationship that will also bring relief for our economy." But in Japan, Foreign Minister Fukuda said that the upward change in the yen's parity was "the greatest economic shock" Japan had suffered since the end of World War II, and the opposition parties were quick to criticize Premier Sato.

10. THE VOLCKER AGREEMENT (FEBRUARY 1973)

The Smithsonian agreement had responded to the immediate situation, but the major questions of a new world monetary order had not been answered. Sources of potential instability remained. The dollar was still inconvertible. No new reserve asset was created; indeed, when the initial Rio allocation of SDR's was exhausted in 1972, there had been no decision on whether another allocation should be made. And instead of greater rate flexibility, the EEC countries actually established in April 1972 a plan whereby intra-EEC rates were to be kept within half the range allowed by the Smithsonian agreement— the "snake" within the "tunnel."

FOREIGN EXCHANGE OPERATIONS IN 1972 *

Following the turn of the year, . . . market optimism shifted to an anxious and even skeptical mood as traders began to ponder the long negotiating path to a restructured international financial system. Market concern focused particularly on the risk that certain foreign central banks might suddenly withdraw from their Smithsonian commitments to defend their currencies at the new upper limits, and successive waves of speculation in January and February drove the mark, the guilder, the Belgian franc, and the yen close to or hard against their official ceilings.

The central banks concerned intervened decisively and without hesitation, however, and this demonstration had a reassuring effect. In early March, expeditious Congressional action on a "clean" gold price bill removed another source of uncertainty that had been breeding unsettling market rumors. Simultaneously, the German government took action to discourage borrowing abroad by German business firms, which had been a major source of buying pressure on the mark over

* Charles A. Coombs, "Treasury and Federal Reserve Foreign Exchange Operations," *Monthly Review of Federal Reserve Bank of New York*, September 1972, pp. 210–11.

the previous three years, while the Japanese government reinstated controls on speculative buying of the yen. Finally, the interest rate gap between Europe and the United States began to be squeezed out from both sides. As recessionary tendencies continued in Europe, discount rate cuts were announced in Germany, Belgium, and the Netherlands, while the United States Treasury bill rate rose significantly.

The dollar showed growing strength and resiliency throughout most of the spring months, as a return flow of short-term funds largely offset continuing deficits in other components of the United States balance of payments. This encouraging trend was abruptly reversed midway in June, however, as sterling was suddenly swept off its Smithsonian parity by a speculative wave that had been gathering force for many months past. In allowing sterling to float on June 23, the British authorities indicated that the defense of sterling during the previous six days had cost the equivalent of $2.6 billion.

Such official intervention to defend sterling was almost entirely conducted in Common Market currencies, in accordance with a British undertaking on May 1 to join with its prospective Common Market partners in maintaining a spread of no more than 2¼ per cent between sterling and any other Common Market currency. This European Community (EC) agreement had thus created a dual system of exchange rate limits in which the 2¼ per cent Common Market band became colloquially described as the "snake" in the "tunnel" represented by the 4½ per cent Smithsonian band. A critical feature of the Common Market 2¼ per cent band was that intervention in dollars was to be confined to circumstances in which a weakening Common Market currency should decline the full distance to its Smithsonian floor or a strong currency should rise to its Smithsonian ceiling. Otherwise, maintenance of the 2¼ per cent Common Market band was to be carried out by intervening in each other's currencies.

As sterling came under selling pressure in June, the Bank of England accordingly was called upon to offer marks and whatever other Common Market currencies were being quoted at rates 2¼ per cent above sterling, while its European partners bought sterling with their currencies. The general effect of such intervention to maintain the 2¼ per cent Common Market band was to brake the decline of sterling toward its Smithsonian floor of $2.5471, while simultaneously pulling down the stronger EC currencies well below their Smithsonian ceilings. In this strained pattern of rates, the markets may have sensed a two-way speculative opportunity to go short of sterling and long of Continental currencies in the hope of profiting on both. Most of the outflow from London seems to have ended up in the Common Market.

On June 23 the British authorities announced their decision to float the pound, in effect temporarily suspending their participation in the Smithsonian and EC agreements. Following that announcement, other European currencies immediately rebounded to their Smithsonian ceilings, reflecting market fears of a severe tightening of capital import controls, a joint float of the Common Market currencies, or some combination of both. The European currency markets were then closed down, and an emergency meeting of the Community Finance Ministers was set for the following Monday in Luxembourg. At that meeting Denmark formally withdrew from the EC monetary agreement, while Italy secured a temporary authorization to keep the lira within the 2¼ per cent band by intervening in dollars rather than European currencies. The Finance Ministers then reaffirmed their determination to defend both the Smithsonian parities and the Common Market band.

Despite this reaffirmation and subsequent drastic controls imposed by Switzerland and Germany to ward off unwanted capital inflows, rumors of a European joint float continued to incite heavy speculative selling of dollars against the stronger European currencies and the yen. By Friday, July 14, the sterling crisis had generated not only the previously noted flight of $2.6 billion of funds from sterling into other Common Market currencies but also additional flows totaling over $6 billion from dollars into various European currencies and the yen.

Meanwhile, the United States authorities had been considering the advisability of renewed operations in the exchange markets, involving, if necessary, Federal Reserve swap drawings which had been suspended on August 15, 1971. On United States initiative and with the approval of the Bundesbank, the first of such exchange operations was launched on July 19 in the form of repeated offerings by the Federal Reserve Bank of New York of sizable amounts of German marks on the New York market. This intervention, which was continued briefly on the following day, was described by Chairman Burns as a move by the United States authorities to play their part to restore order in foreign exchange markets and to do their part in upholding the Smithsonian agreement, just as other countries were doing. The Chairman also indicated that the operation would continue on whatever scale and whenever transactions seemed advisable. The United States Treasury also confirmed the intervention, stating in part that: "The action reflects the willingness of the United States to intervene in the exchange markets upon occasion when it feels it is desirable to help deal with speculative forces. The action indicates absolutely no change in our basic policy approach toward monetary reform and the necessary efforts on all fronts to achieve a sustainable equilibrium in our balance of payments."

The Council of Economic Advisers interpreted the United States balance-of-payments position in essentially optimistic terms—but they admitted that devaluation had so far been disappointing. At the end of 1971, the monetary reserve assets of the United States were down to $12 billion—the lowest year-end level in the post-World War II period. This total included $10.2 billion in gold, essentially unchanged from August 15; $1.1 billion in SDR's, also unchanged; $276 million in foreign currencies; and $585 million in automatic drawing rights in the IMF.

U.S. BALANCE OF PAYMENTS *

The overall balance-of-payments position of the United States, while still far from equilibrium, began to improve in 1972. The improvement, which was all in the capital account, was largely the result of a sharp reduction over 1971 in speculative outflows of capital. Domestic economic policies which curtailed the rate of inflation, the realignment of exchange rates, and renewed confidence in international monetary relationships all contributed to this improvement. The trade and current account deficits of the United States, however, were considerably larger in 1972 than in 1971, although they levelled off during the year. The year-over-year deterioration in these accounts stemmed primarily from the rapid growth of the U.S. economy and a lag in the economic recovery of some of the other major countries.

Progress was also made during 1972 on the longer-term reform objective. Agreement was reached on a format for international monetary negotiations. Discussions on the characteristics of a revised international monetary system are now underway, and the United States has set forth a number of proposals. The major industrialized countries have also agreed to initiate multilateral trade negotiations in the fall of 1973. Finally, these same countries have agreed to explore new forms of cooperation on internal policies which affect trade and investment among nations.

As this *Report* goes to press, official data for the U.S. balance of payments are available only for the first 3 quarters of 1972. These figures, shown in Table II, indicate that, at annual rates, Americans imported $76.2 billion in goods and services during the first 9 months of 1972, while foreigners purchased $71.2 billion in U.S. goods and services. On balance, therefore, Americans obtained $4.9 billion more goods and services abroad than they provided to the rest of the world. In addition, U.S. Government grants and other types of unilateral transfers to foreigners exceeded similar transfers to the United States by $3.7 billion, and U.S. investments in long-term assets abroad exceeded foreign investments in U.S. long-term assets by $1.6 billion. Moreover, recorded short-term capital movements, nonrecorded transactions, and allocations of Special Drawing Rights (SDR's) together resulted in a net outflow of $1.4 billion. Overall, therefore, American balance-of-payments expen-

* *Economic Report of the President*, January 1973, pp. 113–15.

TABLE II. U.S. Balance-of-Payments Transactions, 1971–72

[Billions of dollars]

Type of transaction	1971			1972 first 3 quarters [1]		
	Receipts	Payments	Balance	Receipts	Payments	Balance
Goods [2]	42.8	45.5	−2.7	47.4	54.4	−7.0
Services	23.4	19.9	3.4	23.8	21.8	2.1
Military transactions	1.9	4.8	−2.9	1.2	4.7	−3.6
Investment income [3]	12.9	4.9	8.0	13.1	5.7	7.4
Other	8.5	10.2	−1.7	9.6	11.3	−1.8
GOODS AND SERVICES	66.1	65.4	.7	71.2	76.2	−4.9
Unilateral transfers, net [4]		3.6	−3.6		3.7	−3.7
CURRENT ACCOUNT	66.1	69.0	−2.8	71.2	79.9	−8.7
Long-term capital	1.8	8.2	−6.5	5.1	6.7	−1.6
U.S. Government [5]	−.5	1.9	−2.4	.3	1.3	−1.0
Direct investment	−.1	4.8	−4.8	.3	3.3	−3.0
Other private	2.3	1.6	.8	4.4	2.1	2.4
CURRENT ACCOUNT AND LONG-TERM CAPITAL	67.9	77.2	−9.3	76.3	86.6	−10.2
Short-term nonliquid capital	([6])	2.4	−2.4	.1	.7	−.6
Short-term liquid capital	−6.7	1.1	−7.8	2.9	1.4	1.5
Errors and unrecorded transactions, net		11.0	−11.0		3.0	−3.0
Allocations of SDR's	.7		.7	.7		.7
TOTAL	61.9	91.7	[7] −29.8	80.0	91.7	[7] −11.6

[1] Seasonally adjusted annual rates.
[2] Excludes transfers under military grants.
[3] Includes direct investment fees and royalties.
[4] Excludes military grants of goods and services.
[5] Excludes official reserve transactions and includes transactions in some short-term U.S. Government assets.
[6] Less than $0.05 billion.
[7] Equals official reserve transactions balance.
NOTE: Detail may not add to totals because of rounding.
SOURCE: Department of Commerce.

ditures exceeded receipts by $11.6 billion. Virtually the whole deficit in the U.S. balance of payments on the official reserve transactions basis was financed by increased dollar holdings of foreign central banks.

For the goods-and-services account, preliminary estimates are available for the full year 1972. These figures differ slightly from those in Table II, which are annual rates based on data for the first 3 quarters. These preliminary estimates indicate that the United States imported about $4½ billion more goods and services than it exported. U.S. imports of goods exceeded exports by about $7 billion in 1972, while exports of services exceeded imports by about $2½ billion. These figures represent a substantial deterioration in the goods-and-services account from the full year 1971. . . .

The figures just cited give early indications that the dollar devaluation, reinforced by a lower rate of inflation in the United States than in other major industrialized countries in 1972, is beginning to affect U.S. exports and imports. The fact remains, however, that the U.S. trade deficit was much larger in 1972 than had been expected after the realignment of exchange rates. Cyclical developments in the United States and abroad were a major reason for this disappointment. Nominal gross national product (GNP) in the United States grew by nearly 10 per cent in 1972, compared to 7½ per cent in 1971 and 5 per cent in 1970. Thus while changes in relative prices reduced the attractiveness of foreign goods compared to domestic goods, the level of imports continued to increase with the rapid rise in the overall demand for goods in the U.S. economy. At the same time, a number of major industrial countries experienced lower than normal rates of growth in 1972, which tended to hold down the increase in their demand for U.S. goods.

At the same time as the United States encountered a much larger trade deficit than expected in 1972, Japan's trade surplus rose to a surprisingly large figure in spite of the revaluation of the yen: from $7.79 billion in 1971 to a record figure of $8.97 billion for 1972. At the time of the Smithsonian agreement, Japan's gold and foreign exchange reserves amounted to less than $11 billion, but by the end of the following year they were more than $18 billion, second in the world only to those of West Germany. And despite revaluation of the mark, Germany's exports also continued to expand.

Finally, the dollar's inconvertibility remained a major concern. Some authorities continued to urge a joint float by EEC countries against the dollar. The deputy Governor of the Bank of Italy, Rinaldo Ossola, said in a speech in London that "As long as the dollar remains inconvertible—that is, probably during most of the nineteen-seventies—the problem of adjustment between the United States and the European Economic Community should be solved through the free fluctuation of the dollar vis-à-vis the EEC currencies as a whole, these latter's reciprocal relations being based on relatively fixed parities." [45]

The Bank of International Settlements also warned in its annual report, that rather than accept inconvertible dollars or increase the value of their currencies, other countries are likely to impose controls on dollar flows, and that this could split the world into restrictive monetary blocs.

The annual meeting of the IMF also ended with no conclusive consensus—let alone action—on monetary reform. Secretary of the Treasury Shultz outlined the United States proposals for a reformed system, and the new "Committee of 20" high-level government officials, representing all the member countries of the Fund, held its first session to consider a report on the problems of international monetary reform and possible solutions, prepared by the Executive Directors of the Fund. [See pp. 262–74 below.] It was clear that the process of negotiation would be complex and prolonged.

When a further increase in the size of the United States trade deficit was made public at the start of 1973, the outflow of dollars began to reach proportions of another currency crisis. In late January, the Federal Reserve began intervening in the foreign exchange market and sold marks (from holdings of the Federal Reserve, and then the Treasury, and then from a "swap agreement" with the Bundesbank) in an effort to stop—but in vain—the appreciation of the mark. [46] On February 1, the mark reached its ceiling, and the Bundesbank intervened in the exchange market. During the following seven trading days— between February 1 and 9—the Bundesbank had to buy nearly $6 billion to resist another revaluation of the mark. The dollar intake during this period was the highest ever recorded for Germany and compared with $2.2 billion acquired in dollar support during April 29–May 5, 1971.

The Economist stated in its issue of February 10, "What remains of the Smithsonian exchange parities should get a decent burial. The end looks near." This was scarcely prediction, but simply observation: the outflow of dollars was again threatening

45. *New York Times* (February 17, 1972).
46. Charles A. Coombs, "Treasury and Federal Reserve Foreign Exchange Operations," *Federal Reserve Bank of New York Monthly Review* (March 1973).

the values of the mark and the guilder; the Canadian dollar, British pound, and Swiss franc were already floating outside the Smithsonian band; and the French franc, Belgian franc, and Italian lira were operating on two-tier financial markets which observed Smithsonian rules for only some transactions.

The pressure on foreign currencies had become so great that over the weekend it was decided to close the foreign exchange markets in Europe and Japan. And late Monday evening— February 12, 1973—the United States announced another devaluation of the dollar.

DEVALUATION STATEMENT BY SECRETARY SHULTZ *

In consultation with our trading partners and in keeping with the basic principles of our proposals for monetary reform, we are taking a series of actions designed to achieve three interrelated purposes:

(a) to speed improvement of our trade and payments position in a manner that will support our effort to achieve constructive reform of the monetary system:

(b) to lay the legislative groundwork for broad and outward-looking trade negotiations, paralleling our efforts to strengthen the monetary system; and

(c) to assure that American workers and American businessmen are treated equitably in our trading relationships.

For these purposes:

First, the President is requesting that the Congress authorize a further realignment of exchange rates. This objective will be sought by a formal 10 per cent reduction in the par value of the dollar from 0.92106 SDR to the dollar to 0.82895 SDR to the dollar.

Although this action will, under the existing Articles of Agreement of the International Monetary Fund, result in a change in the official relationship of the dollar to gold, I should like to stress that this technical change has no practical significance. The market price of gold in recent years has diverged widely from the official price, and under these conditions gold has not been transferred to any significant degree among international monetary authorities. We remain strongly of the opinion that orderly arrangements must be negotiated to facilitate the continuing reduction of the role of gold in international monetary affairs.

Consultations with our leading trading partners in Europe assure me that the proposed change in the par value of the dollar is acceptable to them, and will therefore be effective immediately in exchange rates for the dollar in international markets. The dollar will decline in value by about 10 per cent in

*Excerpt from the Statement on Foreign Economic Policy issued on February 12, 1973.

terms of those currencies for which there is an effective par value, for example the deutsche mark and the French franc.

Japanese authorities have indicated that the yen will be permitted to float. Our firm expectation is that the yen will float into a relationship vis-à-vis other currencies consistent with achieving a balance of payments equilibrium not dependent upon significant government intervention.

These changes are intended to supplement and work in the same direction as the changes accomplished in the Smithsonian Agreement of December 1971. They take into account recent developments and are designed to speed improvement in our trade and payments position. In particular, they are designed, together with appropriate trade liberalization, to correct the major payments imbalance between Japan and the United States which has persisted in the past year.

Other countries may also propose changes in their par values or central rates to the International Monetary Fund. We will support all changes that seem warranted on the basis of current and prospective payments imbalances, but plan to vote against any changes that are inappropriate.

We have learned that time must pass before new exchange relationships modify established patterns of trade and capital flows. However, there can be no doubt we have achieved a major improvement in the competitive position of American workers and American business.

The new exchange rates being established at this time represent a reasonable estimate of the relationships which—taken together with appropriate measures for the removal of existing trade and investment restraints—will in time move international economic relationships into sustainable equilibrium. We have, however, undertaken no obligations for the U.S. Government to intervene in foreign exchange markets.

Second, the President has decided to send shortly to the Congress proposals for comprehensive trade legislation. Prior to submitting that legislation, intensive consultations will be held with Members of Congress, labor, agriculture, and business to assure that the legislation reflects our needs as fully as possible.

This legislation, among other things, should furnish the tools we need to:

(i) provide for lowering tariff and non-tariff barriers to trade, assuming our trading partners are willing to participate fully with us in that process;

(ii) provide for raising tariffs when such action would contribute to arrangements assuring that American exports have fair access to foreign markets;

(iii) provide safeguards against the disruption of particular markets and production from rapid changes in foreign trade; and

(iv) protect our external position from large and persistent deficits.

It was now clear that in his hurried trip among European capitals and Tokyo, Under Secretary of the Treasury Paul A.

Volcker had negotiated an agreement over the weekend of February 10–11, by which the dollar would be devalued and the yen permitted to float.

HANDLING OF CRISIS *

WASHINGTON—It was a classic demonstration of a domino theory in action. The first domino was the announcement of Phase 3 on Jan. 11. And the last domino was Monday night's devaluation of the dollar.

That, at any rate, is what many analysts outside the Nixon administration are saying now. They claim what the administration people aren't quite prepared to admit—that the devaluation of the dollar was brought about by the administration's own domestic economic policies.

Before the administration unveiled its revamped Phase 3 controls on wages and prices Jan. 11, few analysts were forecasting another international monetary crisis. Indeed, on Jan. 10, no less a luminary than Walter W. Heller, President Kennedy's economic adviser, wrote in a 1973 outlook that "prospects for shrinking payments deficits and a strengthening of the dollar are good" because the U.S. inflation rate had abated.

Then the clicking sounds began from those falling dominoes. The administrations's removal of the mandatory controls from most of the economy sent the stock market tumbling on fears of renewed inflation. Click. The U.S. reported a fat December trade deficit, dashing administration claims that an improvement was under way; the December figure pushed the 1972 total deficit to $6.4 billion, triple that of 1971. Click.

With their currencies under pressure, the Italians introduced a two-tiered currency system, and the Swiss floated the value of their franc. Click, click. Billions of dollars began pouring into West Germany as speculators bought marks, gambling that the German currency would be revalued upward. A very loud click.

A Tall Tale

The tallest man in the Nixon administration, 6-foot, 7-inch Paul A. Volcker, under secretary of the treasury for monetary affairs, was spotted in Bonn, when he was supposed to be at his desk in Washington. The last domino in line was obviously the U.S. dollar.

While the dominoes were falling, the Nixon administration was demonstrating again that government-by-crisis hasn't been abolished even in the new era of the efficiency expert and the supercrat.

The handling of the crisis tells a good deal about a number of things: about Treasury Secretary George Shultz's domination of economic policy making; about President Nixon's penchant for isolation

---

* *Wall Street Journal,* February 14, 1973. Report by James P. Gannon.

from most of his advisers; about how the White House continues to blame the press for its problems; and about the administration's effort to make the international monetary chaos look like a way to solve the nation's economic ills.

The crisis-management team was a small group of very high-level officials, who generally kept their staffs from knowing much about what was going on, insiders say. Led by Mr. Shultz, who has taken the role of the administration's chief economic policy maker, the group included Secretary of State William Rogers, Federal Reserve Board Chairman Arthur Burns, White House economist Herbert Stein and presidential adviser Peter Flanigan, head of the Council on International Economic Policy

According to one participant, the crisis-watchers met "four or five times" in the past two weeks to plot strategy. The first line of defense chosen was for the Federal Reserve to intervene in currency trading to support the dollar by selling German marks, an operation that was conducted for only "a few days."

"This was a kind of contingency decision to intervene and see if the problem would go away," one of the group explains. But it soon became apparent that the flight from the dollar was too massive to be overcome by the Fed action or by heavy dollar purchases by the German central bank.

The Big Decision

When that tactic failed, President Nixon was faced with the big decision. He called in Mr. Shultz and Mr. Burns for the crucial meeting on Tuesday of last week. The decision: to send Mr. Volcker around the world on a secret mission offering to devalue the dollar. In return, however, other major nations must either hold to their present currency values or allow the currencies to "float" upward in free-market currency trading. "We weren't going to devalue if everyone else was going to follow us down" and frustrate the aim of a major realignment of the dollar's value against such currencies as the German mark and the Japanese yen, one strategist said.

Mr. Volcker left the U.S. unnoticed on a military jet crammed with sophisticated communications gear; this allowed him to keep in touch with Treasury Secretary Shultz as Mr. Volcker hopped from Tokyo to London to Bonn to Paris to Rome and back to Bonn. But the highly visible Mr. Volcker's secret mission became public when he was spotted on the street in Bonn. "There had been some discussion of sending a smaller man," a colleague quips.

Mr. Volcker didn't go abroad with a finely detailed proposal all worked out but with the general outlines of a plan, it's understood. The 10% figure for the devaluation evolved as a figure from his discussions.

The undersecretary was back at the Treasury yesterday, looking slightly haggard and showing signs of the "jet-lag syndrome" that plagues intercontinental travelers. "This is Wednesday, so this must be Washington," he quipped to reporters. Then he was corrected. "Oh, is it Tuesday? Well, it's Wednesday in Japan."

Along his 31,000-mile route, Mr. Volcker used various subterfuges to try to remain unnoticed, slipping out of back doors of U.S. embassies and leaving Tokyo in the dark of night. He somehow escaped detection in Japan, even though along the way he lost his hat, which had his name printed inside.

During his mission Mr. Volcker reported to Mr. Shultz, demonstrating how the quiet, pipe-smoking ex-Prof. Shultz has gathered in the reins of economic power in the second Nixon administration. Mr. Shultz's position was symbolically displayed late Monday night at the news conference on the devaluation. A lot of high-powered talent filed into the Treasury press briefing room: Messrs. Rogers, Flanigan, Burns and Stein, but George Shultz did the briefing and answered all the questions. The other eminences, in their dark-blue suits, sat quietly at an adjacent table, like so many supporting actors without lines to read.

Meanwhile, Mr. Nixon maintained his distance from the crisis at his San Clemente retreat. He spoke to Mr. Shultz by telephone frequently and gave the final go-ahead for the devaluation by phone Monday morning, after Mr. Volcker's mission had turned up general agreement on the U.S. plan.

The contrast is striking between Mr. Nixon's handling of this second devaluation and his handling of the devaluation involved in the Smithsonian Agreement of December 1971. At that time, the President swooped down on the Smithsonian building to announce what he then called "the most significant monetary agreement in the history of the world."

There was no presidential hyperbole—or even comment—when the demise of that historic agreement was announced Monday night with the new devaluation of the dollar. As the press gathered to hear Mr. Shultz disclose the move, Mr. Nixon was completing his cross-country flight from California back to Washington. He arrived at the White House at 11:15 p.m., about the time that reporters were racing down the Treasury's corridors to phone their bulletins. The President went to bed.

DOLLAR DEVALUATION TAKES EFFECT *

Exchange markets, closed down in many countries in the previous week, began to reopen promptly following the devaluation, and by the end of the week of February 12 markets had largely regained stability. The Executive Directors of the Fund met on the U.S. action on the

* *IMF Survey*, February 26, 1973, pp. 49, 51–53.

evening of February 12 and met continuously in the days following to consider communications from member countries on responses to the U.S. devaluation. By the end of last week, a new world exchange rate structure had emerged, in a pattern of roughly four groupings: those holding their gold parities, in effect revaluing their currencies upward by 11.1 per cent against the dollar; those following the dollar down with a 10 per cent devaluation; those devaluing by less than 10 per cent; and those floating their currencies. Also, following the devaluation, world financial leaders began to assess the conditions that led to the devaluation and to discuss how it was negotiated among the countries involved. Many placed renewed emphasis on the urgency of the tasks of reform of the international monetary system and of trade relationships.

In a number of television interviews following the U.S. action, Pierre-Paul Schweitzer, the Managing Director of the Fund, remarked on the Fund support for the U.S. action and on the generally favorable reaction to it from Fund member countries. In one such interview, Mr. Schweitzer said, "I think I can say that our Executive Directors who represent all of our member countries have been unanimous in expressing the opinion that the U.S. action was contributing to improving the U.S. balance of payments, and the world monetary system, and was certainly going to strengthen the dollar. . . ."

"Of course," Mr. Schweitzer noted, "no country likes to see its competitiveness reduced, as it happens to the countries whose currency is revalued compared to the dollar, but on the other hand other countries were also not prepared to live indefinitely with a U.S. deficit of the magnitude which we have witnessed last year, and they were obviously also not able to face the inflow of speculative capital which took place last week, so I think they all felt that the U.S. action was perfectly proper and, as you have noticed, they cooperated in either keeping their currency at the former level or even by floating upwards like the Japanese so as to give the United States the full advantage of the devaluation."

On the need for the U.S. action, Mr. Schweitzer commented that while the general realignment achieved in the Smithsonian Agreement of December 1971 contributed to alleviate the strain at the time, it took longer than expected to bring the U.S. balance of payments into equilibrium, while other countries had intractable surpluses. "This generated a lack of faith in the U.S. dollar and made it vulnerable to speculation," he said.

For the future, Mr. Schweitzer expressed optimism. "International finance is a field where cooperation has been most obvious," he said. "We are negotiating an international monetary reform. Everyone has already agreed on one point, namely that the U.S. should have the same freedom of action as everyone else. The latest crisis could be solved so quickly, practically over a weekend, because the U.S. has taken freedom of action. The Fund's Executive Directors met at the same time as the Shultz press conference was held, and they gave their blessing and approval to the steps the U.S. intended to take."

In statements on February 13, following the U.S. Secretary of the Treasury's announcement, a number of governments commented officially on the devaluation of the U.S. dollar. In London, Anthony Barber, Chancellor of the Exchequer, told the House of Commons: "I welcome these new arrangements, and the House will agree that, compared with the events of 1971 (which also led to a realignment of currencies) a solution has on this occasion been found with remarkable speed, having regard to the range of interests involved and the complexities of the issues. This would certainly not have been achieved without the intensive consultations which took place over the weekend. As the House knows, we have throughout kept in close touch with our European colleagues. And I would add in particular that the way in which the United States, whose currency came under such severe pressure, has taken bold and constructive action on consultation with others, augurs well for future relationships across the Atlantic."

"But if the immediate difficulties have been resolved, the clear lesson to be drawn from the events of the past few weeks or so is the paramount need for constructive and speedy progress toward a more efficient international monetary system. We now need resolute determination to achieve results, and this will be my purpose when I attend the meeting of the Committee of 20 next month in Washington," Mr. Barber said.

And in Bonn, on February 13 in a statement issued by Finance Minister Helmut Schmidt, the German Government welcomed the U.S. devaluation as "action at the right place in accord with the international monetary situation. The Government appreciates the close cooperation and consultations during the preparations for this step. The Government also welcomes the decision of the Japanese Government to float the yen, in addition to the devaluation of the U.S. dollar. The Government expects this to produce a straightening out of the exchange rate ratio between the dollar and the yen which has been the main source of the disequilibrium in the American balance of payments."

"The exchange rate of the mark changes only in relation to the dollar. Within Europe, the monetary ratios remain essentially unchanged. The effects of the dollar's devaluation on our export business will be partially compensated by the foreseeable alteration of the exchange rate of the yen. The impairment of the competitiveness of our export economy will be kept to narrow limits. This does not preclude the possibility of the emergence of difficulties in some areas," Mr. Schmidt's statement said.

In discussions with reporters in the days immediately following the U.S. action to devalue the dollar, officials involved in the negotiations leading up to it revealed some of the background considerations. In his February 13 press conference, Mr. Schmidt said that "from the outset, we were not alone . . . we were in very close touch with the countries on which things primarily depended." Mr. Schmidt made special mention of the contacts with the French Finance Minister Giscard d'Estaing. Both Governments, said Mr. Schmidt, agreed from the outset that the only feasible solution was "a European or an international solution, not a national or an autonomous German solution." He also referred particularly to the direct contacts German Chancellor Willy Brandt had had with U.S. President Richard Nixon, British Prime Minister Edward Heath, and French President Georges Pompidou.

Mr. Schmidt said that practically speaking, two models had been considered feasible by the principals involved—including the Americans—as an approach to the solution of the crisis. One was a "European model," the other an "international model." The European approach would have been an agreement by the EEC countries to stop buying dollars and—by interventionary action—to see to it that the EEC exchange rate ratios were maintained. "I must specifically state," he stressed, "that the French Government was fully prepared to put this model into practice. . . ." He added that the French condition—one that he had endorsed—had been that "such action makes no political sense unless it is jointly taken by all EEC partners. At this point there emerged a considerable problem on the U.K. side, which during the first half of last weekend showed much good will and devoted a great deal of energy and thought to this point. It developed that the situation that had prompted the U.K. Government to float the pound beginning last summer did not permit it on this occasion to set a fixed ratio (for the pound) to the franc, the German mark, and the other European currencies.

"The other model," Mr. Schmidt continued, "is what has now been achieved—that is a devaluation of the dollar in relationship to the whole world, plus a keeping still, holding the line on the part of the European states, and an upward movement by the Japanese currency. This solution was reached by cooperation, for which the American Government—which worked together very closely with the partner states concerned—merits express thanks. In practical terms, agreement had been reached between America, France, Germany, the United Kingdom, and Italy on February 11 in Paris when we sat together in Giscard d'Estaing's home. The crucial question then was: How would the Japanese Government align itself? After the Japanese Government's decision came, during the late hours of February 12, the way was paved for the American decision. To my mind, the overall results achieved are a confirmation that we took the right action. This means that the solution goes to the source (of the problem)— that is the currency relationship between America and Japan."

Considering the energetic efforts that Treasury Under Secretary Volcker had devoted to altering exchange rates in the agreement of February 13, 1973, it is ironical to recall an editorial in the *New York Times* almost exactly three years earlier.

STRICTLY ACADEMIC *

Paul A. Volcker, the new Under Secretary of the Treasury for Monetary Affairs, minced few words in dismissing the notion that the international monetary mechanism would work better if exchange rates were free to fluctuate more widely. He told a Paris news conference that there has been much discussion of such ideas "in academic circles, and that's where they can stay."

Mr. Volcker, a bank economist, served in the Treasury in the Kennedy and Johnson Administrations; his defense of rigidly fixed exchange rates—sardonic though it is—comes as no surprise. But winds of change are at work. The idea of floating the pound sterling—cutting it loose from parity and permitting it to find its own levels in the foreign exchange markets—is now openly deliberated in respectable British circles. The farewell report of the Johnson Council of Economic Advisers acknowledged that the flexibility concept was achieving serious analysis in many areas as a possible safeguard against breakdowns of the monetary system. So what is strictly academic today might well be tomorrow's reality.

The day after the devaluation, President Nixon again chose to connect impending trade legislation with monetary reform. He stated, "The devaluation of the dollar in relation to other currencies is at best a temporary solution to the problem. That is why the trade legislation must follow. The trade legislation directs itself to the cause of the problem. . . . We must go up as well as down (on tariffs). That's the only way to get a fair shake for our products abroad." [47]

In Japan, the day after the devaluation marked near-record

---

* *New York Times*, February 17, 1969.
47. United Press International report, (February 13, 1973).

levels of trading volume on the foreign exchange market as the yen was floated. The yen appreciated 14 per cent, at which point the Bank of Japan intervened to prevent the price of the dollar from falling further (the rate had fallen from 301 yen: $1 to 270 yen: $1). The repercussions again extended to Parliament where the opposition demanded the resignation of the Premier and his cabinet. But Premier Tanaka promptly denied any responsibility for the move, placing the blame directly on the United States and pleading ignorance of predevaluation conversations between his Finance Minister and Mr. Volcker.

Many leading Europeans also expressed anxiety over the durability of the latest monetary settlement. The Finance Minister of West Germany and the Common Market's monetary chief both pointed out that the currency realignment following the dollar devaluation was fragile and that there was an urgent need for progress in monetary reform to resolve the problem of excess dollars.[48]

11. THE PARIS AGREEMENT (MARCH 1973)

Speculators in gold also showed little confidence in the new rates. The price of gold began to climb steadily, and only 10 days after its devaluation, new speculation broke out against the dollar as speculative buying of gold reached new heights. On February 22, the price of gold touched $90, rising in London by almost $10 above the previous day's closing quotation.

The outflow of dollars to Germany accelerated, and by February 23 the dollar had again fallen to its floor against the mark. On March 1 the West Germans closed their official foreign exchange market after having to buy $2.7 billion in one day. Other members of the EEC followed suit, and in an unprecedented move the nine members decided on March 4 to close their foreign exchange markets for two weeks while they sought to establish a European defense system in the latest currency crisis.

At the same time, President Nixon reaffirmed that there would not be another devaluation. At his press conference of March 3, this exchange occurred:

48. *New York Times* (February 16, 1973).

Q. Mr. President what kind of trouble is the American dollar in in Europe, in your judgment?

A. Well, the American dollar, I think, is being attacked by international speculators. I know that when I use that term my sophisticates in the Treasury Department shudder, because they believe these great forces are not determined by speculation and unrest, but as I look at the American economy, as I look at the American rate of inflation, I would say that the dollar is a good bet in the world markets today.

The United States has the lowest rate of inflation of any major industrial country. The United States has certainly the strongest economy of the major industrial countries. The United States also has a program, which we believe is going to work, for continuing to control inflation. We have a very tight budget, or I should say, a responsible budget. Let me point out, it is not a budget which is cut; it is a budget, however, which does not go up as much as some would want it to go, and therefore, one that will continue to cool the inflationary fires.

And, of course, under these circumstances, we believe that the dollar is a sound currency and that this international attack upon it by people who make great sums of money by speculating—one time they make a run on the mark and the next time it is on the yen, and now it is on the dollar. We will survive it.

Let me say there will not be another devaluation. I would say, second, we are going to continue our program of fiscal responsibility so that the dollar will be sound at home and, we trust as well, abroad, and we also are going to continue our efforts to get the other major countries to participate more with us in the goal that we believe we should all achieve, which we set out at the time of the Smithsonian and the other agreements, and that is of getting an international monetary system which is flexible enough to take care of these, what I believe are, temporary attacks on one currency or another.

A conference was then hastily scheduled to meet in Paris a week later (March 9) to devise some concerted action by the EEC countries, United States, Japan, Sweden, Switzerland, and Norway. Who was now to exercise responsibility for another monetary settlement? And what would be the character of the response of the fourteen nations in Paris?

Valèry Giscard d'Estaing, the Finance Minister of France, had said it was an American problem and that, therefore, the

Americans should solve it by having the United States authorities enter the foreign exchange markets in support of the dollar. Other finance ministers were stressing the need to control capital movements. And some were again urging a joint float of the Common Market currencies, although both Britain and Italy appeared to have serious reservations over such a linked operation.

One report, the day before the Paris meeting, asserted that the finance ministers of the EEC countries had agreed to submit the following requests to the United States: (1) to intervene in the exchange markets to maintain the existing rate of the dollar against the European currencies, selling reserve assets, such as gold, or borrowing from the IMF; (2) to reduce the total amount of dollars moving around in the currency centers of Europe by creating special long-term treasury bonds with an exchange-rate guaranteed to attract those who hold dollars; and (3) to restrict outflows of capital and to maintain restrictive domestic credit policies to attract dollars. The Europeans also wanted multinational companies to report the composition of their international currency holdings and then commit themselves not to change them.[49]

At the Paris meeting of March 9 there was a more cooperative attitude among the fourteen nations to "insure jointly an orderly exchange-rate system." After a nine-hour meeting, the ministerial conference issued the following communique.

TEXT OF COMMUNIQUE ON CURRENCY TALKS *

PARIS, March 9
The ministers and central-bank governors examined the international monetary situation in the light of the present crisis and had a broad exchange of views, both on the origins of the crisis and on ways of dealing with it in a spirit of cooperation.

They agreed that the crisis was due to speculative movements of funds. They also agreed that the existing relationships between parities and central rates, following the recent realignment, correspond, in their view, to the economic requirements and that these relationships will make an effective monetary contribution to a better balance of international payments.

49. *New York Times* (March 9, 1973).
* *New York Times*, March 10, 1973.

In these circumstances, they unanimously expressed their determination to insure jointly an orderly exchange-rate system.

The ministers and governors are agreed that, for this purpose, a set of measures needs to be drawn up.

As to the procedure, the ministers and governors considered that the formulation of these measures required a technical study, which they have instructed their deputies to undertake forthwith.

The ministers and governors have decided to meet again on Friday, March 16, to draw joint conclusions on the basis of this study and take the decisions which are called for, so as to make it possible for the European Economic Community countries and Sweden to reopen their exchange markets on Monday, March 19.

Finally, the ministers and governors considered that the recent disturbances underline the urgent need for an effective reform of the international monetary system. They decided to take the necessary steps to accelerate the work of the Committee of Twenty of the International Monetary Fund.

Two days later the EEC countries announced they had decided to float their currencies against the dollar in three separate groups. Six countries would float together: West Germany, France, Belgium, Holland, Luxembourg, and Denmark. Their currencies would be locked within a 2.25 per cent margin of each other, while floating as a unit against the dollar. Britain and Ireland would float together separately from the others, and Italy would float alone. But these other countries were to study ways to bring their currencies into line with the joint float of the six in the future. And a European monetary fund was to be established by mid-year, representing a large fund of pooled reserves of the six in the joint float.

On two other occasions—May 1971 and August 1971—the EEC countries had been unable to agree to a joint float, but now the EEC had indicated its intention to take at least a half-step toward monetary union. Chancellor Willy Brandt had led the way to an economic agreement at Paris through his political determination that West Germany "cannot pursue unilateral concepts," but must insist on a solution "as European as possible." [50] Germany revalued the mark by 3 per cent, and fixed it in relation to Special Drawing Rights instead of to the dollar—a deliberate "prelude to an international currency reform," according to a Bonn government spokesman.[51] In contrast to the

50. *New York Times* (March 12, 1973).
51. *New York Times* (March 15, 1973).

earlier policy whereby the United States offered Europeans the choice of supporting the dollar themselves or letting their currencies appreciate, the Paris agreement now pledged the United States and each of the other countries to "be prepared to intervene at its initiative in its own market, when necessary and desirable, acting in a flexible manner" to support its currency.

Following is the communique issued at the conclusion of the fourteen-nation meeting in Paris.

TEXT OF COMMUNIQUE ON CURRENCY TALKS *

PARIS, March 16

[1]

The ministers and central bank governors of the 10 countries participating in the general arrangements to borrow and the member countries of the European Economic Community met in Paris on March 16, 1973, under the chairmanship of Valèry Giscard d'Estaing, Minister of the Economy and of Finance of France. P. P. Schweitzer, managing director of the International Monetary Fund, took part in the meeting, which was also attended by Nello Celio, head of the Federal Department of Finance of the Swiss Confederation; E. Stopper, president of the Swiss National Bank; W. Haferkamp, vice president of the Commission of the European Economic Community; E. Van Lennep, secretary general of the Organization for Economic Cooperation and Development; René Larre, general manager of the Bank for International Settlements, and Jeremy Morse, chairman of the deputies of the Committee of 20 of the I.M.F.

[2]

The ministers and governors heard a report by the chairman of their deputies, Rinaldo Ossola, on the results of the technical study which the deputies have carried out in accordance with the instructions given to them.

[3]

The ministers and governors took note of the decisions of the members of the E.E.C. announced on Monday. Six members of the E.E.C. and certain other European countries, including Sweden, will maintain 2¼ per cent margins between their currencies. The currencies of certain countries, such as Italy, the United Kingdom, Ireland, Japan and Canada, remain for the time being, floating. However, Italy, the United Kingdom and Ireland have expressed the intention of associating themselves as soon as possible with the decision to maintain E.E.C. exchange rates within margins of 2¼ per cent and meanwhile of remaining in consultation with their E.E.C. partners.

[4]

The ministers and governors reiterated their determination to ensure jointly an orderly exchange-rate system. To this end, they agreed on the basis

* *New York Times*, March 17, 1973.

for an operational approach toward the exchange markets in the near future and on certain further studies to be completed as a matter of urgency.

[5]

They agreed in principle that official intervention in exchange markets may be useful at appropriate times to facilitate the maintenance of orderly conditions, keeping in mind also the desirability of encouraging reflows of speculative movements of funds. Each nation stated that it will be prepared to intervene at its initiative in its own market, when necessary and desirable, acting in a flexible manner in the light of market conditions and in close consultation with the authorities of the nation whose currency may be bought or sold. The countries which have decided to maintain 2¼ per cent margins between their currencies have made known their intention of concerting among themselves the application of these provisions. Such intervention will be financed when necessary through use of mutual credit facilities. To ensure adequate resources for such operations, it is envisaged that some of the existing "swap" facilities will be enlarged.

[6]

Some countries have announced additional measures to restrain capital inflows. The United States authorities emphasized that the phasing out of their controls of longer-term capital outflows by the end of 1974 was intended to coincide with strong improvement in the United States balance-of-payments position. Any step taken during the interim period toward the elimination of these controls would take due account of exchange-market conditions and the balance-of-payments trends. The United States authorities are also reviewing actions that may be appropriate to remove inhibitions on the inflow of capital into the United States. Countries in a strong payments position will review the possibility of removing or relaxing any restrictions on capital outflows, particularly long-term.

[7]

Ministers and governors noted the importance of dampening speculative capital movements. They stated their intentions to seek more complete understanding of the sources and nature of the large capital flows which have recently taken place. With respect to Eurocurrency markets, they agreed that methods of reducing the volatility of these markets will be studied intensively, taking into account the implications for the longer-run operation of the international monetary system. These studies will address themselves, among other factors, to limitations on placement of official reserves in that market by member nations of the I.M.F. and to the possible need for reserve requirements comparable to those in national banking markets. With respect to the former, the ministers and governors confirmed that their authorities would be prepared to take the lead by implementing certain undertakings that their own placements would be gradually and prudently withdrawn. The United States will review possible action to encourage a flow of Eurocurrency funds to the United States as market conditions permit.

[8]

In the context of discussions of monetary reform, the ministers and governors agreed that proposals for funding or consolidation of official currency balances deserved thorough and urgent attention. This matter is already on the agenda of the Committee of 20 of the I.M.F.

[9]

Ministers and governors reaffirmed their attachment to the basic principles which have governed international economic relations since the last war— the greatest possible freedom for international trade and investment and the avoidance of competitive changes of exchange rates. They stated their determination to continue to use the existing organizations of international economic cooperation to maintain these principles for the benefit of all their members.

[10]

Ministers and governors expressed their unanimous conviction that international monetary stability rests, in the last analysis, on the success of national efforts to contain inflation. They are resolved to pursue fully appropriate policies to this end.

[11]

Ministers and governors are confident that, taken together, these moves will launch an internationally responsible program for dealing with the speculative pressures that have recently emerged and for maintaining orderly international monetary arrangements while the work of reform of the international monetary system is pressed ahead. They reiterated their concern that this work be expedited and brought to an early conclusion in the framework of the Committee of 20 of the I.M.F.

How long would confidence in the Paris Agreement be maintained? No sooner was the joint float announced than *The Economist* predicted a "breakdown" and "another currency crisis." "An attempt to maintain fixed exchange rates today is like an order to walk upon the water. Proponents of a joint float somehow think that it will be safer if some of us join hands while doing so." [52]

Within four months it was true that the joint float was tested by another revaluation of the mark. On June 29, 1973, the West German government appreciated the mark by 5.5 per cent against the other European currencies participating in the joint float (technically the new central rate of the mark was raised in terms of the SDR). In explaining the revaluation, Germany's Finance Minister said that in the previous twelve days West Germany had had to absorb foreign currencies (mainly Belgian francs, Dutch guilders, and French francs) worth 4 billion marks (more than $21.5 billion) to keep the mark within the 2.25 per cent "snake" of the joint float. Once again, exchange-rate

52. *The Economist* (March 13, 1973).

pressure was frustrating the efforts of the government and the Bundesbank to control domestic inflation. In yielding to a revaluation, however, the German authorities did not yet reject a continued joint float; the government formally reconstituted the "snake" with a new value for the mark, instead of letting the mark float independently.

While the French remained anxious to maintain fixed currency relationships among the EEC members (mainly to support the European community's common agricultural policy), the French Finance Minister took the occasion of the second revaluation of the mark within a year to urge an end to freely floating rates in the world at large: "the speculative forces which can push a currency within a few weeks from its floor to its ceiling with no rational basis" shows the "unrealistic character of a reform of the international monetary system based on permanent flexibility. The lesson is eloquent. It is high time that it should be heeded." [53]

The future course of international monetary negotiations still had to involve not only the complexities of technical economic issues but also the difficult questions of relinquishing some national sovereignty in monetary matters and forgoing some domestic autonomy in economic policy-making. Of all the political-economic problems requiring collective decision-making by many states, the problem of international monetary reform remained most acute. If the world's monetary system was to cease being characterized as in "suspended animation" or an "evolving status quo," a new Bretton Woods agreement would have to be reached.

But what was to be the substantive content of that new agreement? How soon could the international community agree to it? And for how long? The Bretton Woods agreement had lasted for twenty-seven years, but the Smithsonian agreement disintegrated after only fourteen months, and the Volcker agreement had a duration of merely eighteen days. The Paris agreement had met the latest challenge of financial crisis-management, but few thought it removed the need for more basic measures of international monetary reform.

53. *New York Times* (June 30, 1973).

C. QUESTIONS

1. Writing in 1964, John Kenneth Galbraith said, "Few public problems can ever have been so ingeniously contrived to maximize difficulty as that of the balance of payments. There has been a puzzling choice between real and spurious solutions. And each of the real solutions has been protected by a stout framework of vested ideological and economic interest reinforced, in some cases, by distinctly nonsecular conviction. The sources of difficulty may be dealt with under the following heads: (1) the question as to whether there is a problem; (2) the tendency to technical escape; (3) the temptation to cosmetic or public relations action; (4) the vested resistance to action." (J. K. Galbraith, "The Balance of Payments: A Political and Administrative View," *Review of Economics and Statistics,* May 1964.)

Does the history of the dollar problem since 1964 illustrate the four "sources of difficulty" that Galbraith lists?

2. a. If the United States balance of payments had not been in deficit during the 1960's, do you think there would have been sufficient international liquidity? If the United States succeeds in removing its balance-of-payments deficit in "three or four years," as forecast by Federal Reserve Chairman Arthur Burns, will there be sufficient international liquidity? Is it helpful in answering these questions to distinguish between trend liquidity, market liquidity, and crisis liquidity?

b. If foreign official monetary authorities had refused to accumulate dollar reserve balances during the 1960's, what difference would it have made for United States military expenditures in Vietnam? For American direct foreign investment in France? For United States restrictions on imports? For United States foreign aid? For the unemployment rate in the United States?

c. In what sense can it be said that the dollar problem is even more a political problem than an economic problem?

3. a. President Nixon's action on August 15, 1971, stopped the convertibility of dollars into gold. Would it have been better for the United States to restrict its purchases of gold against dollars,

while continuing to sell gold for dollars at the then existent $35 an ounce price?

b. On what grounds can it be argued that the use of the dollar as a reserve asset, together with the use of gold as a reserve asset, must mean that sooner or later the monetary price of gold must be raised or else gold must be demonetized? Do the events of March 1968 and August 1971 support this argument?

c. Should foreign official dollar holdings again be made convertible into gold? Or into some other "ultimate" international reserve asset? Or remain inconvertible?

d. If a system of limited exchange-rate flexibility is established, and the dollar is the intervention currency, would your answer to c be the same. (You may wish to consider this after reading the next Problem.)

4. Professor Ronald I. McKinnon has suggested the following: "The simple way out is for the United States to abandon completely any payments targets of its own and to permit the other N-1 countries in the world to set their own payments targets unhindered.

"This abandonment should take the form of removing all American restrictions or taxes on portfolio purchases, direct investments, or bank lending abroad, as well as avoiding the tying of foreign aid and the hindering of imports of goods and services. It would also imply that the Department of Commerce should publish international-payments statistics much as it now does but *without* adding up any subset of accounts as a measure of the "deficit." This last entry should be omitted as a casualty to a changing technology. There is no plausible definition of a deficit in the balance of payments of the Nth country which is also a reserve center." (McKinnon, *Private and Official International Money: The Case for the Dollar*, Princeton Essays in International Finance No. 74, April 1969, p. 31.)

Would you have subscribed to McKinnon's position in 1969? On August 14, 1971? Now?

5. It has been said that "It is crucial to remember that the United States destroyed the existing international monetary system in August 1971 because it decided that devaluation served its national economic interests, not because of any collapse of confidence in the dollar by other countries, as so long

predicted by Professor Triffin and others." (C. Fred Bergsten, *Reforming the Dollar*, Council on Foreign Relations, 1972, p. 7.)

Do you agree? How do the events after August 1971 support your position?

6. Would you argue that the dollar problem is an "adjustment problem" in the United States trade balance? Or is it related to the role of the United States as an international financial intermediary? Or to the large stock of internationally mobile capital? How does your diagnosis of the dollar problem affect your proposed remedies?

7. Engage in some writing of imaginary history, and suppose that all the EEC countries had agreed on March 9, 1973, to a joint float against the dollar. What do you think would have been the consequences?

8. a. In reviewing international monetary developments from August 15, 1971, through the Paris agreement, can you distinguish different objectives in an "American solution," "a European solution," and "an international solution?"

b. How do the international monetary developments of this period illustrate the need for harmonization of domestic economic policies as a prerequisite to the maintenance of a system of stable and orderly exchange rates?

9. A GATT working party produced a report (September 12, 1971) which condemned the United States import surcharge as illegal under GATT rules and called for its early removal. Although the IMF found that the United States' balance-of-payments situation was sufficiently critical to justify the surcharge, the GATT working party objected to the use of the surcharge device as detrimental to trade while being aimed at a problem which is essentially monetary.

a. Do you think it is proper international economic conduct to use the threat of import tax surcharges or tariff increases to bring about exchange-rate adjustments? Should matters of trade policy be mixed up with matters of international monetary reform?

b. Should the GATT be reformed along with the IMF?

10. After the breakdown of the Volcker agreement (the second devaluation of the dollar), the *New York Times* stated: "It is

now clear that, in the present environment of distrust and uncertainty, no system of rigidly fixed exchange rates can survive as long as the international money market is able to move huge sums at the least excuse. It can all be as irrational as a mouse stampeding a herd of elephants, but the effect is the same. . . . We need only consider the over-all numbers involved to be suitably awed—a $268 billion pool of liquid assets held by banks and corporations in the international money market, stacked up against $88.5 billion in the monetary reserves of the industrial nations for the defense of currency values." (*New York Times,* March 11, 1973.)

a. Just who are the speculators in the international money market? Should the "international speculators" be blamed as President Nixon did in his press conference of March 3, 1973?

b. What measures can the United States take to curb speculative international capital movements? What measures can other countries take? Were the exchange rate variations of August 1971 and February 1972 the best way to deal with the problem of short-term capital flows?

c. "The one lesson that should be learned from the past year's experience [after the Smithsonian agreement] is that an embittered, politically bargained pact on exchange parities is utterly untenable and merely gives an invitation to what central bankers like to call speculators but are only astute managers of money." (*The Economist,* February 10, 1973, p. 69.)

Would your assessment of the period between the Smithsonian Agreement and the Paris Agreement be the same as the above statement?

D. READINGS

Aliber, Robert Z., *Choices for the Dollar* (1969).

Cooper, Richard N., "The Dollar and the World Economy," in Kermit Gordon (ed.), *Agenda for the Nation* (1968).

Fellner, W., "The Dollar's Place in the International System," *Journal of Economic Literature* (September 1972).

Haberler, Gottfried, "The U.S. Balance of Payments: Freedom or Controls," *Banca Nazionale del Lavoro* (March 1970).

Hearings before the Subcommittee on International Ex-

change and Payments of the Joint Economic Committee, annual.

IMF, *International Financial Statistics,* monthly.

Kennen, Peter B., "The International Position of the Dollar in a Changing World," *International Organization* (Summer 1969).

Kindleberger, Charles P., *Europe and the Dollar* (1966).

Krause, Lawrence B., "A Passive Balance of Payments Strategy for the U.S." *Brookings Papers on Economic Activity,* No. 3 (1970).

Lary, Hal, *Problems of the United States as World Trader and Banker* (1963).

Machlup, Fritz, *Plans for Reform of the International Monetary System* (Princeton International Finance Section, 1964).

Mikesell, R. F., *U.S. Balance of Payments and International Role of the Dollar* (1970).

Triffin, Robert, *The Evolution of the International Monetary System: Historical Reappraisal and Future Perspectives* (Princeton Studies in International Finance, No. 12, 1964).

———, *Gold and the Dollar Crisis: The Future of Convertibility* (1960).

Problem III
International Monetary Reform: Exchange-Rate Flexibility

A. THE CONTEXT

Since the New Economic Policy of August 1971 and the Smithsonian arrangements in December 1971, there has been open discussion of long-forbidden subjects like exchange-rate flexibility, inconvertibility, and gold demonetization. But even after the Paris agreement of March 1973, there still remained many different viewpoints on the controlling principles of international monetary reform—let alone agreement on any one particular institutional arrangement. Even if it is believed that world monetary order is being tested by a lack of international liquidity and a restriction of national economic autonomy, still there can be opposing views on whether the problem of the present system is to be interpreted essentially as a "liquidity problem" or rather as an "adjustment problem."

If it is a "liquidity problem," what are the relative advantages and disadvantages of having liquidity increase through a rise in the price of gold in terms of all currencies? Or creating other reserve assets that can substitute for gold (for example, extending international credit facilities or instituting a different type of reserve-generating system based on the dollar)? How should the creation of liquidity be distributed? Questions concerning the liquidity problem are obviously many.

So too are questions involving any new arrangements to ease the "adjustment problem." Should there be greater exchange-rate flexibility? How can this flexibility be achieved? Through a widening of the band? And a "sliding parity," or "crawling peg?" Or fully flexible rates?

1. INADEQUACY OF RESERVES

Various proposals have been offered since the early 1960's for international monetary reform. Some of these have concentrated on preserving the par-value (or adjustable peg) system of the International Monetary Fund and gold-dollar standard, while providing a more "adequate" supply of international reserves. A Report of the Joint Economic Committee summarized a number of these proposals as early as 1961.[1] It emphasized that "A major policy objective should be to build up confidence in the permanence of the structure of exchange rates by avoiding any future changes in currency parities among the principal industrial and trading countries of the free world."

VARIOUS PLANS *

The plans that are to be considered here range from a mere continuation of the present practice of making ad hoc central bank arrangements to extend credit in order to meet particular "hot money" crises as they arise, to the creation of an international central bank.

(a) *Ad hoc mutual support arrangements*

Representatives of the major central banks or perhaps the various national treasuries could strengthen existing arrangements by providing for agreements for mutual support among the principal trading and financial countries. Such arrangements would deal primarily with short-term capital movements and in particular would protect the reserve centers (and their creditors) against the damaging effects of withdrawals of short-term funds. They might also be used, of course, to protect currencies against strains arising from other causes.

Such arrangements might take a wide variety of forms. Without going into detail, it will be enough to set out some of the dimensions of variations:

(a) Amount of support commitment.
(b) Duration of support.

---

[1] Joint Committee Print, *International Payments Imbalances* (1961).
* Joint Committee Print, *International Payments Imbalances* (1961), pp. 14–18.

(c) Conditions of support: Is there any dependable, advance commitment, or must the conditions be separately negotiated for each new situation, including satisfying lenders as to credit-worthiness of the borrower, satisfying them that the borrower is taking proper steps to rectify the basic cause of the strain, and so on?

(d) Intergovernmental or intercentral bank arrangements.

(e) Bilateral or multilateral arrangements.

(f) Form of support: Agreement to hold borrower's currency, or loan lender''s currency (or possibly gold or a third currency).

(g) Exchange risk: If support takes form of holding borrower's currency, the currency holdings might be subject to a gold or exchange rate guarantee. Or a similar result could be accomplished by making the support take the form of a swap transaction; e.g., at a time of heavy pressure against the pound, the Swiss National Bank buys and holds sterling, but contracts to sell it 3 months forward to Bank of England at a specified rate of exchange.

It will be apparent that arrangements of this kind do not change the basic structure. Reserves would still consist of gold and reserve currencies. But particularly if the arrangements are intended to relieve a key-currency country, a commitment of this type is tantamount to a commitment to hold, and indeed to extend holdings of the reserve currency. From this standpoint, then, it could be regarded as a device for supplementing reserves at least temporarily.

(b) *The Bernstein plan*

The Bernstein plan has earned strong support. Like the arrangements described above, it provides for no change in the form in which reserves are kept and the role of the key-currency countries would not be altered. It contains two elements:

(i) *The integration of Fund quotas with members' own reserves.*—Access to Fund resources would be entirely free, rather than restricted and discretionary, within the limits laid down in the articles of agreement: in the normal case, a member could draw 25 percent of its quota per year up to the point where total drawings were equal to 125 percent of its quota. Drawings in excess of 25 percent a year or 125 percent of quotas would require a waiver. Members would then treat their quotas as virtually an addition to their own reserves and would presumably meet deficits by drawing on the Fund pari passu with drawing on reserves.

(ii) *Increasing Fund resources in members' currencies.*—Free access to Fund resources on this basis would not be possible today. One of the weaknesses of the Fund is that its holdings of the currencies of some of its members are limited unduly and may easily be exhausted. The reserve currency countries have contributed disproportionately to the Fund's resources; other Western European countries not enough. Consequently, the Fund is poorly equipped to deal with a shift of funds from one of the reserve centers to continental European countries. . . .

One way of strengthening its position would be to increase all members' quotas. But while this would increase Fund holdings of all members' currencies (including many for which it has no use), it would also increase members' drawing facilities correspondingly. Moreover, the objection might be raised that such a step was taken as recently as 1959.

Bernstein (and others) have also suggested that certain of the Fund's members agree to lend the Fund additional amounts of their currencies should its holdings of these currencies fall too low. These standby credits need be negotiated only with the leading countries whose currencies are most likely to be in demand, though there is no reason why other Fund members with convertible currencies should not join. Currency borrowed in this way would be employed to meet needs caused by destabilizing short-term capital movements from one financial center to another, rather than to finance deficits in a member country's underlying balance of payments. In order to keep such transactions separate from ordinary Fund transactions, Bernstein proposes that they take place through a subsidiary reserve settlement account. . . .

(c) *The Zolotas plan, and others like it*

Similar proposals which would give the Fund standby borrowing facilities, but under article VII rather than through a separate subsidiary, have been made by Professor Zolotas, Governor of the Bank of Greece, by Maxwell Stamp, as an alternative plan B to his more ambitious and preferred plan (described below); and by Per Jacobsson in his annual report to ECOSOC, April 1961.

(d) *The Franks-Radcliffe Committee proposals*

Sir Oliver Franks and the Radcliffe Committee have proposed that the International Monetary Fund be authorized to accept deposits from its members, which they would treat as reserves. These deposits could be created either by the Fund's lending operations, or by deposit with the Fund by its members of reserves now held in the form of dollars, sterling, or gold. Under this arrangement, the present reserve base would be supplemented by deposit balances with the Fund. Triffin, whose full proposals will be discussed below, has also urged this step as a desirable transition toward his full plan. His idea in proposing it is (a) that countries might be more willing to hold gold-guaranteed deposits with the Fund than unguaranteed sterling or dollars, and thus the structure of reserves would be rendered more stable, and (b) that the acceptance of voluntary deposits by the Fund would be a steppingstone toward the full Triffin plan.

(e) *The Stamp plan*

Maxwell Stamp has proposed that the Fund issue certificates up to a specified amount in any period, e.g., $3 billion a year, to an international agency to aid economic development. This agency would allocate the certificates to developing countries, and the latter would spend them at will. No country, however, would be required to accept the certificates. Countries which did agree to accept them would find their exports stimulated.

(f) *Payments union for developed economies of free world*

The success of the operations of the European Payments Union has suggested still another series of proposals which, if implemented, would give rise to a new form of reserve to supplement gold and the reserve currencies. The members of the OECD (and Japan and possibly Australia and New Zealand) would form a clearing or payments union. Deficits and surpluses of the members on ordinary account would be settled at an agreed ratio (e.g., half or two-thirds) in gold or foreign exchange acceptable to the payee. The remainder would be settled in the form of debits and/or credits on the books of the clearing union. . . .

(g) *The Triffin plan*

Under the plan proposed by Triffin, claims against the International Monetary Fund, or other international institutions, are used as national reserves in place of the dollars and sterling now held as reserves. The essential elements are:

(a) Countries would agree to discontinue holding any reserves in the form of national currencies.

(b) Countries would agree to hold a minimum portion of their reserves in the form of deposits with the International Monetary Fund. (Triffin has suggested 20 percent as the initial percentage.)

(c) The International Monetary Fund would be authorized to expand its deposits by loans and "open market operations" subject to some appropriate limitation on the rate of expansion. Triffin has suggested that this expansion, together with the increase in monetary gold stocks, be limited to an annual increment in total reserves at some agreed rate, say 3 percent.

Thus the present International Monetary Fund would be converted into an international central bank, holding deposits and able to create credit. (The present IMF is a fund, not a bank. It can lend only the pool of currencies and gold represented by members' subscriptions.) The international central bank's deposit liabilities as well as its assets would be subject to a gold guarantee (or, strictly, a maintenance of gold value guarantee), as the present Fund's assets and liabilities are.

These are the bare essentials. There is room for considerable variation in their implementation. The point of prime importance is the transition from the present arrangement to the operation of the Triffin plan. Countries would initially acquire IMF deposits required to meet the minimum requirement by transferring to the IMF gold or foreign currencies they now hold as reserves, and by exchanging their present credit balances with the IMF for new deposits. To the extent that they do not choose to convert existing foreign exchange reserves into IMF deposits, they would liquidate them, by conversion into gold. (Triffin provides a minor exception for "working balances" in key currencies, and another exception for that portion of balances now held in sterling which is not convertible into gold.)

The transition from the present arrangements to the Triffin Fund-Bank would profoundly affect the international financial position of the reserve-currency countries. Their liabilities to other central banks and governments would be eliminated. In part, they would be replaced by liabilities to the Fund-

Bank (maybe entirely in case of pounds). In part, they would be canceled against gold payments (perhaps only for the dollar). . . .

Certain aspects of the Triffin plan are subject to modification. The Fund's "open market operations" might be directed to the purchase of Government obligations of advanced countries or instead to bonds issued by the International Bank for Reconstruction and Development. Likewise, the requirement for minimum deposits and the arrangements for the transfer and subsequent amortization of existing holdings of reserve currencies could of course be modified.

(*h*) *Raising price of gold*

Finally, it has been proposed that the problem could be handled most easily by means of a general increase in the price of gold. This would, of course, mean an increase in the monetary value of the existing reserves of the major gold-holding countries and it might, by increasing the ratio of gold reserves in the key-currency countries to their demand liabilities to foreigners, increase the readiness of these other countries to acquire dollars and sterling for reserve purposes.

Such a step would, however, have other effects which would have to be kept in mind. It would give a subsidy to the largest gold producers—South Africa and the Soviet Union. The incidence of windfall gains would be highly arbitrary, and it would "penalize" countries which had been willing to keep their reserves in the form of dollars and sterling, while favoring those which had insisted upon holding gold. Finally, it would provide a large windfall gain to private gold hoarders and probably stimulate speculative interest in gold. It might lead in the future to very large movements of funds out of the major currencies into gold in anticipation of further increases in its price, thereby vastly increasing the future need for reserves. In those Middle Eastern and Asian countries where gold hoarding has been endemic and has interfered with productive uses of saving, it would serve to enhance gold's prestige as a means of storing wealth.

A major argument for additional reserves is that while fixity of exchange rates is desirable because it reduces the risks of international trade and investment, there must be sufficient financing of deficits to allow more time for corrective forces to operate in the deficit country—especially for the gradual correction of structural "imbalances." This view has been expressed as follows:

> An improved system, which would provide enough means of financing to permit countries to restore equilibrium slowly, must have four characteristics. First, it should provide enough international reserves and credit facilities at the outset to finance substantial imbalances while adjustments are

taking place, and it should provide for increases in these means of financing as the need for them grows. . . . Second, the financing which takes the form of credit should be available readily and promptly, and for a period long enough to permit the country's deficit to be eliminated. . . . Third, the possibility of shifting resources from weak to strong currencies, which is a major source of instability when national currencies are held as reserves, must be prevented. So long as such reserves can be shifted, the countries whose currencies are being used as reserves will regard themselves as vulnerable to their withdrawal and will be subject to the very constraints that should be avoided. . . . Fourth, the principal financial and industrial countries should consult fully and frequently and coordinate their national policies that have substantial effects on international payments, including wage-price policies and commercial policies, not only monetary and fiscal policies.[2]

2. CREATION OF SDRs

The IMF meeting in Rio de Janeiro in 1967 was historic for approving the outline agreement of "a facility based on special drawing rights in the fund." The new special drawing rights (popularly called "paper gold") are simply entries in the IMF ledgers that allow deficit countries to settle part of their payments imbalances with allotments of SDRs. Over the three-year period of distribution, certain countries with surplus positions, designated by the IMF, undertake to accept up to twice the amount of their own SDR allotments in SDRs from other countries. Deficit countries must maintain an average of 30 per cent of their allotment in their reserves over the full, three-year distribution period; in other words, they can use 70 per cent over the entire period to settle their international accounts, although in any one year they can use the entire allotment.

The Rio agreement is significant because it involved international negotiation among many countries to determine the required decisions on the basic period for, the timing of, and the amount and distribution of the new reserve asset.

[2] Walter S. Salant, *Does the International Monetary System Need Reform?* (1964), p. 18.

2.1 *Outline of SDR Agreement*

THE AGREEMENT *

Introduction

The facility described in this Outline is intended to meet the need, as and when it arises, for a supplement to existing reserve assets. It is to be established within the framework of the Fund and, therefore, by an Amendment of the Fund's Articles.

I. Establishment of a Special Drawing Account in the Fund

A. An Amendment to the Articles will establish a Special Drawing Account through which all the operations relating to special drawing rights will be carried out. The purposes of the facility will be set forth in the introductory section of the Amendment.

B. The operations of and resources available under the Special Drawing Account will be separate from the operation of the present Fund which will be referred to as the General Account.

II. Participants and Other Holders

1. Participants. Participation in the Special Drawing Account will be open to any member of the Fund that undertakes the obligations of the Amendment. A member's quota in the Fund will be the same for the purposes of both the General and the Special Drawing Accounts of the Fund.

2. Holding by General Account. The General Account will be authorized to hold and use special drawing rights.

III. Allocation of Special Drawing Rights

1. Principles for decisions. The Special Drawing Account will allocate special drawing rights in accordance with the provisions of the Amendment. . . .

2. Basic period and rate of allocation. The following provisions will apply to any decision to allocate special drawing rights.

(i) The decision will prescribe a basic period during which special drawing rights will be allocated at specific intervals. The period will normally be five years in length, but the Fund may decide that any basic period will be of different duration. The first basic period will begin on the effective date of the first decision to allocate special drawing rights.

(ii) The decision will also prescribe the rate or rates at which special drawing rights will be allocated during the basic period. Rates will be expressed as a percentage, uniform for all participants, of quotas on the date specified in the decision. . . .

* J. Keith Horsefield (ed.), *The International Monetary Fund*, Vol. III: *Documents* (1969).

V. Use of Special Drawing Rights

1. Right to use special drawing rights.

A. A participant will be entitled, in accordance with the provisions of V, to use special drawing rights to acquire an equivalent amount of a currency convertible in fact. A participant which thus provides currency will receive an equivalent amount of special drawing rights.

B. Within the framework of such rules and regulations as the Fund may adopt, a participant may obtain the currencies referred to in A either directly from another participant or through the Special Drawing Account.

C. Except as indicated in V.3.C, a participant will be expected to use its special drawing rights only for balance of payments needs or in the light of developments in its total reserves and not for the sole purpose of changing the composition of its reserves.

D. The use of special drawing rights will not be subject to prior challenge on the basis of this expectation, but the Fund may make representations to any participant which, in the Fund's judgment, has failed to observe the expectation, and may direct drawings to such participant to the extent of such failure.

2. Provisions of currency. A participant's obligation to provide currency will not extend beyond a point at which its holdings of special drawing rights in excess of the net cumulative amount of such rights allocated to it are equal to twice that amount. However, a participant may provide currency, or agree with the Fund to provide currency, in excess of this limit.

3. Selection of participants to be drawn upon. The Fund's rules and instructions relating to the participants from which currencies should be acquired by users of special drawing rights will be based on the following main general principles, supplemented by such principles as the Fund may find desirable from time to time:

A. Normally, currencies will be acquired from participants that have a sufficiently strong balance of payments and reserve position, but this will not preclude the possibility that currency will be acquired from participants with strong reserve positions even though they have moderate balance of payments deficits.

B. The Fund's primary criterion will be to seek to approach over time equality, among the participants indicated from time to time by the criteria in A above, in the ratios of their holdings of special drawing rights, or such holdings in excess of net cumulative allocations thereof, to total reserves.

C. In addition, the Fund will, in its rules and instructions, provide for such use of special drawing rights, either directly between participants or through the intermediary of the Special Drawing Account, as will promote voluntary reconstitution and reconstitution under V.4.

D. Subject to the provisions of V.1.C, a participant may use its special drawing rights to purchase balances of its currency held by another participant, with the agreement of the latter.

4. Reconstitution.

A. Members that use their special drawing rights will incur an obligation to reconstitute their position in accordance with principles which will take account of the amount and the duration of the use. These principles will be laid down in rules and regulations of the Fund.

B. The rules for reconstitution of drawings made during the first basic period will be based on the following principles:

i. The average net use, taking into account both use below and holdings above its net cumulative allocation, made by a participant of its special drawing rights calculated on the basis of the preceding five years, shall not exceed 70 percent of its average net cumulative allocation during this period. Reconstitution under this subparagraph i will be brought about through the mechanism of transfers, by the Fund directing drawings correspondingly. . . .

VI. Interest and Maintenance of Gold Value

A. *Interest.* A moderate rate of interest will be paid in special drawing rights on holdings of special drawing rights. The cost of this interest will be assessed against all participants in proportion to net cumulative allocations of special drawing rights to them.

B. *Maintenance of gold value.* The unit of value for expressing special drawing rights will be equal to 0.888671 grams of fine gold. The rights and obligations of participants and of the Special Drawing Account will be subject to an absolute maintenance of gold value or to provisions similar to Article IV, Section 8 of the Fund's Articles.

2.2 *Implementation*

By mid-1969 a sufficient number of Fund members had ratified the agreement to allow it to take effect. The allocation of a specific amount of SDRs was then in order. The Group of 10—the leading industrial nations—finally reached a mutually agreeable formula for a three-year allocation of SDRs, with a total of $3.5 billion to be allocated for 1970 and $3 billion in each of the two succeeding years. After this initial three-year period, the SDR operation was to be reassessed.

Table I indicates the allocation and distribution of SDRs over the period 1970–72. The initial allocation was according to each country's size of quota in the IMF—so that the United States received more than 25 per cent of the total, the Group of 10 approximately 60 per cent, and all the less-developed countries only 25 per cent.

Some hailed SDRs as a "landmark in monetary evolution." And it could certainly be claimed that the securing of official

TABLE 1. Participants' SDR Positions
(As of February 28, 1973.
Amounts expressed in millions of SDRs)

Participants	Allocation				SDR Holdings		
	Jan. 1, 1970	Jan. 1, 1971	Jan. 1, 1972	Total to Date	Net Acquisition or Net Use (−)	Amount	Percent of Allocations
Industrial countries	2,276.2	1,954.8	1,946.7	6,177.7	397.0	6,574.7	106
United States	866.9	716.9	710.2	2,294.0	−490.9	1,803.1	79
United Kingdom	409.9	299.6	296.8	1,006.3	−401.9	604.4	60
Industrial Europe	753.3	692.2	695.9	2,141.4	1,136.0	3,277.4	153
Canada	124.3	117.7	116.6	358.6	106.7	465.3	130
Japan	121.8	128.4	127.2	377.4	47.1	424.5	112
Other developed areas	284.8	247.0	257.3	789.1	−140.5	648.5	82
Less developed areas	853.1	747.5	747.4	2,348.0	−843.7	1,504.2	64
Latin America	330.0	275.8	273.3	879.1	−270.9	608.2	69
Middle East	77.4	81.0	81.0	239.4	−115.4	124.0	52
Other Asia	277.7	242.4	244.9	765.0	−276.8	488.2	64
Other Africa	168.0	148.3	148.2	464.5	−180.7	283.9	61
Country total	3,414.0	2,949.2	2,951.5	9,314.8	−587.4	8,727.4	

SOURCE: IMF, *International Financial Statistics*.

agreement to the international negotiation of a new reserve asset was the most notable accomplishment in international monetary cooperation since Bretton Woods. Nonetheless, some economists called attention to the opportunity cost of the SDR agreement. To those who believed that the adjustment process remained the fundamental problem of the international monetary system, the limited increase in liquidity was merely a diversionary tactic. A few others regarded the agreement

> as positively harmful . . . [because] it would distract attention from the more fundamental problems facing the world system and . . . while its long-run potential for good or bad was substantial, the major hurdle was to get beyond the immediate short run. Solution of the short-run problem would involve substantial changes in the structure of the system and the long-run creation of a new international money should be integrated into or evolve out of this short-run reconstruction of the system.[3]

As to the crucial question of whether SDRs would become in fact an effective supplement to the present international monetary system, Professor Johnson replied

> time alone will tell. Some authors still hark back to the idea of returning to gold as the basic international monetary reserve, by means of a general increase in its monetary price. Others are convinced that gold has been superseded by the new invention of SDRs. Still others argue that the dollar, as a "natural" outcome of the evolution of the world economy since World War II, will dominate the SDRs and prevent any return to gold at a higher monetary price. My own view is that gold has had its day and that the problem for the future lies between the dollar and the Special Drawing Rights.[4]

An early advocacy of an SDR-standard came at the 1971 meeting of the governors of the IMF. The British Chancellor of the Exchequer, Anthony Barber, proposed that SDRs replace both gold and dollars as the main reserve assets and as the central

[3] Robert Mundell, "Toward a Better International Monetary System," *Journal of Money, Credit, and Banking* (August 1969), p. 626.

[4] Harry G. Johnson, *Efficiency in Domestic and International Money Supply*, International Economics Series, No. 3, University of Surrey (1970), p. 15.

pivot of the international currency system. An advantage claimed for the Barber plan was that the dollar and pound would be reduced to normal national currencies and would no longer have to bear the costs of being reserve currencies. Another advantage, according to the Chancellor, was that "the parity of the dollar would be expressed in terms of the SDR in the same way as any other currency; this would give the United States government an important instrument of adjustment policy which it has hitherto ruled out, that is, the possibility of changing the parity of its currency." The Barber plan was, however, more suggestive than detailed—and it did not begin to answer such difficult questions as what would be the actual parity rates in terms of the SDR, what would be the amount and distribution of the SDRs, and to what extent and by what means would existing dollar and sterling balances be funded into SDRs.

3. DEVELOPING COUNTRIES' RECOMMENDATIONS

The future of the international monetary system is as important to the Third World countries as it is to the United States, EEC, and Japan. The gold-exchange and dollar standard—characterized by limited liquidity, requirements of balance-of-payments discipline, and successive currency crises—had restrained international economic expansion during the 1960's and early 1970's. The developing countries were therefore anxious for monetary reforms that would allow a higher rate of growth throughout the world economy, with indirect benefits to the late-developing nations. Even more, these countries sought direct benefits from some plan that would provide a link between the creation of additional liquidity and additional development assistance. They were also concerned about reform of the adjustment mechanism and how greater exchange-rate flexibility would affect the course of their development.

3.1 *Linking Reserve Creation and Development Assistance*

THE "LINK" *

Chairman REUSS. Good morning.

The Subcommittee on International Exchange and Payments will be in order for a hearing to consider a new facility for increasing financial assistance to developing nations.

While the proposals under discussion today are new in the sense that they are not now in being, the idea of using the multilateral creation of reserves not only to ease the liquidity problem but also to finance real transference to developing countries has been discussed for almost ten years.

Today we hope to consider the arguments for and against the so-called "link," what the form of such a mechanism might be, the advantages and disadvantages of alternative mechanisms, and the benefits that the less developed countries might potentially get from such a facility.

We have an exceptionally distinguished panel of witnesses to participate in our discussion this morning. . . .

All of you gentlemen have prepared most valuable statements which under the rule and without objection will be admitted into the record and made part of the proceedings in full.

I would like each one of you, starting with Mr. Dell, to give or summarize the points that you wish to make, and then I would hope that we can have some discussion not only among members of the subcommittee but also among members of the panel on this most important question.

Mr. Dell?

STATEMENT OF SIDNEY DELL
Director, New York Office of UNCTAD

Mr. DELL. Mr. Chairman, among the indispensable conditions for a healthier world economy is a willingness on the part of the industrial countries to assist in the development of the less-developed countries.

It is generally recognized that, as the World Bank has lately reaffirmed, the current flow of capital to the less-developed countries is well below the capacity of these countries to make effective use of it. Among the reasons frequently cited by donor countries for curtailment of aid programs is the fear of losing reserves, and if action is taken to increase the world level of reserves, it is to be presumed that one of the deterrents to an enlargement of aid would be pro tanto removed.

---

* Joint Economic Committee, *Hearing Before the Subcommittee on International Exchange and Payments,* 91st Congress, 1st Session, 1969, pp. 1–5, 16–19, 29–30.

It cannot, however, be taken for granted that restrictions on aid, once imposed, will be readily relaxed. Such limitations on aid have by now acquired a life of their own, and all kinds of reasons have been found to justify them. There is therefore no assurance that an easing of the world's liquidity position will be accompanied by an increase in the flow of resources to the less-developed countries, unless specific steps are taken to insure that this occurs.

This is the basic rationale for a link between liquidity creation and the provision of aid to less-developed countries. Such a link would enable donor countries to respond to the need for more aid, without running the risk of incurring any loss of reserves, and without having to increase taxes for this purpose, although not of course without increasing the transfer of real resources.

One contention commonly advanced against the link is that liquidity creation is not designed to effect a permanent transfer of real resources from one group of countries to another, a contention that would apparently rule out the gold standard as well, since countries acquiring gold for their reserves have always had to transfer real resources to the gold producing countries in exchange. This argument would also rule out the newly established system of SDR's, which allows participating countries to maintain as little as 30 percent of their net cumulative allocation of SDR's, and use the balance to acquire real resources from other participants.

Another objection is that linking liquidity creation with the provision of assistance to less-developed countries may tend to generate pressures for excessively large amounts of SDR creation in relation to world liquidity needs.

It is important to note, however, that throughout the discussion of this matter by both industrial and less-developed countries in UNCTAD, the point has never been questioned that the amount of any new reserve creation should be determined by the monetary requirements of the world economy, and not by the need for development finance.

In any case, there is very little risk of excessive creation of SDR's in circumstances in which a mere 15 percent of the total vote in the International Monetary Fund suffices to prevent a proposed act of liquidity creation.

Finally, it has been suggested that if the industrial countries are not prepared to expand their aid by direct means, that is by direct contributions to bilateral and multilateral aid programs, they are not likely to be willing to do the same thing indirectly, that is through the link.

Now although the real burden of aid is the same, whether the transfer takes place by conventional methods or through such methods as the link, governments may see some advantages in the latter method.

As I have already mentioned, two advantages of this method are that it avoids any risk of reserve losses, and that it makes it possible to expand aid programs without having to increase taxes.

The possibility that introduction of the link would tempt governments to reduce other forms of aid cannot be entirely dismissed. It is, however, unlikely that the opening up of new channels of aid adds nothing at all to the total flow. The net increase in the total level of aid resulting from the link may turn out to be less than the direct allocations of SDR's or their equivalents in national currencies for lending to less-developed countries, but there would probably be some net increase, and my own impression is that the net increase would be considerable.

We come finally to the question of the most suitable form for the link. Although there are important advantages in establishing the link as an integral part of the mechanism through which SDR's are distributed, we have to face the fact that in the immediate future this has been ruled out by the terms of the new amendment to the articles of agreement of the International Monetary Fund, which preclude the holding of SDR's by any such agency as the World Bank group.

There is therefore a strong case for considering a voluntary form of the link, as suggested by Professor Triffin, and by Dr. I. G. Patel, economic adviser to the Ministry of Finance of India and one of the members of the UNCTAD expert group on international monetary issues. . . .

What Dr. Patel suggests is that every act of international liquidity creation should be accompanied by voluntary contributions to IDA by all the Part One member countries of IDA, the size of the voluntary contribution being a certain uniform proportion of the share of every Part One country in international liquidity creation.

Most of the objections to the link in its organic form do not apply to this alternative version. From a legal standpoint, there is nothing in the amendment to the articles of agreement of the IMF that would preclude such an arrangement, and from the standpoint of economic and banking policy, this alternative version of the link would provide for a clear separation between liquidity creation and development assistance as recommended by the critics of the organic link. . . .

As to the possible ratio of IDA contributions to the newly created reserves, this is a a matter for discussion and negotiation just as the obligation to reconstitute 30 percent of cumulative SDR allocations was a matter for discussion and negotiation.

Ideally one would like to see IDA contributions equal to the value of the newly created reserves, but one might have to settle for less than this. . . .

All in all, the link would significantly increase the efficiency of new reserve creation in improving the international economic environment.

Thank you, Mr. Chairman.

STATEMENT OF HARRY G. JOHNSON

*Professor of Economics,
University of Chicago, and the London School of
Economics and Political Science*

Mr. JOHNSON. Thank you, Mr. Chairman.

The proposal of the link does have a lot of attraction at the present time for two reasons, one being that the balance of payments deficits for the United

Kingdom and the United States have been used as justifications for reducing the flow of aid. The other is that the developing countries have become much more capable of absorbing aid, just at a time when the flow of aid relative at least to the capacity to bear the burden has been falling.

Nevertheless, it seems to me that there are fairly strong arguments against the general proposal to link international reserve creation and development assistance. One which I have advanced in the past is that development assistance and the creation of international reserves are separate issues, each with its own economics and, more important, with its own politics.

One can argue that the linkage of these two problems in policy discussions is really a matter of willingness of governments to link them, and that perhaps at the present time this possibility is greater than it has been in the past, and that is a matter on which I am not competent to pass a judgment.

The more fundamental argument against the proposal, I think, is that contrary to widely held views the creation of international reserves does not need to involve the generation of a pool of resources which have to be allocated somehow and on which the less developed countries have a moral claim.

Perhaps some years ago this view was more plausible, in the sense that plans for international monetary reform at that time were generally modeled on the concept of a bank, with liabilities which would constitute the reserve assets, being backed by assets in the form of loans and securities, but it has come to be understood in the course of the discussion that what is required of international reserves is acceptability to those who have to hold them, and that the quality of acceptability does not require that there be assets to back the reserve instrument. And that principle is in fact embodied in the SDR scheme which from that point of view constitutes a considerable advance on earlier discussions.

The fact that it is embodied in the SDR scheme makes it much more difficult to disguise the fact that linking reserve creation to development assistance does demand a deliberate choice to transfer real resources from the developed countries which want to hold larger stocks of reserves to the less developed countries which would benefit either by initially receiving the reserve assets or by receiving the funds paid in exchange for them.

Now the real transfer involved is entirely unnecessary from the standpoint of creating new international reserve assets, and you could only justify it either on the political feasibility argument, which I have already mentioned, or else by creating some sort of fiction to the effect that it is more desirable that countries earn their additional reserves than that they simply create them.

Creating reserves is a costless procedure, at least in economic terms. On the other hand, giving reserves away and then earning them back does involve a very substantial real cost in terms of transferring real resources and it seems to me that countries would be unlikely to accept that unless they already had a strong desire to increase their transfers of resources to the promotion of the economic growth of the less developed countries, and in that case the question is whether the linkage is the best way of doing this.

Well, the specific proposal before the subcommittee is for the linkage of creation of SDR's in addition to those created under the present agreed scheme to the financing of the development of the less developed countries.

Now the basic argument for that proposal has to rest on the assumption that under the agreement, the creation of new reserves in the form of SDR's will promote the healthy development of the international economy and that the creation that is prospective will be insufficient to the needs of the international economy. Otherwise the proposal to create additional SDR's is really a proposal for financing economic development by world inflation, and the policy of promoting development by inflation is not usually regarded as a good policy in the context of single nation's policies.

Well, the whole thing has to rest then on the assumption that reserve creation would otherwise be inadequate, and this raises two problems. The first is to establish that in fact it will be inadequate by some kind of economic standard, and this raises difficulties, because in spite of the alleged seriousness of the international liquidity problem, the world economy has been characterized by a mild but marked inflation of prices since World War II.

That inflationary trend of world prices has been much more resented on the European Continent than it has been here and in the United Kingdom, and the assertion that the reserve creation will be inadequate could simply be the assertion that United Kingdom and United States views on inflation versus unemployment are correct, and that the world would be better off being forced to accept those views than it would be if it had less inflation with less reserve creation.

The second difficulty, while it is a political one, is one which I do feel competent to discuss, and that is that if the developed countries having negotiated the present scheme then negotiate a sizable increase of reserves in the form of SDR's, then even if it is true that those new reserves will be inadequate and will prove to be inadequate, I do not see the countries involved accepting a renegotiation of their decision in the form of extra SDR's. Rather I expect them to insist on seeing what happens with the reserves they create, and if necessary correcting their decision in the event of experience.

Well, these considerations suggest that in the light of the questions posed by the subcommittee for these hearings, that aid-linked SDR's would virtually have to be and should be created as an integral part of the decision to create new international reserves, and that they would not constitute a net addition to the total of SDR's created, only a redistribution of a predetermined quantity of SDR's.

Now in connection with the proposal that creation of extra SDR's should be on a voluntary purchase basis there is I think a real question of how many might be purchased. As reserve assets, SDR's will be significantly inferior to U.S. dollars, and though I am not very confident at the moment, they might even be inferior to sterling, because the SDR's carry a very low rate of interest on accumulations additional to a country's quota.

The development of the use of SDR's as an international reserve asset will depend on the establishment of a central bank preference for them, and it is not altogether clear that such a preference will in fact be established. It is possible that the rest of the world will get used to the present de facto dollar standard, and that the use of dollars as reserve assets rather than being terminated as is assumed in many of these discussions, may in fact revive.

Another consideration is that it would be perfectly possible for countries, if they want to accumulate reserves and also want to have the accumulation of reserves matched by contributions to the less developed countries, to do that entirely apart from the SDR scheme itself. It is possible, as I suggest in my statement, that this could be done simply by purchasing World Bank bonds, and using them as reserve assets.

They would be less liquid, obviously, than SDR's. On the other hand, they would offer a rate or return substantially superior.

Now, this consideration—and I had not read Mr. Dell's paper before I came this morning—but the proposal that you should couple the creation of SDR's with contributions to IDA, for example, really accepts this point, and I do not see that to say that that is a proper procedure really amounts to accepting any link at all other than some sort of moral obligation to contribute to the developing countries.

If we accept my argument that aid linked SDR's would simply be a redistribution of a predetermined total of SDR's, it is obvious that the benefit of aid linking to the developing countries is going to depend on the total size of the SDR's created and the proportion of them which are linked to aid. This is an answer to another one of the subcommittee's questions which is how much benefit the developing countries would get from this.

Insofar as SDR's are decided on the basis of how much extra money the world needs, then the amount of them created would have to depend among other things on how much use of the dollar as a source of additional reserves is made, and also on the estimate of how many extra reserves the world needs.

Again I would say that it is not all that clear that the dollar is finished as an international reserve asset. Some of my colleagues have argued on the contrary that the dollar is going to be the currency of the future, and in that case, the amount of SDR's required will be rather substantially less than current estimates indicate.

As to the proportion of SDR's to be aid linked, this depends very much on the scheme of linking, but it seems to me very unlikely that the developed countries would really make a major proportion of the SDR subject to the linkage.

STATEMENT OF RAUL PREBISCH

Former Secretary-General
of UNCTAD, and Director-General of the United
Nations Latin American Institute for Economic
and Social Planning

Mr. PREBISCH. Thank you, Mr. Chairman.

Undoubtedly, international monetary reform and the transfer of resources to developing countries are two different things, and we should not mix them. However, this does not mean that they cannot be combined. What we are trying to do, therefore, is take advantage of the reform in order to add more resources to developing countries.

But it is obvious that the amount of new monetary resources to be created should be considered quite independently of any consideration as to the external financial needs of developing countries. This is essential in order to avoid monetary inflation in the use of this reform.

I think that, given the voting power of the different countries in the IMF, there is no risk of developing countries exercising a very effective pressure on developed countries. As you know, the latter have the real power to decide the amount of resources to be created. Indeed, I am afraid that if there is any risk of bias, this risk would be in favor of an insufficient rather than an excessive creation of resources.

The question of whether the link should be organic or not, as Mr. Dell already said, has been considered. The amendment of the articles of the Fund has not entailed an organic link, and in order to introduce an organic link, it would be necessary to amend the amendments. This could be a very serious difficulty. But it is perfectly conceivable to make a parallel agreement whereby developed countries receiving additional resources would put part of the equivalent of these resources at the disposal of the World Bank, or IDA, or regional banks, in order to increase the amount of their resource transfers to developing countries.

There is nothing unsound in the transfer of real resources in that way; this was the nature of the transfer of resources during the golden age of the gold standard. There is nothing new in this. Countries willing to capture part of the increment of gold supplies would exercise all their competitive power through their exports of goods and services to obtain a part of the new gold resources. The results of this SDR scheme, if the idea of a link was accented, would be the same. Instead of gold, countries could capture these new instruments which are representative of gold.

As to the proportion of resources to be transferred to developing countries, Mr. Chairman, I have suggested in my short paper that it be a 50-percent proportion. There is, of course, nothing dogmatic about this. It is a matter of negotiation, as Mr. Dell has said. But the final target should be 100 percent at some future date.

As to conditions of transfer, Mr. Chairman, I consider that it would be unfair to charge a rate of interest to developing countries in this operation, except in exceptional cases. On the contrary, I would like to see this new resource as an element to alleviate the already heavy load of services plaguing developing countries in the form of interest, amortization, and related capital remittances.

It is a well known fact that many developing countries are in a very critical situation in this matter of a substantial and still rising debt-servicing burden. Especially in Latin America. This concerns me very much, not only in regard to the present, but also to the critical situations that would appear in the course of the next few years, if present tendencies continue, and worse yet, if they are aggravated, as seems to be the case.

There is, naturally, the risk that this new transfer of financial resources to

developing countries would diminish in a parallel fashion the resources that
are presently transferred and which are very scarce indeed. However, I would
rather see this as part of the policy commitment accepted by developed
countries at the UNCTAD Conference in New Delhi a year ago, whereby in principle they agreed to transfer 1 percent of their gross product to developing
countries. I think that this new operation, through the link, can and should
help developed countries achieve that target as soon as possible.

3.2 General Aspects of Monetary Reform

After the events of August 15, 1971, the LDCs expressed a
strong determination for an active role in international monetary negotiations, as evident in the Lima Action Program and
statements of UNCTAD. The following extract conveys some
general attitudes on reform of the system.

THE DEVELOPING WORLD AND MONETARY REFORM *

In the establishment of a new monetary system, the following main
objectives and criteria should be borne in mind:

(a) The system should permanently guarantee a situation of international liquidity appropriate for the expansion of world trade and for
the acceleration of the growth of the exports and economies of the developing countries. This means that from its inception the system—
unlike that established at Bretton Woods—should incorporate a body
of rules taking due account of the special problems of the developing
countries. This call for differential treatment should not be considered
in any way unusual, since it simply means extending to the monetary
and financial field a principle which has already been accepted in the
sphere of trade. Steps should be taken to see that this principle is put
into full practical effect. . . .

(b) It is a matter of crucial importance that the developing countries
should participate effectively from the outset in the negotiations concerning the reform of the monetary system and, later, in its actual
operation. . . . Moreover, the Lima Action Programme notes that it is
"entirely unacceptable that vital decisions about the future of the international monetary system which are of concern to the entire world
community are sought to be taken by a limited group of countries outside the framework of the International Monetary Fund."

So far, the reconstruction of the monetary system is being decided
exclusively within the framework of the Group of Ten, although the
Group's meetings are attended by the Managing Director of the Fund.
This procedure, which is completely contrary to the principle of participation in the negotiations by developing countries, strengthens the

* *Economic Bulletin for Latin America*, United Nations, Vol. XVII, No. 1 (1972).

need for the establishment of an intergovernmental group to represent the views sustained by the Group of 77, as advocated in the guiding principles agreed upon in the Lima Programme. If this course or another with the same end in view is not followed, the developing nations will continue to operate within a monetary organization in which all they can do is to ratify in the last stage of the reform process what has already been laid down and decided by a few industrialized nations.

(c) In the Lima Action Programme it was agreed that "the role and authority of the International Monetary Fund should be reestablished and strengthened in all matters that concern the whole international community, as an effective way of safeguarding the interests of all countries especially of the developing countries." It was further agreed that "the voting power of the developing countries in the International Monetary Fund should be increased by introducing provisions in the Articles of Agreement of the International Monetary Fund in order to increase the number of votes allocated to these countries. . . ."

The Attitude of the Developing Countries to a New Monetary System

The Lima Action Programme, which stipulates with great precision the main features that should be introduced in the new monetary system, states that: "The following considerations and guidelines, among others, should be taken into account in the exploration of solutions to the crisis:

"(a) It is indispensable to the restoration of stability and confidence in the world monetary system that a satisfactory structure of exchange rates maintained within narrow margins should be established;

"(b) The new system must provide a mechanism for creating additional international liquidity, through truly collective international action, in line with requirements of an expanding world economy and the special needs of developing countries, and with such safeguards as will ensure that the total supply of international liquidity is not unduly influenced by the balance-of-payments position of any single country or group of countries;

"(c) The creation of a link between SDRs and additional resources for financing development should be made an integral part of the new international monetary system;

"(d) The adherence of the developing countries to a new international monetary system necessarily presupposes the existence of a permanent system of guarantees against exchange losses affecting the reserves of these countries. In any case a mechanism should be worked out to compensate developing countries against involuntary losses they have suffered because of currency speculations in certain currencies of developed countries."

With regard to paragraph (a), it is obvious that a system where parities fluctuate within fairly wide margins would have an unfavourable impact on developing countries. This is particularly so because excessive fluctuations introduce a permanent factor of instability in international trade which has a more serious effect on countries which are less prepared and lack the experience to contend with problems of this kind, i.e., precisely the less developed countries.

Bearing in mind that short-term capital movements are the main determining factors in parity fluctuations, it is particularly important that the industrialized countries should attach more importance to the adoption of internal measures to curb such movements. This course was actually envisaged at Bretton Woods but, with few exceptions, the developed countries never put it into practice.

In order to comply with paragraph (b) of the excerpt from the Lima Action Programme reproduced above, it would seem necessary to include an additional feature in the new system. As strongly maintained by the Latin American spokesman at the last meeting of the International Monetary Fund in Washington, the basic source of international liquidity and the central instrument of reserves should not be identified with national currencies and should increasingly become a fiduciary instrument like SDRs.

Clearly this feature is of particular importance because it would enable the dollar-standard system with all its limitations to be gradually eliminated and the stability and independence of the new monetary system to be progressively enhanced. In this latter respect, the IMF would obviously have a better chance of effectively directing the operation of this system if its base unit is a fiduciary instrument which is created independently of the member countries and is issued and circulated under the supervision and control of the IMF itself.

If a more important role is assigned to Special Drawing Rights it becomes more urgent to adopt procedures whereby the developing nations can have greater access to them. The first step, as already suggested, would be to adopt a different criterion for the distribution of SDRs when they are next allocated, so that developing countries may receive a bigger proportion than that determined by the IMF quotas. The adoption and implementation of this formula is not an alternative to the establishment of a link between the allocation of SDRs and additional development finance, but on the contrary complements such a measure. An important fact to remember is that, in view of the slowing-up of the expansion of international trade, an increase in the purchasing power of developing regions in the near future would be a much-needed stimulus.

The second step would be to establish a link between the allocation of Special Drawing Rights and the provision of additional finance to developing countries, a point which was also included in the Lima Action Programme. . . .

Thirdly, it is necessary that the international community should accept the principle that the balance-of-payments deficits which may give rise to the use of SDRs must be only temporary, and it should be specified as far as possible exactly what is meant by this. The aim of this would be to try to limit the use of SDRs by developed countries which have balance-of-payments deficits over long periods. What happened in 1970 and 1971 was instructive in this respect: the United States and the United Kingdom have been the main users of SDRs, and the EEC has been the principal acceptor. In other words, because the established procedure provides simply that SDRs may be used by deficit countries, and because there is no clear limitation as to what kind of deficits may be financed, a curious situation has arisen in which two of the greatest industrialized countries—one of them being the basis of the system—were the main beneficiaries under the system created at the end of 1969.

Lastly, in paragraph (*d*) of the section of the Lima Action Programme quoted above it is affirmed that the existence of a permanent system of guarantees against exchange losses affecting the reserves of developing countries is necessary in the new system.

The importance of the adoption and implementation of this principle cannot be overemphasized, having in mind the reduction in the real value of international reserves resulting from the exchange-rate realignments approved in December. It must not be forgotten that since the developing countries' reserves were kept mainly in dollars—not in gold or European currencies—they were severely affected by the changes in parities. It would not be fair if this were to happen again, since it would mean introducing disruptive elements into the system itself and encouraging speculation with different forms of reserves by national monetary authorities in order to protect the real value of their holding.

It is therefore a matter of urgency to adopt specific measures in this connexion, including the approval of compensation for losses incurred by developing nations as a result of the recent currency realignments.

4. FLEXIBILITY OF EXCHANGE RATES

Instead of emphasizing the reserve problem, other proposals have sought to improve the adjustment process by advocating greater flexibility of exchange rates. At the extreme end of the spectrum of flexibility are fully flexible or freely floating rates. A strong statement in favor of this type of exchange-rate regime was made in the early 1960's by Professor Milton Friedman.

4.1 *Case for Fully Flexible Rates*

PROFESSOR FRIEDMAN'S STATEMENT *

[L]et us consider the national objective with which our payments system is most directly connected: the promotion of a healthy and balanced growth of world trade, carried on, so far as possible, by private individuals and private enterprises with minimum intervention by governments. This has been a major objective of our whole postwar international economic policy, most recently expressed in the Trade Expansion Act of 1962. Success would knit the free world more closely together, and, by fostering the international division of labor, raise standards of living throughout the world, including the United States.

Suppose that we succeed in negotiating far-reaching reciprocal reductions in tariffs and other trade barriers with the Common Market and other countries. Such reductions will expand trade in general but clearly will have different effects on different industries. The demand for the products of some will expand, for others contract. This is a phenomenon we are familiar with from our internal development. The capacity of our free enterprise system to adapt quickly and efficiently to such shifts, whether produced by changes in technology or tastes, has been a major source of our economic growth. The only additional element introduced by international trade is the fact that different currencies are involved, and this is where the payment mechanism comes in; its function is to keep this fact from being an additional source of disturbance.

An all-around lowering of tariffs would tend to increase both our expenditures and our receipts in foreign currencies. There is no way of knowing in advance which increase would tend to be the greater and hence no way of knowing whether the initial effect would be toward a surplus or deficit in our balance of payments. What is clear is that we cannot hope to succeed in the objective of expanding world trade unless we can readily adjust to either outcome.

Suppose then that the initial effect is to increase our expenditures on imports more than our receipts from exports. How could we adjust to this outcome?

One method of adjustment is to draw on reserves or borrow from abroad to finance the excess increase in imports. The obvious objection to this method is that it is only a temporary device, and hence can be relied on only when the disturbance is temporary. But that is not the major objection. Even if we had very large reserves or could borrow large amounts from abroad, so that we could continue this expedient for many years, it is a most undesirable one. We can see why if we look at physical rather than financial magnitudes.

* Professor Friedman's 1963 statement before the Joint Economic Committee, 88th Congress, 1st Session, *The United States Balance of Payments*, Part 3, November 14, 1963, pp. 452–59. Another portion of Friedman's statement appears on pp. 121–22 above.

The physical counterpart to the financial deficit is a reduction of employment in industries competing with imports that is larger than the concurrent expansion of employment in export industries. So long as the financial deficit continues, the assumed tariff reductions create employment problems. But it is no part of the aim of tariff reductions to create unemployment at home or to promote employment abroad. The aim is a balanced expansion of trade, with exports rising along with imports and thereby providing employment opportunities to offset any reduction in employment resulting from increased imports.

Hence, simply drawing on reserves or borrowing abroad is a most unsatisfactory method of adjustment.

Another method of adjustment is to lower U.S. prices relative to foreign prices, since this would stimulate exports and discourage imports. If foreign countries are accommodating enough to engage in inflation, such a change in relative prices might require merely that the United States keep prices stable or even that it simply keep them from rising as fast as foreign prices. But there is no necessity for foreign countries to be so accommodating, and we could hardly count on their being so accommodating. The use of this technique therefore involves a willingness to produce a decline in U.S. prices by tight monetary policy or tight fiscal policy or both. Given time, this method of adjustment would work. But in the interim, it would exact a heavy toll. It would be difficult or impossible to force down prices appreciably without producing a recession and considerable unemployment. To eliminate in the long run the unemployment resulting from the tariff changes, we should in the short run be creating cyclical unemployment. The cure might for a time be far worse than the disease.

This second method is therefore also most unsatisfactory. Yet these two methods—drawing on reserves and forcing down prices—are the only two methods available under our present international payment arrangements, which involve fixed exchange rates between the U.S. dollar and other currencies. Little wonder that we have so far made such disappointing progress toward the reduction of trade barriers, that our practice has differed so much from our preaching.

There is one other way and only one other way to adjust and that is by allowing (or forcing) the price of the U.S. dollar to fall in terms of other currencies. To a foreigner, U.S. goods can become cheaper in either of two ways—either because their prices in the U.S. fall in terms of dollars or because the foreigner has to give up fewer units of his own currency to acquire a dollar, which is to say, the price of the dollar falls. For example, suppose a particular U.S. car sells for $2,800 when a dollar costs 7 shillings, tuppence in British money (i.e., roughly £1 = $2.80). The price of the car is then £1,000 in British money. It is all the same to an Englishman—or even a Scotsman—whether the price of the car falls to $2,500 while the price of a dollar remains 7 shillings, tuppence, or alternatively, the price of the car remains $2,800, while the price of a dollar falls to 6 shillings, 5 pence (i.e., roughly £1 = $3.11). In either case, the car costs the Englishman £ 900 rather than

£1,000, which is what matters to him. Similarly, foreign goods can become more expensive to an American in either of two ways—either because the price in terms of foreign currency rises or because he has to give up more dollars to acquire a given amount of foreign currency.

Changes in exchange rates can therefore alter the relative price of U.S. and foreign goods in precisely the same way as can changes in internal prices in the United States and in foreign countries. And they can do so without requiring anything like the same internal adjustments. If the initial effect of the tariff reductions would be to create a deficit at the former exchange rate (or enlarge an existing deficit or reduce an existing surplus) and thereby increase unemployment, this effect can be entirely avoided by a change in exchange rates which will produce a balanced expansion in imports and exports without interfering with domestic employment, domestic prices, or domestic monetary and fiscal policy. The pig can be roasted without burning down the barn.

The situation is, of course, entirely symmetrical if the tariff changes should initially happen to expand our exports more than our imports. Under present circumstances, we would welcome such a result, and conceivably, if the matching deficit were experienced by countries currently running a surplus, they might permit it to occur without seeking to offset it. In that case, they and we would be using the first method of adjustment—changes in reserves or borrowing. But again, if we had started off from an even keel, this would be an undesirable method of adjustment. On our side, we should be sending out useful goods and receiving only foreign currencies in return. On the side of our partners, they would be using up reserves and tolerating the creation of unemployment.

The second method of adjusting to a surplus is to permit or force domestic prices to rise—which is of course what we did in part in the early postwar years when we were running large surpluses. Again, we should be forcing maladjustments on the whole economy to solve a problem arising from a small part of it—the 5 percent accounted for by foreign trade.

Again, these two methods are the only ones available under our present international payments arrangements, and neither is satisfactory.

The final method is to permit or force exchange rates to change—in this case, a rise in the price of the dollar in terms of foreign currencies. This solution is again specifically adapted to the specific problem of the balance of payments.

Changes in exchange rates can be produced in either of two general ways. One way is by a change in an official exchange rate: an official devaluation or appreciation from one fixed level which the government is committed to support to another fixed level. This is the method used by Britain in its postwar devaluation and by Germany in 1961 when the mark was appreciated. This is also the main method contemplated by the IMF which permits member nations to change their exchange rates by 10 percent without consultation and by a larger amount after consultation and approval by the Fund. But this method has serious disadvantages. It makes a change in rates a matter of major moment, and hence there is a tendency to postpone any change as long as possible. Difficulties cumulate and a larger change is finally needed than would have been required if it could have been made promptly. By the time the change is made, everyone is aware that a change is pending and is certain about the direction of the change. The result is to encourage a flight from a currency, if it is going to be devalued, or to a currency, if it is going to be appreciated.

There is in any event little basis for determining precisely what the new rate should be. Speculative movements increase the difficulty of judging what the new rate should be, and introduce a systematic bias, making the change needed appear larger than it actually is. The result, particularly when devaluation occurs, is generally to lead officials to "play safe" by making an even larger change than the large change needed. The country is then left after the devaluation with a maladjustment precisely the opposite of that with which it started, and is thereby encouraged to follow policies it cannot sustain in the long run.

Even if all these difficulties could be avoided, this method of changing from one fixed rate to another has the disadvantage that it is necessarily discontinuous. Even if the new exchange rates are precisely correct when first established, they will not long remain correct.

A second and much better way in which changes in exchange rates can be produced is by permitting exchange rates to float, by allowing them to be determined from day to day in the market. This is the method which the United States used from 1862 to 1879, and again, in effect, from 1917 or so to about 1925, and again from 1933 to 1934. It is the method which Britain used from 1918 to 1925 and again from 1931 to 1939, and which Canada used for most of the interwar period and again from 1950 to May 1962. Under this method, exchange rates adjust themselves continuously, and market forces determine the magnitude of each change. There is no need for any official to decide by how much the rate should rise or fall. This is the method of the free market, the method that we adopt unquestioningly in a private enterprise economy for the bulk of goods and services. It is no less available for the price of one money in terms of another.

With a floating exchange rate, it is possible for governments to intervene and try to affect the rate by buying or selling, as the British Exchange Equalization Fund did rather successfully in the 1930's, or by combining buying and selling with public announcements of intentions, as Canada did so disastrously in early 1962. On the whole, it seems to me undersirable to have government intervene, because there is a strong tendency for government agencies to try to peg the rate rather than to stabilize it, because they have no special advantage over private speculators in stabilizing it, because they can make far bigger mistakes than private speculators risking their own money, and because there is a tendency for them to cover up their mistakes by changing the rules—as the Canadian case so strikingly illustrates—rather than by reversing course. But this is an issue on which there is much difference of opinion among economists who are agreed in favoring floating rates. Clearly, it is possible to have a successful floating rate along with governmental speculation.

The great objective of tearing down trade barriers, of promoting a worldwide expansion of trade, of giving citizens of all countries, and especially the underdeveloped countries, every opportunity to sell their products in open markets under equal terms and thereby every incentive to use their resources efficiently, of giving countries an alternative through free world trade to autarky and central planning—this great objective can, I believe, be achieved best under a regime of floating rates. All countries, and not just the United States, can proceed to liberalize boldly and confidently only if they can have reasonable assurance that the resulting trade expansion will be balanced and will not interfere with major domestic objectives. Floating exchange rates, and so far as I can see, only floating exchange rates, provide this assurance. They do so because they are an automatic mechanism for protecting the domestic economy from the possibility that liberalization will produce a serious imbalance in international payments.

Despite their advantages, floating exchange rates have a bad press. Why is this so?

One reason is because a consequence of our present system that I have been citing as a serious disadvantage is often regarded as an advantage; namely, the extent to which the small foreign trade sector dominates national policy. Those who regard this as an advantage refer to it as the discipline of the gold standard. I would have much sympathy for this view if we had a real gold standard, so the discipline was imposed by impersonal forces which in turn reflected the realities of resources, tastes, and technology. But in fact we have today only a pseudo gold standard and the so-called discipline is imposed by governmental officials of other countries who are determining their own internal monetary policies and are either being forced to dance to our tune or calling the tune for us, depending primarily on accidental political developments. This is a discipline we can well do without.

A possibly more important reason why floating exchange rates have a bad press, I believe, is a mistaken interpretation of experience with floating rates, arising out of a statistical fallacy that can be seen easily in a standard example. Arizona is clearly the worst place in the United States for a person with tuberculosis to go because the death rate from tuberculosis is higher in Arizona than in any other State. The fallacy in this case is obvious. It is less obvious in connection with exchange rates. Countries that have gotten into severe financial difficulties, for whatever reason, have had ultimately to change their exchange rates or let them change. No amount of exchange control and other restrictions on trade have enabled them to peg an exchange rate that was far out of line with economic realities. In consequence, floating rates have frequently been associated with financial and economic instability. It is easy to conclude, as many have, that floating exchange rates produce such instability.

This misreading of experience is reinforced by the general prejudice against speculation, which has led to the frequent assertion, typically on the basis of no evidence whatsoever, that speculation in exchange can be expected to be destabilizing and thereby to increase the instability in rates. Few who make this assertion even recognize that it is equivalent to asserting that speculators generally lose money.

Floating exchange rates need not be unstable exchange rates—any more than the prices of automobiles or of government bonds, of coffee or of meals need gyrate wildly just because they are free to change from day to day. The Canadian exchange rate was free to change during more than a decade, yet it varied within narrow limits. The ultimate objective is a world in which exchange rates, while free to vary, are in fact highly stable because basic economic policies and conditions are stable. Instability of exchange rates is a symptom of instability in the underlying economic structure. Elimination of this symptom by administrative pegging of exchange rates cures none of the underlying difficulties and only makes adjustment to them more painful.

The confusion between stable exchange rates and pegged exchange rates helps to explain the frequent comment that floating exchange rates would introduce an additional element of uncertainty into foreign trade and thereby discourage its expansion. They introduce no additional element of uncertainty. If a floating rate would, for example, decline, then a pegged rate would be subject to pressure that the authorities would have to meet by internal deflation or exchange control in some form. The uncertainty about the rate would simply be replaced by uncertainty about internal prices or about the availability of exchange; and the latter uncertainties, being subject to administrative rather than market control, are likely to be the more erratic and unpredictable. Moreover, the trader can far more readily and cheaply protect himself against the danger of changes in exchange rates, through hedging operations in a forward market, than he can against the danger of changes in internal prices or exchange availability. Floating rates are therefore far more favorable to private international trade than pegged rates.

Though I have discussed the problem of international payments in the context of trade liberalization, the discussion is directly applicable to the more general problem of adapting to any forces that make for balance-of-payments difficulties. Consider our present problem of a deficit in the balance of trade plus long-term capital movement. How can we adjust to it? By one of the three methods outlined: first, drawing on reserves or borrowing; second, keeping U.S. prices from rising as rapidly as foreign prices or forcing them down; third, permitting or forcing exchange rates to alter. And, this time, by one more method: by imposing additional trade barriers or their equivalent, whether in the form of higher tariffs, or smaller import quotas, or extracting from other countries tighter "voluntary" quotas on their exports, or "tieing" foreign aid, or buying higher priced domestic goods or services to meet military needs, or imposing taxes on foreign borrowing, or imposing direct controls on investments by U.S. citizens abroad, or any one of the host of other devices for interfering with the private business of private individuals that have become so familiar to us since Hjalmar Schacht perfected the modern techniques of exchange control in 1934 to strengthen the Nazis for war and to despoil a large class of his fellow citizens.

Fortunately or unfortunately, even Congress cannot repeal the laws of arithmetic. Books must balance. We must use one of these four methods. Because we have been unwilling to select the only one that is currently fully consistent with both economic and political needs—namely, floating exchange rates—we have been driven, as if by an invisible hand, to employ all the others, and even then may not escape the need for explicit changes in exchange rates. . . .

4.2 *Case Against Fully Flexible Rates*

If for some economists the merit of freely floating rates is that the price of foreign exchange would be determined daily in the market for foreign currency by the forces of demand and supply, to others this is its very disadvantage because the exchange rate is considered too strategic a price to be determined freely.

If the exchange rate is left to market forces, its impact would be general—in effect, the scale changes for all prices, whereas a government may want to alter only some prices of specific exportables and importables. Depreciation, for instance, will have a general effect on all prices in the foreign trade sector, acting as an ad valorem subsidy on all exportables and an ad valorem tax on all importables. The capacity for selective price changes is lost.

Another serious concern for some governments is the domestic price instability that might result from fluctuating rates. Countries with high ratios of foreign trade to domestic production might find that price changes in the foreign sector can dominate their entire domestic economy. And this domination may bear no relation to any need for general price changes. A short-term capital outflow, for example, might cause a depreciation in the exchange rate and have a general inflationary impact on the domestic economy.[5]

Critics also claim that freely floating rates would fluctuate widely, and the uncertainty that this creates would inhibit international transactions. "Under some circumstances, exchange markets might degenerate into chaos if they are set adrift without guidance. What is feared is destabilizing speculation: a massive buying or selling wave fed by capital movements which could force exchange rates to extreme movements and wild

---

[5] Lawrence B. Krause, "Fixed, Flexible and Gliding Exchange Rates," *Journal of Money, Credit, and Banking* (May 1971), p. 332.

fluctuations." [6] The counter-argument to this fear is that "speculators who engage in genuinely destabilizing speculation—that
is, whose speculations move the exchange rate away from rather
than toward its equilibrium level—will consistently lose
money, because they will consistently be buying when the rate
is "high" and selling when it is "low" by comparison with its
equilibrium value." [7] This reply is not completely satisfying to
critics who still persist in arguing that professional speculators
may be able to profit by leading amateur speculators who are
the herd-like followers into destabilizing speculation. As long
as new groups of amateur speculators can be attracted to the
market, the instability can be perpetuated, and the professional
speculators can continue to profit. [8]

Even if the exchange-rate fluctuations are not severe, there is
nonetheless some uncertainty that increases the risk of doing
international business. True, "traders averse to uncertainty
would be able to hedge their transactions through forward exchange markets, which would, if necessary, develop in response to demand." [9] But critics reply that "even assuming that
forward cover is available, the added cost of buying it will reduce the volume of international trade. . . . Furthermore, forward cover will be very difficult to obtain for transactions with
long lead times such as custom designed machinery, jet planes,
or ships. Also certain services like insurance involve assuming
liabilities well into the future and the absence of forward cover
for exchange risks could easily seriously inhibit the supplying
of this service on an international basis. Thus some degree of
international specialization might have to be sacrificed. Some
productive capital movements like bond flotations would also
be seriously inhibited." [10]

Another major argument against freely fluctuating rates is that
the free market would establish an inappropriate exchange rate
that promotes inflation. This is because the discipline against

---

[6] Ibid. p. 331.

[7] Harry G. Johnson, "The Case for Flexible Exchange Rates, 1969," *Report*, Federal
Reserve Bank of St. Louis (June 1969), p. 20.

[8] Krause, "Fixed, Flexible and Gliding Exchange Rates," p. 331.

[9] Johnson, "The Case for Flexible Exchange Rates," p. 20.

[10] Krause, "Fixed, Flexible and Gliding Exchange Rates," p. 331.

inflationary policies would be lost if the consequence of inflationary policies is only exchange-rate depreciation. Central
banks would lose their leverage on governments concerning fiscal matters that would have led to reserve losses in the absence
of rate flexibility.[11] Moreover, fluctuations in exchange rates are
in themselves inflationary. If effective, depreciation will lead to
an increase in exports and a decrease in imports that will be
inflationary through the impact on aggregate demand. In addition, there may be a cost-push type of inflation to the extent that
imports rise in price, are inputs, and firms have sufficient market power to raise prices. With a rising cost of living, wages will
also tend to rise, and another round of price increases will
ensue. In contrast, when a currency appreciates, not all cost
reductions are translated into price reductions. Wage rates are
sticky downward, and part of the appreciation gain will simply
be absorbed in higher real wages; and instead of reducing their
prices, producers may simply raise profit margins when their
import costs fall. This asymmetric adjustment to exchange-rate
movements—depreciation leading to higher prices and appreciation to higher real factor returns—will on balance leave the
price level higher than it would be in the absence of exchange-
rate fluctuations.[12]

For these reasons—its overly general impact, creation of uncertainty, and fostering of inflation—a freely fluctuating exchange market can be criticized as establishing an inappropriate price. A free market exchange rate will adjust to price and
cost disparities—but the price and cost disparities may be fostered by the system itself, and the rate established by the uncontrolled market need not be considered any more appropriate
than a rate that is managed in a constrained market. Just because it is not an ordinary but such a special price, the critics
contend that the determination of the exchange rate should not
be left to market forces. A domestic analogy is the interest rate
structure—again, the price of money—which is determined by
national monetary authorities.

Another set of arguments is based on the contention that no

[11] Ibid. p. 332.
[12] Ibid.

change in price—whether determined by market forces or the government—would be appropriate for some sources of balance-of-payments disequilibria. Exchange-rate variations do not fit the situations of inflation coupled with a balance-of- payments deficit or unemployment coupled with a balance-of-payments surplus. In the former situation, disinflationary measures are appropriate—not currency depreciation that would in itself be inflationary. Freely fluctuating rates might set in motion a spiral of depreciating exchanges, subsequent wage increases to meet the rise in cost of living, further price increases, balance-of-payments deterioration, and further exchange depreciation. In the opposite situation of unemployment and an international surplus, the appropriate policies are domestic reflationary measures and not currency appreciation which would be deflationary.

An alteration of the exchange rate would also be unsuitable for cases of structural disequilibrium. If there is a loss of export markets for nonprice reasons, it is of little avail to reduce the price of exports through currency depreciation. When an external deficit is not caused by inappropriate relative prices, a change in the exchange rate is ineffective as a remedial policy. If the source of the deficit is an outflow of capital, it may also be considered inappropriate to place the burden of adjustment in the current account. In a world of volatile short-term capital movements, this consideration carries special force.

One can also argue against exchange-rate changes out of an interest in maintaining the benefits of international money. Thus, Professor Kindleberger has stated that his

> basic regret about [the] second devaluation [of the dollar] is that the world is now left without an international money. Most international economists lack interest in this. Their concern is with the medium-of-exchange function of money only, and this they believe can be discharged effectively by fluctuating exchange rates. Strong believers for the most part in the services of money within national economies, they see little need beyond the exchange function in the international sphere. I believe this is a mistake. We need money internationally not only as a medium of exchange but as a unit of account, store of value, and standard of deferred payment, that is, to calculate world prices in, for holding international liq-

uid balances, and for fixing long-term contracts. The devaluation of August 1971 produced upsets in the world markets for oil, coffee, airfares, tanker construction, that is in long-term contracts and commodity agreements which need to fix prices over a considerable period of time. The elasticities economists brush aside this problem by referring airily to forward markets. They do not solve it. And they ignore the need for an international money as a store of value, a vehicle currency which countries can hold to balance temporal excesses against deficiencies. International lending and borrowing will suffer without an international money.[13]

Freely floating rates are also criticized as causing a deficit country to bear excessive costs of adjustment. No mechanism of adjustment is without its costs, but the problem is to minimize the burden and distribute it equitably among deficit and surplus countries. For a deficit country that has to undergo currency depreciation, the costs may be considered unduly burdensome in entailing resource reallocation, deterioration in the country's terms of trade, change in the distribution of income, and reduction in the total amount of resources available for home consumption and investment. For a surplus country, currency appreciation will weaken the country's competitive position in world markets, to the disadvantage of exporters and domestic competitors with imports. The burden of adjustment will be heavier when price elasticities are low, responses are slow, and the economy's capacity to transform is limited.

A regime of freely fluctuating rates may be especially undesirable for the less-developed countries. Beyond the previously mentioned disadvantages, there are several other considerations of special concern to LDCs: freely fluctuating rates could inhibit regional integration unless the countries could agree to a joint float or a common currency; the creation of uncertainty for the foreign investor who wants to reconvert funds into the creditor's currency may be a significant deterrent to capital inflow; the increased burden of servicing external debt

---

[13] Statement of C. P. Kindleberger, Hearings before the Subcommittee on International Finance of the Subcommittee on Banking and Currency, House of Representatives, 93rd Congress, 1st Session, p. 313. For elaboration, see also Kindleberger, "The Benefits of International Money," *Journal of International Economics* (September 1972), pp. 425–42.

could be severe; the calculation and management of development plans would be made more complex; and the facilities for a forward market may be extremely thin in a developing country. Exchange-rate depreciation would also be ineffective to the extent, as is often true, that domestic inflation persists; the demand for imports is a function of output and is unresponsive to price changes; the marginal propensity to save is a constant that can not be readily altered by relative price changes; and exports have a low price elasticity of demand.

In the final analysis, the merits of the case for or against freely floating rates will depend in reality on how gradual the exchange-rate adjustments would be, how predictable, how effective and rapid the adjustment process, and what would be the costs of feasible alternative policies. No a priori judgment is possible, and no general answer would apply to all countries.

What is evident, however, from the post-1971 experience is that countries have been reluctant to allow unlimited flexibility. This has been demonstrated in competitive "nonrevaluations" and in "dirty floats" since August 15, 1971. In practice, the essential question is what degree of flexibility is feasible—what is the acceptable and desirable range of "managed floating" or limited flexibility short of fully flexible rates?

4.3 *Limited Flexibility*

Although the movement toward unlimited flexibility did not gain strength in the events after August 15, 1971, there were developments more sympathetic to greater flexibility in rates. The band was actually widened in the Smithsonian Agreement, and the degree of flexibility was further increased in the Paris Agreement (see pp. 199–206 above). It may well be asked: If greater flexibility of exchange rates is so desirable, why not go all the way to freely flexible rates? The answers amount to the belief that fully flexible rates would cause far more problems than limited flexibility, so that even if a fully flexible regime could be instituted, countries would revert to more limited flexibility in practice; accordingly, it seems more sensible to move consciously in that direction from the outset.[14] There is much

---

[14] C. Fred Bergsten, *Reforming the Dollar: An International Monetary Policy for the United States* (1972), p. 61.

appeal in a course of evolutionary experimentation along a route from wider margins and a band of nonintervention to the eventual conversion of the system into freely fluctuating rates.[15]

Although countries may not yet be ready for unlimited flexibility, nonetheless it is feasible to have greater—albeit limited—flexibility. And as stated in the 1970 Report of the Executive Directors of the IMF, greater flexibility could be accommodated under the Fund's par-value fixed-rate system (see pp. 252–59 below).

Table II below indicates the distinguishing characteristics of different exchange-rate regimes—fixed rates, fully flexible, or limited flexibility. Fully flexible rates are distinguishable from fixed-rate and limited-flexibility systems by the absence of a commitment to a formal parity, to specific intervention points, and to conditions that must be met before a change in parity can be made. The fixed-rate and limited-flexibility systems have in common the commitment to a formal parity and to announced

TABLE II. Rate Flexibility Under Alternative
Exchange-Rate Systems

	Exchange-Rate System		
Characteristic	*Fixed Rates*	*Full Flexibility*	*Limited Flexibility*
Formal parity	Formal	None	Formal
Formal intervention limits	Announced	None	Announced
Conditions for change in parity	"Last resort"	None	"Fundamental disequilibrium" or "objective indicators"
Exchange values in short run	Fixed	Unlimited market flexibility	Limited flexibility within "band"
Desired exchange values in long run	Fixed	Unlimited market flexibility	"Internationally managed flexibility"

SOURCE: Adapted from Samuel I. Katz, *The Case for the Par-Value System, 1972,* Princeton Essays in International Finance, No. 92, March 1972, p. 3.

[15] Lawrence B. Krause, *Sequel to Bretton Woods* (1971), p. 50.

intervention points in the short run. But in the long run, a fixed-rate system (such as the pre-1914 international gold standard) would not undergo a change in parity except as a "last resort" measure after reserves and credits had been exhausted. Under limited flexibility, in contrast, a change in parity over the longer run would be more readily possible under conditions of "fundamental disequilibrium" (as in the original IMF agreement) or under other guidelines for adjustment, such as the "objective indicators" suggested in the United States proposals for international monetary reform (see pp. 266–73 below).

To the extent that countries were unwilling to revert to a fixed-rate system and were not yet ready for fully flexible rates, monetary reform had to focus on the limits of rate flexibility. If there were to be predetermined limits of flexibility in the short run, how were the limits to be set? And in terms of what reserve asset were the support points to be defined—gold, the dollar, or the SDR?

If regional integration is desired, can the member countries maintain a sufficient degree of monetary cooperation and policy harmonization to form an "optimum currency area"? Which exchange rates, if any, should be allowed to fluctuate?

Finally, if there is to be exchange-rate variations in the longer run, how are the changes to be determined? By what presumptive rules or objective indicators? And by what form of collective monitoring or "internationally managed" flexibility?

Some of the major issues of international monetary reform have centered on these questions.

5. AGENDA FOR MONETARY REFORM

Against the background of international currency crises and the dollar problem, the Executive Directors of the IMF published a study in 1972 on *Reform of the International Monetary System*. This report identified five main problem areas of the international monetary system which may call for new arrangements through international discussion and negotiation:

    (i) the exchange-rate mechanism, including both the indications of when changes in par-values are necessary and the respective responsibilities of the deficit and surplus countries for making par-value changes;

    (ii) the re-establishment of convertibility and the arrangements for the settlement of imbalances among countries;

   (iii) the position in the system of the various reserve assets and in particular the status and function to be given to foreign exchange reserves, gold, and SDRs;

   (iv) the problem of disequilibrating capital movements and what might be done to lessen the intense market pressures that accompany them, and

   (v) the possibility of new provisions in the Fund arrangements for the special needs of developing countries.

This is a succinct summary of the agenda for monetary reform. It will be useful to keep it in mind as we now turn to the actual course of international negotiations and consider what progress these negotiations have made in moving toward a new world monetary order.

B. THE ISSUES

Issues relating to greater exchange-rate flexibility and the relationships between reform of adjustment and reform of liquidity came to dominate discussions in the international financial community by the end of the 1960's. The IMF recognized in its 1969 annual report that "if exchange rates that are no longer appropriate are nevertheless maintained, they contribute to the persistence of balance of payments disequilibria, the encouragement of speculation and crises in the foreign exchange markets."

In an editorial headed "Currencies Should Not Be Virility Symbols," the London *Times* stated that the IMF's report

> is understandably cautious, but it does point in the right direction when it calls for continuing study of "greater flexibility in the adjustment of exchange rates or of par values" and at the same time emphasizes that "any changes that might be made should preserve the essential characteristics of the par value system. . . ." Inevitably the move toward greater flexibility will be a slow one. The once powerful gold lobby in international monetary discussions is now a dwindling band of diminishing importance, but many countries still prefer to err on the side of extreme (and sometimes foolish) caution in taking decisions in this area. In the interim period it is important

that countries cease regarding their currencies as a national virility symbol. When a country's payments position is in fundamental disequilibrium it is wholly proper that it should change the par value of its currency.

6. THE BÜRGENSTOCK COMMUNIQUE

At an important international conference in Bürgenstock, Switzerland, a number of academic economists and practitioners from the banking and business world considered the possibility of improving the adjustment mechanism through greater exchange-rate flexibility. The opinion of the majority of the participants is reflected in the following press release.

COMMUNIQUE *

Twenty officials of banking and business firms and eighteen academic economists from ten different countries have been reviewing proposals for increasing flexibility in exchange rates. Various methods by which countries could adjust the parities of their currencies in terms of the US dollar were considered, as well as possibilities for widening the range of permissible fluctuation in the market rates of these currencies. . . .

After reviewing the recent experience of the international monetary system, the participants recognized that structural changes in international supply and demand and in capital movements, as well as divergent rates of economic growth, differences in economic objectives and policies, and varying price and cost trends among nations would from time to time call for changes in the exchange rates of particular currencies. There was a consensus that such changes when appropriate should take place sooner, and thus generally be smaller and more frequent, than during the past two decades. Following their analysis of all of the current proposals for change, some participants pointed toward a need for greater readiness by countries to adjust the established parities of their currencies within the existing framework. A majority favored both widening the range (or "band") within which exchange rates may respond to market forces, and permitting a more continuous and gradual adjustment of parities. They stressed that such innovations should be so framed as to facilitate continued international economic co-operation while leaving individual countries or groups of countries free to adapt their own approach to their own individual circumstances.

* Extracts from a Press Communique released from Bürgenstock, Switzerland, on June 30, 1969.

Throughout, the participants had in mind the need for improvements which would facilitate balance of payments adjustment in ways consistent with the domestic objectives of governments and the elimination of many restrictions on trade, current payments, and capital movements.

7. IMF REPORT—1970

In 1970 the Executive Directors of the IMF issued a report which sought to narrow the range of possible improvements in the mechanism of exchange-rate adjustment "to various methods of achieving a limited increase in potential flexibility through modification in institutional arrangements or in policy attitudes consistent with the underlying philosophy of the Bretton Woods system." The report reiterated IMF support of the par-value system, but it went on to acknowledge that, in certain specific forms, rate flexibility greater than that provided by the existing arrangements would be consistent with the Fund's Articles of Agreement. The central principle was that the distinctive characteristic of the par-value system is the acceptance of flexibility of exchange rates within a specified margin (2 per cent, or at most 3 per cent, against an intervention currency) and in accordance with internationally agreed-upon criteria and procedures. Portions of the report follow.

THE ROLE OF EXCHANGE RATES IN THE ADJUSTMENT OF INTERNATIONAL PAYMENTS *

The basic achievements of the par value system and of its operation hitherto, may be summarized under the following three heads.

(1) Acceptance of the principle that the determination of the rate of exchange for each currency is a matter of international concern; and implementation of that principle in the formulation of policy actions by the relevant authorities.

(2) Attainment of a high degree of stability in exchange rates of major currencies, with a limited number of exceptions in cases where continued exchange stability was clearly not consistent with the circumstances of member countries; this general degree of exchange stability permitting countries that are in a position to do so to focus their policies of domestic and external financial management on their par value as a fixed point of reference.

* A Report by the Executive Directors, International Monetary Fund, 1970.

(3) Maintenance of generally orderly exchange arrangements, and avoidance of competitive exchange depreciation.

The main areas in which improvements in the operation of the par value system may be sought, may in turn be summarized under two heads.

(1) Reducing delays in needed adjustment of par values, while minimizing the risk of encouraging premature or unnecessary adjustments; a particularly important consideration in this context would be to minimize recourse to restrictions on trade and current payments.

(2) Effecting needed adjustment in exchange rates more smoothly, and with smaller attendant movements of speculative funds in a disequilibrating direction.

In addition, there has been discussion of what would be, over time, an appropriate relationship between downward and upward adjustments in parities.

The central issue is to determine the extent to which progress along these lines might be secured while maintaining the basic achievements of the par value system summarized above. The following explains why three radical proposals for alteration of the mechanism of exchange rate adjustment have been found unacceptable.

Regimes Inconsistent with the Par Value System

a. Freely Floating Exchange Rates

The essential advantage claimed for a system of freely floating exchange rates is that it leaves decision making on the appropriate pattern of exchange rates to automatic forces of the market. It could thereby, in theory, do away with the need for countries to hold official reserves for the purpose of influencing the exchange rate or the balance of payments, and could also in theory remove the need for other official policies directed to the balance of payments. An essential drawback of such a system is that national authorities could not be expected in modern conditions to adopt a policy of neutrality with respect to movements in an economic variable of such importance to the domestic economy as the rate of exchange, with its effects on prices, incomes, employment, and the structure of industry as between domestic and foreign sectors. For this reason, assurance of market equilibrium in the overall balance of payments, through such variation in the exchange rate as is necessary to attain it, would not remove the possible sources of concern that national authorities may legitimately feel about their external finances. Speculative capital movements would at times tend to exaggerate rather than to offset underlying payments disequilibria, and at such times, fluctuations in rates would be substantial in the absence of official intervention. The fluctuations in exchange rates that occurred, and the absence of any limits on the scope for potential fluctuations, would involve damaging uncertainties for international trade.

For the reasons indicated in the previous paragraph, the determination of exchange rates would in practice not be left entirely to market forces. In place of a system of freely floating rates, there would emerge a system of fluctuating rates, influenced by official intervention. National authorities would continue to formulate and to implement policies directed to their country's balance of payments; yet the absence of par values and of the associated international procedures for adjusting exchange rates would leave a vacuum in the necessary provisions for international coordination of exchange rate policies. Countries would need to find a new set of safeguards, comparable to the safeguards that have been built up under the par value system, against arbitrary actions and conflicts between national policies in the determination of exchange rates. Yet construction of international safeguards adequate to ensure that intervention by national authorities in exchange markets was mutually compatible and acceptable would either lead quickly back to a regime of par values, or would involve international supervision and control of national exchange rate actions, and perhaps also of other aspects of national policies, to a degree that seems unlikely to be acceptable to national authorities.

A general system of fluctuating rates would have special consequences for small countries and countries with particular regional associations. Such countries would in many cases seek to maintain a fixed currency link with certain other countries, and this would involve the establishment or strengthening of regional currency areas.

b. Substantially Wider Margins

Proposals for a substantial widening of the permitted margins of fluctuation around parity—to, say, 5 per cent compared with the present maximum of 1 per cent against an intervention currency—aim at achieving in many respects the same objectives as those of freely fluctuating rates. The system is, however, subject to the constraint of an internationally agreed parity; accordingly, the basic feature of the present system, international agreement on exchange rates, is preserved in principle, although the significance of the par value inevitably tends to decline as margins become wider. The main operational difference between substantially wider margins and freely fluctuating rates would be in the existence of limits to the fluctuation of the rate, at which the exchange authorities would be committed to intervene.

The main advantages claimed for a system of substantially wider margins are (a) encouragement of market equilibration, and discouragement of disequilibrating speculation, lessening the need for reserve movements and providing greater scope for independent monetary policies, through influences of the kind discussed [below] in the context of a slight widening of margins; (b) attainment of a smoother transition between changes in par value; and (c) achievement of some equilibrating effects on current account transactions, permitting a more gradual adjustment to incipient long-term disequilibria. However, if the substantial widening of margins were to increase the likelihood of parity changes of a given amount taking place, the equilibration noted under (a) above could in certain conditions be replaced by disequilibrating influences.

Perhaps the most serious problem that would be posed by a substantial widening of margins would be the risk that countries would find their competitive positions subjected to sudden and inappropriate changes as a result of temporary market developments or of administrative actions of other countries through official intervention in exchange markets. While the permitted margin for deviations in exchange rates around parity remains relatively narrow, the safeguard against such a risk resides in the international procedures by which these parities are adjusted. If the permitted margins were widened to a point at which movements in rates within the margins could be expected to affect international competitiveness in a significant degree, the safeguard provided by the procedure of parity adjustment would no longer be adequate. Special problems would also arise for countries with particular regional relationships. . . .

A widening of the margins by substantial amounts would also provide more leeway for continuous fluctuation in exchange rates than would be desired by many countries on domestic grounds. Such countries could of course abstain from taking advantage of the new facility to the full extent, since the provisions on exchange margins have always been permissive, authorizing maximum deviations rather than requiring national authorities to allow deviations to the indicated amount. However, even countries that made no change in their own arrangements would be affected indirectly by an increase in fluctuation in their exchange rates against the currencies of countries that did take advantage of the permissible wider margin, especially where trade with these latter countries comprised a substantial share of external trade and national product of the country making no change in its exchange arrangements.

The principle that the rate of exchange of each currency is a matter of international concern, which is an essential safeguard provided by the par value system, would therefore not be compatible with a widening of permitted fluctuations around par that reached substantial proportions, at least in the absence of an elaboration of a new set of rules relating to official intervention in exchange markets. A substantial widening of scope for fluctuation around par values might also be considered inconsistent with another basic characteristic of the par value system, the stability of exchange rates at realistic levels.

On these grounds, neither fluctuating exchange rates nor a substantial widening of margins can recommend themselves as advantageous for the Fund membership at large.

This is not necessarily to preclude the possibility that, in exceptional circumstances, a fluctuating rate or a substantial widening of margins might be helpful to a country with special problems, and that such an expedient might be found internationally acceptable for a temporary period. If the international community were prepared to grant a special dispensation in such a case, this might need to be supported by the application of special conditions, to take the place of the safeguards residing in the basic provisions which were no longer being observed.

c. Automatic Adjustment of Parities

The proposals for new institutional arrangements to effect parity changes automatically and at fixed intervals in accordance with the movement of selected indicators include a number of variants, which in some cases allow a measure of discretion in the application of the relevant formula. Under one family of proposals, the parity of a currency would be determined by a mathematical formula based on an average of spot market rates over a predetermined previous period; the formula would be applied so as to result in parity changes at frequent intervals—quarterly, monthly, or even weekly—and would limit the maximum cumulative movement in parity to a modest annual amount, such as 2 or 3 per cent in one direction. Under other proposals, parities would be determined by a formula based on movements in reserves over some recent period (and perhaps also in relation to certain trend or target movements in reserves for the country concerned). A third series of proposals envisage a formula based on a composite indicator including data on reserve movements, spot market rates, and perhaps also forward rates. Variants of each of these three families of proposals would introduce an element of discretion (itself of varying degree) on the extent to which the chosen formula were followed in adjustment of parities; thus, the indicators of reserve movements and of market rates might be regarded as "presumptive criteria," which would be followed in the absence of good reasons to the contrary. In certain proposals, such discretion would be exercised at least in part by an international authority such as the Fund. Virtually all the main proposals allow for the possibility of a larger adjustment in parity, which could override the automatic or discretionary indicator, but this provision is intended to be confined to exceptional or emergency use.

By basing the criteria of parity adjustment in the normal case on some objective quantitative indicator of the balance of payments, rather than on a general judgment of whether an exchange adjustment is necessary in connection with a fundamental disequilibrium in the economy, proponents of such schemes look for three main benefits. Firstly, movement in parities in a more continuous way is expected to be less disruptive, and less exposed to disequilibrating speculation, than less frequent adjustments by larger amounts. Secondly, more continuous movement in parities in response to financial indicators is expected to make adjustment of exchange rates more readily accepted by the public and less sensitive to political considerations. Thirdly, the possibility for exchange rates to move more freely, provided by the first two influences, is expected to reduce the pressure for suppression of disequilibria through restrictions on trade or payments or through distortion of domestic policies; it is also expected to reduce the pressure and need for undue reliance on financing of payments imbalances. However, it is recognized that substantial needs for official financing may remain.

Against these possible benefits, the automatic or near automatic linkage of exchange rate adjustment to balance of payments indicators would involve overriding disadvantages. The need for adjustment of the exchange rate cannot be judged from the position of the balance of payments alone, without reference to the condition of the domestic economy. Movements in market exchange rates and in reserves at any time are influenced by cyclical factors and other temporary phenomena which have no enduring effect on competitiveness and call for no adjustment in the exchange rate. If the parity is made to respond automatically to market forces of this kind, this will involve continuous movement in parities in cases where absolute stability might otherwise be achieved, and is likely in some cases to involve movements in an inappropriate direction. Moreover, the removal of political and psychological constraints on adjustment of exchange rates will not be advantageous in cases where such constraints have strengthened the hands of the domestic authorities in securing acceptance of necessary domestic adjustments that would otherwise be resisted. Finally, national authorities might choose to avoid what they regarded as an inappropriate movement in their exchange rate. In that event they might either suppress the payments disequilibrium through restrictions on external trade or payments; or they might prefer to adjust the exchange rate, independently of the formula or indicators, by an amount sufficient, with any necessary accompanying domestic measures, to correct the disequilibrium at once.

On these grounds, a regime under which parities would be adjusted automatically at fixed intervals on the basis of some predetermined formula would not be consistent with the basic principles of the par value system and does not recommend itself as advantageous.

Proposals for Adapting the Par Value System

The conclusion that the par value system is the most suitable general exchange rate regime for the members of the Fund carries with it a duty for the Fund and its members to make this system as effective as possible for achieving the purposes of the Fund. This implies, for the Fund, the need to review and where necessary to adjust its criteria, procedures and operational practices to ensure that they are as well suited as possible to this end. For the members of the Fund, this implies, first, pursuit of internal policies that will keep the growth in aggregate demand in line with the development of available resources; for while inflationary pressures are not the only sources of exchange rate difficulties, they have certainly been the most frequent sources in the past. Second, it implies a willingness, in instances where exchange rate changes are appropriate to restore equilibrium, to make such changes at a time and in a manner most likely to enhance their effectiveness. The latter consideration is of particular importance because in present conditions of international mobility of capital, expectations that parities may be changed can lead to large and disruptive movements of funds. The impact of such expectations has been increased because of the much larger role that international capital movements now play in the working of the international monetary system than was envisaged when the Bretton Woods system was established.

The counterpart to a policy of prompt changes in parities when changes are needed is the defense of any parity that is appropriate to a country's underlying situation, even though it may at a particular time be buffeted by strong movements in reserves. Where the reserve movement is a heavy inflow, the problem will be to deal with the inflow without provoking undesirable effects on the domestic economy. Pressures on a parity may be still greater where the country is faced by a large outflow of reserves. In either case, and depending on circumstances that may differ from country to country, it may or may not be desirable and possible to alleviate the situation by recourse to controls on capital movements. The country whose currency is under downward pressure will in any event have to be able to use adequate reserves to defend the rate. In terms of national policies, this requires the persistent pursuit by countries of balance of payments and reserve policies that will result over time in adequate reserves. Internationally, it requires an appropriate policy on reserve creation that makes it possible for countries to realize reasonable reserve aims. The facility for special drawing rights is intended to provide the means of meeting this requirement. Where movements of funds are very large, however, reserves that are adequate for normal purposes may not suffice. To supplement them, the countries that are most subject to large short-term capital flows have instituted a network of swap credit facilities among themselves. All members of the Fund, moreover, can have recourse to controls on capital movements. The fact that such use is conditional has the advantage from the international point of view that access to the higher credit tranches involves inter alia an international judgment as to the appropriateness of the exchange rate in defense of which balance of payments assistance is being sought. . . .

A Slight Widening in the Margins Around Parity

For the reasons developed [earlier], a substantial widening of the permitted margins for market rates would risk the erosion of the safeguard that internationally agreed parities provide against changes in a country's competitive position as a result of actions by other countries. The same objection would not apply to the introduction of a possibility for members to adopt slightly wider margins, if they wanted to do so, under which fluctuations in market rates continued to be confined to magnitudes that could be expected to have only a minor effect on countries' competitive positions. It would be difficult to determine how far one could go beyond the present margins before the potential disadvantages of a widening of margins would outbalance any potential benefits from such widening, and the Executive Directors have not reached a common view on this question. The answer to this question could depend inter alia on whether Fund approval would be required before an individual member could apply wider margins.

[A] slight widening of margins could have three possible advantages. First, by increasing the scope for movements in exchange rates around par, it would somewhat reduce the sensitivity of short-term capital movements to divergences in conditions in national money markets, and would thereby allow somewhat greater independence for national monetary policies. Second, the increased scope for market movements around par could, in certain circumstances, reduce pressure on official reserves, by encouraging anticipatory movements of private funds in a stabilizing direction. Thirdly, the moderate increase in scope for market rates to move in response to market pressures would slightly reduce the prospective profitability of speculation on possible parity changes, and could be of some help in smoothing the transition from one parity to another; this influence would be significant only where the typical size of parity changes was relatively small. Against these possible advantages, a slight widening in margins could also involve certain disadvantages both for the member adopting them and for other countries. Since all provisions for the widening of margins under discussion would leave each member the option not to adopt margins wider than those applied at present, any members or groups of members that considered such margins disadvantageous to themselves could refrain from adopting them for their own currencies. Members that did not themselves adopt wider margins might be unfavorably affected by the effects of the adoption of such margins by other members; the increased scope for fluctuation of market rates, which could often be considered advantageous in its effect on capital movements, might have unwelcome effects especially on trade and current payments, though these effects would not be expected to be substantial with a widening of margins that remained relatively slight. In addition, a widening of margins, even by slight proportions, could introduce undesired disturbances in the economic and financial relations among certain groupings of members and might create special difficulties for many primary producing countries.

It may be recalled that the present arrangements, under which member countries are permitted margins of up to one per cent against their intervention currency and cumulated margins against other currencies of up to 2 per cent, are validated under the Fund's jurisdiction to give temporary approval of multiple currency practices, in accordance with an Executive Board Decision of 1959. It would not be possible for the Fund, however, to approve a further widening of margins that would involve margins against the member's intervention currency in excess of one per cent. The Executive Directors have considered the 1959 Decision in connection with the question whether it would be desirable to amend the margin provisions so as to allow a slight widening in the effective permissible margins. Further study is needed to determine whether any such amendment, if it were to be judged desirable, should take the form of a provision establishing new margins, or permitting the Fund to establish appropriate margins for all currencies or in individual cases. A related question that would need to be considered concerns the safeguards and conditions that the Fund might impose.

8. IMF MEETING—1971

At their meeting in Washington a month after President Nixon's action of August 15, 1971, the Governors of the 118 member countries of the IMF were confronted with both a risk and a challenge. The risk, in the words of the Fund's managing director, "was that if common understandings were not reached, the situation would drift and deteriorate further. There was also a challenge for the international community to agree on the appropriate course of action."

To initiate discussions on the future of the monetary system, the Fund's Board of Governors requested its Executive Directors to prepare a report on necessary or desirable measures for improvement of the monetary system. Subsequently, the Executive Directors published their study *Reform of the International Monetary System.* The five aspects of the system about which changes were to be considered have already been summarized on pp. 249–50 above.

In closing the meeting, the managing director of the Fund emphasized the need for a collaborative approach to devise a durable solution to the problems of the international monetary system.

CLOSING REMARKS OF THE MANAGING DIRECTOR OF THE IMF *

Mr. Chairman, I have been most impressed by the general atmosphere of our meeting, resulting from the tenor of the statements made by Governors. Understandably, Governors have voiced deep concern about the current international monetary picture. But they have also taken a constructive view. Many Governors, and foremost among them you, Mr. Chairman, in your opening statement, have stressed the challenge which the present situation offers—the challenge to devise and adopt new measures, both for the immediate future and for the longer run, that will lead to a strengthening in the performance and structure of the international monetary system. Moreover, the atmosphere of this meeting in the world-wide forum provided by the Fund's Board of Governors has been one of cooperation. Emphasis has been placed on the need for international collaboration in the approach to present problems. Several Governors have noted the importance of cooperation with the United States in the task it has undertaken to strengthen its balance of payments position—a view which is, of course, in no way inconsistent with the widely stated belief that the U.S. import surcharge should be removed as quickly as possible.

In reviewing the proceedings of the week, Mr. Chairman, let me now indicate five issues on which there has been a substantial measure of agree-

* *International Financial News Survey,* October 6, 1971, pp. 321–22.

ment. These pertain to the character of the present international monetary situation and the steps that should be taken to correct it.

First, to elaborate a point that I made a moment ago, the importance that Governors have attached to international collaboration in their statements reflects their general view that the failure to find a common solution would entail real dangers. These dangers are related to disorder in currency and trade relationships sufficiently serious to damage world trade and thus to have a marked economic impact on member countries. There is a clear consensus that international action is required to resolve the present difficulties, and that such action would serve the economic interest of all members—and not least the developing countries, whose vulnerability in the present crisis is generally recognized.

Second, I have heard no dissent from the proposition that a substantial adjustment is required to deal adequately with the present imbalance in world payments. This adjustment, it is agreed, would require the establishment for the major currencies of a realistic new structure of parities or official exchange rates. This currency realignment, it is further agreed, should take place as expeditiously as possible.

Third, there would appear to be a concurrence in the view that the realignment of currencies should be accompanied by the introduction of some temporary widening of margins. It is generally felt that this would be helpful in the present situation of uncertainty.

Fourth, Governors have expressed concern about the impact of the present situation on the operations of the Fund. There is broad agreement that it is important to all members that normal conduct of Fund operations should be resumed as promptly as possible.

Fifth, Governors are in agreement that improvement or reform of the international monetary system will require the study of all aspects of the system, including the roles of reserve currencies, gold, and special drawing rights; convertibility; the provisions of the Articles of Agreement with respect to exchange rates; and the problems caused by destabilizing capital movements. In the discussions this week, many Governors expressed their belief that the longer-term evolution of the international monetary system should include a major increase in the role played by an internationally managed reserve asset—specifically, SDRs—in the world reserve system. This is seen as contributing both to the effectiveness of the international adjustment process and to the improvement in control over the volume of international liquidity.

Let me also say how gratified I was by the general recognition that all member countries should participate in the work and the decision-making involved in the reform of the international monetary system.

Mr. Chairman, I want to emphasize again that this meeting has been constructive. However, its lasting value will depend on translating into action the principles of international cooperation on which we have all agreed this week. I believe we have made a good start in marking out a generally acceptable path toward solution of the present difficulties, but the world will judge us solely by our actions. I continue to feel the sense of urgency that I expressed in my opening remarks last Monday.

9. IMF MEETING—1972

During the following year there was little substantive progress toward monetary reform while the countries sought to designate the appropriate forum for discussing reform measures. The United States wished to broaden the composition of the major negotiating parties to include countries other than the Group of 10. And at the third session of UNCTAD in Chile (May 1972), a resolution was adopted strongly supporting "the view that there should be effective participation of the developing countries in the decision making process of the international monetary system and its reform to ensure that due consideration is given to the interests of developing and developed countries alike."

A major step taken by the IMF's Board of Governors, prior to their 1972 annual meeting, was the agreement to establish a Committee of 20 to advise the Board on issues related to international monetary reform.

9.1 Committee of 20

INAUGURAL MEETING *

The inaugural meeting of the Committee of 20 was held during the Annual Meetings week. The Committee made procedural decisions preparing for substantive talks on reform of the international monetary system to begin this year.

Ali Wardhana, Minister of Finance of Indonesia, was selected to serve as Chairman of the Committee of 20, the formal name of which is the Committee of the Board of Governors of the Fund on Reform of the International Monetary System and Related Issues.

The Committee consists of one member appointed by each country or group of countries appointed or electing an Executive Director of the Fund. Pierre-Paul Schweitzer, the Managing Director of the Fund, is a participant. Each member of the Committee may appoint two Associates and name two Deputies.

The Committee's task is to advise and to report to the Board of Governors on all aspects of reform of the international monetary system, including pro-

* *IMF Survey*, October 9, 1972, p. 65.

posals for amendments of the Articles of Agreement of the Fund. The Committee will give full attention to the interrelation between these matters and existing or prospective arrangements among countries—including those that involve international trade, the flow of capital, investment, and development assistance—that could affect attainment of the purposes of the Fund under the present or amended Articles of Agreement.

Mr. Wardhana convened the September 28 meeting of the Committee as Chairman of the Governors of the Fund, as provided for in the Resolution of the Governors establishing the Committee of 20. The Resolution was prepared by the Executive Directors and adopted by a mail vote of the Governors during July. Following the selection of Mr. Wardhana, the Committee selected C. Jeremy Morse, an Executive Director of the Bank of England, to serve as Chairman of the Deputies.

The Committee took note of the report of the Executive Directors on *Reform of the International Monetary System*. They exchanged views on the future work of the Committee, and expressed determination to make rapid progress toward agreement on reform.

9.2 United States' Proposals for Reform

The most important development at the 1972 meeting was the presentation of the United States' proposals for reform. Treasury Secretary Shultz outlined these proposals as follows.

SECRETARY SHULTZ'S ADDRESS *

The Exchange Rate Regime

We recognize that most countries want to maintain a fixed point of reference for their currencies—in other words, a "central" or "par" value. The corollary is a willingness to maintain and support these values by assuring convertibility of their currencies into other international assets.

A margin for fluctuation for market exchange rates around such central values will need to be provided sufficiently wide to dampen incentives for short-term capital movements and, when changes in central values are desirable, to ease the transition. The Smithsonian Agreement took a major step in that direction. Building on that approach in the context of a symmetrical system, the permissible outer limits of these margins of fluctuation for all currencies—including the dollar—might be set in the same range as now permitted for non-dollar currencies trading against each other.

We also visualize, for example, that countries in the process of forming a monetary union—with the higher degree of political and economic integration that implies—may want to maintain narrower bands among themselves, and should be allowed to do so. In addition, an individual nation, particularly

* *IMF Survey*, October 9, 1972, p. 70.

in the developing world, may wish to seek the agreement of a principal trading partner to maintain a narrower range of exchange rate fluctuation between them.

Provision needs also to be made for countries which decide to float their currencies. However, a country that refrains from setting a central value, particularly beyond a brief transitional period, should be required to observe more stringent standards of behavior in other respects to assure the consistency of its actions with the basic requirements of a cooperative order.

The Reserve Mechanism

We contemplate that the SDR would increase in importance and become the formal numeraire of the system. To facilitate its role, that instrument should be freed of those encumbrances of reconstitution obligations, designation procedures, and holding limits which would be unnecessary in a reformed system. Changes in the amount of SDRs in the system as a whole will be required periodically to meet the aggregate need for reserves.

A "central value system" implies some fluctuation in official reserve holdings of individual countries to meet temporary disturbances in their balance of payments positions. In addition, countries should ordinarily remain free to borrow or lend, bilaterally or multilaterally, through the IMF or otherwise.

At the same time, official foreign currency holdings need be neither generally banned nor encouraged. Some countries may find holdings of foreign currencies provide a useful margin of flexibility in reserve management, and fluctuations in such holdings can provide some elasticity for the system as a whole in meeting sudden flows of volatile capital. However, careful study should be given to proposals for exchanging part of existing reserve currency holdings into a special issue of SDRs, at the option of the holder.

The suggested provisions for central values and convertibility do not imply restoration of a gold-based system. The rigidities of such a system, subject to the uncertainties of gold production, speculation, and demand for industrial uses, cannot meet the needs of today.

I do not expect governmental holdings of gold to disappear overnight. I do believe orderly procedures are available to facilitate a diminishing role of gold in international monetary affairs in the future.

The Balance of Payments Adjustment Process

In a system of convertibility and central values, an effective balance of payments adjustment process is inextricably linked to appropriate criteria for changes in central values and the appropriate level, trend, and distribution of reserves. Agreement on these matters, and on other elements of an effective and timely adjustment process, is essential to make a system both practical and durable.

There is, of course, usually a very close relationship between imbalances in payments and fluctuations in reserve positions. Countries experiencing large deterioration in their reserve positions generally have had to devalue their currencies or take other measures to strengthen their balance of payments. Surplus countries with disproportionate reserve gains have, however, been under much less pressure to revalue their currencies upward or to take other policy actions with a similar balance of payments effect. If the adjustment process is to be more effective and efficient in a reformed system, this asymmetry will need to be corrected.

I believe the most promising approach would be to insure that a surfeit of reserves indicates, and produces pressure for, adjustment on the surplus side as losses of reserves already do for the deficit side. Supplementary guides and several technical approaches may be feasible and should be examined. Important transitional difficulties will need to be overcome. But, in essence, I believe disproportionate gains or losses in reserves may be the most equitable and effective single indicator we have to guide the adjustment process.

As I have already indicated, a variety of policy responses to affect the balance of payments can be contemplated. An individual country finding its reserves falling disproportionately would be expected to initiate corrective actions. For example, small devaluations would be freely permitted [to] such a country. Under appropriate international surveillance, at some point a country would have a prima facie case for a larger devaluation.

While we must frankly face up to limitation of the use of domestic monetary, fiscal, or other internal policies in promoting international adjustments in some circumstances, we should also recognize that the country in deficit might well prefer—and be in a position to apply—stricter internal financial disciplines rather than devalue its currency. Only in exceptional circumstances and for a limited period should a country be permitted direct restraints and these should be general and nondiscriminatory. Persistent refusal to take fundamental adjustment measures could result in withdrawal of borrowing, SDR allocation, or other privileges.

Conversely, a country permitting its reserves to rise disproportionately could lose its right to demand conversion, unless it undertook at least limited revaluation or other acceptable measures of adjustment. If reserves nonetheless continued to rise and were maintained at those higher levels over an extended period, then more forceful adjustment measures would be indicated.

For a surplus as for a deficit country, a change in the exchange rate need not be the only measure contemplated. Increasing the provision of concessionary aid on an untied basis, reduction of tariffs and other trade barriers, and elimination of obstacles to outward investment could, in specific circumstances at the option of the nation concerned, provide supplementary or alternative means. But, in the absence of a truly effective combination of corrective measures, other countries should ultimately be free to protect their interests by a surcharge on the imports from the chronic surplus country.

For countries moving toward a monetary union, the guidelines might be applied on a collective basis, provided the countries were willing to speak with one voice and to be treated as a unit for purposes of applying the basic rules of the international monetary and trading system.

Capital and Other Balance of Payments Controls

It is implicit in what I have said that I believe that the adjustment process should be directed toward encouraging freer trade and open capital markets. If trade controls are permitted temporarily in extreme cases on balance of payments grounds, they should be in the form of surcharges or across-the-board taxes. Controls on capital flows should not be allowed to become a means of maintaining a chronically undervalued currency. No country should be forced to use controls in lieu of other, more basic, adjustment measures.

Secretary Shultz' address was followed by a memorandum to the Committee of 20 that elaborated how movements in monetary reserves should serve as "objective indicators" to guide the balance-of-payments adjustment process.

ELABORATION OF UNITED STATES' PROPOSALS *

The Need for Objective Criteria

The U.S. proposals take as a point of departure that the stability and durability of a new monetary system will be crucially dependent on finding an equitable and effective means of promoting the adjustment of external imbalances.

In approaching that objective, we believe success is dependent upon finding an appropriate blend among three possible approaches, each of which contains some advantages, but none of which is satisfactory by itself. The three approaches are:

a) national discretion—a degree of which is essential in a world of sovereign nations and desirable in allowing maximum practicable freedom of action among individual countries, but which, relied on alone, assures neither equilibrium nor an equitable sharing of adjustment responsibilities;

b) discretionary authority of a central institution—which can bring to bear the influence and collective wisdom of the entire world community on particular adjustment problems, but which can lead to endless debate, indecision, or unbalanced decisions in a potentially politically charged atmosphere, and which requires at least the appearance of ceding more authority to an international body than nations will yield at this stage of international development;

c) objective criteria—which can be helpful in establishing measurements for indicating adjustment needs for various nations and various situations on a standardized basis, but which do not unerringly point to appropriate adjustments or permit needed discretion by national authorities.

* Memorandum on "The U.S. Proposals for Using Reserves as an Indicator of the Need for Balance-of-Payments Adjustment," submitted to Committee of 20, November 1972; reprinted in *Economic Report of the President*, January 1973, pp. 162–71.

The U.S. proposal aims at a balance among these approaches—to utilize the advantages of each, while avoiding the disadvantages which might result from excessive or singleminded reliance on any of the three. We propose that objective criteria be established to note and locate the existence of an undesirable degree of balance-of-payments disequilibrium, and to create a strong presumption that effective adjustment policies should be implemented. But we would leave to the country concerned substantial discretion in determining the composition of those adjustment policies. And international consultations would be utilized to determine the applicability of the criteria to particular situations and to consider exceptional cases in which the rules might be overridden. . . .

Adjustment, Reserves, and Convertibility

The U.S. proposals assume that most nations will want to maintain established values for their exchange rates—par values or central rates—in conjunction with a generalized system of convertibility of national currencies into international reserve assets. In a system of established exchange values and convertibility, there is a close relationship between balance-of-payments disequilibria and reserve changes. Accordingly, in our view the single most valid indicator that a country is in actual or emerging disequilibrium—as well as the most readily available, the most comprehensive, and the least ambiguous—is a persistent movement of its reserves in one direction or another.

To be viable, a convertibility system must be capable of satisfying the sum of individual countries' normal needs for and secular growth in reserves. Nations individually, either explicitly through formulation of overt balance-of-payments objectives, or more implicitly through their behavior, express an effective demand for reserves. Unless the international monetary system is capable of meeting these national demands in the aggregate and changing the level of reserves to meet changes in such needs over time, a satisfactory reconciliation of national balance-of-payments aims, and therefore sustained balance-of-payments equilibrium, cannot be assured. For if reserves are not adequate to these demands in the aggregate, nations are incapable by definition of reaching their desired reserve positions simultaneously. A decision to provide the system with too few reserves induces—and sanctions—a destabilizing and ultimately fruitless competition for scarce reserves. Creation of too many reserves pushes too great a share of the adjustment pressures onto surplus countries and facilitates world inflation.

A critical defect of the system in the past was that while it tried to promise unlimited convertibility, and while fundamentally it required a broad measure of balance-of-payments equilibrium for sustained operation, it did not provide the supply of acceptable reserve assets or the discipline on adjustment policies necessary to achieve these objectives. A basic feature of the U.S. proposal is that nations must, through the process of negotiation, reach a collective decision on the appropriate normal stock and rate of increase of reserves, and be prepared to accept the consequences of that decision in terms of their own individual reserve positions and their own freedom of action to run surpluses or deficits.

It would be essential in the proposed system that countries regard their balance-of-payments disequilibria, whether surplus or deficit, as a source of concern before the agreed indicators came into play. In other words, countries would not be expected to ignore imbalances blithely until their disequilibria had become so extreme as to prompt strong *international* concern through the indicator mechanism. Reserve fluctuations would signal emerging disequilibria; movement to outer indicators signalling strong *international* concern would occur only when countries failed to make the appropriate responses as the disequilibria built up.

Convertibility itself cannot promote adequate or equitable adjustment. Convertibility is in that sense an asymmetrical tool, operating only on deficit countries. In the framework of the U.S. proposal, the inherent link of convertibility to reserve fluctuations would result in broadly symmetrical pressures upon surplus and deficit nations.

In short, the logic of the U.S. proposals is that a) better balance-of-payments adjustment is required and is essential to the maintenance of a convertibility system; b) such an adjustment process, in turn, requires recognition by both surplus and deficit countries of their obligations and responsibilities to take action; c) in that context, objective indicators of the need for adjustment are essential; d) a broad equality between the availability of, and demands for, reserves in the system must be satisfied; and e) all of these needs can be brought together, in the context of a system of established exchange rates supported by convertibility, by the use of reserve movements as the main indicator of the need for adjustment.

Description of the Proposed Adjustment/Reserve/ Convertibility System

These principles could be incorporated into several alternative operational frameworks. Such alternative formulations could, for example, (a) emphasize the use of net or gross reserves as the basis for measuring fluctuations in reserves; (b) focus attention largely on changes in reserves from an existing starting level or on an appropriate distribution of individual countries' reserves in relation to some "objective" standard; and (c) provide for either relatively narrow or relatively wide ranges of fluctuation in reserves before international disciplines come into play. While the underlying principles and logic of the various approaches would be broadly similar, the particular formulation chosen would determine the speed, force and manner with which the adjustment pressures would operate. For its part, the United States wishes to continue to examine the advantages and disadvantages of the alternatives with care, and would welcome the contribution toward this effort that others can make.

The use of fluctuations in countries' reserves as the main indicator of adjustment need requires a judgment about a "base" level and trend of reserves for each country. Abstracting from transitional problems (noted later), these "base levels" could be established in several different ways. For instance, the distributional pattern of national quotas in the IMF (allowing for any agreed revisions in the future) might represent one approach toward determining a broadly acceptable distribution of reserves in normal circumstances. Another approach would be to give heavy weight to the actual level of reserves at the start of the system for the majority of countries, relying on separate negotiations for those countries whose reserves at the start of the system were judged to be seriously excessive or inadequate. Countries' "base levels," in any case, would be expected to rise over time, consistent with collective decisions about world SDR creation. The manner in which "base levels" should be calculated would clearly be a matter for careful negotiation. What is necessary is that *some* pattern be accepted that is generally satisfactory.

Use of reserve fluctuations to achieve an evenhanded stimulus to adjustment will require a broad consistency between the total of established "base levels" for individual countries and the actual supply of reserves in the system as a whole. Conceptually, in a system which did not provide for reserve currencies, this need could be met simply by assuring that the aggregate of gold, SDR's and IMF positions—that is, "primary reserves"—equaled the aggregate of countries' "base levels" of reserves. If in such a system aggregate "base levels" were above total primary reserves, a destabilizing and potentially deflationary competition for reserves could result; if "base levels" were below the total of primary assets, too large a share of adjustment pressures would be shifted toward surplus countries and world inflation might be facilitated.

In practice, we assume that some nations will wish to hold foreign exchange in their reserves and should be permitted to do so. Some nations will want flexibility of reserve management, and the system as a whole will benefit from an ability to respond flexibly to sudden and reversible increases in the need for liquidity during periods of strain related to speculative or other factors. Thus, in structuring the proposed system consideration will need to be given to the complication introduced by the existence of a possibly fluctuating margin of foreign exchange holdings. In a convertibility system, foreign exchange holdings are potential claims on primary reserves. Consequently, a stable system must provide enough primary reserves in relation to the whole to meet reasonable demands for conversion of these potential convertibility claims and/or must limit demands for conversion by individual countries that would otherwise claim an excessive proportion of the available supply of primary reserves.

There are a number of complementary approaches which could reconcile the existence of foreign exchange holdings in reserves with the stability and evenhanded working of a system of reserve indicators. One approach would be to equate the aggregate of "base levels" with the total of primary reserves and provide limits on the disproportionate accumulation of primary reserves by a country above its base level. Some assurance against excessive claims for primary reserves growing out of past accumulation of foreign exchange could also be provided by arrangements providing for bilateral or multilateral funding of existing foreign exchange reserves to the extent the holder wished to fund such balances, or by a facility for exchange of such balances—initially or over time—into SDR's. These aspects of the question should receive careful study, but are not further considered here.

Under a reserve-indicator system, certain points would be established above and below each country's base level to guide the adjustment process and to assure even-handed convertibility disciplines. Such points would be set according to uniform procedures for each country, and could be described as follows, again abstracting from special arrangements that would be appropriate during a transitional period.

(a) A "low point" would be set at some point below the "base level." In concept, this might approximate a level of reserves considered to be close to the minimum level ordinarily necessary to maintain confidence and to guard against extreme emergencies. If a country's reserves fell below its "low point" for a period of time, definite adjustment pressures would be anticipated and acceptable adjustment measures would be expected. In the absence of adequate policies over a specified period, international sanctions— for example, refusal to provide credit, or loss of scheduled SDR allocations— might become effective. Such sanctions would be avoided only if the IMF, through approval of a satisfactory program of adjustment, made a finding that sanctions were not warranted. Negotiated credits to deficit countries would ordinarily be permitted—but excessive or prolonged borrowing to circumvent the indicators would not be allowed.

(b) A "lower warning point" would be set at a point between a country's "base level" and the "low point." Small devaluations would be freely permitted a country at any time its reserves were below its base level. Proposals for larger devaluations would always require IMF approval; such proposals would not ordinarily be looked upon with favor unless a country's reserves had fallen below its "lower warning point."

(c) An "outer point" would be established above a country's "base level." As a country moved toward its "outer point," it would be expected to apply adjustment measures of progressive intensity. If reserves rose to the "outer point," remained at or above that level for a specified period, and an adequate program of adjustment were not in place, international action to induce adjustment would take effect. For example, the IMF might authorize other countries to impose general import taxes or surcharges against the country concerned, there might be a loss of scheduled SDR allocations, or there might be a tax on the country's excess reserve holdings with proceeds to go to development assistance. Such sanctions could be avoided, or postponed, only if the IMF made a positive finding they were not warranted, on the basis of an agreed program of adjustment—involving, for example, major moves toward liberalization of import restrictions, removal of any controls on the outward flow of capital, provision of concessional untied aid, or revaluation. Standards should be developed for judging the adequacy of such programs and their consistency with progress toward a liberal world economic order. If reserve gains persisted despite the agreed program, authorization for sanctions would, after a further period, take effect. In any event, the IMF would review the country's position periodically, and make such recommendations and authorizations as it deemed appropriate.

(d) An "upper warning point" would be set between the "base level" and the "outer point," analogous to the lower warning point, representing an international judgment that adjustment is called for. The IMF would be expected to report on the country's balance-of-payments position and prospects, and revaluation or other adjustment measures would be anticipated.

(e) Depending on the volume of total reserves relative to primary reserves in the system, this "upper warning point" might coincide with a "convertibility point" representing the maximum accumulation of *primary* reserves for each country that would be justified, consistent with the level of aggregate primary reserves in the entire system, for the convertibility mechanism to operate equitably with respect to both deficit and surplus countries. Both to provide an incentive for adjustment, and to prevent countries from placing further convertibility pressures on others, a country reaching such a "convertibility point" would be unable to acquire additional primary reserves, through either purchase or SDR allocation.

A reserve-indicator system such as the one sketched above should be supplemented and elaborated by consultative procedures within the IMF concerning adjustment programs and problems. For such procedures to be effective, national policy officials at a politically responsive level should be drawn into the process. Such IMF review could take into account supplementary criteria in considering the nature and magnitude of any need for adjustment.

Countries would not be expected to delay adjustment action until they had reached the indicator points. The purpose of a reserve-indicator system is to provide strong incentives for countries to act in limited steps, using a variety of tools suited to their circumstances before their situation becomes so urgent as to involve international concern and action. Moreover, while countries would at given points be brought under overt international pressure for adjustment, they would still have a range of policy options at their disposal. The range of "acceptable adjustment measures" for the system would, however, be limited to those consistent with market mechanisms and a liberal world trade and payments order. Exchange rate changes are not seen as the only, or necessarily the most desirable, means of adjustment in all cases.

Even though the aim of the system is to promote equilibrium, some scope for fluctuation in reserves is obviously necessary and desirable. No workable system can or should try to assure lock-step economic performance from 124 nations differing greatly in size, stage of development, and economic circumstance. Through the process of negotiation, an international consensus should be reached in defining the indicator points so as to get "enough" elbow room for some fluctuation in reserves to meet transitory payments imbalances, but not "so much" that adjustment is inappropriately delayed.

The reserve-indicator system should be designed to permit countries maximum flexibility to the extent compatible with maintaining the system's basic principles:

(a) As noted, a *small* devaluation without requirement for approval might be permitted at any time a country's reserves were below base level. Small revaluations might be permitted at any time. While in practice, situations would seldom, if ever, arise for withholding international approval from larger revaluations, restraint will continue to be necessary to guard against competitive devaluation.

(b) A country could opt for a transitional float, under agreed rules, in lieu of a discrete exchange rate change. If it intended to reestablish and maintain a central value for its currency within a given period, a reserve-deficient country could be permitted, under suitable guidelines, to increase its reserves toward its base level. If a country's reserves were above its base level at the time of initiation of the transitional float, it would not be permitted further reserve accumulation.

(c) A country could depart from the regime of established parities to float for a period of indefinite duration but only if it adhered to internationally agreed standards that would assure the consistency of its actions with the basic requirements of a cooperative order. These standards would relate, for example, to movements in its reserves, its intervention policies, elimination of controls on the inward flow of capital, avoidance of restrictive trade controls imposed for balance-of-payments purposes and elimination of any existing extraordinary balance-of-payments measures. Exchange rate systems nominally establishing a central or par value but envisaging very frequent changes such as those now in force in some less developed countries, could be integrated with this rule.

(d) Any group of countries in the process of forming a monetary union— with an implicit high degree of political and economic integration—could choose to operate as a unit. In this instance, the relevant criteria would be applied to the unit as a whole, which would be expected to speak with one voice in international forums. The reserve norms for the unit would have to be recalculated to reflect external trade and appropriate treatment of intra-unit assets.

(e) On a selective basis, consideration should be given to special arrangements for exclusion from reserves, and thus from measurements of adjustment need, of an "investment fund" of foreign securities or other foreign assets held by official agencies. Such funds might be appropriate for selected countries that wanted to hold over a prolonged period of time within official accounts (or with official inducements), foreign assets for long-term investment purposes. Such countries could be asked to observe certain criteria with respect to term, size and nature of the holdings. Oil producing countries with relatively large external assets would be candidates for such arrangements.

(f) Negotiated official credits (including IMF credits) should be permitted. Satisfactory procedures for the recording of such credits under the reserve-indicator system would need to be devised.

(g) In general, the system should neither ban nor encourage official holdings of foreign exchange. However, in the context of the proposed system, such holdings would presumably not loom so large relatively as in recent years. Each country should have the right to place limits on the further accumulation of its own currency of issue by official institutions in any other individual country or group of countries. Each country that chose to permit foreign official holdings of its currency must provide reasonable and normal investment facilities for those holdings.

The United States proposal neither gives special rights to nor imposes special obligations on any country or group of countries. It assumes a monetary system in which all countries are treated equally. All would have the same freedom to use the full exchange rate margins permitted in the system. All would have the same rights to allow their currencies to float, transitionally or indefinitely, under the same internationally agreed rules of behavior and surveillance. All maintaining established values for their currencies would have the same obligation to assure convertibility of their currencies—meaning that officially held balances of foreign currencies could be freely presented to the issuing country for conversion into primary reserve assets, with the choice among SDR's, reserve positions in the IMF and gold to be made by the issuing country.

DEVELOPING COUNTRIES' VIEWS *

The overwhelming concern of the Fund Governors from the developing countries at the Annual Meetings was the need for greater recognition of their interests in the reform of the international monetary system. As Indonesia's Minister of Finance, Ali Wardhana, noted in his opening address as Chairman of the Annual Meetings, monetary reform "provides an unprecedented, and probably unique, opportunity to assist at the same time in dealing with the problems of the developing countries."

Speaking for the countries of Latin America, the Governor of El Salvador's Central Reserve Bank, Eduardo Suarez C., said that "the objectives of the reform should include appropriate priority for development problems and the mechanisms which will facilitate and ensure a greater transfer of real resources to the developing countries."

In broad terms, Senegal's Minister of Finance, Babacar Ba, spoke for the seven African member states of the West African Monetary Union, and stressed the need to "avert the disastrous effects of a natural tendency for both riches and poverty to grow."

This means, he said, that "Through decisions taken without consulting them and applied without consideration for the harm they cause them, the developing countries last year lost a part of the value of their meager foreign exchange reserves, had the burden of their external indebtedness aggravated, and saw a general fluctuation of currencies introduced into both the financial calculation of their investments and into the marketing of their products and payments for the imports,

* *IMF Survey*, October 9, 1972.

over and above all the other elements of uncertainty affecting them now and in the future." . . .

On the whole, the Governors representing the developing countries agreed that their interests would be served by an enlargement of financial assistance on softer terms and a modification of trade policies in the developed countries favoring an expansion of the developing countries' exports. These views were reflected in the communiqué of the Ministers of the Intergovernmental Group of 24 on International Monetary Affairs: ". . . a reformed monetary system must have as one of its basic aims the facilitation of a substantial transfer of real resources from the developed to the developing countries and the financing of such transfers on appropriate terms designed to avoid problems of excessive debt burdens on the developing countries."

The transfer of resources, in the views expressed by the Governors, can best be served by the maintenance of stable exchange rates with some degree of flexibility.

10. MEETINGS OF THE COMMITTEE OF 20

During the year prior to the Fund's annual meeting in Nairobi in September 1973, the Committee of 20 held a number of sessions in an effort to negotiate a draft outline of reform. After their sixth session in July 1973, the chairman of the Committee stated that the Committee had been able to advance toward the draft outline, "identifying the main alternative choices, the main points of dispute, the major issues that have got to be decided in the reform."

It is instructive to consider the course of the Committee's progress, as summarized in the following set of press briefings given by the Chairman.

THE EXPLORATORY STAGE *

MR. MORSE: I think the substantive discussion that we did have was orderly and pretty effective. . . .

I would say just one or two things about the quality of the discussion: We definitely began a debate. That implies that people were talking sufficiently the same sort of language to be able to debate about it. Well, of course, within that debate, as you well know, there are differences of view. There were differences of view on the answer

---

* Press briefing given by C. Jeremy Morse, Chairman of the Deputies of the Committee of 20, after the first meeting of the Committee; *IMF Survey*, December 11, 1972.

to some of the precise points that we were talking about in the adjustment process, and there are also differences of approach. And, as one of the Deputies put it rather well, he said, "There is a tension between the desire for stability and the desire for flexibility, which we have to resolve."

So we have only just begun the debate, and it is in the coming meetings that we have to try to resolve that tension and work toward some kind of consensus.

But I would stress that we shan't, of course, get to consensus on any of these big subjects easily or early; and we shan't, in fact, get to consensus until we have covered the whole ground. [There] are a variety of topics in the reform, and different governments and different parts of the world are interested in different parts of the reform in different ways; and not until they see the whole will they be able to come to a conclusion about it. And that, indeed, was what we looked to in the program of work that we proposed—namely, that the Deputies should seek, with the help of the Committee as given, to cover the whole scope of the terms of reference in their discussions, so that we can report for the Committee on the subject as a whole, and in the hope of arriving at some kind of draft outline, in time for Nairobi—on which Ministers will then see whether they are able to agree or not.

Well, at our next meeting in Paris we shall come back, I think, to the adjustment process, and try to take it a stage further. And we also intend to embark on the other big area of debate for the reform; the whole area of reserve assets, the role of reserve assets, and the convertibility, and the questions that are consequent on that.

QUESTION: *Mr. Morse, was there any discussion on the link between the special drawing rights to the problem of the developing countries?*

MR. MORSE: Yes, it was mentioned quite a bit in the general exchange of views, and not so much of course in the discussion on the adjustment process. It is a view on which there are now a great variety of opinions and a spectrum of opinions among both developed and developing countries, and it is certainly one of the topics that we have to tackle at a later meeting.

QUESTION: *Mr. Morse, some of your delegates are committed to a monetary union, yet you are talking about a more flexible exchange rate system; I wonder how you reconcile the two ideas.*

MR. MORSE: I don't know if it is for me to reconcile them, but I don't think either those outside the European Union or those inside it are having too much difficulty with that in the general concept of the system, because if we are talking about a system in which a number of countries have to coexist it is obviously perfectly possible for some of those countries to group together or to split apart as time goes on.

Well—so in a general theory of the reform, I don't think that raises any great difficulties. That is not to say that it may not raise some difficulties in practice for individual countries, but you perhaps leap a little ahead in saying that we are definitely going to have a more flexible system, as it were; we are going to have a less rigid system. But it is a matter still for debate as to what the degree of fixity is.

QUESTION: *Did you sense any support, outside of the U.S., on the matter of sanctions at some point, or is that going too far ahead?*

MR. MORSE: Well, it was a subject that we touched on—and people used that word. I think the way we approached it was that if you make a general assessment in international consultation of a country's position and decided that there is a need for adjustment, can you help that general assessment by these indicators; and, if the indicators light up, should that trigger consultation. And then if a situation after consultation still looks disagreeable to the other countries of the world, should there be positive guidance, either from the Fund or from countries meeting within the Fund, and ultimately should there be some kind of pressures or sanctions. And, of course, some of those have been mentioned—some possibilities have been mentioned in various speeches, including some in Secretary Shultz's address to the Annual Meeting. We didn't go very deeply into it, but it certainly isn't true that everybody rejects the idea that there might have to be pressures at the end of the line.

QUESTION: *Did only one country advocate reserves as the prime objective indicator?*

MR. MORSE: Well, I said I wouldn't talk about national positions. Only one country?

(Laughter)

QUESTION: *Did any other country?*

MR. MORSE: I think one country has certainly developed its thoughts further about it than other people have, yes, and is more convinced of the primacy of that particular kind of indicator, yes.

QUESTION: *What other objective indicators have been proposed in this meeting?*

MR. MORSE: Well, other objective indicators which have been mentioned—befor the meeting really—you will find them mentioned in the Report of the Executive Board, would include exchange market movements and also include the movement of the basic balance to which some countries attach importance. They would include price movements, and also a rather different kind of indicator which has been sometimes mentioned is the divergence between balance of payments aims and their outturn. So a variety of indicators were touched on by the speakers.

SECOND-STAGE DISCUSSION *

MR. MORSE: . . . Once again we've devoted almost all of our meeting to questions of substance, and only spent a very short time on matters of procedure. . . . We had a first round of discussion on one of the big subjects of the monetary reform—the reserve assets and convertibility—and I'll say a little about what the particular subjects under that heading are.

We were looking at what kind of long-term reserve asset system we might want, how to adjust the need for reserve creation and how we would control, better than in the past, reserve creation. We were also looking at what should be the roles in such a long-term system of the various reserve assets we have, the three principal ones being gold, SDRs, and reserve currencies; and we also looked glancingly at positions in the Fund. We were considering how we might come back to a system of general convertibility, in the form of what we call, in the technical jargon, asset settlement. Asset settlement is a system in which countries settle their imbalances by losing or gaining reserve assets rather than by running up and down their reserve liabilities as in a reserve currency system. We are also examining whether the long-term system should move toward what is technically known—it's rather a difficult term—as multicurrency intervention. Essentially the meaning of this is that all currencies would be treated equally for intervention processes and the special position notably of the United States dollar would be reduced. Pro tanto, the United States would of course gain more freedom of maneuver, perhaps wider margins and, hopefully, more room to move its exchange rate when necessary.

We looked at all these components of a long-term system; but also in this field there are a number of very important short-term or transitional questions that have to be considered—how to get to such a system—and we were looking at those transitional questions in the light of the long-term system that we would like to have. Some of the objectives of the system, like a return to general convertibility and possibly the establishment of a multicurrency intervention system might perhaps have to be achieved by stages—they might take some time. And then in relation to each of the main reserve assets that I mentioned there are transitional problems. . . .

Now, on the last day, we had a different kind of discussion—we had a second stage discussion on the adjustment process, building on our first discussion of that subject that we had in Washington in November . . . we looked again at various ways of improving the techniques of the adjustment process, including the question of indicators, which

* Press briefing after third meeting of the Committee of 20, *IMF Survey*, February 12, 1973.

we had broached last time and on which a good deal of reflection had taken place and papers had been written, and we also looked fairly closely at procedures and improvement of procedures. Both these are positive ways of improving the adjustment process, recognizing that probably in some ways it's going to be—certainly not easier—maybe more difficult than in the recent past to maintain a smooth adjustment process, partly because of inflation, and even if that is curbed, more fundamentally because in the new system that we envisage there would be less scope than before for the aims of other countries to be accommodated by U.S. deficits or deficits of other reserve centers. We also continued our examination of whether there were obstacles in the existing system that could be removed, including a better balance between surplus and deficit countries in taking action—and all this on a very general plane of adjustment. I would like to repeat what I said at the last press conference, that we have not been talking about exchange rate changes only. We have been talking about the whole range of adjustment and about the relative roles of different types of adjustment action, the relative roles of domestic action and external action, and within external action the different roles of exchange rate changes and also of capital controls and trade controls. . . .

QUESTION: *Mr. Chairman, would you say that there is agreement towards any kind of convergence of views on the question of objective indicators or criteria to rule on parity changes?*

MR. MORSE: I think I spoke to you last time in the sense that there was a general willingness to look at this proposition and examine it further. It is quite a difficult question and it's going to need a good deal of analysis. Despite some statements that I have seen, the difficulty does not arise from any proposal for the automatic use of indicators to trigger parity changes. As I think you know, that is not the proposal we are debating. I mentioned this last time. What we are debating is the possible use of indicators for various purposes at various stages in the general adjustment process—in the first stage to indicate or to identify an imbalance that might require examination and perhaps subsequently action. And I think there is a general agreement that there is no necessary conflict between the greater use of such indicators and continuing qualitative or discretionary assessment. . . .

QUESTION: *Now could I ask another question? May I ask you, Mr. Chairman, whether you think that the other countries of the world are willing to give the United States the type of adjustment that it needs to make the dollar convertible?*

MR. MORSE: I don't know whether they are, but that's the essence of the reform. If they are, well then we shall have a nice reform; if they're not, then we shall have something else. . . .

QUESTION: *Have any of the staff which are at your disposition— which you mentioned earlier—so far been able to make any analytical studies of how the various indicators would have worked had they operated at various times in the past—and is it yet clear from any such study whether any indicators seem to perform better than any other indicators?*

MR. MORSE: Well, the answer to that is, Yes, there have been studies— particularly by the Fund staff on this subject—and certainly in those studies the indicators don't all perform exactly the same—but if the implication of your question is—is there any one indicator or one type of indicator that absolutely stands out—I think probably No, but equally I don't think those studies are by any means fully refined yet. You can group indicators—as you probably know perfectly well. There are some indicators related to reserves, and different definitions of reserves; there are some indicators related to diminishing components of the basic balance, the basic balance itself, down to the current account, say, at the other end. Then there is quite a different family of indicators related to prices and costs; and there are the old indicators that were popular two or three years ago related to exchange rates—as in some of the automatic versions of the crawling peg—either spot exchange rates or forward exchange rates. Not only are these all rather different but also the information on them is available with different time lags and for some countries but not for others. Plainly this is a subject that needs a lot of study. The United States' position—which I'm not supposed to talk about but which was mentioned last time is, as you know, to give considerable weight to the reserve indicator and there is a widespread feeling that some indicator in this field—if indicators are used—is an important criterion.

QUESTION: *Have the Deputies accepted the concept of cyclical adjustment for balance of payments . . . ?*

MR. MORSE: . . . I think it's recognized that where cyclical adjustment can be made it is useful, despite the imperfection of the art. Particularly, I think (and this is a fruit of work that's been done in OECD here in Paris over the last few years), there is the importance in the international group of looking at situations on the basis that every country is cyclically adjusted. We saw this very much in the debate leading up to Smithsonian. Most people will make allowance for their own cyclical adjustment if they want to keep on the safe side and at the same time not take enough account of the cyclical position of other countries. It's a very important part, I think, of improving the technique of international discussion on these technical matters to get the staff of the IMF or the OECD—or whatever institution—to present the figures in a consistent way—all cyclically adjusted together. So this is certainly an important part of the technique that we will have to use. . . .

THE STAGE OF NEGOTIATION *

QUESTION: *Can you indicate any area where there is a consensus? Have you got a consensus on anything?*

MR. MORSE: I think you ask me that question every time. We won't get consensus in any major area until we come to the end of the line. We have all the subjects in play. On many minor points, no doubt, there was consensus. And on some of the broader areas we probably came closer together. But, as on former occasions, I don't want to elaborate that in detail. I would simply say this. Let's take two of the main subjects: The adjustment process, on which, as you know, the Americans have made detailed proposals, which have been published including an indicator system; and, on the other hand, settlement or convertibility—a subject in which the other countries (and particularly the Europeans) have been interested from the start. The advance we made in discussing these two subjects is that both sides really began to work on each other's positions, to look into them closely, to interact on them; maybe coming together somewhat in the process—one would have to reflect on a lot of detail to analyze that precisely.

This process I describe, as you will see, is a beginning of bargaining on these major issues. It illustrates what I call the move from exploration to negotiation, the beginning of bargaining; in some cases, perhaps, drawing a little closer together; in others, sharpening up differences which will probably only be ultimately resolved by Ministers in these major areas; and the same would apply to other areas as well.

QUESTION: *Mr. Morse, will you please explain to us what special commission, technical commission, was set on the link problem?*

MR: MORSE: This is a working group of the Deputies similar to the ones that we had between the last two meetings on the questions of indicators and disequilibrating capital flows. It is a working party—to which each of the 20 constituencies sends one or two people—to thrash through some of the outstanding questions, arguments, technical problems involved in different proposals for the link, etc.—set up, of course, without prejudice to the question of whether there will be a link or not, just as we set up a working party on indicators without prejudice to the question of what their role would be in the system. The purpose is to elaborate the work a little farther—this being a case where there is still some more elaboration to do.

QUESTION: *Mr. Morse, was there—would you agree that there was a substantial European cooperation at this time, more than at the other meetings?*

* Press briefing after fifth meeting of the Committee of 20, *IMF Survey,* June 11, 1973.

MR. MORSE: On quite a few subjects the Europeans have established a common position. I would certainly say, looking back to the SDR negotiations in which, of course, I was involved as a national delegate, that there is far more of a European common position now. The change seems to me rather marked. To stretch your question a little further, they are also very cooperative in a general sense. Indeed, the spirit in the meeting was extremely good, which was the reason why we were able to get on with the debate.

QUESTION: *How much support is there for an abstract SDR?*

MR. MORSE: A good deal of support and a good deal of increased interest in it, and a good deal of technical advance in elaborating what is involved in it. By an abstract SDR we mean making the SDR the numeraire of the system—founding the system on one SDR = one SDR—and we discussed what that would imply for the relationship of the SDR to currencies, both in terms of par vaues and in the use of SDRs in transactions and, therefore, in relation to market rates; and also of course, when we discussed the question of the numeraire and gold, [what it would imply for] the relationship between the SDR and gold. It is certainly a subject in which there is a lively interest and a good deal of debate.

QUESTION: *Mr. Morse, you mentioned that in this process of bargaining some opinions were coming closer together and some differences, I believe you said, appeared to be sketched more sharply. Would you illustrate one of the latter for us?*

MR. MORSE: Consistent with my practice, I don't want to go into detail on what points there was consensus on and what points not. But in general, to take the example I gave you on the whole complex of the adjustment process—on how tight it should be or how loose it should be in relation to the settlement system, and how tight or loose that should be—there are still different positions. There is the American position on the adjustment process and there are other positions. Similarly on the settlement side there are perhaps two or three broad positions on what kind of system people want—whether they view it in relation to reserve centers or other countries. And we have a much clearer idea of what those positions are for a wide range of countries, and what the weight of them is—sufficient, in fact, to enable us to feel that we can make a shot at what the package might be. So if I said that differences were sharper, I really meant we knew more about them rather than they were necessarily more antagonistic.

QUESTION: *Is it true, on the question of controls in the Euro-market, that there is a difference of interests between reserve centers and other countries?*

MR. MORSE: I wouldn't say particularly between the traditional reserve centers and other countries, but rather the new reserve centers;

by which I mean the countries that are recipients of inflows which they don't want. As you know, this is a debate which has been going on among the developed countries for a long time, with those countries that have suffered inflows which upset their domestic economy—and even perhaps their external position—feeling that the Euro-markets have been a very important channel for these flows. There is also a debate about whether there is endogenous credit creation in these markets as well. But the argument really turns on balancing the harmful effect of the inflows into those countries and the beneficial effects of the Euro-market for other countries, particularly those who have borrowed in it. Developing countries, by and large, have found the Euro-market a good source of funds, and feel that they have got a lot of benefits from it.

QUESTION: *How do you prevent the Euro-market moving elsewhere if you put controls on the regional basis? Is it possible?*

MR. MORSE: That is one of the long-debated questions, but it is not one that we debated here at any length. It is a question which I used to be particularly interested in before I forgot what it was to be English.

A STAGE FORWARD *

QUESTION: *So you won't be disappointed, I will ask my questions again this time about consensus on anything beyond what you have already indicated.*

MR. MORSE: I might mention one area in which we took a step forward. It is not an absolutely crucial area, but it may be quite important in the future system, and that is multicurrency intervention. There was evinced a general desire to pursue studies of the possibility of establishing such a system, into which a number of the leading countries might enter. The motive behind this is the desire to have a more symmetrical system than the dollar intervention system—the United States getting out of it more freedom in its exchange rate action and more freedom on margins and, on the other side, removing the dollar from the special position, which many people think was a fault of the old system and led to over-dependence and breakdown. . . .

QUESTION: *Mr. Morse, at your last meeting, if memory serves me right, you delegated the IMF Board to work out ground rules for the floats. Whatever happened to that exercise?*

MR. MORSE: The Deputies in their May meeting looked at the question of rules for floating, whether by individual countries or general floating, in the reformed system. In general the feeling has been that it is difficult to lay down in advance rules about the main things which

* Press briefing after sixth meeting of the Committee of 20, *IMF Survey*, July 23, 1973.

countries are interested in in a floating regime—intervention and the use of controls; that you have to treat each situation *ad hoc* as it arises, as indeed is being done at the present time. We haven't found any way to lay out an elaborate system of rules for floating for the future system. So we shall have to rely on an improved procedure for consultation and surveillance, which is part of our proposals for the future adjustment process; and whether countries are all on a pattern of fixed rates or one or two are floating or there is more general floating, all important situations of imbalance would be brought into the surveillance and examined. In this way you would look at intervention in cases of floating—where rates were going, who was building up reserves or losing reserves in situations of dirty floating—managed floating, perhaps I should call it, because we vowed that we would no longer talk about dirty floating or clean floating.

QUESTION: *What would be the real political issues which would have to be settled by the Ministers, where there is a clear division and you don't see any convergence, as you phrased it?*

MR. MORSE: In the adjustment field, as I said, there is the question about what role indicators should play, how far they should be an automatic or not—"automatic" is the wrong word because provisions for overriding, etc., have been written in—but how far there should be a presumption of the need for adjustment created by indicators, or how far it should be a matter of general assessment which leads the Fund to say to a country, "You should adjust." That is mainly a political question as to how the international community makes its will known to national governments. In the settlement system, the question whether you have a rather tight system, imposing fairly severe restrictions on any further increase in reserve currency holdings, or whether you have a rather looser system, is plainly one of major importance for the character of the system. The question of the SDR becoming the center of the system, and its character, how it should perform in relation to other currencies that might be rival reserve assets and what interest rate it should carry, that is plainly a question of major interest to governments as well as to technicians. And finally the SDR/aid link question is also one which has strong political interest.

QUESTION: *I am not clear on your comment about the United States, and the others, that are coming together on this adjustment process. Do you mean that it is not the United States against everybody else at this stage? Or has something changed?*

MR. MORSE: No. I said that the positions had been brought closer together; the position of the United States on the one hand (I think there might be one or two others with the United States, but essentially it is the United States' position); and the position of others. That convergence didn't take place in this meeting; it had taken place by the end of the May meeting.

QUESTION: *In what sense coming together? What is there in common?*

MR. MORSE: Well, for instance, both sides envisage a system in which there will be an important use of indicators. And both sides envisage that there will have to be assessment cross-checking those indicators. The essential difference is whether movements in the indicator should create a presumption that countries should take adjustment action, unless it is decided otherwise; or whether the indicator is simply one important factor which has to be taken seriously into account in arriving at a judgment on the matter.

QUESTION: *Is there to be a discussion some time of a system of indicators that are to be used? If so, what indicators are to be used, except the reserve indicator?*

MR. MORSE: The general feeling is that the other indicator which is the most important and should be taken account of in the new system is the basic balance indicator. There is a general feeling that if the basic balance is going in a contrary direction to the reserves, that would be an important reason to make one pause before acting on the reserve indicator.

QUESTION: *Would you say that there is a consensus on symmetry in the new system, that is, presumption that surplus countries have an obligation to act, as well as deficit countries?*

MR. MORSE: I think, on symmetry, there really is a consensus, a meaningful consensus on both the main aspects of symmetry; both on the aspect you mentioned (that surplus countries have an equal duty to adjust with deficit countries); and also on the question of symmetry as between the United States and all the other countries; namely, that we should move to a system in which there is less of a special position for the dollar. I think that on these two points we have a genuine change in the system which is genuinely desired by all concerned.

QUESTION: *Mr. Morse, how do you see the concept for after Nairobi, time-wise?*

MR. MORSE: Well, I see it—assuming that we can achieve an important part of this kind of agreement by Nairobi—assuming that the Committee wishes to do so, and achieves that—then I see it as I have set it out to you before, namely, that we have up to a year's more work. That work would partly consist of pursuing questions which have not yet been fully worked out, like the multicurrency intervention question. It will partly consist of working out the detail, on an assured basis, of questions which have been decided; for instance, if and when this question about adjustment and indicators is decided, there will be important details to be worked out about the numbers of the system. And it will partly consist of the Executive Board drafting into amendments of the Articles what has been decided on reform. I see all that as a process which will take up to a year.

QUESTION: *Then, the ratification process?*

MR. MORSE: Then, the ratification process takes about a year after that.

Of course, there are parts of the reform which could be introduced earlier, because they wouldn't involve amendments of the Articles. For instance, one could set up some of the surveillance procedure on the basis of the new adjustment system without waiting for ratification, because it doesn't involve amendment. It is not the case that the whole reform is something for '75. But, of course, how and when the reform will be implemented will tie in with how the current scene develops; and when it is possible, in the adjustment area, to return to stable rates. In the SDR area, there are some things that could be applied whether we have already returned to stable rates or not.

11. ASSESSMENT OF PROGRESS TOWARD REFORM

The progress of the Committee of 20, and in particular the impact of events on the task of reform since the Committee began its deliberations, was assessed in the following excerpt from the Annual Report of the Bank for International Settlements.

UNRESOLVED ISSUES OF ADJUSTMENT AND LIQUIDITY *

Assuming that the object of the exercise is to re-establish a par value system with more effective adjustment incentives, it might be said that . . . the convertibility of currencies and the methods of settling imbalances, was the primary task before the Committee. It was indeed the suspension of convertibility by the United States on 15th August 1971, without provision for its restoration in the Smithsonian agreement, which really spelt the end of the Bretton Woods conception and rules. But with the huge amassing of dollar reserves that has taken place in the last four years, it is generally accepted that re-establishment of dollar convertibility will be complicated and will at least require a considerable transitional period. Hence the discussions so far have centred around the prospective exchange rate system, including the function of exchange rate changes in the adjustment process, and the future status of the various kinds of reserves.

On the former of these problems there was from the outset general agreement on the desirability of retaining a fixed exchange rate system, but with some greater flexibility of rates than in the past. As a matter of fact, by the time the Committee of Twenty first met, exchange rates had already shown much more flexibility. From November 1967 until the time when the Committee began its work, there had been eleven adjustments of fixed parities by Group of Ten countries. . . .

* Bank for International Settlements, *Forty-Third Annual Report*, June 1973, pp. 32–37.

This incrased flexibility was not due to any improvement in the rules, however, nor did it bring about a nicely managed implementation of the adjustments. On the contrary, the changes in exchange rates had been unduly delayed and the adjustment processes were set in motion by the force majeure of market crisis.

Against this background, recent discussions have been concerned less with the principle of greater flexibility than with its application—that is, with improving and speeding up adjustment decisions and, more specifically, with identifying cases in which changes in exchange rates are called for. The main proposal has been put forward by the United States; it is that "disproportionate" changes over a given time in a country's official monetary reserves should be taken as an "objective indicator" of the existence of a payments disequilibrium requiring corrective action. Such action need not involve a change in the exchange rate if a correction can be secured by other means.

The proposal accepts certain objectives for the reformed monetary system that had received rather general support in recent years. One is that the system should make it feasible for all currencies, including the dollar, to maintain convertibility into the basic reserve assets of gold and SDRs by assuring that losses of reserves could be subsequently recouped. The second is to prevent exaggerated increases in foreign exchange reserves. And the third is that the future growth of official reserves should be largely through new allocations of SDRs, which likewise should be kept under international control and be limited to the global needs of the system. It is a system which requires that both deficit and surplus countries maintain discipline to keep their changes of reserves in line with the set limits or to adjust quickly to reverse excessive movements.

It was evident in the Bretton Woods system that persistent reserve losses which could not be corrected by domestic policy measures inevitably lead sooner or later to devaluation of the currency; undue delays in devaluing arose through excessive granting of official credit and through excessive accumulation of dollars by surplus countries (in a sense also granting of credit). To make the system more symmetrical, the proposal contemplates a comparable obligation on surplus countries to control their surpluses by either internal adjustment or revaluation of the currency—it being clear that one country's surplus is another country's deficit.

While the US proposal has been taken seriously and seen to be a logical scheme, it has met with rather strong objections on the grounds that a reserve loss or gain is not necessarily a sign of fundamental disequilibrium; it may originate from cyclical developments, from excess or deficiency of demand, from interest rate differentials or from speculative flows of money. Besides, a country's reserves can be affected by another country's misdeeds. It was therefore suggested that a better objective indicator would be the deficit or surplus of the basic balance of payments adjusted for the relative position of the country in the business cycle. Further objections, voiced by various countries, to the use of reserves as the key indicator were that this would put the onus of taking action on the surplus countries, that it would hurry countries into using the exchange rate as the main adjustment instrument and that it would frustrate countries' objectives with regard to the structure of their balance of payments.

It is apparent from past experience that a satisfactory working of a fixed exchange rate system requires that the concept of fundamental disequilibrium be made as concrete as possible. It is not likely, however, that really objective criteria can enable such situations to be identified simply by rule of thumb. There seems generally to be a need for a judgement case by case, based on a careful analysis of all the relevant factors, which will of course differ from one case to another. And as in some such cases, particularly those involving the dollar, both gains and losses of reserves will have occurred, there is also no avoiding a judgement on which countries should have responsibility for taking corrective action.

The recent breakdown of the fixed rate system has inevitably placed the whole discussion of the exchange rate régime in a rather different context. After this traumatic experience the opinion has been expressed that it might be better not to return to fixed rates at all. . . .

However, official opinion by and large remains favourable to the ideal of a fixed rate system, for the same reasons as in the past. On the one hand, it is considered useful in the management of economic affairs that governments be subject to the discipline of the balance of payments so that it acts as a brake on domestic inflationary forces. In addition, it is thought that fixed rates make it politically easier to limit direct controls on trade and payments, such as might be imposed under a régime of floating in order to avoid shocks to the structure of the external sector. None the less, the idea of floating for some years has many adherents. The main reason for this is the reluctance of the authorities within a system of fixed rates to have their external reserves and their domestic monetary policies affected against their will by any substantial external imbalance that may continue even after a realignment. This could happen, given the huge potential size of leads and lags and of other private liquid capital flows, if at a time when confidence was still at a low ebb new fixed rates were simply to afford a target for speculation. It could also happen as a result of the sluggishness of the response of the current account to changes in exchange rates, although the existence of such lags is also a forceful argument against completely free floating because the necessary conditions for stability may not be fulfilled. Finally, there are some who believe that a new fixed rate system cannot be built on the basis of an inconvertible dollar.

As to the second problem mentioned above, namely the future of the various reserve assets, there are many who start from the idea that the future growth of reserves should be controlled, so that the increase may be in accordance with global needs. This of course assumes a fixed rate system, as otherwise there would be little need for reserves at all. The idea of control stems from the belief that excessive reserve growth contributes to inflation and at the same time is a clear sign of inadequate adjustment policies.

In recent discussions also it has been fairly generally accepted that SDRs should in future be the principal means of reserve growth, partly—though not entirely—as an aid to global reserve management. There is more to this idea, however, than just accepting it and proceeding to allocate SDRs, as became clear during the first three years of SDR allocation. It has in fact important implications for the nature of the SDR, for the future of other reserve assets, for the adjustment process and indeed for the feasibility of maintaining fixed exchange rates as the normal relationship among currencies.

With regard to the nature of the SDR, it means first of all that SDRs must carry a rate of interest which makes them attractive to hold. This is of particular concern to countries which now hold their reserves mainly in foreign exchange because of the importance they attach to the income earned on them. Secondly, it means making SDRs a more independent reserve asset, which implies substituting some other guarantee for the link with gold as well as changing the rules at present governing their use, such as the holding limits and the reconstitution provisions.

As for other types of reserves, attention has naturally been focused on controlling the growth of foreign exchange reserves, with the idea that any further increases should be strictly limited. Even on the assumption that the adjustment process will work better and more promptly in the future, this proposal appears premature. To adopt it could require an over-adjustment process, in which exchange rate changes would be destabilising from the standpoint of trade and of the domestic economy—a cure which would be worse than the disease. Any management of global reserves will have to allow for some play in the system—in fact for some unmanaged growth of reserves; otherwise the adjustment of parities may need to be so frequent that confidence in a fixed rate could not be maintained. It would in any case not be easy to secure agreement on limiting exchange holdings, nor would it be difficult to get round such limits in one way or another if they existed.

The question of the place of gold in the reformed monetary system is of course quite different from that of exchange reserves. Gold does not involve the risk of an excessive increase in reserves. However, gold reserves are virtually frozen because no central bank will give up gold at the present official value with the market price soaring above it. There is also the probability that so long as that situation persists, countries will be cautious about using their gold-guaranteed claims on the IMF, which at the present include their SDRs. In addition, the glaring discrepancy between over $100 for gold in the market and its nominal legal value of $42 is an obstacle to the restoration of confidence in, and the convertibility of, the dollar.

As to what to do about gold in the new monetary system, the only point of agreement seems to be that the share of gold in global reserves will tend to decline as that of SDRs increases. For the rest there is a whole gamut of opinion. Some believe that gold should be "phased out" of the system, though without having yet indicated how this should be done; on the other hand, many countries believe that gold should be retained in the system, and even that the SDR link with gold should be kept. Likewise, opinions are divided between maintaining the present official value of gold and raising it to a realistic relationship with the market price. A view heard recently is that the fixed official value should be abolished or ignored, leaving countries free, if they wished, to use gold in official settlements at or about the market price. It is also held that the understanding reached in Washington in March 1968 should be lifted in order that monetary authorities may be free to sell gold to the market, as allowed under the Fund's Articles, or even free to buy and sell. However, whatever the effect of these proposals might be, the intention behind them is simply that gold be unfrozen, not that it should again become a positive component in the growth of reserves.

It is in this respect that the system has already undergone a profound change. Formerly the inflow of new gold into the system served not only to increase global reserves but to finance net payments surpluses for the system as a whole, because new gold was a current-account export of gold-producing countries whereas its receipt was a means of balance-of-payments settlement. Gold thereby contributed to exchange rate stability by allowing some play in the adjustment process. Allocations of SDRs, on the other hand, do not finance payments surpluses in this way. Rather, they simply create surpluses—and that only if one ignores the implicit liabilities—still leaving true payments surpluses to be financed in one way or another. Hence an SDR system demands more rapid and effective adjustments of payments deficits and surpluses, unless both persistent transfers of SDRs are permitted and allocations are on a sufficient scale.

On the subject of the large movements of funds that have agitated the exchange markets, not much in the way of positive ideas has emerged as yet—except to call them destabilising. In fact, however, the destabilisation has mostly come from resistance to changing parities that were clearly unrealistic or from the extreme pursuit of domestic monetary policy on closed economy assumptions. It seems to be expected that the adjustment process will work better in the future, though many milliards of dollars were bought over the past year before the authorities abandoned the Smithsonian exchange rates. As to limitations on the operation of monetary policy, there are no signs that it figures very much in official thinking. Hence emphasis is likely to be on controls, though they have not been conspicuously effective, not even the extreme measures used by the Japanese authorities.

The idea that the reformed system should have special provisions for the benefit of developing countries has meant so far that they should be allocated, by one technique or another, more SDRs than would result from allocations proportionate to their quotas in the IMF. This idea has come to be called the "link" between SDRs and development aid. It is not yet clear what could be done on these lines, but there is strong political pressure behind it. On strictly monetary grounds the link raises some difficult questions. SDRs were not intended to finance persistent deficits but to finance swings in payments, as is clear from the provisions for reconstitution of SDR debtor positions. Hence there remains in the SDR idea some sense of a credit facility. And should the developing countries tend to become the main debtors to the SDR system, it is not apparent that confidence in the SDRs could be maintained, particularly if their share in the total allocations was large. Just how the link may affect other channels of aid is another aspect of the problem that needs to be considered.

Thus it can be seen that there are very difficult issues to be resolved, which moreover, have to be resolved in such a way that the pieces fit together to make a workable system. Hence the negotiation is likely to be a time-consuming process.

A more pointed summary of the progress—or lack of progress —toward reform was offered by C. Fred Bergsten in testimony before the House Subcommittee on International Finance. Dr. Bergsten emphasized the need for common and concerted action to promote the "speedy creation of a new international economic order."

THE SYSTEMIC CRISIS OF WORLD MONEY *

[My] statement attempts to make only three basic points. The first one is . . .
that we face what I would call a systemic crisis. What we see going on in the international money markets is not just an attack on the dollar, though it is partly that, but a collapse of confidence in the functioning of the entire monetary system and the ability of national governments and central banks to collaborate sufficiently to make that system work. . . .

We do have a systemic crisis, and one cannot deal with it by tinkering around the margins. You must get to the core of the system, which rested in the past on fixed exchange rates, gold and the dollar, none of which are satisfactory bases for a monetary system in the future.

I then go on to urge early and immediate action to achieve monetary reform. Technically, there are several ways to restore a stable system. Clean floats, with their purity governed by intensive international surveillance, would do it. So might truly fixed exchange rates, backed by massive financing to assure the defeat of speculative runs on any currency. An intermediate approach would preserve fixed parities but let actual rates fluctuate within wide margins (at least 5 percent on either side of parities), assure timely changes in parities through agreed rules backed up by international sanctions for countries to take action when action was required, create enough SDR's to meet countries' needs for reserves, and provide short-term credits

---

* Statement of C. Fred Bergsten, Senior Fellow, Brookings Institution, before the Subcommittee on International Finance of the Committee on Banking and Currency, House of Representatives, 93rd Congress, 1st Session, Hearings, March 7, 1973, pp. 134–36.

to deal with interest sensitive and speculative flows which do not call for parity adjustments.

Indeed, it makes little substantive difference whether the new system is based on (a) floating rates under multilateral surveillance, or (b) rates fixed within wide margins and changed frequently by small amounts. The same kind of rules would provide a basis for sanctioning or forbidding market intervention under the former approach, and for prompting or denying parity shifts under the latter. The basic choice is between such flexibility in exchange rates, however labeled, and truly fixed exchange rates with the resulting transfer of resources among countries financed through private capital flows and official reserves and credits. The fixed-rate system would generate intolerable unemployment for many deficit countries and intolerable inflation for many surplus countries. I would certainly opt for one of the flexibility variants. . . .

The third point is that the officials around the world know all of these difficulties, they know the different options that confront them, and they know what has to be done to achieve reform of the system. But more important than any of their specific differences is the failure of the major countries to perceive the urgent, even critical, need for them to act together immediately to take common and concerted action to place a new system in effect at once. Some Americans may still wistfully believe that U.S. interests are served by the indefinite suspension of dollar convertibility, and that we cannot be hurt by the crises which are an important part of its result. Some Europeans may still blissfully believe that world monetary disorder promotes European unity, but the events of the past week should make it totally clear that such disorder destroys any hope of European unity which existed theretofore. Some Japanese may still hope that the problems will all go away, and just let them go on piling up surpluses.

But any such view at this point would be incredibly myopic and naive. To be sure, no new system is going to solve all international economic problems forever. But no international economic problems are going to be solved, even temporarily, without a new system. In the absence of rapid and purposive movement toward implementing such a system, massive speculation will continue to break out at the slightest provocation. Controls over capital movements will continue to proliferate. Trade protectionism will continue to rise. The generation of economic peace which we have experienced since World War II will collapse and international political relations will soon be affected as well.

Fundamental reform will require concessions on all sides, and I do not mean to imply that it will be painless. Some countries will have to give up their allegiance to fixed exchange rates. A few will have to give up their attachment to gold. The United States will have to place the international role of the dollar squarely on the negotiating table. All will have to recognize that they can no longer run large surpluses or deficits indefinitely. But the costs of these concessions pale beside the costs of disintegration of the world economy. The case for fundamental reform is overwhelming.

12. IMF MEETING—1973

Although many economists did believe that "the case for fundamental reform is overwhelming," the long-anticipated meeting of the Board of Governors of the IMF in Nairobi in September 1973 failed to provide more than a tentative "first outline of reform."

Prior to the Nairobi meeting of the 126 Fund member nations, the Fund's Executive Directors issued their 1973 Annual Report which observed that international currency relationships now lack firm foundation in an internationally agreed set of rules or code of conduct. Despite continuing consultation and a substantial degree of cooperation among national monetary authorities, this situation is not consistent with one of the prime conceptions in the founding of the Fund—that exchange rates are intrinsically a matter of international concern. The Report therefore re-emphasized that an essential aspect of international monetary reform was the need to bring exchange rate policies and practices under the framework of a system founded on international agreement and commanding general support, whatever may prove to be the particular characteristics of that system.

In Nairobi, at his first press conference since becoming the IMF's new managing director, H. Johannes Witteveen stated that it is "rather optimistic" to expect that even the IMF annual meeting in 1974 would be ready to adopt formally a newly negotiated set of monetary rules. He said "there is still a large distance to be bridged" in the negotiations. At the opening session of the Nairobi meeting, the new managing director also stated that recent experience shows that floating currency-exchange rates "offer no panacea for the problems confronting us . . . Freely floating exchange rates cannot be relied upon to reflect underlying payments trends and thus to achieve appropriate currency relationships." He welcomed the beginning of modest intervention in foreign exchange markets, and added his "hope this will prove to be the first step in a gradual move toward a situation in which intervention is more widely used to stabilize exchange rates and to support an appropriate and internationally agreed set of currency values." He stated that he saw "much benefit in collaboration aimed at a gradual move toward more stable and orderly exchange arrangements . . . without waiting for formal ratification of reform." [16]

The most significant development at the Nairobi meeting was the release by the Committee of 20 of its report on the "First Outline of Reform." This draft outline was intended to define the general shape of the reformed system. The most important area of agreement related to the adjustment process, but the details of objective indicators or presumptive rules were not yet worked out. While emphasizing "stable but adjustable par values," the outline also expressed agreement that the SDR, not gold, should be the numeraire for the new international monetary system, and that the SDR should become the principal reserve asset. Regarding the role of gold in a reformed system, the outline offered three alternatives for consideration, all of which would permit central banks to sell their monetary gold in the free market. Under one plan, the central monetary authorities could also buy gold. In none of the three alternatives would there be any increase in the official price of gold. Two of the plans would abolish the official price altogether.

Excerpts from the draft outline by the Committee of 20 deputies follow.

FIRST OUTLINE OF REFORM *

This First Outline of Reform, which is forwarded to the Board of Governors under cover of a report by the Chairman of the Committee on Reform of the International Monetary System and Related Issues, has been prepared by the Chairman and Vice-Chairmen of the Deputies. It reflects in the view of the Chairman of the Committee the stage reached in the Committee's discussions. It records agreement on some issues, and disagreement on others to which further consideration will have to be given. In a number of cases it records suggestions which are not generally accepted or points to the need for further detailed study. Where agreement is recorded, it is subject, particularly in the fields of adjustment and convertibility, to further agreement on operational provisions as well as to eventual agreement on the reform as a whole.

Introduction

1. It is generally agreed that there is need for a reformed world monetary order, based on cooperation and consultation within the framework of a strengthened International Monetary Fund, that will encourage the growth of

---

[16] *New York Times* (September 25, 1973), p. 57.

* A complete text of the draft is printed in *IMF Survey*, October 8, 1973, pp. 305–308.

world trade and employment, promote economic development, and help to avoid both inflation and deflation. The main features of the international monetary reform should include:

(a) an effective and symmetrical adjustment process, including better functioning of the exchange rate mechanism, with the exchange rate regime based on stable but adjustable par values and floating rates recognized as providing a useful technique in particular situations;

(b) cooperation in dealing with disequilibrating capital flows;

(c) the introduction of an appropriate degree and form of convertibility for the settlement of imbalances, with symmetrical obligations on all countries;

(d) better international management of global liquidity, with the SDR becoming the principal reserve asset and the role of gold and of reserve currencies being reduced;

(e) consistency between arrangements for adjustment, convertibility, and global liquidity;

(f) the promotion of the flow of real resources to developing countries. . . .

Adjustment

3. There shall be a better working of the adjustment process in which adequate methods to assure timely and effective balance of payments adjustment by both surplus and deficit countries will be assisted by improved international consultation in the Fund, including the use of objective indicators. Countries will take such prompt and adequate adjustment action, domestic or external, as may be needed to avoid protracted payments imbalances. Countries should direct their policies to keeping their official reserves within limits which would be internationally agreed from time to time in the Fund and which would be consistent with the volume of global liquidity. For this purpose a reserve indicator structure should be established, subject to a more detailed study of the operational provisions involved. In choosing among different forms of adjustment action, countries should take into account repercussions on other countries as well as internal considerations.

4. In connection with adjustment it is envisaged that the Fund will introduce new procedures, involving special meetings, at regular intervals, of a Fund consultative body at an appropriate level ("the consultative body"). It has been suggested that the consultative body might be the resident Executive Board or, alternatively, a body to which constituencies could or would send representatives from capitals. In these special meetings:

(a) the world payments situation would be surveyed in relation both to the general working of the adjustment process and to developments affecting global liquidity. These surveys would allow for periodic consideration of balance of payments aims and for a review of the aggregate flow of real resources to developing countries and its financing; and

(b) particular cases of imbalance that individually or collectively have significant international repercussions, as determined by criteria to be established, would be examined.

5. A country would become subject to examination under paragraph 4(b) if either:

(a) there had been a disproportionate movement in its official reserves; or

(b) in the judgment of the Managing Director, following informal soundings among Executive Directors, there was prima facie evidence that the country was facing significant imbalance, even though this was not indicated by a disproportionate movement in the country's official reserves.

6. In the process of examination under paragraph 4(b), representatives of the country examined would be expected to comment on the country's economic prospects, including particularly its basic balance of payments position and prospects, on its external objectives, and on what domestic or external action, if any, it had taken or intended to take. An assessment by the consultative body would establish whether there was a need for adjustment. In making this assessment, the consultative body would take account of all relevant considerations, including the factors mentioned above; it would examine the consistency of the country's reserve and current account aims and policies with those of other countries, and would attach major importance to disproportionate movements of reserves. Account would be taken of the special characteristics of developing countries that make it difficult for them to achieve prompt adjustment without seriously damaging their long-term development programs. Following an assessment the consultative body would, where appropriate, call upon the country concerned to adopt or reinforce policies to correct its imbalance. A country in choosing between different forms of policy should take account of views expressed in the course of the examination on the form and size of policy action. . . .

Pressures

9. Provision will be made for graduated pressures to be applied to both surplus and deficit countries in cases of large and persistent imbalance. Proposals have been made for both financial pressures and other pressures. Further study will be needed of these proposals. In particular, it is not agreed how financial pressures should be activated and whether or not there should be other pressures as described in paragraph 11.

10. It has been suggested that pressures would start with financial pressures of a mild form, such as penalty rates of interest on net creditor or net debtor positions in the Fund. A more severe financial pressure which has been suggested is that, if a country's reserves rise to a predetermined point, that country would lose the right to convert further accruals of currency balances, and would be required to deposit such further accruals with the Fund at progressively increasing negative interest rates. There will be further consideration of these possible forms of financial pressures, including the question of penalty or negative interest rates in the case of the more severe pressure mentioned above. There will also be further consideration of the basis on which financial pressures might be activated. Such pressures could be activated by a positive decision of the Fund, at an appropriate level, following a

finding that the country had failed to take adequate corrective measures after it had been called upon to do so. It is not agreed whether or not they could be activated on the basis of a disproportionate movement in a country's reserves, either presumptively (i.e., unless the Fund decides that pressures are unwarranted) or—in the case of the more severe pressure mentioned above—automatically.

11. It has also been suggested that, for cases of more extreme imbalance, other pressures should be available, such as the publication of a Fund report on the position of the country concerned, and trade or other current account restrictions against countries in persistent large surplus. If there were to be pressures of this sort, they would be activated by a positive decision of the Fund following a finding that the country had failed to take adequate corrective measures after it had been called upon to do so; the authority to activate these pressures would rest ultimately, either directly or upon appeal, with a Committee of Fund Governors.

The Exchange Rate Mechanism

12. In the reformed system exchange rates will continue to be a matter for international concern and consultation. Competitive depreciation or undervaluation will be avoided. The exchange rate mechanism will remain based on stable but adjustable par values, and countries should not make inappropriate par value changes. On the other hand, countries should, whether in surplus or deficit, make appropriate par value changes promptly. Changes in par values will continue to be subject to Fund approval. Further consideration will be given to whether or not there should be simplified procedures, under appropriate safeguards, for small par value changes.

13. Countries may adopt floating rates in particular situations, subject to Fund authorization, surveillance, and review. Authorization to float will relieve a country of its obligation to observe the margins mentioned in paragraph 14. There will be further study of the possibility both of defining in advance particular situations in which countries might adopt floating rates and of developing a code of conduct, to be observed both by countries with floating rates and by other countries in relation to a floating currency, which would be designed to ensure consistency with international payments equilibrium. This study will cover the question of whether Fund authorization to float should depend upon a judgment in each particular case or whether it should be readily granted to countries undertaking to observe such a code of conduct or other agreed rules.

14. Except when authorized to adopt floating rates, countries will maintain the market exchange rates for their currencies within agreed maximum margins in relation to their parities. It is agreed that it would be desirable that there should be a symmetrical system in which the maximum margins for all currencies, including intervention currencies, should be the same, and should be 2¼ per cent on either side of parity. There will be further study of how symmetry can be achieved. An appropriate Fund body should be empowered to change the agreed maximum margins on a qualified majority.

Multicurrency Intervention

15. A detailed examination will be made of the practicality and desirability of establishing a system of multicurrency intervention in which countries whose currencies are widely traded in exchange markets might participate. The object of such a system would be to promote greater symmetry among participating countries with regard to exchange rate policy and intervention and settlement obligations; and it would make possible the establishment of symmetrical margins as mentioned in paragraph 14. Attention will be paid to the implications of such a system for nonparticipating countries.

Controls

16. There will be a strong presumption against the use of controls on current account transactions or payments for balance of payments purposes. In this connection arrangements will be made for continuing close coordination between the Fund and GATT. Countries will not use controls over capital transactions for the purpose of maintaining inappropriate exchange rates or, more generally, of avoiding appropriate adjustment action.

17. Wherever possible, developing countries will be exempted from controls imposed by other countries, particularly from import controls and controls over outward long-term investment. The special circumstances of developing countries will be taken into account by the Fund in assessing controls which these countries feel it necessary to apply.

Disequilibrating Capital Flows

18. Countries will cooperate in actions designed to limit disequilibrating capital flows and in arrangements to finance and offset them. Actions that countries might choose to adopt could include a more satisfactory degree of harmonization of monetary policies, subject to the requirements of domestic demand management; prompt adjustment of inappropriate par values, use of wider margins, and the adoption of floating rates in particular situations; and the use of administrative controls, including dual exchange markets and fiscal incentives. There should be improved consultation in the Fund on actions designed to limit disequilibrating capital flows, with the following objectives: first, to increase their effectiveness and to minimize harmful effects on third countries; and secondly, to avoid unnecessary proliferation and escalation of controls and the additional flows which might be prompted by anticipation thereof.

19. Insofar as countries use controls to limit disequilibrating capital flows, they should avoid an excessive degree of administrative restriction which could damage trade and beneficial capital flows and should not retain controls longer than needed. Such controls should be applied without discrimination except as stated in paragraph 17; in this connection there will be further consideration of the special position of countries which maintain close financial ties.

Convertibility

20. It is agreed that the basic objectives to be accommodated in the reformed convertibility system should be symmetry of obligations on all countries, including those whose currencies are held in official reserves; the better management of global reserves and the avoidance of uncontrolled growth of reserve currency balances; adequate elasticity; and as much freedom for countries to choose the composition of their reserves as is consistent with the overall objectives of the reform.

21. All countries maintaining par values will settle in reserve assets those official balances of their currencies which are presented to them for conversion. It is not agreed whether, beyond this, there should be more mandatory settlement arrangements in which countries whose currencies are held in official reserves would settle imbalances fully in reserve assets, with some accompanying limitation on other countries' accumulation of reserve currency holdings. It is, however, agreed that the amount of international liquidity and, in particular, the aggregate volume of official currency holdings should be kept under international surveillance and management, taking into account any necessary increase over time in official currency holdings in relation to the growth of international transactions.

22. There will be further consideration of the mechanism for settlements, including consideration of whether there should be direct settlement between countries or whether it should be wholly or partly centralized in the Fund. There will also be further consideration of means, including a possible substitution facility as envisaged in paragraph 31, to protect the system from any net conversion of the overhang of existing reserve currency balances.

23. It is generally recognized that there is a need for some elasticity within the settlement system, particularly to finance disequilibrating capital flows, and that provision for such elasticity should be consistent with other aspects of the reform. There will be further consideration of the appropriate degree and form of elasticity, which it has been suggested might:

(i) be limited to credit facilities, including Fund credit and official bilateral short-term credit, under international surveillance;

(ii) include, in addition to (i), a provision that the right of member countries to present currency balances for conversion into reserve assets would be suspended when their primary reserves exceeded a predetermined level and that the settlement obligation of the issuer would be correspondingly suspended; or

(iii) include, in addition to (i), provision for relaxation of the normal convertibility obligations by a collective decision in the Fund.

24. Provision could be made, if necessary, to permit the introduction of convertibility by stages.

Primary Reserve Assets

25. The SDR will become the principal reserve asset, and the role of gold and reserve currencies will be reduced. The SDR will also be the numeraire in terms of which par values will be expressed.

26. Allocation of SDRs will be such as to ensure that the volume of global reserves is adequate in conformity with the adjustment and settlement systems. There will be further discussion of appropriate procedures for determination of global reserve needs and for decision-making on SDR allocation and cancellation.

27. The effective yield on the SDR should be high enough to make it attractive to acquire and hold but not so high as to make countries reluctant to use the SDR when in deficit. For this purpose, it has been suggested that the value of the SDR in transactions against currencies should be maintained equal to an average of a group of currencies and that the SDR should carry an average market interest rate. Alternatively, it has been suggested that the value of the SDR in transactions against currencies should be maintained equal to an average of a group of strong currencies and that the SDR should carry an interest rate lower than an average market interest rate. Another suggested alternative is that the value of the SDR in transactions against currencies should be maintained by the balance of revaluations and devaluations of currencies in general and that the SDR should carry a low or zero rate of interest.

28. Further thought will be given to the question of a possible provision to permit the Fund uniformly to change the value of the SDR in transactions against currencies in a manner appropriate to the alternative adopted under paragraph 27.

29. In the light of the agreed objective that the SDR should become the principal reserve asset, consideration will be given to revising the rules governing its use with a view to relaxing existing constraints. Consideration will be given to other aspects of the SDR, including its name, with a view to promoting public understanding.

30. Appropriate arrangements will be made for gold in the reformed system in the light of the agreed objective that the SDR should become the principal reserve asset. Under one alternative, monetary authorities, including the Fund, would be free to sell, but not to buy, gold in the market at the market price; they would not undertake transactions with each other at a price different from the official price, which would be retained and would not be subject to a uniform increase. Under another alternative, the official price of gold would be abolished and monetary authorities, including the Fund, would be free to deal in gold with one another at a market-related price and to sell gold in the market. Another alternative would modify the preceding one by authorizing monetary authorities also to buy gold in the market.

Consolidation and Management of Currency Reserves

31. In order to facilitate a resumption of general convertibility, provision will be made for consolidation of outstanding reserve currency balances at the outset of the reform, provided that satisfactory terms can be agreed. This consolidation could take the form of

(a) bilateral funding in amounts and on terms to be agreed between holders and issuers; and/or

(b) substitution into SDRs through a facility in the Fund, on the basis of terms to be negotiated. . . .

33. Countries will cooperate in the management of their currency reserves so as to avoid disequilibrating movements of official funds. Among the possible provisions for achieving this objective, the following have been suggested:

(i) A country whose currency is held in official reserves should be able to require other countries to limit or convert into other reserve assets further increases in their holdings of its currency.

(ii) Countries should periodically choose the composition of their currency reserves and should undertake not to change it without prior consultation with the Fund.

(iii) Countries should not add to their currency reserve placements outside the territory of the country of issue except within limits to be agreed with the Fund.

The Link and Credit Facilities in Favor of Developing Countries

34. In the light of the agreed objective to promote economic development, the reformed monetary system will contain arrangements to promote an increasing flow of real resources from the developed to developing countries. If these arrangements were to include a link between development assistance and SDR allocation, this could take one of the following forms:

(a) A link would be established between development finance and SDR allocation, the total volume of which will be determined exclusively on the basis of global liquidity needs. This link would take the form of the direct distribution to developing countries of a larger proportion of SDR allocations than they would receive on the basis of their share in Fund quotas. Link resources so allocated would be distributed to all developing countries in such a way as to be relatively favorable to the least developed countries.

(b) A link would be established between development finance and SDR allocation, the total volume of which will be determined exclusively on the basis of global liquidity needs. This link would take the form of direct allocation to international and regional development finance institutions of a predetermined share of SDR allocations. Link resources distributed to development finance institutions would be disbursed to developing countries on the basis of development need and in such a way as to be relatively favorable to the least developed countries. The use of link funds by development finance institutions, including their distribution and terms, would reflect the nature and purpose of these resources.

35. A detailed examination will be made of proposals for establishing a new facility in the Fund to provide longer-term balance of payments finance for developing countries.

The Board of Governors of the IMF merely "took note" of the outline draft, commended the Committee of 20 for its efforts, and urged the Committee to complete its task as soon as possible. Even on the areas of agreement in the draft, there was still need to establish operational principles and technical details of implementation. In addition, several complex issues remained unresolved—most notably, the rule for convertibility of holdings of dollars and other currencies into primary reserve assets such as SDRs; the way that the SDR will be valued and the amount that will be created; the role of gold; and whether there will be a link between new allocations of SDRs and aid to developing countries.

The Committee of 20 set a deadline of July 31, 1974 for agreement on the issues still outstanding. After that would come a period of legal drafting of amendments to the Articles of the IMF and then parliamentary ratification.

With extensive negotiations still necessary, it was clear that a new "Nairobi system" was not yet ready to replace the disintegrating Bretton Woods system.

C. QUESTIONS

1. Consider the following quotation: "The fixed exchange rate system . . . leaves much to be desired. The efficiency of the adjustment mechanism implied by it depends on how well the authorities understand it. Inept policies by national authorities have led to substantial criticism of the system and to arguments for an alternative regime based on flexible exchange rates. Careful examination of the arguments for flexible exchange rates, however, show them to be rather weak. . . . My conclusion is that the fixed exchange system is the worst system, except for all the others." (Robert Mundell, "Toward a Better International Monetary System," *Journal of Money, Credit and Banking*, August 1969, p. 633.)

   a. Would you agree with this conclusion if the monetary system were a reformed system of "managed floating" in which intervention in exchange markets by national exchange authorities was constrained and coordinated in some way by international agreement? How does the present system differ from such a system?

b. If you had been a member of the Committee of 20, would you have argued for a wider band of exchange margins to provide an improved adjustment mechanism? If so, by how much?

c. If parity is permitted to slide, is there still an argument for a widened band? Would you have argued for a sliding parity? If so, how would you determine what should be the value of the sliding parity?

2. Consider the debate over objective indicators for adjustment. The financial ministers of the European Economic Community opposed an automatic adjustment mechanism as unworkable and argued that many indicators should be used to decide when parity changes are needed. (*New York Times*, March 24, 1973.)

a. What do you consider to be the different implications of mandatory or automatic measures of adjustment as contrasted with presumptive rules that merely request a country to consult with the IMF on possible policy readjustments? How is this problem related to international sanctions?

b. Do you think that a "normal" level of reserves is a sufficient indicator? How should "normal" be measured? What other indicators might merit consideration?

c. Does the problem of quantitative or objective indicators involve judgments of fact? or value? or both?

3. In the United States government's memorandum explaining its proposals (see pp. 266–73, above), it was recognized that three questions might be raised about the operational feasibility of the United States proposal: "The first question is: Is it possible to define reserves so as to assure they are useful and accurate criteria? The second question is: How do we deal with problems of heavy speculative capital flows? The third question is: Aren't reserve indicators retrospective and insufficiently refined, pointing to past maladjustments rather than present or future needs and unable to take account of the composition of the balance of payments?"

How would you answer these questions? (For the government's answers, see *Economic Report of the President*, January 1973, pp. 172–74.)

4. While recognizing that prompter readjustment of clearly un-

dervalued as well as overvalued exchange rates will have to be encouraged in the reconstruction of the international monetary system, Professor Robert Triffin has also stated: "Equally, or more important, will be a system of reserve creation and management, adjusting the total levels of reserves to world needs and making use of them for internationally agreed objectives." (*The Times*, September 13, 1971).

a. Do you think international monetary negotiations have given enough attention to reserve creation—its amount, composition, and distribution?

b. Would you agree with Triffin's proposal that "reserve accounts with the IMF should become the basic instrument for all international settlements and reserve accumulation" while "holdings of foreign national currencies should be strictly limited to an agreed ceiling (5 per cent of annual imports or 15 per cent of global reserves) and any currency balances acquired from the market and exceeding this ceiling should be immediately exchanged into the IMF reserve accounts?" (*New York Times*, January 23, 1972.)

c. If you had been a member of the Committee of 20, what measures would you have recommended for handling the large volume of outstanding official dollar holdings?

5. Recall the two-tier gold system negotiated in March 1968 (see pp. 129–31, above). Since that time the University of Alaska has offered an "introductory course in gold prospecting." More significantly, the private market price of gold has risen remarkably—rising above $140 an ounce in European markets in January 1974, while the official price was only $42.

What do you think should be the future position of gold in the international monetary system? Do you think gold should be demonetized? If so, by what specific measures should this be accomplished?

6. Would you agree that "the increasing size and mobility of short-term capital and changes in geographical patterns of production by international firms might be the main cause of endemic world monetary instability?" What problems do these capital movements present for a world monetary order? Have international monetary negotiations squarely faced these problems?

7. Consider what transpired at the IMF's meeting in Nairobi in

1973. In light of international monetary events that preceded it
and the negotiations of the Committee of 20, what is your assessment of the significance of that meeting? If the Bretton
Woods conference in 1944 represented "the coincidence of the
hour and the men," could the same be said about the Nairobi
meeting in 1973?

8. Consider more broadly the recent history of international
monetary negotiations, especially those conducted in the Committee of 20 and at the IMF meeting of 1973. What does this history reveal about the political economics of policy formation in
international monetary affairs? Has the trend been toward increased international integration at the economic and political
levels, with additional inroads into national economic sovereignty?

9. Would you have any suggestions for improving the process
of collective decision-making in international monetary affairs?

D. READINGS

Acheson, A. L. K. et al., *Bretton Woods Revisited* (1972).

Bergsten, C. Fred et al., *Approaches to Greater Flexibility of Exchange Rates: The Bürgenstock Papers* (1970).

——, *Reforming the Dollar* (1972).

Bhagwati, Jagdish N. et al., "The International Monetary System: A Symposium," *Journal of International Economics*, September 1972.

Council on Foreign Relations, *The Smithsonian Agreement and Its Aftermath: Several Views* (1972).

de Vries, T., *An Agenda for Monetary Reform* (1972).

Fellner, William et al., *Maintaining and Restoring Balance in International Payments* (1966).

Fleming, J. M., "The SDR: Some Problems and Possibilities," *IMF Staff Papers*, March 1971.

Grubel, H. G. (ed.), *World Monetary Reform* (1963).

Hirsch, Fred, *An SDR Standard*, Princeton Essays in International Finance, No. 99, June 1973.

Johnson, Harry G., *The International Monetary Problem* (1969).